Lecture Notes in Computer Science   13005

More information about this subseries at http://www.springer.com/series/7410

Wenlian Lu · Kun Sun · Moti Yung ·
Feng Liu (Eds.)

Science of Cyber Security

Third International Conference, SciSec 2021
Virtual Event, August 13–15, 2021
Revised Selected Papers

Springer

Editors
Wenlian Lu
Fudan University
Shanghai, China

Kun Sun
George Mason University
Fairfax, VA, USA

Moti Yung
Computer Science Department
Columbia University
New York, NY, USA

Feng Liu
Institute of Information Engineering
Chinese Academy of Sciences
Beijing, China

ISSN 0302-9743 ISSN 1611-3349 (electronic)
Lecture Notes in Computer Science
ISBN 978-3-030-89136-7 ISBN 978-3-030-89137-4 (eBook)
https://doi.org/10.1007/978-3-030-89137-4

LNCS Sublibrary: SL4 – Security and Cryptology

This Springer imprint is published by the registered company Springer Nature Switzerland AG
The registered company address is: Gewerbestrasse 11, 6330 Cham, Switzerland

Preface

The third annual International Conference on Science of Cyber Security (SciSec 2021) was held successfully online during August 13–15, 2021. The mission of SciSec is to catalyze the research collaborations between the relevant scientific communities and disciplines that should work together in exploring the foundational aspects of cybersecurity. We believe that this collaboration is needed in order to deepen our understanding of, and build a firm foundation for, the emerging science of cybersecurity discipline. SciSec is unique in appreciating the importance of multidisciplinary and interdisciplinary broad research efforts towards the ultimate goal of a sound science of cybersecurity, which attempts to deeply understand and systematize knowledge in the field of security.

SciSec 2021 solicited high-quality, original research papers that could justifiably help develop the science of cybersecurity. Topics of interest included, but were not limited to, the following:

- Cybersecurity Dynamics
- Cybersecurity Metrics and Their Measurements
- First-principle Cybersecurity Modeling and Analysis (e.g., Dynamical Systems, Control-Theoretic Modeling, Game-Theoretic Modeling)
- Cybersecurity Data Analytics
- Quantitative Risk Management for Cybersecurity
- Big Data for Cybersecurity
- Artificial Intelligence for Cybersecurity
- Machine Learning for Cybersecurity
- Economics Approaches for Cybersecurity
- Social Sciences Approaches for Cybersecurity
- Statistical Physics Approaches for Cybersecurity
- Complexity Sciences Approaches for Cybersecurity
- Experimental Cybersecurity
- Macroscopic Cybersecurity
- Statistics Approaches for Cybersecurity
- Human Factors for Cybersecurity
- Compositional Security
- Biology-inspired Approaches for Cybersecurity
- Synergistic Approaches for Cybersecurity

SciSec 2021 was hosted by the Fudan University, Shanghai, China. Due to the intensification of the COVID-19 situation all around the world, SciSec 2021 was held totally online through Tencent Conference and VooV Meeting. The Program Committee selected 22 papers — 17 full papers and 5 poster papers — from a total of 50 submissions for presentation at the conference. These papers cover the following subjects: detection for cybersecurity, machine learning for cybersecurity, and dynamics, network and inference. We anticipate that the topics covered by the program in the future will be more systematic and further diversified.

The Program Committee further selected the paper titled "Detecting Internet-scale Surveillance Devices using RTSP Recessive Features" by Zhaoteng Yan, Zhi Li, Wenping Bai, Nan Yu, Hongsong Zhu, and Limin Sun and the paper titled "Dismantling Interdependent Networks Based on Supra-Laplacian Energy" by Wei Lin, Shuming Zhou, Min Li, and Gaolin Chen for the Distinguished Paper Award. The conference program also included four invited keynote talks: the first keynote titled "Layers of Abstractions and Layers of Obstructions and the U2F" was delivered by Moti Yung, Google and Columbia University, USA; the second keynote titled "Progresses and Challenges in Federated Learning" was delivered by Gong Zhang, Huawei, China; the third keynote titled "SARR: A Cybersecurity Metrics and Quantification Framework" was delivered by Shouhuai Xu, University of Colorado Colorado Springs, USA; while the fourth keynote was titled "Preliminary Exploration on Several Security Issues in AI" and was delivered by Yugang Jiang, Fudan University, China. The conference program presented a panel discussion on "Where are Cybersecurity Boundaries?"

We would like to thank all of the authors of the submitted papers for their interest in SciSec 2021. We also would like to thank the reviewers, keynote speakers, and participants for their contributions to the success of SciSec 2021. Our sincere gratitude further goes to the Program Committee, the Publicity Committee, and the Organizing Committee, for their hard work and great efforts throughout the entire process of preparing and managing the event. Furthermore, we are grateful to Fudan University for their generosity to enable free registration for attending SciSec 2021.

We hope that you will find the conference proceedings inspiring and that it will further help you in finding opportunities for your future research.

August 2021

Wenlian Lu
Kun Sun
Moti Yung
Feng Liu

The original version of the book was revised: the affiliation of Feng Liu was presented incorrectly. This was corrected. The correction to the book is available at
https://doi.org/10.1007/978-3-030-89137-4_19

Organization

Steering Committee

Guoping Jiang   Nanjing University of Posts and Telecommunications, China
Feng Liu   Institute of Information Engineering, Chinese Academy of Sciences, China
Shouhuai Xu   University of Colorado Colorado Springs, USA
Moti Yung   Google and Columbia University, USA

Program Committee Co-chairs

Wenlian Lu   Fudan University, China
Kun Sun   George Mason University, USA
Moti Yung   Google and Columbia University, USA

Organization Committee Chair

Lei Shi   Fudan University, China

Publicity Co-chairs

Habtamu Abie   Norwegian Computing Center, Norway
Guen Chen   University of Texas at San Antonio, USA
Noseong Park   George Mason University, USA
Chunhua Su   University of Aizu, Japan
Jia Xu   Nanjing University of Posts and Telecommunications, China
Xiaofan Yang   Chongqing University, China
Jeong Hyun Yi   Soongsil University, South Korea
Lidong Zhai   Institute of Information Engineering, Chinese Academy of Sciences, China
James Zheng   Macquarie University, Australia

Program Committee Members

Habtamu Abie   Norwegian Computing Centre, Norway
Richard Brook   Clemson University, USA
Sara Foresti   University of Milan, Italy
Ying Fan   Beijing Normal University, China
Xinwen Fu   University of Massachusetts Lowell, USA
Jianxi Gao   Rensselaer Polytechnic Institute, USA

Dieter Gollmann	Hamburg University of Technology, Germany
Yujuan Han	Shanghai Maritime University, China
Debiao He	Wuhan University, China
Daojing He	East China Normal University, China
Wei Huo	Institute of Information Engineering, Chinese Academy of Sciences, China
Zbigniew Kalbarczyk	Coordinated Science Laboratory, USA
Arash Habibi Lashkari	University of New Brunswick, Canada
Lingguang Lei	Institute of Information Engineering, Chinese Academy of Sciences, China
Cong Li	Fudan University, China
Xiwei Liu	Tongji University, China
Zhuo Lu	University of South Florida, USA
Pratyusa K. Manadhata	Hewlett Packard Laboratories, USA
Thomas Moyer	University of North Carolina at Charlotte, USA
Andrew Odlyzko	University of Minnesota, USA
Kazumasa Omote	University of Tsukuba, Japan
Noseong Park	George Mason University, USA
Kouichi Sakurai	Kyushu University, Japan
Lipeng Song	North University of China, China
Chunhua Su	Osaka University, Japan
Longkun Tang	Huaqiao University, China
Lingyu Wang	Concordia University, Canada
Zhi Wang	Nankai University, China
Chengyi Xia	Tianjin University of Technology, China
Min Xiao	Nanjing University of Posts and Telecommunications, China
Xin-Jian Xu	Shanghai University, China
Jia Xu	Nanjing University of Posts and Telecommunications, China
Maochao Xu	Illinois State University, USA
Guanhua Yang	Binghamton University, USA
Xiaofan Yang	Chongqing University, China
Chuan Yue	Colorado School of Mines, USA
Jun Zhao	Nanyang Technological University, Singapore
Sencun Zhu	Pennsylvania State University, USA
Cliff Zou	University of Central Florida, USA

Web Chair

| Weixia Cai | Institute of Information Engineering, Chinese Academy of Sciences, China |

Organizing Committee Members

| Dandan Yuan | Fudan University, China |
| Chenyao Zhang | Fudan University, China |

Contents

Keynote Report

SARR: A Cybersecurity Metrics and Quantification Framework (Keynote)

Shouhuai Xu[✉]

Laboratory for Cybersecurity Dynamics Department of Computer Science,
University of Colorado Colorado Springs, Colorado Springs, USA
sxu@uccs.edu
https://xu-lab.org/

Abstract. Cybersecurity Metrics and Quantification is a fundamental but notoriously hard problem and is undoubtedly one of the pillars underlying the emerging Science of Cybersecurity. In this paper, we present an novel approach to addressing this problem by unifying Security, Agility, Resilience and Risk (SARR) metrics into a single framework. The SARR approach and the resulting framework are unique because: (i) it is driven by the *assumptions* that are made when modeling, designing, implementing, operating, and defending systems, which are broadly defined to include infrastructures and enterprise networks; and (ii) it embraces the *uncertainty* inherent to the cybersecurity domain. We will review the status quo by looking into existing metrics and quantification research through the SARR lens and discuss a range of open problems.

Keywords: Cybersecurity metrics · Cybersecurity quantification · Security · Agility · Resilience · Risk · Cybersecurity management

1 Introduction

Effective cybersecurity design, operations, and management ought to rely on quantitative metrics. This is because effective cybersecurity decision-making and management demands cybersecurity quantification, which in turn requires us to tackle the problem of metrics. For example, when a Chief Executive Officer (CEO) decides whether to increase the enterprise's cybersecurity investment, the CEO would ask a simple question: What is the estimated return, ideally measured in dollar amount, if we increase the cybersecurity budget (say) by $5M this year? Unfortunately, the status quo is that we cannot answer this question yet because cybersecurity metrics and quantification remains one of the most difficult yet fundamental open problems [10,32,38], despite significant efforts [3,4,6–8,21,30,33,35,37,39,40,59].

Our Contributions. In this paper, we propose a systematic approach to tackling the problem, by unifying Security, Agility, Resilience, and Risks (SARR) metrics into a single framework. The approach is *assumption*-driven and embraces the

© Springer Nature Switzerland AG 2021
W. Lu et al. (Eds.): SciSec 2021, LNCS 13005, pp. 3–17, 2021.
https://doi.org/10.1007/978-3-030-89137-4_1

uncertainty inherent to the cybersecurity domain. Moreover, we evaluate existing cybersecurity metrics through the SARR lens and propose a range of open problems for future research. Our findings include: (i) it is essential to explicitly and precisely articulate the assumptions made at the design and operation phases of systems; (ii) it is important to understand and characterize the relationships between cybersecurity assumptions, because they may not be independent of each other; (iii) uncertainty is inherent to cybersecurity because defenders cannot directly observe whether or not assumptions made at the design phase are violated in the operation phase; (iv) the current understanding of cybersecurity agility and resilience metrics is superficial, even if defenders can be certain about which assumptions are violated; (v) cybersecurity risk metrics emerge from the uncertainty inherent to assumptions.

Related Work. From a conceptual point of view, the present study corresponds to one pillar of the Cybersecurity Dynamics framework [47,48,53,56], which aims to quantify and analyze cybersecurity from a holistic perspective (in contrast to the building-blocks perspective). This approach stresses the importance of considering the *time* dimension in cybersecurity, leading to *time-dependent* metrics and analysis methods (e.g., [11,18,26,49–51,54,57,58,60]). The SARR framework is partly inspired by the STRAM framework [8], which systematizes security metrics, trust metrics, resilience metrics, and agility metrics. The SARR framework goes far beyond the STRAM framework [8] because STRAM does not present the underlying connections between the families of metrics. In contrast, SARR uses *assumptions* and *uncertainty* to unify families of metrics, and these two aspects play no roles in STRAM.

From a technical point of view, the present study focuses on characterizing *what* need to be measured, rather than *how* to measure because we treat the measurement of well-defined metrics as an orthogonal research problem. The latter can be challenging as well. For example, when we infer the ground-truth labels of files in the setting of malware detection, we often encounter the situation that malware detectors give conflicting information (e.g., one detector says a file is benign but another says the file is malicious) [1,2,13,23,31].

Paper Outline. Section 2 presents the SARR framework. Section 3 discusses the status quo in cybersecurity metrics and quantification research. Section 4 explores future research directions. Section 5 concludes the present paper.

2   The SARR Framework

2.1   Terminology

Abstractions and Views. Cyberspace is a complex system which mandates the use of multiple (levels of) abstractions to understand them. We use the term *network* broadly to include the entire cyberspace, an infrastructure, an enterprise network, or a cyber-physical-human network of interest. Networks can be decomposed horizontally or vertically, leading to two views:

- In the horizontal view, an network can be decomposed into many networked *devices*, which are combinations of hardware and software with computing and networking capabilities. Devices include computers (e.g., servers, sensors and IoT devices), network devices (e.g., routers and switches), and cybersecurity devices which run (e.g.) intrusion detection systems and firewalls. The horizontal view is often used by cyber defense operators.
- In the vertical view, a network can be decomposed into layers of *components*, which are hardware or software sub-systems, possibly provided by different vendors. Examples of components include operating systems (e.g., Microsoft Windows vs. Linux), applications, and security functions (e.g., intrusion detection systems, malware detectors, and firewalls). We may treat *data* as components as well. Each component may be further divided into layers. For example, the TCP/IP stack can be seen as the communication component, which can be divided into layers of communication protocols. Each component may incorporate or integrate multiple *building-blocks*, such as the machine learning techniques employed by malware detectors. This distinction is important because building-block techniques are often carefully analyzed, components are often proprietary and analyzed only superficially, but networks are analyzed even less thoroughly, perhaps because they are very complex.

Design vs. Operation. In principle, the lifecycle of a network, device, component, or building-block can be divided into a *design* phase and an *operation* phase. The design phase deals with its modeling, design, analysis, implementation, and testing; for ease of reference, we refer to the entities that conduct these activities as *designers*. The operation phase deals with its installation, configuration, operation, maintenance, and defense in the real world; similarly, we refer to the entities that conduct these activities as *operators*. The design vs. operation distinction is important because there can be huge gaps between these two phases, which will be elaborated later.

Cybersecurity vs. Security Properties and Metrics. We use the term *security properties* to describe the standard notions of confidentiality, integrity, availability, non-repudiation, authentication, etc. We use the term *cybersecurity properties* to describe security, agility, resilience, risk and possibly other properties. This means that cybersecurity properties are much broader than security properties. Cybersecurity quantification indicates precise characterization of these cybersecurity properties. For this purpose, we need *cybersecurity metrics*. A metric is a function that maps from a set of objects (e.g., networks, devices, components or building-blocks) to a set of values with a scale (e.g., $\{0, 1\}$ or $[0, 1]$), reflecting security or cybersecurity properties of the objects [35].

2.2 SARR Overview

Figure 1 highlights the framework, which is driven by the *assumptions* that are made at the design and operation phases of an network, device, component or building-block. For a given set of assumptions, there are three kinds of scenarios according to a spectrum of *(un)certainty* in regards to the assumptions.

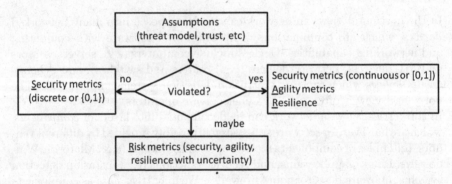

Fig. 1. The SARR framework is driven by *assumptions* and embraces *uncertainty*.

1. It is *certain* that the assumptions are not violated. This often corresponds to the analyses that are conducted at the design phase, where designers consider a range of security properties (e.g., confidentiality, integrity, availability, authentication, and non-repudiation) with respect to a certain system model and a certain threat model. Essentially, these security properties are often defined over a binary scale, denoted by $\{0, 1\}$, indicating whether a property holds or not under the system model and the threat model.
2. It is *certain* that some or all assumptions are violated. This often corresponds to the operation phase, where security properties may be partially or entirely compromised. Therefore, security properties may be defined over a continuous scale, such as $[0, 1]$ (e.g., the fraction of compromised computers in an network). In this case, detection of violations would trigger the defender to take countermeasures to "bounce back" from the violations, leading to the notion of *agility* and *resilience* metrics, which will be elaborated later.
3. It is *uncertain* whether assumptions are violated or not (i.e., assumptions may be violated). This naturally leads to *risk* metrics by associating uncertainties to security, agility and resilience metrics.

In the rest of the section we will elaborate these matters.

2.3   Assumptions

In order to tame cybersecurity, assumptions may be made, explicitly or implicitly, during the design and operation phases of an network, device, component or building-block. They are fundamental to cybersecurity properties.

Assumptions Associated with the Design Phase. At this phase, assumptions can be made with respect to system models, vulnerabilities, attacks (i.e., threat models) and defenses. For example, designers often use *system models* to describe the interactions between the participating entities, the environment and the interaction with it (if appropriate), the communication channels between the participating entities (e.g., authenticated private channel), and the trust that is embedded into the model (e.g., a participating entity is semi-honest or honest).

Designers use *threat models* with simplifying assumptions when specifying security properties, proposing systems architectures, selecting protocols and mechanisms, analyzing whether a property is attained or not under those assumptions. Programmers and testers detect/eliminate bugs and vulnerabilities in the course of developing software, while making various (possibly implicit) assumptions (e.g., competency of a bug/vulnerability detection tool).

Assumptions Associated with the Operation Phase. During this phase, various kinds of (possibly implicit) assumptions are often made (e.g., competency of configurations or defense tools). One example of assumptions that are often made at the design phase and then inherited at the operation phase is the attacker's capability. For example, Byzantine Fault-Tolerance (BFT) protocols, which can be seen as a building-block, work correctly when no more than one-third of the replicas are compromised [29]. However, there is no guarantee in the real world that the attacker cannot go beyond the one-third threshold, effectively compromising the assurance offered by these powerful building-blocks. This can be further attributed to the limited capabilities of cyber defense tools, such as intrusion detection systems and malware detectors.

2.4   Metrics When Assumptions Are Certainly Not Violated

Under the premise that assumptions are complete and are not violated, cybersecurity metrics may degenerate to security metrics in the sense that agility, resilience and risk may become irrelevant. Moreover, it may be sufficient to use binary metrics, namely $\{0, 1\}$, to quantify security properties. This serves as a starting point towards tackling cybersecurity metrics because it would be rare to ascertain in the real world that assumptions are certainly not violated and that the articulated assumptions are sufficient.

Metrics Associated with the Design Phase. At the design phase, we need to define metrics to precisely describe the desired security properties. Textbook knowledge would teach us that the desired properties include confidentiality, integrity, availability, authentication, non-repudiation, etc. However, they may not be sufficient. We advocate accurate and rigorous definitions (or specifications) of metrics, ideally as accurate and rigorous as the definitions given in modern cryptography [16]. This is important because when accurate and rigorous definitions are not given, it is not possible to conduct rigorous analysis to establish desired properties. This means that each security property must be precisely defined with respect to a system model and a threat model. For example, when we specify an availability property, we should specify it as a property of a *service* (e.g., the service offered at port #80) vs. *data* (e.g., a file in a computer) in the presence of some attack.

Metrics Associated with the Operation Phase. We need to define metrics to precisely describe the required security properties of an network, device, component, or building-block at the operation phase. For example, availability metrics at the operation phase may include service response time and service throughput. Metrics associated with the operation phase are less understood than their counterparts associated with the design phase.

2.5 Metrics When Assumptions Are Certainly Violated

When assumptions are violated, some or all of the security properties are compromised. In order to describe how defenders respond to such violations of assumptions or compromises of security properties, agility and resilience properties emerge. Intuitively, agility quantitatively characterizes how *fast* a defender responds to cybersecurity situation changes [8,30], and resilience quantitatively characterizes whether and how the defender can make the network, device, component or building-block "bounce back" from the violation of assumptions (i.e., correcting the violations) and the compromise of security properties (i.e., making them hold again). The state-of-the-art is that the notions of *agility-by-design* and *resilience-by-design* are less investigated and understood than *security-by-design*. Agility and resilience are inherently associated with the operation phase because (i) assumptions are the starting point of a design process and (ii) assumptions are violated in real-world operations but not at the design phase. When assumptions are violated, we propose quantifying *security*, *agility*, and *resilience* properties.

For quantifying security properties, examples of metrics are described as follows. (i) To what extent may an assumption have been violated? This may require quantifying the extent to which a network, device, component, or building-block is compromised. This is important for example when using BFT protocols to tolerate attacks, where the fraction of devices that are compromised (e.g., 35% vs. 50%) would make a difference in the defender's response to the attacks. (ii) To what extent is a security property compromised? This is important because a security property may not be *all-or-nothing*, meaning that a violation of assumptions may only cause a degradation of a security property. For example, when a network (or device) is compromised, the attacker may only be able to steal some, but not all, of the data sorted on the network (or device), causing a partial loss of the confidentiality property.

For quantifying agility, example metrics are described as follows. (i) How agile is the defender in detecting the violation of an assumption? One assumption can be that an employed intrusion prevention system can effectively detect a certain class of attacks. Another assumption can be that the attacker does not identify any 0-day vulnerability or use any new attack vector that cannot be recognized by defense tools. (ii) How fast do the desired security properties degrade because of the violation of assumptions? (iii) How quickly does the defender react to the violation of assumptions or successful attacks? (iv) How quickly does the defender bring the network to the required level of security properties?

For quantifying resilience, example metrics are described as follows. (i) What is the maximum degree of violation in terms of the assumptions or security properties that would make it possible for the defender to recover the network (or device or component) and its services without shutting down and re-booting it from scratch? In order to quantify these, we would need to quantify the maximum degree of violation with respect to the assumptions that can be tolerated. (ii) Does a security property degrades gradually or abruptly when assumptions are violated? (iii) How does the degradation pattern, such as gradual vs. abrupt, depend on the degree of violations of the assumptions?

2.6   Metrics When Assumptions May Be Violated

The preceding two scenarios correspond to the two ends of the spectrum of (un)certainty about the assumptions being violated or not. In the real world, it is rare that the defender would be certain about whether an assumption is violated or not. As a consequence, it is rare for the defender to be certain about whether a security property is compromised or not. Since *uncertainty* is inherent to the cybersecurity domain, we have to embrace the uncertainty, meaning that cybersecurity metrics must be defined while bearing in mind the uncertainty factor. We use the term *risk* to accommodate the security, agility and resilience metrics that can cope with uncertainty. Some examples of risk metrics are described as follows. (i) What is the degree of certainty that a security property is compromised? In order to quantify this, the defender would need to quantify the degree of certainty that an assumption is violated. (ii) What is the degree of certainty when a defense tool flags an event as an attack (e.g., an incoming network connection is an attack or a file is malicious) or anomaly? This may be measured as the conditional probability (or trustworthiness), for example, Pr(the event is indeed an attack|a detector says an event is an attack). (iii) What is the degree of certainty that some software contains a zero-day vulnerability that is known to the attacker but not the defender? (iv) What is the degree of certainty about a threat model (e.g., attacker indeed cannot wage attacks that are not permitted by the threat model)?

Observation 1. *Uncertainty is inherent to cybersecurity, meaning that we must define cybersecurity metrics to help defenders quantify cybersecurity risks and make decisions in their cyber defense operations.*

3   Status Quo

In this section, we use the SARR framework as a lens to look into the cybersecurity metrics that have been proposed in the literature. For this purpose, we leverage survey papers [8,35,37] as a source of metrics, while considering more recent literature published after those survey papers (e.g., [13,30]).

3.1   Assumptions

Assumptions are often articulated more clearly in building-block studies (e.g., cryptography) than the other settings of cybersecurity (e.g., what a chosen-ciphertext attacker can do exactly). However, there are still gaps that are yet to be bridged. First, assumptions may be stated *implicitly*. For example, cryptography assumes that cryptographic keys are kept secret, either entirely or at least for most information of cryptographic keys (i.e., a partial exposure of cryptographic key may be tolerated). However, cryptographic keys in the real world can be compromised in their entirety (see, e.g., [14,20]). As a consequence, the security property of digital signatures, known as unforgeability, under the assumption that the private signing keys are kept secret is compromised. This highlights the importance of coping with the presence of compromised cryptographic keys which have not been revoked yet [12,41,52]. Still, the trustworthiness of digital signatures has yet to be quantified given the uncertainty that the private signing keys or services may have been compromised without being detected.

Second, assumptions may be inadequate or incomplete. One example of inadequacy is the evolution from considering chosen-plaintext attacks to considering chosen-ciphertext attacks. One example of incompleteness is that earlier threat models simply did not consider the presence of side-channel attacks, which are however realistic. This is not surprising because cyber attacks evolve with time, meaning that threat models also evolve with time [47,48,53].

The preceding examples highlight the gaps between the validity of assumptions made at the design phase and the validity of these assumption in the real world. These gaps highlight the importance of explicitly and precisely articulating assumptions because violation of assumptions cause new properties and metrics to emerge (e.g., emergence of agility and resilience metrics). Moreover, the inevitable uncertainty causes the emergence of risk metrics.

Observation 2. *In order to tame cybersecurity, it is essential to explicitly and precisely articulate the assumptions that are made at the design phase and the operation phase. This is far from being achieved and is a big challenge.*

3.2   Security Metrics

In [35], four classes of security metrics are defined: those for quantifying vulnerabilities (including user/human, interface-induced, and software vulnerabilities), those for quantifying attack capabilities (including zero-day, targeted, botnet attacks, malware, and evasion attacks), those for quantifying the effectiveness of defenses (including preventive, reactive, proactive defense capabilities), and those for quantifying situations (e.g., the percentage of compromised computers at a point in time). It is concluded in [35], and re-affirmed in [55], that the problem "what should be measured" is largely open.

Observation 3. *Our understanding of what should be measured in cybersecurity is superficial.*

3.3   Agility Metrics

In a broader context, the existing metrics that can be adapted to measure agility are classified into the following categories [8]: those for quantifying timeliness (including detection time, overall agility quickness) and those for quantifying usability (including ease of use, usefulness, defense cost).

In the narrower context of attack-defense interactions, a novel family of agility metrics are proposed in [30] to quantify the co-evolution (or escalation) of cyber attacks and defenses. Unlike the classification used in [8], the agility metrics defined in [30] accommodate two dimensions of the attack-defense co-evolution, namely *timeliness* and *effectiveness*. Timeliness metrics describe how quickly an attacker is in terms of evolving its attacks in response to the defender's use of new strategy and/or techniques (and comparable metrics from the defender's perspective). These metrics include: *generation-time*, which is the time it takes an attacker (or defender) to evolve its strategies or techniques from one generation to another generation as observed by the defender (or attacker), where a generation may be a new version of a tool (e.g., a new version of malware detector); and *triggering-time*, which is the time it takes an attacker (or defender) to evolve into the next generation of strategy or techniques. Effectiveness metrics quantify how effective a new generation of attacks (or defenses) are, including: *evolutionary-effectiveness*, which describes the effectiveness of the attacker's (defender's) strategy or techniques with respect to defender's (or attacker's); *relative-generational-impact*, which is the effectiveness gain of the current generation of attack (or defense) over the past generation of attack (of defense).

Observation 4. *Our understanding of agility metrics are even more superficial than our understanding of security metrics.*

3.4   Resilience Metrics

By adapting the existing metrics that are defined in other contexts, resilience metrics may be classified into the following families [8]: those for quantifying fault-tolerance metrics (including mean-time-to-failure, percolation threshold, diversity), those for quantifying adaptability (including degree of local decision, degree of intelligent decision, degree of automation), and those for quantifying recoverability (including mean-time-to-full-recovery, mean-time-between-failures, mean-time-to-repair, and intrusion response cost). There are no systematic studies on resilience metrics.

Observation 5. *Our understanding of resilience metrics are even more superficial than our understanding of security metrics.*

3.5   Risk Metrics

Risk is often investigated in the setting of hazards and is often defined as a product of threat (which is a probability estimated by domain expert or other means), vulnerability (which is another probability estimated by domain expert or another means), and consequence (which is the damage caused by the threat when it happens) [22]. This means that risk is quantified as the expected or mean loss. However, this approach is not competent for managing the risk incurred by terrorist attacks [9] because it cannot deal with, among other things, the dependence between many events (e.g., cascading failures). This immediately implies that this approach is not competent for cybersecurity risk management because there are many kinds of dependencies and interdependencies which make cybersecurity risks exhibit emergent properties [17,34,36,46]. In order to deal with these problems, Cybersecurity Dynamics offers a promising approach, especially its predictive power in forecasting the evolution of dynamical situational awareness attained by first-principle analyses (e.g., [11,18,19,26–28,42,45,49–51,54,60,61]) and data-driven analyses (e.g., [5,15,24,25,43,44,57,58]).

4 Future Research Directions

In order to ultimately tackle the Cybersecurity Metrics and Quantification problem, we highlight some open problems that must be adequately addressed.

Taming Cybersecurity Assumptions. It would be ideal that (i) assumptions are always explicitly and precisely stated, (ii) assumptions are independent of each other, and (iii) assumptions made at the design phase are always valid at the operation phase. However, these are hard to achieve. Alternatively, we should characterize the relationships between related assumptions. For example, an authenticated private communication channel assumes the following: (i) authenticity of the communication parties, (ii) confidentiality of the communication contents, and (iii) integrity of the communication contents. These assumptions further rely on other, often implicitly made, assumptions. Specifically, the preceding assumptions (i)–(iii) would have to be based on the assumption that the communication parties are not compromised when cryptographic mechanisms are used to realize these assumptions; otherwise, assumptions (i)–(iii) are violated. Therefore, when the threat model assumes that the attacker cannot compromise any of the communication parties, the security guarantee rigorously proven in the abstract model may become irrelevant in the real world.

Bridging Design vs. Operation Gaps. There are several gaps between designers' views and defenders' views, especially in terms of their levels of abstractions. In particular, designers often deal with build-blocks and components, but defenders often deal with networks and devices. There are big gaps between these views. First, designers often make assumptions with the mindset that these assumptions will not be violated in the real world. As a consequence, the resulting cybersecurity properties are not only bound to the completeness and accuracy of the assumptions, but also bound to the premise that the assumptions are not violated in practice. Therefore, there is a big gap between the *certainty* of assumptions considered by designers and the *uncertainty* of assumptions being violated or not as perceived by defenders. Second, the network-level and device-level implications of the assumptions that are made when designing building-blocks and components are often unaddressed. This further amplifies the uncertainty encountered by defenders in the real world.

The preceding discussion would explain why security properties are often analyzed in academic research literature but not agility or resilience properties. Moreover, the preceding discussion would also explain why designers often focus on achieving preventive defense with no successful attacks. However, defenders often deal with successful attacks, which break security properties by violating the assumptions made by designers. This explains why real-world cyber defenders need to leverage preventive defenses, reactive defenses, adaptive defenses, proactive defenses, and active defenses collectively in order to achieve effective defenses [47, 48]. This also explains why the motivating question mentioned in the Introduction cannot be answered yet, namely that the current cybersecurity metrics and quantification knowledge is not sufficient to answer the defender's question in regards to the return on cybersecurity investment.

Identifying and Defining Cybersecurity Metrics That Must Be Measured. As mentioned above, the current understanding of what should be quantified is superficial [35, 55]. It is important to define a comprehensive, ideally complete, suite of metrics under each of the security, agility, resilience, and risk pillars. Since the literature study is often geared towards designers' views, existing metrics are often defined for some purposes but rarely for the purposes of cyber defense operations. Since academic research is often geared towards that assumptions are not to be violated, there is a very limited body of knowledge that can help defenders achieve quantitative cyber defense decision-making and cybersecurity risk management. In order to bridge these gaps, one candidate approach is to leverage cybersecurity datasets to define cybersecurity metrics at multiple levels of abstraction: data vs. knowledge vs. application [48]. Using Medical Science as an analogy, data-level metrics may be defined to quantify building-block or "cell" level properties; "cell" level metrics may be leveraged to define sub-system or "tissue" level properties; "tissue" level metrics may be further leveraged to define "organ" level metrics; "organ" level metrics may be further leveraged to define "human body" level metrics. It should be mentioned that a higher level metric would not be any simple aggregation of some lever level metrics, because cybersecurity is largely about emergent properties [46, 55], meaning that the phenomenon observed at a higher level of abstraction is the outcome of interactions between its composing parts.

Seeking Foundations to Distinguish Good from Poor Metrics [35]. It would not be hard to define cybersecurity metrics, but it is certainly hard to define "good" cybersecurity metrics. This is because it is hard to define criteria or seek foundations to evaluate the competency or usefulness of cybersecurity metrics. In order to tackle this problem, we may need to conduct many case studies and define metrics at multiple levels of abstractions [55] before we can draw general insights along this direction. It would be ideal to conduct such case studies on some killer applications; two candidate killer applications are cyber defense command-and-control and quantitative cyber risk management [48].

Fostering a Cybersecurity Metrics Research Community. In order to tackle such a fundamental problem like cybersecurity metrics and quantification, it must take a community effort. This can be justified by how the basic medical science research has supported clinical healthcare practices. For example, the basic medical science research creates knowledge to help understand how the various kinds of metrics (e.g., blood pressure) would reflect a human being's health condition (e.g., presence or absence of certain diseases), and this kind of knowledge is applied to guide the practice of medical diagnosis and treatment. Analogously, cybersecurity metrics research would need to identify, invent, and define metrics (e.g., "cybersecurity blood pressure") that reflect the cybersecurity situations and can be applied to diagnose the "health conditions" of networks or devices.

In order to accelerate the fostering of a research community, we can start with some "grass roots" actions. For example, when one publishes a paper, the author may strive to clearly articulate the assumptions that are needed by the new result. Moreover, the author may strive to define metrics that are important to quantify the progress made by the new result [35]. Furthermore, when we teach cybersecurity courses, we should strive to make students know that much research needs to be done in order to tackle the fundamental problems of cybersecurity metrics and quantification. For this purpose, we would need to develop new curriculum materials.

Developing a Science of Cybersecurity Measurement. Well defined cybersecurity metrics need to be measured in the real world, which would demand the support of principled (rather than heuristic) methods. This problem may seem trivial at a first glance, which may be true for some metrics in some settings. However, the accurate measurement of cybersecurity metrics could be very challenging, which may be analogous to the measurement of light speed or gravitational constant in Physics. To see this, let us consider a simple and well-defined metric: What is the fraction (or percentage) of the devices in an network that are compromised at a given point in time t? The measurement of this metric is challenging in practice when the network is large. The reason is that automated or semi-automated tools (e.g., intrusion detection systems and/or anti-malware tools) that can be leveraged for measurement purposes are not necessarily trustworthy because of their false-positives and false-negatives.

5   Conclusion

We have presented a framework to unify security metrics, agility metrics, resilience metrics, and risk metrics. The framework is driven by the assumptions that are made at the design and operations phases, while embracing the uncertainty about whether these assumptions are violated or not in the real world. We identified a number of gaps that have not been discussed in the literature but must be bridged in order to tackle the problem of Cybersecurity Metrics and Quantification and ultimately tame cybersecurity. In particular, we must bridge the assumption gap and the uncertainty gap, which are inherent to the discrepancies between designers' views at lower levels of abstractions (i.e., building-blocks and components) and operators' views at high levels of abstractions (i.e., networks and devices). We presented a number of future research directions. In addition, it is interesting to investigate how to extend the SARR framework to accommodate other kinds of metrics, such as dependability.

Acknowledgement. We thank Moti Yung for illuminating discussions and Eric Ficke for proofreading the paper. This work was supported in part by ARO Grant #W911NF-17-1-0566, NSF Grants #2115134 and #2122631 (#1814825), and by a Grant from the State of Colorado.

References

1. Charlton, J., Du, P., Cho, J., Xu, S.: Measuring relative accuracy of malware detectors in the absence of ground truth. In: Proceedings of IEEE MILCOM, pp. 450–455 (2018)
2. Charlton, J., Du, P., Xu, S.: A new method for inferring ground-truth labels. In: Proceedings of SciSec (2021)
3. Chen, H., Cho, J., Xu, S.: Quantifying the security effectiveness of firewalls and DMZs. In: Proceedings of HoTSoS 2018, pp. 9:1–9:11 (2018)
4. Chen, H., Cho, J., Xu, S.: Quantifying the security effectiveness of network diversity. In: Proceedings of HoTSoS 2018, p. 24:1 (2018)
5. Chen, Y., Huang, Z., Xu, S., Lai, Y.: Spatiotemporal patterns and predictability of cyberattacks. PLoS ONE **10**(5), e0124472 (2015)
6. Cheng, Y., Deng, J., Li, J., DeLoach, S., Singhal, A., Ou, X.: Metrics of security. In: Cyber Defense and Situational Awareness, pp. 263–295 (2014)
7. Cho, J., Hurley, P., Xu, S.: Metrics and measurement of trustworthy systems. In: Proceedings IEEE MILCOM (2016)
8. Cho, J., Xu, S., Hurley, P., Mackay, M., Benjamin, T., Beaumont, M.: STRAM: measuring the trustworthiness of computer-based systems. ACM Comput. Surv. **51**(6), 128:1–128:47 (2019)
9. National Research Council: Review of the Department of Homeland Security's Approach to Risk Analysis. The National Academies Press (2010)
10. INFOSEC Research Council. Hard problem list. http://www.infosec-research.org/docs_public/20051130-IRC-HPL-FINAL.pdf (2007)
11. Da, G., Xu, M., Xu, S.: A new approach to modeling and analyzing security of networked systems. In: Proceedings HotSoS 2014, pp. 6:1–6:12 (2014)
12. Dai, W., Parker, P., Jin, H., Xu, S.: Enhancing data trustworthiness via assured digital signing. IEEE TDSC **9**(6), 838–851 (2012)
13. Du, P., Sun, Z., Chen, H., Cho, J.H., Xu, S.: Statistical estimation of malware detection metrics in the absence of ground truth. IEEE T-IFS **13**(12), 2965–2980 (2018)
14. Durumeric, Z., et al.: The matter of heartbleed. In: Proceedings IMC (2014)
15. Fang, Z., Xu, M., Xu, S., Hu, T.: A framework for predicting data breach risk: leveraging dependence to cope with sparsity. IEEE T-IFS **16**, 2186–2201 (2021)
16. Goldreich, O.: The Foundations of Cryptography, vol. 1. Cambridge University Press (2001)
17. Haimes, Y.Y.: On the definition of resilience in systems. Risk Anal. **29**(4), 498–501 (2009)
18. Han, Y., Lu, W., Xu, S.: Characterizing the power of moving target defense via cyber epidemic dynamics. In: HotSoS, pp. 1–12 (2014)
19. Han, Y., Lu, W., Xu, S.: Preventive and reactive cyber defense dynamics with ergodic time-dependent parameters is globally attractive. IEEE TNSE, accepted for publication (2021)
20. Harrison, K., Xu, S.: Protecting cryptographic keys from memory disclosures. In: IEEE/IFIP DSN 2007, pp. 137–143 (2007)

21. Homer, J., et al.: Aggregating vulnerability metrics in enterprise networks using attack graphs. J. Comput. Secur. **21**(4), 561–597 (2013)
22. Jensen, U.: Probabilistic risk analysis: foundations and methods. J. Am. Stat. Assoc. **97**(459), 925 (2002)
23. Kantchelian, A., et al.: Better malware ground truth: techniques for weighting anti-virus vendor labels. In: Proceedings AISec, pp. 45–56 (2015)
24. Li, D., Li, Q., Ye, Y., Xu, S.: SoK: arms race in adversarial malware detection. CoRR, abs/2005.11671 (2020)
25. Li, D., Li, Q., Ye, Y., Xu, S.: A framework for enhancing deep neural networks against adversarial malware. IEEE TNSE **8**(1), 736–750 (2021)
26. Li, X., Parker, P., Xu, S.: A stochastic model for quantitative security analyses of networked systems. IEEE TDSC **8**(1), 28–43 (2011)
27. Lin, Z., Lu, W., Xu, S.: Unified preventive and reactive cyber defense dynamics is still globally convergent. IEEE/ACM ToN **27**(3), 1098–1111 (2019)
28. Lu, W., Xu, S., Yi, X.: Optimizing active cyber defense dynamics. In: Proceedings GameSec 2013, pp. 206–225 (2013)
29. Lynch, N.: Distributed Algorithms. Morgan Kaufmann (1996)
30. Mireles, J., Ficke, E., Cho, J., Hurley, P., Xu, S.: Metrics towards measuring cyber agility. IEEE T-IFS **14**(12), 3217–3232 (2019)
31. Morales, J., Xu, S., Sandhu, R.: Analyzing malware detection efficiency with multiple anti-malware programs. In: Proceedings CyberSecurity (2012)
32. Nicol, D., et al.: The science of security 5 hard problems, August 2015. http://cps-vo.org/node/21590
33. Noel, S., Jajodia, S.: A suite of metrics for network attack graph analytics. In: Network Security Metrics, pp. 141–176. Springer, Cham (2017). https://doi.org/10.1007/978-3-319-66505-4_7
34. Park, J., Seager, T.P., Rao, P.S.C., Convertino, M., Linkov, I.: Integrating risk and resilience approaches to catastrophe management in engineering systems. Risk Anal. **33**(3), 356–367 (2013)
35. Pendleton, M., Garcia-Lebron, R., Cho, J., Xu, S.: A survey on systems security metrics. ACM Comput. Surv. **49**(4), 62:1–62:35 (2016)
36. Pfleeger, S.L., Cunningham, R.K.: Why measuring security is hard. IEEE Secur. Priv. **8**(4), 46–54 (2010)
37. Ramos, A., Lazar, M., Filho, R.H., Rodrigues, J.J.P.C.: Model-based quantitative network security metrics: a survey. IEEE Commun. Surv. Tutor. **19**(4), 2704–2734 (2017)
38. National Science and Technology Council: Trustworthy cyberspace: strategic plan for the federal cybersecurity research and development program (2011). https://www.nitrd.gov/SUBCOMMITTEE/csia/Fed_Cybersecurity_RD_Strategic_Plan_2011.pdf
39. Wang, L., Jajodia, S., Singhal, A.: Network Security Metrics. Network Security Metrics, Springer, Cham (2017). https://doi.org/10.1007/978-3-319-66505-4
40. Wang, L., Jajodia, S., Singhal, A., Cheng, P., Noel, S.: k-zero day safety: a network security metric for measuring the risk of unknown vulnerabilities. IEEE TDSC **11**(1), 30–44 (2014)
41. Xu, L., et al.: KCRS: a blockchain-based key compromise resilient signature system. In: Proceedings BlockSys, pp. 226–239 (2019)
42. Xu, M., Da, G., Xu, S.: Cyber epidemic models with dependences. Internet Math. **11**(1), 62–92 (2015)
43. Xu, M., Hua, L., Xu, S.: A vine copula model for predicting the effectiveness of cyber defense early-warning. Technometrics **59**(4), 508–520 (2017)

44. Xu, M., Schweitzer, K.M., Bateman, R.M., Xu, S.: Modeling and predicting cyber hacking breaches. IEEE T-IFS **13**(11), 2856–2871 (2018)
45. Xu, M., Xu, S.: An extended stochastic model for quantitative security analysis of networked systems. Internet Math. **8**(3), 288–320 (2012)
46. Xu, S.: Emergent behavior in cybersecurity. In: Proceedings HotSoS, pp. 13:1–13:2 (2014)
47. Xu, S.: Cybersecurity dynamics: a foundation for the science of cybersecurity. In: Proactive and Dynamic Network Defense, pp. 1–31 (2019)
48. Xu, S.: The cybersecurity dynamics way of thinking and landscape (invited paper). In: ACM Workshop on Moving Target Defense (2020)
49. Xu, S., Lu, W., Xu, L.: Push- and pull-based epidemic spreading in networks: thresholds and deeper insights. ACM TAAS **7**(3), 1–26 (2012)
50. Xu, S., Lu, W., Xu, L., Zhan, Z.: Adaptive epidemic dynamics in networks: thresholds and control. ACM TAAS **8**(4), 1–19 (2014)
51. Xu, S., Lu, W., Zhan, Z.: A stochastic model of multivirus dynamics. IEEE Trans. Dependable Secure Comput. **9**(1), 30–45 (2012)
52. Xu, S., Yung, M.: Expecting the unexpected: towards robust credential infrastructure. In: Financial Crypto, pp. 201–221 (2009)
53. Xu, S.: Cybersecurity dynamics. In: Proceedings HotSoS 2014, pp. 14:1–14:2 (2014)
54. Shouhuai, X., Wenlian, L., Li, H.: A stochastic model of active cyber defense dynamics. Internet Math. **11**(1), 23–61 (2015)
55. Xu, S., Trivedi, K.: Report of the 2019 SATC pi meeting break-out session on "cybersecurity metrics: Why is it so hard?" (2019)
56. Shouhuai, X., Yung, M., Wang, J.: Seeking foundations for the science of cyber security. Inf. Syst. Front. **23**, 263–267 (2021)
57. Zhan, Z., Xu, M., Xu, S.: Characterizing honeypot-captured cyber attacks: statistical framework and case study. IEEE T-IFS **8**(11), 1775–1789 (2013)
58. Zhan, Z., Maochao, X., Shouhuai, X.: Predicting cyber attack rates with extreme values. IEEE T-IFS **10**(8), 1666–1677 (2015)
59. Zhang, M., Wang, L., Jajodia, S., Singhal, A., Albanese, M.: Network diversity: a security metric for evaluating the resilience of networks against zero-day attacks. IEEE Trans. Inf. Forensics Secur. **11**(5), 1071–1086 (2016)
60. Zheng, R., Lu, W., Xu, S.: Active cyber defense dynamics exhibiting rich phenomena. In: Proceedings HotSoS (2015)
61. Zheng, R., Lu, W., Xu, S.: Preventive and reactive cyber defense dynamics is globally stable. IEEE TNSE **5**(2), 156–170 (2018)

Detection for Cybersecurity

Detecting Internet-Scale Surveillance Devices Using RTSP Recessive Features

Zhaoteng Yan[1,2] (ID), Zhi Li[1,2(✉)] (ID), Wenping Bai[2] (ID), Nan Yu[2] (ID),
Hongsong Zhu[1,2] (ID), and Limin Sun[1,2]

[1] School of Cyber Security, University of Chinese Academy of Sciences,
Beijing, China
{yanzhaoteng,lizhi,zhuhongsong,sunlimin}@iie.ac.cn
[2] Institute of Information Engineering, Chinese Academy of Sciences, Beijing, China
{baiwenping,yunan}@iie.ac.cn

Abstract. In recent years, fingerprinting online surveillance devices has been a hot research topic. However, large-scale devices still can not be identified their brands in previous studies and mainstream search engines. In this work, we propose a novel neural network-based approach for automatically discovering surveillance devices and identifying their brands in cyberspace. Moreover, by using the deep semi-supervised learning algorithm, the most unlabeled samples with new-explored recessive features can be learned of RTSP protocol. In the global IPv4 space, we implement an evaluation on $3,123,489$ active RTSP-hosts for training and testing. The experimental results demonstrate our approach can discover $2,803,406$ surveillance devices, which are eight times and three times more than those discovered by Shodan and Zoomeye. Moreover, the number of identified brand-level devices by our approach is $2,457,661$ devices with their brands, which is at least four times more than existing methods. The performance of these results with precision and recall can both achieve 93%.

Keywords: RTSP · Video surveillance devices · Fingerprinting

1 Introduction

Video surveillance devices, including IP camera, Network Video Recorder(NVR), Digital Video Recorder (DVR), etc., can intuitively grasp the real-time image and audio of the target monitoring area. For convenience, massive surveillance devices are connecting to the Internet. Meanwhile, these online embedded devices bring huge threats to cyberspace because of their lack of enough security protection [2]. The most effective measurement of security assessment is identifying their manufacturers. Therefore, previous studies [5,7,10,14] and search engines [13,18] on discovery and fingerprinting these devices have been implemented.

However, there is existing a problem that most online surveillance devices still can not be identified. As an example, this work focus on the video surveillance devices which are opening RTSP service in cyberspace. As a kind of classic video

© Springer Nature Switzerland AG 2021
W. Lu et al. (Eds.): SciSec 2021, LNCS 13005, pp. 21–35, 2021.
https://doi.org/10.1007/978-3-030-89137-4_2

transmission protocol, RTSP is the most used application protocol which can be implemented by manufacturers as the remote video transmission service between their video surveillance products. According to the statistics in 2019, there are 2, 290, 633 hosts were opening RTSP service on the Internet [18]. However, only 526, 241 can be identified as surveillance devices and there is a large remaining number of RSTP-hosts (1, 764, 392, about 77% of the total) were tagged as *Unknown*. Even the remaining unknown RSTP-hosts may include some RTSP streaming servers or honeypots, however, the number of un-identified surveillance devices is still too huge.

According to our analysis, the two main reasons of most RSTP-hosts can not be identified are as follows: (1) *Single probing load.* Current mainstream search engine (such as Shodan [13], Zoomeye [18], Censys [5]) and previous studies [10] employed one kind method OPTIONS request as the only probing load to obtain protocol banners. Actually, this is only one of the 11 methods which were originally designed for RTSP request packets [12]. This caused the identification source is unitary. (2) *Simple dominant feature.* Previous approaches employed the obvious characteristic field (commonly using the name of manufacturers, such as Hikvision, Dahua) as the fingerprinting feature. This kind of feature is simple and intuitive, but most effective. However, only a few parts of video surveillance devices provide these dominant keywords in their protocol banners. Moreover, more and more manufacturers have modified their obvious vendor/model name from the responses in their new products. This caused the scope of identification becomes much smaller and the difficulty of fingerprinting is highly increased.

Motivation: In this paper, we aim to detect these *Unknown* RSTP-hosts on the Internet whether are surveillance devices or not, and then identify their manufacturers if they are. The key of our work is mining new effective non-dominant features and generating accurate fingerprints on the RTSP protocol banners. We observe that every surveillance manufacturer implements the RTSP service between its product and a streaming server with *distinction*. That caused that there are a variety of response packets when these surveillance devices received the same sequential standard request methods (including OPTIONS, DESCRIBE, SETUP, etc.). Therefore, these *distinctions* can be employed as a new kind of recessive feature to distinguish the surveillance brands, even if the various response packets do not contain obvious characteristic keywords.

Challenges: To achieve this end, we need to address three main challenges as follows:

- *Un-standard products:* each manufacturer respectively implements RTSP in its diverse serial of surveillance products, which caused the difficulty of feature extraction is greatly increased.
- *Too few labeled-samples:* there are no publicly labeled surveillance devices by using RTSP recessive features as ground truth for training neural networks.
- *Unevenly sample distribution:* unbalanced market occupancy of various brands caused the distribution of training and testing samples are uneven.

Method: To address these challenges, we employ a novel method consists of three parts: Text-CNN, DS^3L, Open-world SSL, and the name is abbreviated to TDO. Firstly, we use enhanced Text- Convolutional Neural Network(CNN) to extract recessive features from encoded consequential and normal $Response >$ matrixes against un-standard samples. Then we use DS^3L (Deep Safe Semi-Supervised Learning) for extending the labeled samples. In particular, the open-world SSL (Semi-Supervised Learning) algorithm is employed to clustering unseen classes which may not be contained in the labeled brands on the Internet.

Results: To evaluate the performance, we implement our approach to the real Internet-wide public data. We generate the experimental dataset which contains $3,011,237$ active RTSP-hosts. After training and testing, $2,803,406$ can be classified as discovered surveillance devices. The highly increased identification rate (89.75%) is about eight and three times than famous search engines of Shodan and Zoomeye [13,18]. Moreover, $2,457,661$ discovered devices can be identified in their diverse 35 brands, including 8 new brands of unseen classes. And the number of identified brand-lever devices is 7.2 times and 4.7 times more than representative previous approaches by ARE and IoTtracker [7,14]. The results show that the precision and recall keep high comparable performance as 93.39% and 93.12%.

Contributions: Overall, we make the following desirable contributions:

- *New recessive feature:* we propose a method TDO for identifying online surveillance devices using recessive features of RTSP protocol.
- *Active learning :* we propose the first neural network-based approach to encoding RTSP $Responses >$ into consequential vectored matrixes for recessive feature extraction.
- *Effective evaluation in the real experiment:* we generate the first data set which contains $2,803,406$ labeled surveillance devices, about four times as many as commercial search engines. Among which, $2,457,661$ brand-level samples are identified over 35 different brands, almost four times than previous approaches.
- *High precision and recall:* the evaluation demonstrates that our approach can achieve higher precision and recall (93%) than six comparable classification algorithms.

2   Related Work

Internet-Wide Discovering of Surveillance Devices. As a video surveillance device is the most typical IoT device, previous studies on discovering surveillance devices in cyberspace were also along with fingerprinting online IoT devices. Durumeric *et al.* proposed ZMap which decreased Internet-wide scanning time from two years to one hour [6]. Based on ZMap, researchers proposed many fast Internet-wide scan mechanisms for IoT devices, including webcams [3]. At the same time, device search engines such as Shodan [13] and Censys [5] emerged in succession and provided Internet-wide device searching services to the public. Due to the online surveillance devices were the most Mirai-infected bonnets in 2016 [2], Antonakakis *et al.* determined hundreds of thousands of IP cameras and DVRs were infections. A specific study on discovering almost 1.6 million surveillance devices in cyberspace, which comes closest to our work, was given by Qiang *et al.* [10]. Although Qiang'*et al.* also discussed RTSP as one application service of video surveillance devices, they only used HTTP webpages as the main fingerprinting target source data.

The above-mentioned previous works mainly focus on fingerprinting surveillance devices using dominant features, such as obvious vendor and product names [5,7], or visible webpages [10]. However, these approaches only can cover a part of target devices that carried dominant features. To the complex and irregular cyberspace, the ideal dominant features obviously inadequate.

Protocol Recessive Features. For augmented cognition, a new field on intending to extract recessive features has come out in recent years. Xu *et al.* used HTML Doomtree and CSS style as enhancing recessive features [14], that increased 40.76% identifiable devices than using obvious vendor and product names [7]. Kai *et al.* and Zhaoteng *et al.* proposed neural network to learn deep recessive features in protocol banners, such as special string field [16,17]. These works have partly added the number of identifiable online IoT devices. However, previous works still performed helpless on RTSP-service surveillance devices. That is exactly the issue what this paper aimed to resolve.

3   Protocol Analysis on RTSP

In this section, we first describe RTSP $<Request, Response>$ method. Then, we introduce recessive feature extraction for Internet-wide measurements on surveillance device discovery.

3.1 $<Request, Response>$ Methods of RTSP

As a standard C/S model application protocol, there is a total of 20 methods. On one hand, there are 6 required or recommended methods, and 5 optional methods defined by RTSP [12]. There are 6 serialize required or recommended methods are commonly implemented in video surveillance devices as streaming servers. On the other hand, there are 9 abnormal methods (including `bad_method`, `bad_option_url`, etc.) and one `HTTP Get` method. These special methods are generated by us to extend the identification data source.

Each request method carries out a unique function [12], which caused its corresponding response is also different. Meanwhile, the $<Request, Response>$ packets explore HTTP-structure format. As shown in Fig. 1, there are two examples of `Hikvision` and `Uniview` IP camera. We observe that different brands of devices typically have unique six *Response* packets(status code, layout, and content, even some *Response* is null). What's more, even the same brand, *Response* packets are also different from diverse product serials or device types. For example, Hikvision NVRs and IP cameras may be loaded with different firmware in different production years. Consequently, the diverse and normalized response packets present two characteristics: invariant and distinct, which provide us the opportunity to extract these useful features for identification.

	Hikvision	Uniview
OPTIONS Response	RTSPV/1.0 200 OK\r\n CSeq: 1000\r\n Public: OPTIONS, DESCRIBE, PLAY, PAUSE, SETUP, TEARDOWN, SET_PARAMETER, GET_PARAMETER\r\n Date: Wed, May 08 2019 11:12:32 GMT\r\n\r\n	RTSPV/1.0 200 OK\r\n CSeq: 1000\r\n Public: SETUP,TEARDOWN,OPTIONS,PLAY,ANNOUNCE,DESCRIBE, SET_PARAMETER,\r\n\r\n
DESCRIBE Response	RTSPV/1.0 401 Unauthorized\r\n CSeq: 1000\r\n WWW-Authenticate: Digest realm=\"54c4155fbb2a\", nonce=\"30e10b28c57c6c54b16963f75c6d5ce0\", stale=\"FALSE\"\r\n WWW-Authenticate: Basic realm=\"54c4155fbb2a\"\r\n Date: Wed, May 08 2019 11:12:32 GMT\r\n\r\n	RTSPV/1.0 401 ClientUnAuthorized\r\n CSeq: 1000\r\n WWW-Authenticate: Digest realm=\"48ea631dc359\", nonce=\"15577112237111119411311411615845996 1687\", stale=\"FALSE\"\r\n WWW-Authenticate: Basic realm=\"48ea631dc359\"\r\n\r\n
SETUP Response	RTSPV/1.0 401 Unauthorized\r\n CSeq: 1000\r\n WWW-Authenticate: Digest realm=\"54c4155fbb2a\", nonce=\"12631c5955aff087d4444dc61b9229b7\", stale=\"FALSE\"\r\n WWW-Authenticate: Basic realm=\"54c4155fbb2a\"\r\n Date: Wed, May 08 2019 11:12:32 GMT\r\n\r\n	RTSPV/1.0 401 ClientUnAuthorized\r\n CSeq: 1000\r\n WWW-Authenticate: Digest realm=\"48ea631dc359\", nonce=\"155711112571519136121111143115834677461\", stale=\"FALSE\"\r\n WWW-Authenticate: Basic realm=\"48ea631dc359\"\r\n\r\n
PLAY Response	RTSPV/1.0 454 Session Not Found\r\n CSeq: 1000\r\n Session: 0\r\n Date: Wed, May 08 2019 11:12:32 GMT\r\n\r\n	RTSPV/1.0 401 ClientUnAuthorized\r\n CSeq: 1000\r\n WWW-Authenticate: Digest realm=\"48ea631dc359\", nonce=\"155711324911521172121171351611601686410\", stale=\"FALSE\"\r\n WWW-Authenticate: Basic realm=\"48ea631dc359\"\r\n\r\n
PAUSE Response	null	RTSPV/1.0 401 ClientUnAuthorized\r\n CSeq: 1000\r\n WWW-Authenticate: Digest realm=\"48ea631dc359\", nonce=\"1557181329421119428111111148175893361 15\", stale=\"FALSE\"\r\n WWW-Authenticate: Basic realm=\"48ea631dc359\"\r\n\r\n
TEARDOWN Response	RTSPV/1.0 500 Internal Server Error\r\n CSeq: 1000\r\n Session: 0\r\n Date: Wed, May 08 2019 11:12:32 GMT\r\n\r\n	RTSPV/1.0 401 ClientUnAuthorized\r\n CSeq: 1000\r\n WWW-Authenticate: Digest realm=\"48ea631dc359\", nonce=\"15571131114111295121122121191514158364 19\", stale=\"FALSE\"\r\n WWW-Authenticate: Basic realm=\"48ea631dc359\"\r\n\r\n

Fig. 1. Two examples of 6 irregular response packets.

Most significantly, non-interruption is the basic guideline to choose *Request* methods. For example, benefited from OPTIONS does not influence server state, existing search engines use the OPTIONS *Response* as identification of source data [13,18]. Thanks to the authentication of RTSP, the other *Requests* will not bring any interrupt to target devices unless authentication passed. Moreover, these un-authentication *Responses* still contain useful contents for identification, as shown in Fig. 1. Therefore, there is no need to worry about the influence of getting response packets on online surveillance devices.

3.2   Features Selection

To identify the brand of a surveillance device besides direct brand name keywords as observe feature, we choose three-dimensional recessive features in *Response* packets. First, we use the diverse responses of 20 sequential *Request* methods. Take Fig. 1 as two typical examples, two different IP cameras from two manufacturers return diverse responses. Among which, the contents on each header field show obvious contrast. Second, we explore the diverse respond mechanisms of different brands. As shown in Fig. 1, PAUSE *Response* of a Uniview camera display a normal packet while Hikvision responses null. This non-responding is a characteristic in itself to distinguish with other brands. Third, status code is another useful feature. There are 44 kinds of RTSP status codes, which have been implemented by diverse manufacturers. Such as "454" in Hikvision PLAY *Response* and "401" in Uniview PLAY *Response*.

With regard to the stability of feature source data, these *Responses* of a device rarely change (except for data, time, and temporary strings in the "nonce" field) until its firmware is updated.

3.3 Challenges of Internet-Wide Measurement

Although the above-mentioned displays that it is possible to use diverse and structural RTSP *Responses* for fingerprinting. There are reminding three difficulties to hold in cyberspace. First, not all surveillance devices of one brand respond same sequential *Response* packets because of diverse serials, device types, and updating firmware. That caused the *Responses* complex and irregular. Second, market share of different manufacturers determine their respective proportion of different products in cyberspace. That caused the samples distributed uniformly, which easily lead to classification on some brands of less market share over-fitting. Third, there are not labeled online samples, among which one common case is that unlabeled data contains classes that are not seen in the labeled data.

As our goal is to identify online surveillance devices and detect their brands which are tagged as the *Unknown* by existing search engines, we focus on obtaining *Responses* from accessible devices which open their RTSP services in cyberspace without protection. With regard to the meticulously protected devices, we will not attempt any disallowed probing packets to comply with ethics. To achieve this aim, we need to address the three difficulties as our main novelty and contribution.

4   Methodology

In this section, we introduce a new architecture of TDO for fingerprinting online surveillance devices base on mixed neural networks and deep learning methods.

As illustrated in Fig. 2, the workflow of our architecture consists of six steps: (1) Data collection: we firstly send 20 sequential RTSP *Request* methods to the hosts with port 554 opening both on our private Intranet and the public Internet. Simultaneously, we collect these *Responses* from these offline and online devices. (2) Pre-processing: we clean and normalize each *Response* as a matrix sample in the unified format. (3) Input: depending on manual labeling experience and fingerprints, we tag the known device a label with surveillance type and its brand. Thus, these samples can be divided into two categories: labeled and unlabeled, which can be respectively used as the training and testing dataset. (4) Training: based on deep learning algorithms, we train the classification model. (5) Classification and (6) Identification: the trained module can identify the unlabeled sample whether a surveillance device and its brand.

4.1 Data Collection

As illustrated in Fig. 2, our data sources are obtained from two environments: offline and online. First, concerning the offline data source, we constructed a private surveillance Intranet which contains 67 popular surveillance devices we purchased. In the white-box testing environment, we can explore <*Request, Response*> methods of RTSP and ensure the non-interruption in

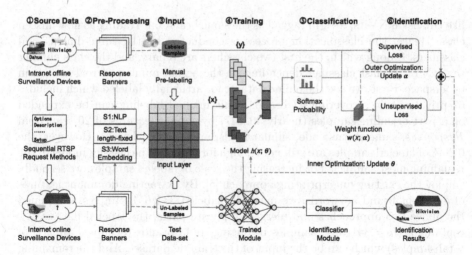

Fig. 2. The Main System Architecture.

detail. Most significantly, we have evaluated the feasibility of fingerprinting these devices by using *Responses* as a data source. Meanwhile, these few well-labeled samples can be used as seeds for fingerprinting in cyberspace. Second, for reducing unnecessary Internet-wide scans and respecting network ethics, we collected active hosts which were opening RTSP service on port 554 from search engine [13,18]. Then, we sent 20 *Request* methods to these hosts and collected respecting *Responses* as online data source.

4.2 Pre-processing

Although RTSP *Response* packets are typically semi-structured and specially RTSP-format text content, the packets still need to be processed. As shown in Fig. 1, the *Response* packets contain some useless symbols, such as *"="*, *":"*. To make useful characteristics more efficient, we firstly transform these symbols as ASCII codes and clean by them NLP (Natural Language Processing) [1]. Then, considering the texts vary in length, we set the fixed length of each response no exceeding 200. Most significantly, we process each response in standard RTSP *Response* format with 44 fields. Among which, we fill *null* for the empty field. After the above steps, each response is processed as a unified text-matrix. Thus, each sample is constructed by 20 sequential matrixes for every host.

4.3 Labeling

The normalized samples need to be tagged a label in two previous approaches by using common features. And the label of each host contains three attributes: whether surveillance device (T), whether can be identified by dominant feature (A), and its brand name (B). For instance, a label $y_i = \{A_i, T_i, B_i\}$ of one Hikvision IPcam (i) is $\{Yes, Yes, Hikvision\}$. With regard to the different class like Hikvision NVRs, we still tagged as the same brand but trading as new unseen class. Hence, the classification process is conducted by the three-dimensional classifiers. Among which, the first two classifiers are binary, and the class number ($c \in C$) of the last classifier depending on the actual number of real brands in cyberspace. First, we use the offline dataset for artificially labeled which includes 67 private devices covering 43 brands. This manual labeling can be expended on a part of online samples (nearly $30, 147$) by similar features of 20 sequential *Responses*: same status code, similar fields, and similar content. However, the 0.96% of labeled samples are still not enough for training the classier model of the remaining most samples. For increasing the scale of labeled samples, we secondly employ the existing fingerprinting approach [5]. By extracting dominant features of apparent brand keywords, we manually labeled $334, 651$ samples. Combined the above two approaches and merged duplicate parts, the labeled dataset X_n contains n ($n = 341, 324$) samples belonging to 43 brands (occupied 10.93% of total samples) which can be the input of the training dataset. And the remaining m ($m = 2, 782, 165$) unlabeled samples construct the testing dataset Y_m.

4.4   Training

Considering the *Response* packet is different from common text, we employ CNN-enhanced instead of CNN for better learning recessive features from sequential and logic *Responses*. As we discussed above, we aim to use three recessive features (status code, content, response-method), which may be processed as ordinary word vectors based on classic CNN models. In a trial test by using the TextCNN program in Tensorflow [9], the over-fitting problem appears after only one round of the training process, and the learned feature focuses on the samples of 9 big brands. Integrating the two main reasons, we propose an enhanced-CNN model [15], directed at the extraction of all recessive characteristics of the text-matrixes. Hence, we trade the 20 sequential matrixes of each host like 20 continuous photographs, which produced the reduced global feature map (x_i) in the input layer. In the convolutional layer, the sub-sampling is followed to extract local features by mapping several feature maps. Then, the two-dimension feature maps in the fully connected layer, which can be used to linking the positional relationship of each map. Consequently, global and local recessive features can be fully learned by the CNN-enhanced algorithm.

To address another challenge of unevenly distribution in the Internet-wide samples, we employ DS^3L to strengthen the minority samples of small brands and maintain the majority samples of big brands [8]. According to our statistics of the final Internet-wide experimental result, the samples of Top 5 brands (Dahua, Hikvision, Xiongmai) occupy nearly two-thirds of the total samples ($3, 123, 489$) and the remaining one-third samples are belong to more than 32 brands. For instance, the number of Bottom 10 brands (including Sony, Axis, Netgear, etc.) surveillance devices is 317, which is less than 0.02% of Dahua (Top 1) samples. Thus, we use DS^3L for two stages. First, we set a weight function $w(x_i; \alpha)$ parameterized by α for the unlabeled samples and find the optimal model $\hat{\theta}(\alpha)$ as following:

$$\hat{\theta}(\alpha) = \min_{\theta \in \Theta} \sum_{i=1}^{n} \ell(h(x_i; \theta), y_i) + \sum_{i=n+1}^{n+m} w(x_i; \alpha)\Omega(x_i; \theta) \tag{1}$$

where $\theta \in \Theta$ denotes a training parameter and $h(x_i; \theta)$ denotes the training model. ℓ refers to the loss function and $\Omega(x_i; \theta)$ refers to the regularization term.

Then for maintaining the generalization performance of the labeled samples of big brands, we attempt to find the optimal parameter $\hat{\alpha}$ as following:

$$\hat{\alpha} = \arg \min_{\alpha \in \mathbb{B}^d} \sum_{i=1}^{n} [\ell(h(x_i; \hat{\theta}(\alpha)), y_i] \tag{2}$$

where $\alpha \in \mathbb{B}^d$ denotes to a sample to a weight. The training process is synchronously optimizing the weighted loss $\hat{\alpha}$, which can be minimizing the supervised degradation performance of well-labeled samples.

On the other hand, To address another challenge of unseen classes in the unlabeled samples, we partly employ the open-world SSL algorithm to enhance the DS^3L semi-supervised algorithm for discovery novel classes of unlabeled-brands in the real cyberspace [4]. As above-mentioned, the labeled samples cover 43 brands, which are only a few parts of more than thousands of diverse brands on the Internet [7]. However, DS^3L may reject new classes of *Unknown* brands to be discovered. Therefore, we denote the number (u) of novel classes as an unknown parameter. By clustering unknown classes (c_u), we calculate the similarity of the new class with labeled classes (C) of samples using Levenshtein distance [11]. Note that if $c_u \notin C$, we assign the class c_u as a novel class. After fingerprinting by artificial experience, we would try to manually label the novel class as a new brand and add one of the total numbers as $(c + 1)$.

4.5 Classification

After the training process, the trained models can be built for prediction as three-dimensional classifiers. As mentioned in Sect. 4.3, three classifiers are logically associated as follows: the first classifier is for determining whether a host is a surveillance device, then the second classifier is for detecting whether it can be identified by using the dominant feature, the third classifier is for identifying its brand. We have investigated the 4 typical classification of machine learning algorithms, including support vector machine(SVM), decision trees, and neural networks. Considering the logic relationship of two classifiers and the actual performance(see Sect. 5.2), we select the neural network for classification and three-dimensional logistic regression. Consequently, the unlabeled sample of testing dataset can be predicted whether is a surveillance device by the trained classification neural network. Towards finally identifying its manufacturer, a multi-class classifier needs to interpret.

4.6 Identification

In the identification module, we utilize the multi-class (c-class) classifier to detect the brand B_j of an unknown sample from an online surveillance device. In theory, the number (j) of brands decides the number c of classes. While in practice, each manufacturer may produce multiple series of surveillance devices in different decades. This problem ($j < c$) results that multiple clusters that may belong to the same brand, but can not be classified as the same class. For instance, Hikvision DS-2CD-xx IP camera and DS-xx NVR have two different superficial characteristics. As a result, we introduce pseudo-labeling for these particular clusters. With regard to the cluster having a similar feature on the neural network, we add a middle step of tagging the same pseudo-labels for these samples. Then according to the similarity of neurons, we labeled the final brand for these clusters based on dual-clustering and their similarity. Finally, the multi-class classifier determines the certain brand of the sample by calculating the probability $p(x_i)$ and using Argmax function to detect the most corresponding class.

5 Real-World Experiments and Result

In this section, we implement the real-world experiments on the Internet to perform the actual validity and accuracy of our approach.

5.1 Experimental Data

Step1: Data Collection. For offline data, we acquired 67 popular surveillance devices (including 58 IP cameras, 5 NVRs, and 4 DVRs) from 43 brands, see Fig. 3, keeping their original firmware and their manufacture years range from 2012 to 2020, aiming to emulate the real-usage as possible.

Fig. 3. Acquired surveillance devices in our experimental Intranet.

For online experiment, we utilized the bulk data in 2020 from search engine [13,18], which contains $5,046,671$ active hosts via HTTP-Get requests on port 554.

After $<Request, Response>$ methods, we received $3,123,489$ *Responses* hosts as online data source (other $1,923,182$ hosts may not return *Responses* because the access were blocked by firewalls or network address translators).

Step2&3: Pre-processing and Labeling. Then, the $3,123,489$ *Responses* consequential banners were processed as $3,123,489$ normal matrixes. After manually and previous labeling approach [7], there are $341,324$ samples that can be tagged with their labels as $\{Device - Type, Feature - Type, Brand\}$ which cover 27 brands. With regard to the other 16 surveillance brands of our acquired devices (such as Zavio, Tiandy, etc.), there are no available samples that have been found opening RTSP service on the Internet. Thus, the remaining unlabeled samples $(2,782,165)$ occupy nearly 89.07% of all samples.

Step4: Training. As shown in Table 1, we implemented the training process for extending the labeled samples by three stages. (1)By using the enhanced-TextCNN algorithm, $800,251$ samples can be added into the labeled dataset. (2)By using the DS^3L algorithm, $271,566$ samples can be added into the labeled dataset, which increases more than double than the previous stage. (3)By using the open-world SSL algorithm, $98,096$ samples can be added to the labeled dataset. These additional samples were labeled from unseen-class samples which cover 8 "new" brands. Totally, there are $1,511,237$ samples (occupying 48.38% of all samples) that can be labeled by learning recessive features and the semi-supervised learning algorithm.

Table 1. Label samples of Three Stages in Training Process.

	# of pre-labels	TextCNN	DS^3L	Openworld SSL
Labeled samples	341,324	1,141,575	1,413,141	1,511,237
Un-Labeled samples	2,782,165	1,981,914	1,710,348	1,612,252

Step5&6: Classification and Identification. As shown in Table 3, the total of $2,803,406$ samples can be classified in the final testing process as surveillance devices. Among which, $2,457,661$ samples can be identified their brands which cover 35 brands. And the other $345,745$ surveillance devices only can be identified their device-type as H264 DVR which can not be identified their detail brands (a part of these DVRs belong to Xiongmai, Dahua, etc.).

5.2 Evaluation

Measurement. To evaluate the performance, we introduce two evaluation indexes: precision and recall. Precision reflects the rating of devices correctly classified, recall reflects the number of Other devices incorrectly classified, and the harmonic means of F1-score is calculated using as follows:

$$Precision = \frac{TP}{TP + FP}, Recall = \frac{TP}{TP + FN}, F1 = \frac{2 * Precision * Recall}{Precision + Recall}$$

$$(3)$$

where True Positive (TP) denotes the number of surveillance devices correctly classified, False Positive denotes the number of devices incorrectly classified and False Negative (FN) reflects the number of surveillance devices incorrectly classified. Naturally, high precision and recall are the desirable outcomes.

Performance. As shown in Fig. 4, the changing trends of `precision` and `F1-score` were similar with the number of training samples, and the diversification of `recall` is opposite. When the number of training samples reach to 150 thousands, the performance is becoming to stabilize.

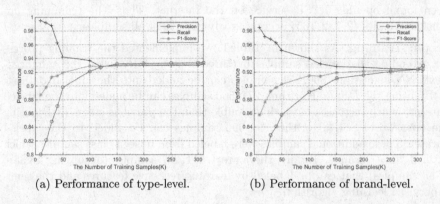

(a) Performance of type-level.   (b) Performance of brand-level.

Fig. 4. Trend of classification performance along with the number of training samples.

For performance comparison, we also evaluate other six classification algorithms: Naive Bayes, Boosting, Support Vector Machine (SVM), K-Means, C4.5 Decision Tree, simple Neural Network. As shown in Table 2, which indicates our approach TDO has the best performance. The main reason is our approach mixed neural network and deep semi-supervised algorithm, which separately ensure the high precision and recall, and especially for classifying un-seen classes.

Table 2. Performance of seven classification algorithms.

Approach	{Surveillance, -, null}			{Surveillance, -, Brand}		
	Precision(%)	Recall(%)	F1 score(%)	Precision(%)	Recall(%)	F1 score(%)
Naive Bayes	74.71	69.35	71.93	72.19	71.03	71.61
Boosting	71.92	73.22	72.56	72.45	70.38	71.40
SVM	85.36	90.44	87.83	86.33	87.55	86.94
k-Means	83.41	81.87	82.63	81.39	82.34	81.86
C4.5	78.75	81.55	80.13	77.99	80.10	79.03
Neural Network	90.23	91.61	90.91	91.68	90.51	91.09
TDO	**93.39**	**93.12**	**93.25**	**92.97**	**92.33**	**92.65**

5.3   Comparison

To evaluate the further effectiveness of meeting the above-mentioned challenges, we carry out two comparative trials on type-level and brand-level.

Comparison with Search Engine.   Due to the difference in probing methods and periods, the number of collected samples also differs from each search engine. We choose the comparative samples in the year 2020 to ensure as fair as possible. Then, we compare the number of identified surveillance devices on type-level. Table 3 shows that the identification rate of our approach is eight times and three times more than those discovered by Shodan and Zoomeye respectively. The underlying reasons are two fold: using recessive features and the deep semi-supervised algorithm help our approach to achieve the higher classification results.

Comparison with Existing Approaches.   Table 3 shows the comparison between our approach and ARE [7]/IoTtracker [14]. Using the same dataset of $3,123,489$ samples, The surveillance devices which can be identified with their brands by our approach are 7.2 times and 4.7 times more than those identified by ARE [7] and IoTtracker [14] respectively. With regard to ARE by generating fingerprints based on dominant feature [7], our recessive features on twenty consequential *Responses* approach added new feature space. With regard to IoTtracker by using recessive features on semi-structured contents similarly, our approach added the identification results benefiting from mixed enhanced-TextCNN, DS^3L and open-world algorithms.

Table 3. Comparison with popular search engines and approaches.

{Surveillance, -, null}				{Surveillance, -, Brand}		
Search Engine	# of Devices	# of Samples	Rate (%) of Identification	Approach	# of Devices	Rate (%) of Identification
Shodan	435,641	4,145,206	10.51	ARE	341,324	10.93
Zoomeye	708,184	2,224,485	31.84	IoTtracker	520,317	16.66
TDO	2,803,406	3,123,489	89.75	TDO	2,457,661	78.68

5.4   Distribution

We analyzed the distribution of identified results in two dimensions: geography and brand.

Distribution of Countries.   We locate the identified type-level results over 97 countries, with the Top10 countries accounting for 84% of $2,803,406$ surveillance devices. Table 4 indicates that the maximum devices (nearly one-third) belong to China. The two main reasons are: (1) most brands of identified results (see right part of Table 4) are manufactured by China; (2) the statistical results (including Taiwan, Hongkong, etc.) are combined to China because these domains belong to China.

Table 4. Distribution of Top10 brands and countries.

{Surveillance, -, null}		{Surveillance, -, Brand}	
Country	# of (%) Devices	Brand	# of (%) Devices
China	946,215(33.75)	Dahua	1,041,941(42.39)
America	416,457(14.85)	Hikvision	654,036(26.61)
Vietnam	239,185(8.53)	Xiongmai	348,293(14.17)
Korea	239,104(8.53)	TVT	119,322(4.85)
Japan	101,411(3.62)	D-Link	101,951(4.15)
Australia	98,509(3.51)	Foscam	50,886(2.07)
France	81,301(2.90)	Hisilicon	43,460(1.77)
Brazil	80,101(2.86)	iCatch	42,717(1.74)
Russia	77,654(2.77)	Uniview	23,323(0.95)
Canada	55,748(1.99)	Samsung	16,195(0.66)
Other	467,721(16.68)	Other	15,537(0.63)
Total	2,803,406(100)	Total	2,457,661(100)

Distribution of Brands. With regard to the uneven sample distribution, we analyzed the distribution of found brand-level surveillance devices with their brands. Table 4 indicates the Top10 brands occupy 99.37% of the identified results(2, 457, 661). Among which, Dahua is the Top1 brand which has the maximum number of devices. Meanwhile, the Chinese brands (including Xiongmai, TVT, Foscam, etc.) undoubtedly have occupied more surveillance devices than the brands of the other countries. There are also two main reasons: (1) most offline labeled samples of acquired surveillance devices in our local Intranet were bought from China; (2) the distribution is a reflection that China has the biggest manufacturing power of surveillance devices.

6   Discussion and Conclusion

In this paper, the main limitation is that our work focus on fingerprinting surveillance devices by using recessive features of RTSP protocol. It seems that the target device and protocol are too simple, and our approach seems to lack generality. However, in fact, our approach can be widely extended to other common (like Network Time Protocol) and complex protocols (like industrial protocols). Consequently, these similar protocols can be evaluated as future work. Meanwhile, attempting on decrease requests/responses (like six irregular packets in Fig. 1) may be another improving work.

In this paper, we presented a new approach for automatically and accurately fingerprinting surveillance devices in cyberspace. We novelly explored new recessive features from RTSP responses. Moreover, we creatively used neural networks and deep semi-supervised algorithms for classification. Combined with the two effective methods, we found 2, 803, 406 surveillance devices in the wild which accounting for 89.7% of all samples. Most significantly, the performance of precision and recall of our experimental results both reach up to 93%.

Acknowledgments. Supported by the science and technology project of State Grid Corporation of China(No. 521304190004).

References

1. Nltk: the natural language toolkit. http://www.nltk.org/
2. Antonakakis, M., et al.: Understanding the mirai botnet. In: Proceedings of 26th USENIX Security Symposium (2017)
3. Bouharb, E., Debbabi, M., Assi, C.: Cyber scanning: a comprehensive survey. In: IEEE Communications Surveys and Tutorials. vol. 16, pp. 1496–1519 (2014)
4. Cao, K., Brbić, M., Leskovec, J.: Open-world semi-supervised learning. In: arXiv:2102.03526 (2021)
5. Durumeric, Z., Adrian, D., Mirian, A., Bailey, M., Halderman, J.A.: A search engine backed by internet-wide scanning. In: Proceedings of 22nd Computer and Communications Security (2015)
6. Durumeric, Z., Wustrow, E., Halderman, J.A.: Zmap: fast internet-wide scanning and its security applications. In: Proceedings of 23th USENIX Security Symposium (2013)
7. Feng, X., Li, Q., Wang, H., Sun, L.: Acquisitional rule-based engine for discovering internet-of-thing devices. In: Proceedings of 27th USENIX Security Symposium (2018)
8. Guo, L.Z., Zhang, Z.Y., Jiang, Y., Li, Y.F., Zhou, Z.H.: Safe deep semi-supervised learning for unseen-class unlabeled data. In: III, H.D., Singh, A. (eds.) Proceedings of the 37th International Conference on Machine Learning Proceedings of Machine Learning Research, vol. 119, pp. 3897–3906. PMLR (2020)
9. Kim, Y.: Convolutional neural networks for sentence classification. In: Empirical Methods in Natural Language Processing, pp. 1746–1751 (2014)
10. Li, Q., Feng, X., Wang, H., Sun, L.: Automatically discovering surveillance devices in the cyberspace. In: Proceedings of 8th ACM International Conference on Multimedia System (2017)
11. Michael Gilleland, M.P.S.: Levenshtein distance, in three flavors. https://people. cs.pitt.edu/ (2006)
12. Schulzrinne, H., Rao, A., Lanphier, R.: Real time streaming protocol (rtsp). In: RFC2326 (1998)
13. Shodan: https://www.shodan.io/explore/tag/webcam
14. Wang, X., Wang, Y., Feng, X., Zhu, H., Sun, L., Zou, Y.: Iottracker: an enhanced engine for discovering internet-of-thing devices. In: Proceedings of IEEE WoW-MoM (2019)
15. Yan, X., Jacky, K., Bennin, K.E., Qing, M.: Improving bug localization with word embedding and enhanced convolutional neural networks. Inf. Softw. Technol. **105**, 17–29 (2019)
16. Yan, Z., Lv, S., Zhang, Y., Zhu, H., Sun, L.: Remote fingerprinting on internet-wide printers based on neural network. In: Proceedings of IEEE GLOBECOM (2019)
17. Yang, K., Li, Q., Sun, L.: Towards automatic fingerprinting of IOT devices in the cyberspace. Comput. Netw. **148**, 318–327 (2019)
18. Zoomeye: https://www.zoomeye.org/

An Intrusion Detection Framework for IoT Using Partial Domain Adaptation

Yulin Fan[1,2]([✉]), Yang Li[1,2], Huajun Cui[1], Huiran Yang[1], Yan Zhang[1,2], and Weiping Wang[1,2]

[1] Institute of Information Engineering, Chinese Academy of Sciences, Beijing, China
`fanyulin@iie.ac.cn`
[2] School of Cyber Security, University of Chinese Academy of Sciences, Beijing, China

Abstract. With the rapid development of the Internet of Things (IoT), the security problem of IoT is becoming increasingly prominent. Deep learning (DL) has achieved success in network intrusion detection systems (NIDS) for IoT. Its capability of automatically extracting high-dimensional features from data and finding the association between data make it easy to identify abnormal activity from network traffic. However, DL method requires a large amount of labeled data, which is very time-consuming and expensive. Due to the privacy of IoT data, it is hard to collect enough data to train models. Also, the heterogeneity of IoT makes the NID model trained from the data collected from one IoT unable to be directly applied to another one. To address the problem, domain adaptation (DA) has been used by transferring the knowledge from the domain with huge amounts of labeled data to the domain with less or unlabeled data. However, previous DA methods generally assume the same label spaces between source and target domain, which is not feasible in a complex real environment of IoT. In this paper, we propose a NID framework using a weighted adversarial nets-based partial domain adaptation method to address this problem of inconsistent label spaces by mapping two domains to a domain-invariant feature space. The proposal can train a highly accurate NID model through the knowledge transfer from the abundant public labeled dataset of the traditional Internet to the unlabeled dataset of IoT. In addition, the proposed scheme can detect unknown attacks in the IoT with the help of knowledge from the traditional Internet. Moreover, the proposed scheme is an online NID detection which is more suitable for real IoT application. The experiments results demonstrate that our proposed scheme can achieve a good performance to detect attacks.

Keywords: IoT · Intrusion detection · Partial domain adaptation

1 Introduction

The Internet of things (IoT) is actively shaping the world. It combines various sensors and end-devices with the Internet to realize the interconnection of people, machines and things at any time and place [1]. As the application of IoT will involve various fields and influence all walks of life, the importance of its network security is self-evident. Due to the open deployment environment, limited resources, the inherent security loopholes of the network and the vulnerability of IoT terminal equipment, the harm and loss of attacks will be greater than the similar situation in traditional Internet. Therefore, the research of IoT security technology is particularly important.

Network intrusion detection (NID) is a kind of security defense technology, which can actively collect and analyze the network information, trying to find out whether there is a violation of security policy. Many researches in NIDs have made great efforts based on machine learning (ML) and deep learning (DL). These methods capture packets from network layer and extract the characteristics based on packets or flows to train a NID model. They do not consider underlying protocol and can provide a good adaptive ability. At present, there are some available public NID datasets for research, such as DARPA [4]and KDD [3]. However, the privacy and distributed features of IoT make it difficult to collect typical datasets of the IoT. Therefore, some NID schemes of IoT are based on those traditional NID data rather than IoT data [8]. However, labeled data from traditional Internet may not be suited for training DL models for IoT. Moreover, due to heterogeneity, different IoT have different network traffic patterns. Even the NID model trained by data collected from one IoT network often has poor generalization performance and cannot be applied to another IoT networks directly.

In order to solve the scarcity of labeled data and differences in data distribution, domain adaptation (DA) has been used in NIDs recently [10–12]. DA is a branch of transfer learning [13] that enable to transfer knowledge gained from source domain with an adequate labeled data to a different but similar target domain with few and unlabeled data [14]. In our case, the source domain refers to a large amount of labeled NID dataset collected from traditional Internet, while the target domain is a relative smaller unlabeled NID dataset drawn from a specific IoT network. On one hand, our source domain and target domain are different since they have different traffic patterns due to the different network protocols, architectures and application modes. On the other hand, the attack pattern in IoT is similar to the traditional Internet, such as Man-in-the-middle Attack and Botnet. DA tries to use the similarity between data to apply the knowledge previously learned in source domain to the new unknown domain (target domain). Since most DA methods try to map source and target domains to a common domain-invariant space, the label spaces of the two domains are required to be the same for feasible transfer. However, if they have different label spaces, the effect of DA will be greatly damaged, which is called **negative transfer**. Ignoring its negative transfer effect will lead to many false positives and even performance degradation. Therefore, the inconsistent label spaces of source and target domain is necessary to be considered.

In reality, the source domain and target domain often have the different label spaces, especially in our IoT research problem. For example, the traditional Internet contains various attack including Web Attack, such as XSS and

SQL Injection, DDoS, Botnet etc. Due to the large number of end-devices, the IoT is also vulnerable to DDoS and Botnet attacks. However, many resource-constrained IoT networks such as remote meter reading and smart parking hardly suffers from Web Attack. So, it is reasonable to assume that the attack types in IoT domain is a subset of that in tradition Internet domain. Here, the classes that both the domains have constitute the **shared label spaces**, while the classes not contained in the target domain but only in the source domain constitute the **private label spaces**. If the knowledge containing private label spaces (like Web Attack) and shared label spaces (like DDoS) is directly transferred to the IoT, it may cause negative transfer. Fortunately, Partial Domain Adaptation (PDA) [18] method has been proposed to solve the problem of inconsistent label spaces. PDA is a DA technique that allows to find the common parts (shared label spaces) and restrain the private label spaces of source domain that has little relationship with target domain to improve transfer performance.

In this paper, we apply a weighted adversarial nets-based PDA [19] in NIDs of IoT. It can transfer knowledge from one to another dataset although the label spaces of the two domains are different. It uses adversarial network structure to map two domains to a common domain-invariant feature space to complete domain adaptation, and reduce weight of the samples from private label spaces to restrain negative transfer. Our contributions are as follows:

- To the best of our knowledge, we are the first to address the problem of the inconsistent label spaces between Internet and IoT and apply PDA method into NIDs of IoT. We use PDA to train a highly accurate NID model with unlabeled dataset for IoT, with the knowledge transfer of the abundant public labeled datasets in the traditional Internet, in a specific scenario that source and target datasets own different label spaces. To foster further research, the source code is public[1].
- The proposed NID scheme can identify unknown attacks in IoT, with the help of the abundant public labeled datasets in the traditional Internet.
- We design an online NID framework by offline training to detect attack automatically in real-time, which is quite suitable for real IoT application.
- We implement the methods on two available NID datasets from traditional Internet and IoT respectively. Experiment results show that, with the few unlabeled data of IoT, the proposed PDA based NID approach can achieve a good performance to detect attacks.

2   Background

2.1   Generative Adversarial Networks (GAN)

In GAN framework [21], two models are trained simultaneously: the generation model G and the discriminant model D. G is responsible for capturing data distribution and D is responsible for estimating the probability of samples coming

---

[1] Our code is public available at https://github.com/rainforest2378/IoT-PDA.git.

from the true distribution. G and D play with each other and self-strengthen effect will be produced on both of them through the game.

In computer vision, G is a network that generates pictures. It receives a random noise z and generates pictures through this noise, which is denoted as $G(z)$. The goal of G is to generate pictures as real as possible to deceive D. D takes the real and fake generated images as input, and outputs the probability that x is a real picture (comes from the distribution of real images). The closer the output $D(x)$ is to 1, the more likely the input image is to be real. The goal of D is to separate images generated by G from the real image as much as possible. In this way, G and D form a dynamic "game process". So the minimax loss of GAN can be denoted as:

$$\min_G \max_D V(D, G) = E_{x \sim P_{data}}[log(D(x))] + E_{x \sim P_G}[log(1 - D(G(z)))] \tag{1}$$

2.2 Domain Adaptation and Partial Domain Adaptation

Domain adaptation (DA) [13] is aimed to solve the problem of difference between the training dataset (source domain) and the test dataset (target domain). Its critical insight is to learn a mapping to find the similarity between the source and the target domain. Since original DA methods rely on the comparison of marginal distributions between the source and target domains, the label spaces between the two domains are required to be the same for feasible adaptation. However, in a realistic scenario, the source domain often has different label spaces with target domain.

In this way, partial domain adaptation (PDA) [18] is required for feasible transfer. A natural and possible way is to strengthen the effect of the source domain samples in the shared label spaces, while restrain that in the private label spaces. J. Zhang et al. proposes a novel Importance Weighted Adversarial Nets architecture for PDA [19], which is based on the idea of GAN. As shown in middle picture of Fig. 1, it consists of two feature extractors, F_s and F_t,(corresponding to generator of GAN) and two domain classifiers, D and D_0, (corresponding to discriminator of GAN). It solves the inconsistent label spaces problem with the help of the first domain classifier D. D measures the importance of source samples, and assigns appropriate weights to them. For example, if samples are from private label spaces, lower weights will be assigned to them to restrain the negative transfer. The details will be introduced in next section.

3   The Proposed Framework

The main goal of the proposed scheme is to use PDA to learn a NID model that can accurately predict the samples classes (benign or specific attack) in the target domain. In our research, the source domain is Internet with labeled NID data, and target domain is IoT with insufficient and unlabeled NID data. Our proposal can be divided into three phases as shown in Fig. 1. First, we process the original PCAP packets and extract flow-based statistical features to prepare the source data and target data. Then feature extractor F_s and classifier are trained for source domain. Second, we perform the PDA to train feature extractor F_t of target domain and two domain discriminators (D and D_0). Third, an online intrusion detection model is designed to mark target samples as benign or known attack classes, or even identify unknown attacks.

3.1   System Model

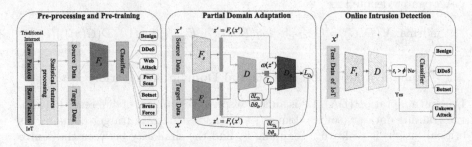

Fig. 1. The overview of three phases of our scheme, including pre-processing and pre-training, partial domain adaptation and online intrusion detection. The blue trapezoid F_s indicates the feature extractors of source domain. The green trapezoid F_t represents feature extractors of target domain. The pink trapezoid D indicates domain classifier that producing weights while the brown one D_0 indicates domain classifier that identify the source and target samples. The block filled with slashes indicates its model is fixed and its parameters will not be updated during current phase. (Color figure online)

We start with the description of our system model. In this paper, source domain with labeled data is denoted as $D_s = \{x_i^s, y_i^s\}_{i=1}^{n_s}$. x_i^s is a sample of source domain, which is drawn from the Internet distribution $P_s(x)$, where i is the index of source samples. Target domain with unlabeled data is denoted as $D_t = \{x_j^t\}_{j=1}^{n_t}$. x_j^t is a sample in target domain which is drawn from the IoT distribution $P_t(x)$, where j is the index of target samples. n_s and n_t are respectively the number of source samples and target samples. Our proposal focuses on datasets with sufficient source data and limited target data, so $n_s > n_t$. Assume that feature space of two domains are the same, that is, $X_s = X_t$. Assume that the attacks in IoT are a subset of traditional Internet attacks. So, the label spaces are different and the label space of the target domain is contained in the label space of the source domain, that is, $Y_s \subseteq Y_t$. The edge distributions of these two domains are different, namely $P_s(x) \neq P_t(x)$. Our task is to train a NID model for target IoT domain D_t to predict the labels $y^t \in Y_t$ with the help of source Internet domain D_s.

3.2   Pre-processing and Pre-training

As shown in left figure of Fig. 1, we first preprocess the raw network packets of the traditional Internet and IoT network and pretrain classification model for traditional Internet. We use the same tool to extract the same statistical features so that the source domain and the target domain have the same feature spaces. CICFlowMentor [22] is an open-source tool that generates bidirectional flows (bi-flows) from PCAP files, and extracts the statistical time-related features from these flows. In general, a unidirectional flow refers to a set of packets with the same protocol type, source IP address, destination IP address, source port and destination port. So, a bi-flow can be defined as a set of network packets that move forward or back forward between two endpoints. In order to obtain time-related statistics, bi-flows are supposed to be counted in a limited period of time. Concretely, TCP bi-flows are terminated by the end of TCP connection (signed by FIN packet) while UDP bi-flows are terminated by a flow timeout. The flow timeout value can be set arbitrarily.

We also pre-train NID model $C(F_s(x^s))$ of source domain in this phase. The feature extractor F_s of source domain is constructed with two convolutional layers (with 64 and 128 filters), two maximum pool layers, one flatten layer and two full connection layer (with 128 and 64 neurons) activated by ReLU function. The attack classifier C consists of some neurons (the number of the neurons corresponds to number of attack classes of source samples) activated by sigmoid function. F_s is used to extract superior features of source domain and C is used to classify the source samples into benign or attack classes y^s, such as DDoS, Web Attack, Port Scan, Botnet, Brute Force. Note that F_s and C will be used (fixed) in the following PDA training and online intrusion detection phases respectively. The model $C(F_s(x^s))$ for source domain is obtained by minimizing the loss function and learning the parameters of F_s and C, denoted as:

$$\min_{F_s,C} L_s = E_{x,y \sim P_s(x,y)} L(C(F_s(x)), y) \tag{2}$$

where L_s is the cross-entropy loss of multi-classes classification task for source domain.

3.3   Partial Domain Adaptation

This phase aims to realize knowledge transfer with partial domain adaptation. A weighted adversarial nets-based PDA method [19] is applied to boost shared label spaces alignment. Two domain classifier D, D_0 and two feature extractors F_s, F_t are adopted. F_s is obtained in pre-training phase. F_t share the same network structure but different network parameters with F_s. The output of the feature extractors will be fed into D and D_0. D and D_0 are common neural networks. D consists of 2 fully connected layers with 20, 10 neurons in that order and D_0 consists of 3 fully connected layers with 50, 40, 10 neurons in that order.

The training process is shown in Algorithm 1, including three training parts (learning D, D_0 and F_t). First of all, F_s and F_t take samples from the source and target data x^s, x^t respectively and output z^s, z^t. D takes z^s labelled by 1 and target data z^t labelled by 0 as input and output $D(z) = p(y = 1|z) = \sigma(a(z))$. σ is the logistic sigmoid function and $a(z)$ is the output of the last fully connection layer. The value of $D(z)$ is the predictive probability of the sample coming from source distribution. Maximizing the loss L_D with respect to D is used to improve its ability to distinguish the source and target samples, denoted as:

$$\max_D L_D(D, F_s, F_t) = E_{x \sim P_s(x)}[log D(F_s(x))] + E_{x \sim P_t(x)}[log(1 - D(F_t(x)))] \quad (3)$$

After above training, D has converged to its optimal value. Therefore, $D(z)$ can indicate the likelihood of the sample coming from shared label spaces or private label spaces of source domain. An importance weight $\omega(z^s)$ should be assigned to each source sample to adjust its effect on transfer process. The weight is inversely related to $D(z)$ [19], denoted as

$$\omega(z^s) = 1 - D(z^s) = \frac{1}{\frac{P_s(z^s)}{P_t(z^s)} + 1} \quad (4)$$

If the $\frac{P_s(z^s)}{P_t(z^s)}$ is high, the sample can be perfectly discriminated from the target IoT domain, which means it is more likely coming from the private label spaces distribution of source Internet domain. Therefore, a smaller value $w(z^s)$ will be gotten. For example, the samples belong to Web Attack and Brute Force classes in our case will be assigned smaller weights to restrain their effect on knowledge transfer in PDA. In contrast, a small $\frac{P_s(z^s)}{P_t(z^s)}$ means that samples are more likely to come from the shared label spaces, such as, DDoS, Botnet and Scan classes in our case. These kinds of samples are really needed because they will give positive effect for domain adaptation. Hence, higher weights are assigned to them.

In order to distinguish weighted source features z^s and target features z^t and optimize F_t, D_0 is introduced as the second domain classifier. F_t and D_0 play a two-player game to align shared label spaces, that is to say, to reduce the shift on the shared label spaces. After importance weights obtained, the objective function can be described as following. Maximizing the loss with respect to the parameters of D_0 attempts to identify the difference between distributions of the source and target samples,

$$\min_{F_t} \max_{D_0} L_\omega(D_0, F_s, F_t) = \lambda E_{x \sim P_s(x)} w(z^s) log D_0(F_s(x)) + E_{x \sim P_t(x)} log(1 - D_0(F_t(x))) \quad (5)$$

where λ is a tradeoff parameter that measures the inhibition degree of private label spaces. Note that importance weights $w(z)$ have been added to the source samples to restrain effect of samples from private label spaces. Minimizing the loss with respect to F_t is to minimize the divergence between the weighted z^s and z^t to confuse D_0, described as

$$\min_{F_t} L_\omega(D_0, F_s, F_t) = E_{x \sim P_t(x)}[log(1 - D_0(F_t(x)))] \quad (6)$$

Note that only the gradient of D_0 will be back-propagated to update F_t, since they are learned from the weighted source samples. The procedure is repeated for several times. After the training, the distribution divergence of two domains on shared label spaces is reduced so that the extracted features of target data by F_t can be put into C directly to perform classification.

Algorithm 1. The PDA training procedure

Input: traditional NID data $D_s = \{x_i^s\}_{i=1}^{n_s}$, IoT data $D_t = \{x_j^t\}_{j=1}^{n_t}$

Output: feature extractor of IoT F_t

1: **Initialization:** Train a CNN model $C(F_s(x^s))$ with D_s to minimize L_s, as described in formulation (2).

2: **for** iteration = 1, 2,..., i **do**

3:     **learning D:**

4:     m samples $\{x_1^s, x_2^s, \cdots, x_m^s\}$ from D_s and m samples $\{x_1^t, x_2^t, \cdots, x_m^t\}$ from D_t

5:     Obtaining generated data $\{z_1^s, z_2^s, ..., z_m^s\}$, $z_i^s = F_s(x_i^s)$ and $\{z_1^t, z_2^t, ..., z_m^t\}$, $z_i^t = F_t(x_i^t)$

6:     Update parameters θ_d of discriminator D to maximize
$V = \frac{1}{m} \sum_{i=1}^{m} log D(z_i^s) + \frac{1}{m} \sum_{i=1}^{m} log(1 - D(z_i^t))$
$\theta_d \leftarrow \theta_d + \eta \bigtriangledown V$

7:     **learning D_0:**

8:     Update parameters θ_{d_0} of discriminator D_0 to maximize
$V = \lambda \frac{1}{m} \sum_{i=1}^{m} \omega(z_i^s) log D_0(z_i^s) + \frac{1}{m} \sum_{i=1}^{m} log(1 - D_0(z_i^t))$
$\theta_0 \leftarrow \theta_{d_0} + \eta \bigtriangledown V$

9:     **learning F_t:**

10:     m samples $\{x_1^t, x_2^t, \cdots, x_m^t\}$ from D_t

11:     Update parameters θ_{f_t} of feature extractor F_t to minimize
$V = \frac{1}{m} \sum_{i=1}^{m} log(1 - D_0(z_i^t))$
$\theta_{f_t} \leftarrow \theta_{f_t} + \eta \bigtriangledown V$

12: **end for**

3.4   Online Intrusion Detection

After the above two phases, the classifier C and trained F_t, D are obtained. They are combined to design a novel online intrusion detection model, as shown in the right figure of Fig. 1. **This NID model can not only detect the specific attacks in shared label spaces of IoT, but also detect unknown attacks that belong to private label spaces of source Internet domain with the help of D.**

In this phase, we fixed F_t, D and C and do not update any of their structure and internal parameters. The new coming test data are passed through F_t to perform feature extraction first. Then put the result $F_t(x_j^t)$ into D and get an Anomaly Score, denoted as $s_j^t = D(F_t(x_j^t))$, which is the probability value representing the similarity degree between the target data in testing process and training process. The anomaly score s_j^t measures the samples abnormality.

Specifically, samples belonging to shared label spaces will produce a lower value (close to 0), while samples that come from private label spaces will produce a larger value, which reflect corresponding sample is more likely a new and unseen attack class in IoT. The larger the score, the greater the difference to the distribution of shared label spaces. In order to detect unknown attack, a cutoff threshold ϕ is required. In this case, a simple approach is to set ϕ to the average score $E(s_j^t) = \frac{1}{n_t} \sum_{j=1}^{n_t} D(F_t(x_j^t)), j = 1, \cdots, n_t$ of target training samples, which we assume represent data from shared label spaces. Hence, $\phi = E(s_j^t) + \epsilon$, where ϵ means numerical fluctuation, that is to say, ϕ can be designed flexibly according to the distinct condition.

The execution procedure of our online intrusion detection is presented in Algorithm 2. If new samples come from private label space appear in test phase, such as Brute Force, their scores are very likely to be higher than the threshold ϕ so they will be labeled as unknown attack. On the contrary, if the scores are lower than ϕ, we consider the corresponding samples come from shared label spaces. Since the classifier C learns the matching from output of feature extractor to specific attack classes, it can be directly used to predict the samples types. In this case, we put $F_t(x_j^t)$ into C directly to perform classification and obtain the specific class y_j^t of x_j^t, such as DDoS, Scan and Botnet.

Another merit of our proposal is that it supports online detection. After offline training, a personalized NID model is obtained for each IoT. The NID model does not need to change any parameters in the online intrusion detection phase. Therefore, it is suitable for real-time intrusion detection, which can meet the lightweight deployment requirements of IoT.

Algorithm 2. The online intrusion detection procedure

Input: Feature extractor of IoT F_t, classifier C, the first discriminator D. IoT data
    to be tested $D_t = \{x_j^t\}_{j=1}^{n_o}$, n_o is number of test samples.
Output: class y_j^t that sample x_j^t belongs to, where $j = 1, 2, 3, \cdots, n_o$
  1: *thereshold* $\phi = \frac{1}{n_t} \sum_{j=1}^{n_t} D(F_t(x_j^t)) + \epsilon$
  2: **for** $j = 1, 2, 3, \cdots, n_o$ **do**
  3:    $z_j^t = F_t(x_j^t)$, $s_j^t = D(z_j^t)$
  4:    **if** $s_j^t > \phi$ **then**
  5:       $y_j^t = attack_{unknown}$
  6:    **else**
  7:       $y_j^t = C(z_j^t)$
  8:    **end if**
  9: **end for**

---

4   Evaluation

In this section, we evaluate the performance of the proposed approach via three experiments on known and unknown attacks detection.

4.1 Datasets and Experiment Setup

We use CIC-IDS2017 [22] as source domain. It is drawn from traditional Internet and contains benign and up-to-date common attacks. Its data collection lasted for five days. Monday is a normal day including only normal traffic and the other four days contain various attacks including Brute Force, Web Attack, Port Scan, Botnet, DDoS, etc. We select IoT datasets [8] as target domain. It is drawn from IP cameras video surveillance network and smart home network, including benign and several types of attack.

We conduct three experiments to evaluate the effectiveness of our approach. The first is to evaluate the basic ability of multi-class classification for target IoT domain. The second is to prove the ability of unknown attacks detection. The third aims to verify the generality of our method, that is, the effectiveness of our method on the traditional non-partial domain adaptation problem.

In the experiment, the small batch random gradient descent (SGD) is used for optimization. We set the learning rate of batch processing to 0.1 and the training iterations to about 50 with the batch size of 64. In order to verify the effectiveness of our approach, we evaluate the approach with accuracy(ACC), true positive rate(TPR), false positive rate(FPR), f1 score(F1) and area under the ROC curve(AUC).

Table 1. Performance of the NID models trained using our approach

	C6→I2				C6→I3			C6→I4
	Benign SYN DoS	Benign OS Scan	Benign Mirai	Benign SSL R.	Benign OS Scan SYN DoS	Benign SSL R. OS Scan	Benign Mirai OS Scan	Benign SYN DoS Mirai OS Scan
ACC	0.9778	0.9557	0.9990	0.8455	0.8677	0.6885	0.9022	0.7630
TPR	0.9978	0.9807	0.9999	0.9758	0.7515	0.7293	0.8999	0.7872
FPR	0.0021	4.00E-05	6.00E-05	0.0241	0.0444	0.0139	0.0203	0.0359
F1	0.9870	0.9999	0.9995	0.9092	0.7432	0.7233	0.8943	0.7448
AUC	0.8745	0.8662	0.6906	0.6614	0.7239	0.6980	0.7480	0.6682

4.2 Detection of Partial Domain Adaptation

To verify whether our method can identify the specific categories of attack for IoT, we choose source labeled data samples including 5 attack categories(Brute Force, Web Attack, DDoS, Botnet and Scan) and a benign category to train a classification model. The Internet and IoT dataset have 3 identical attacks (DDoS, Botnet and Scan). In IoT dataset, DDoS contains two attack types, SYN DoS and SSL Renegotiation (SSL R.). Scan attack refers to OS Scan and Botnet malware refers to Mirai. We choose IoT dataset with different classes as different target domains, and each target domain contains one benign category and less than or equal to 3 attack categories. Hence, the source domain is CIC-IDS2017 with six classes denoted as **C6** and target domain are IoT dataset with n classes denoted as **In**, where $n = 2, 3, 4$ denotes the number of categories.

We model the NID as a multi-class classification problem. The weighted adversarial nets-based PDA is used to train F_t, D, D_0. Finally, we build our online NID classification model by connecting the F_t, D and C in series. We evaluate its performance in detecting categories (benign or certain attack types) that target samples belonging to. We repeat the experiments for 5 times to take the average metric values.

As the results shown in Table 1, our approach gains about 87.42% accuracy in average. It is clear that our method performs well in terms of AUC, too. This shows that even if the label spaces are different, PDA can well align the two domains by assigning different weights to source samples from different label spaces, so that the knowledge obtained from the labeled source Internet domain can be well transferred to the unlabeled IoT domain for accurate classification. We observe that the accuracy maintains 76.30% in case **C6→I4**, even if it is more difficult to distinguish different attacks with the increase of target categories. We performed experiments coded in python and executed on Windows 10 PC with i7-9750H CPU and 8G RAM. Each iteration takes about 210 milliseconds in training phase and the online detection model can handle approx. 47,000 samples per second. The rapid process speed is beneficial in real application environment of IoT.

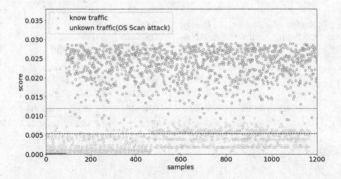

Fig. 2. The result of unknown attacks detection. The red points indicate the samples from unknown classes and blue points indicate samples from known classes. The blue dotted line indicates the average anomaly score of samples from known classes and the orange line indicates the upper limit threshold that might be chosen. (Color figure online)

4.3   Detection of Unknown Attack

In this experiment, we prove that our online NID model can not only classify the known attacks in target samples but also identify the unknown attack that did not occur in the target domain in training phase. As shown in Fig. 2, the blue points are samples (benign and SYN DoS categories) that belong to shared label spaces. As time goes on, IoT discovers a new type of attack OS Scan (red points) that do not appear in IoT network before. Obviously, samples of unknown attack have higher anomaly scores than that of known classes samples. Through setting up a threshold, it is easy to identify the unknown attack categories.

We consider the samples that exceed the threshold as unknown attack. The lower blue line is the average score of known samples coming from shared label spaces. In order to get a better unknown anomaly detector, we can measure the performance of different thresholds around the average value. The upper orange dotted line is the threshold that we might select which detect 98.19% unknown attack and produce 2.50% FPR, better than the performance of average value. Therefore, with the help of D and private space, unknown attacks can be detected effectively, which is very important for intrusion detection.

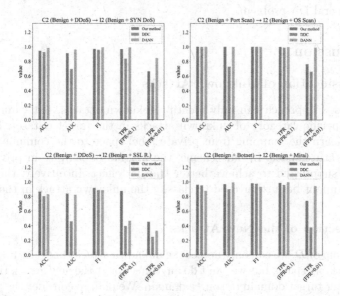

Fig. 3. Comparison of detection performance between our scheme and DDC and DANN. In each subgraph, the source domain is denoted as C2 (one benign and a specific attack), target domain I2 is IoT data with the same label space. (Color figure online)

4.4 Detection of Non-partial Domain Adaptation

Finally, in order to verify the generality of our scheme, we evaluate it on the traditional non-partial DA problem and compare it with two typical DA method DANN [20] and DDC [15]. DANN is a adversarial-based DA method. It trains a feature extractor by maximizing domain classifier loss and minimizing label predictor loss simultaneously. DDC (Deep domain confusion) uses domain distribution difference to extract domain invariant features by minimizing the domain discrepancy loss and classification loss, denoted as: $L = L_C(X_L, y) + \lambda d_{MMD}^2(X_S, X_T)$. d_{MMD} is the most commonly used metric to measure the distribution difference between source and target domain. This distance is added to the objective function of the network for training.

We choose CIC-IDS2017 with benign and one specific attack category as the source domain (C2) and IoT dataset with benign and one attack category as the target domain (I2). We model this as a binary classification problem that predicting the samples belong to benign or attack. In this way, the source and target domain have the same label spaces. The result is shown in Fig. 3. We observe that the NID model trained by our method outperforms DDC method and has no noticeable degradation compared to the DANN method. The result also demonstrate that our method has 45.4% TPR (FPR = 0.01) in the scenario C2 (Benign + DDoS)→I2 (Benign + SSL R.), higher than DANN. Hence, our scheme has good generality that can be used not only for PDA problem, but also for general DA problem.

5   Discussion

5.1   Classification of Unknown Attacks

The proposed approach can only identify unknown attacks, but cannot determine the specific category of unknown attacks in the target dataset. However, it doesn't learn the mapping from private label space to the common domain-invariant feature space. In our scheme, the weights of samples in private label spaces are suppressed to achieve better transfer effect. Intuitively, this part of knowledge might be further used to classify the unknown attack in the future.

5.2   Detection of the New Attacks

With the help of D, we can only detect the unknown attack that once appeared in the private label space, but we can't do anything about the new attack that never seen in either target domain or source domain. We plan to consider the zero-shot learning problem [23] (the sample categories in the test set are completely not available in the training set) to address this problem in the future. Zero-shot learning is designed to imitate the human reasoning process that use the past knowledge to infer the specific form of new objects, so as to identify new objects.

6   Related Work

The domain of IDS for IoT has been extensively studied [2]. For anomaly-based IoT IDS, many researchers are interested in using ML algorithms [5–7,9]. Most of them just use traditional NID dataset for experiment. However, since IoT systems are different from the traditional Internet due to the protocol and application, each IoT has its own characteristics of network traffic. It is necessary to train personalized model for different IoT with few and unlabeled data.

Juan Zhao proposes HeTL [10] and CeHTL [11] that use feature-based transfer learning to detect previously unseen attack based on the known attacks. It finds the similarity of two different attacks, such as DoS and R2L, and learn an optimized representation that is invariant when attack behaviors change. Both approaches are unsupervised DA techniques that consider the same label spaces while our approach focus on different label spaces situation.

Ankush Singla use adversarial DA to address the problem of scarcity of labeled training data in a dataset [12]. The method works on the source and target datasets which have same or different feature spaces. The result demonstrates that their models can achieve good performance even when the number of labeled target samples is significantly small. However, it is a supervised model that requires few labeled target data.

7 Conclusion

In this paper, a PDA method is applied to NID system of IoT with few and unlabeled data. This method solves the problem of different label spaces between source domain (traditional Internet) and target domain (IoT). In training stage, the knowledge of shared label spaces can be well transferred, and the negative impact of samples from private label spaces is restrained. The experimental results show that the proposed method can effectively classify the types of IoT traffic (benign or specific attack classes) and identify the potential unknown attacks. Compared with the other general DA methods (DDC, DANN), it has considerable detection accuracy and low false alarm rate in the non-partial DA problem. In addition, our method is lightweight and suitable for IoT.

Acknowledgment. This work is supported by the Project of Beijing Municipal Science & Technology Plan under Grant No. Z191100007119001 and Z191100007119003.

References

1. Gubbi, J., Buyya, R., Marusic, S., Palaniswami, M.: Internet of Things (IoT): a vision, architectural elements, and future directions. Futur. Gener. Comput. Syst. **29**(7), 1645–1660 (2013)
2. Chaabouni, N., et al.: Network intrusion detection for IoT security based on learning techniques. IEEE Commun. Surv. Tutor. **21**(3), 2671–2701 (2019)
3. Tavallaee, M., Bagheri, E., Lu, W., Ghorbani, A.A.: A detailed analysis of the KDD CUP 99 data set. In: Proceedings of the Second IEEE Symposium on Computational Intelligence for Security and Defence Applications, pp. 1–6 (2009)
4. Lippmann, R., Haines, J.W., Fried, D.J., Korba, J., Das, K.: DARPA off-line intrusion detection evaluation. Comput. Netw. **34**(4), 579–595 (2000)
5. Bostani, H., Sheikhan, M.: Hybrid of anomaly-based and specification-based IDS for Internet of Things using unsupervised OPF based on MapReduce approach. Comput. Commun. **98**, 52–71 (2017)
6. Pajouh, H.H., et al.: A two-layer dimension reduction and two-tier classification model for anomaly-based intrusion detection in IoT backbone networks. IEEE Trans. Emerg. Top. Comput. **7**, 314–323 (2016)

7. Lopez-Martin, M., Carro, B., Sanchez-Esguevillas, A., Lloret, J.: Conditional variational autoencoder for prediction and feature recovery applied to intrusion detection in IoT. Sensors **17**(9), 1967 (2017)
8. Mirsky, Y., Doitshman, T., Elovici, Y., Shabtai, A.: Kitsune: an ensemble of autoencoders for online network intrusion detection. arXiv preprint arXiv:1802.09089 (2018)
9. Hodo, E., et al.: Threat analysis of IoT networks using artificial neural network intrusion detection system. In: 2016 International Symposium on Networks, Computers and Communications (ISNCC), pp. 1–6. IEEE (2016)
10. Zhao, J., Shetty, S., Pan, J.W.: Feature-based transfer learning for network security. In: MILCOM 2017-2017 IEEE Military Communications Conference (2017)
11. Zhao, J., Shetty, S., Pan, J.W., Kamhoua, C., Kwiat, K.: Transfer learning for detecting unknown network attacks. EURASIP J. Inf. Secur. **2019**, Article no. 1 (2019)
12. Singla, A., Bertino, E., Verma, D.: Preparing network intrusion detection deep learning models with minimal data using adversarial domain adaptation. In: The 15th ACM Asia Conference on Computer and Communications Security, pp. 127–140 (2020)
13. Pan, S.J., Yang, Q.: A survey on transfer learning. IEEE Trans. Knowl. Data Eng. **22**(10), 1345–1359 (2009)
14. Wang, M., Deng, W.: Deep visual domain adaptation: a survey. Neurocomputing **312**, 135–153 (2018)
15. Tzeng, E., Hoffman, J., Zhang, N., Saenko, K., Darrell, T.: Deep domain confusion: maximizing for domain invariance. arXiv preprint arXiv:1412.3474 (2014)
16. Ben-David, S., et al.: A theory of learning from different domains. Mach. Learn. **79**(1), 151–175 (2010)
17. Sun, B., Saenko, K.: Deep CORAL: correlation alignment for deep domain adaptation. In: Hua, G., Jégou, H. (eds.) ECCV 2016. LNCS, vol. 9915, pp. 443–450. Springer, Cham (2016). https://doi.org/10.1007/978-3-319-49409-8_35
18. Fan, C., et al.: A review of deep domain adaptation: general situation and complex situation. Acta Automatica Sinica **46**, 1–34 (2020)
19. Zhang, J., Ding, Z.W., Li, W.Q., Ogunbona, P.: Importance weighted adversarial nets for partial domain adaptation. In: IEEE Conference on Computer Vision and Pattern Recognition (2018)
20. Ganin, Y., et al.: Domain-adversarial training of neural networks. J. Mach. Learn. Res. **17**(1), 2096–2030 (2016)
21. Goodfellow, I., et al.: Generative adversarial nets. In: Advances in Neural Information Processing Systems (2014)
22. Sharafaldin, I., Habibi Lashkari, A., Ghorbani, A.A.: Toward generating a new intrusion detection dataset and intrusion traffic characterization. In: 4th International Conference on Information Systems Security and Privacy (ICISSP) (2018)
23. Palatucci, M., Pomerleau, D., Hinton, G.E., Mitchell, T.M.: Zero-shot learning with semantic output codes. In: 23rd Annual Conference on Neural Information Processing Systems, pp. 1401–1408 (2009)

Mining Trojan Detection Based on Multi-dimensional Static Features

Zixian Tang[1,2], Qiang Wang[1,2], Wenhao Li[1,2], Huaifeng Bao[1,2], Feng Liu[1,2], and Wen Wang[1,2(✉)]

[1] State Key Laboratory of Information Security,
Institute of Information Engineering, CAS, Beijing, China
{tangzixian,wangqiang3113,liwenhao,baohuaifeng,liufeng,wangwen}@iie.ac.cn
[2] School of Cyber Security, University of Chinese Academy of Sciences,
Beijing, China

Abstract. The developing technic and the variety of Mining Trojan is increasingly threatening the computational resources from the weak-defend systems. Mining Trojan is illicitly implanted into the systems and mines cryptocurrency such as Bitcon through the hijacked resource. Previous work focuses on performing binary classification to identify a malicious software from the benign ones, but fail to classify the specific Mining Trojan. In order to tackle the above issues, in this paper, we propose a hierarchical detector, called Miner-Killer, to effectively and precisely classify Mining Trojans apart from the benign ones. First, Miner-Killer converts binary codes from Trojan samples to format files, assembly files and string files. Second, the static features are extracted by MSFV Extractor. Then, an ensemble learning model is trained by the extracted features and is applied to classify the unseen Mining Trojans. Experiments on two real-world datasets demonstrate that our proposed method can significantly detect the Mining Trojans, which outperforms the state-of-the-art methods applied to detect malware.

Keywords: Mining Trojan detection · Cryptocurrency · Static analysis · Ensemble learning

1 Introduction

Cryptocurrency is one of the virtual currency based on node network and digital encryption algorithm. It is issued and managed by developers and exchanged among members in specific virtual communities [10]. Bitcon, for example, is one of the virtual encrypted digital Peer-to-Peer (P2P) currency generated by a high-computation-demand algorithm [5]. In order to attain Bitcoin without paying the price, Mining Trojan is developed and illegally implanted into the victim systems. Then the hijacked computing systems execute the Trojan and silently mine Bitcoin for the hackers. Therefore, detecting mechanism should be proposed to protect user privacy and the service life of the computing resources from Mining Trojan.

© Springer Nature Switzerland AG 2021
W. Lu et al. (Eds.): SciSec 2021, LNCS 13005, pp. 51–65, 2021.
https://doi.org/10.1007/978-3-030-89137-4_4

Survey from Tencent Yujian Threat Intelligence Center [26] demonstrates the prosperity of Mining Trojan, of which the number grows exponentially month to month. Meanwhile, state-level Advance Persistent Threat (APT) organizations are diverting attention to embed attacking payload into Mining Trojan. Specifically, Monero Mining Trojan is employed to attack national government agencies in APT32 exposed by the Defender team [18].

With the increasing risk of Mining Trojan attacks, there is an urgent need for a new solution that can prevent and detect Mining Trojans. There have been a lot of in-depth researches on malware detection [3,12,15], which can be summarized as static feature based methods [21] and dynamic running feature [2] based methods. However, few of them have focused their attention on Mining Trojan detection. Many security vendors have the ability to detect Mining Trojan. Their products can be regarded as fingerprint-based and EDR-based (Endpoint Detection & Response). Fingerprint matching methods that use hash value or file name is invalid for the newborn samples; EDR-based detection requires monitoring the utilization rate of hardware resources and process analysis at the terminal to better identify the mining behavior, which cannot directly get the appropriate detection results from the samples.

In order to tackle the limitation of existing methods, we proposed Miner-Killer, a hierarchical system to precisely detect Mining Trojans. Firstly, Miner-Killer extracts multi-dimensional static features, namely MSFV, from three forms of binary files. Then a well-trained ensemble model predict the labels of the input samples and classify to the according categories. The experimental results show that Miner-Killer achieves 97.8% accuracy on the DataCon2020-Malware dataset, and 99.5% accuracy on the Win-Miner dataset.

Our contributions can be summarized as follows:

- We comprehensively analyze Mining Trojan from the aspect of static features, including file header, opcodes and encoded strings and intuitively present the analysis results.
- We propose a novel method, called Multi-dimensional Static Feature Vector (MSFV), to represent Mining Trojan. Well-considered experiments prove the rationality and generalization of our proposed MSFV.
- To the best of our knowledge, we are among the first to tackle the issues of detecting real-world Mining Trojan. Evaluated on real-world datasets, Miner-Killer achieves eye-catching performance and is superior to well-known AVs and the state-of-the-arts.

2   Background and Related Work

2.1   Mining Trojan

Since Bitcoin has received huge attention before, many digital currencies based on blockchain technology have also come out, such as Ethereum and Monero. This type of digital currency is not issued by a specific currency issuer, but is obtained through a large number of calculations based on specific algorithms.

The mining program uses the powerful computing power of the computer to perform a large number of calculations to obtain digital currency. Due to the limitation of hardware performance, digital currency players need a large number of computers to perform calculations to obtain a certain amount of digital currency. Therefore, some criminals use various methods to implant the mining machine program into the victim's computer and use the victim's computer to calculate Strengthen mining. This type of mining program that is implanted into the user's computer is a mining Trojan.

In the industry, many anti-virus software (AV) can effectively fight against mining Trojans. Most of these AVs collect file signatures, fingerprints and other characteristics and use their accumulated virus database to compare and identify malware. Although this approach is efficient and fast, it needs to constantly update the database to adapt to the constantly changing and evolving mining Trojans. For mining Trojans that are simply deformed or newly emerged, AV will fail.

At present, there are few studies on detection of Mining Trojan. Most relevant research contents are aimed at browser-based mining, also known as cryptojacking [6,9]. Hong et al. [11], Rodriguez et al. [23] and others have proposed cryptojacking detection methods for browsers, and found a batch of mining websites based on dynamic features. However, these methods do not involve executable samples. Zareh et al. [27] proposed a dynamic detection method for botnet Bitcoin mining programs, but the samples they chose were not real-world Mining Trojans. The paper also pointed out that there has not been any research on Mining Trojans before this.

2.2 Malware Detection

Although there has been less work on detecting of Mining Trojans, much work has been done on the classification and detection of malware. From early features based on artificial recognition [16] to the use of machine learning [13], deep learning methods [20], the game around malware detection and anti-detection has been going on. All research can be summarized into static feature-based methods and dynamic feature-based methods.

Static Feature Based. Static features refer to the information contained in the sample itself without executing it, such as file header, opcodes, and raw bytes. Shafiq et al. [25] proposed PE-Miner, which automatically extracts distinguishing features from portable executables (PE) to detect previously unknown malware. David et al. [8] proposed a method of using PE file header format specification to identify malicious software, which showed good results in actual emergency response detection. Santos et al. [24] proposed a malicious code detection technology based on fusion features, which identifies malware with the help of supervised learning by integrating opcodes and execution tracking information features. Zhang et al. [28] converted the sequence of opcodes obtained by decompilation of executable files into images, and input them into the convolutional neural network CNN for detection. Raff et al. [20] input the original byte sequence of the sample into the artificial neural network MalConv to train a classifier for identifying whether the file is benign or malicious. The methods based on static features have been proved to be effective for most malwares, but some highly resistant malwares will use packing, code transformations or other obfuscation schemes to obscure static features, which interferes with the effectiveness of the detection.

Dynamic Feature Based. The detection of malicious samples based on dynamic features via runtime behaviors generated. Rieck et al. [22] collected the behavioral features of malware through sandbox, and trained a machine learning model to identify them based on these dynamic features. Bailey et al. [4] proposed to describe the behavior of malware based on system state changes, rather than the order of system calls. Cesare et al. [7] constructs a signature through the control flow chart contained in the malware, and describes the characteristics of the decompiled flow chart on this basis, which can effectively identify malware variants. Kolosnjaji et al. [14] constructed a neural network based on convolutional and recurrent network layers in order to obtain the best features for classification, and achieve an average of 85.6% on precision and 89.4% on recall using this combined neural network architecture. However, all dynamic analysis approaches rely heavily on the support of the environment.

3   MSFV Extraction on Mining Trojans

In this section, we first introduce three static manifestations of sample files. Then, feature engineering for Mining Trojans on three static files and the generation of MSFV are introduced in detail.

3.1   Static Analysis

Generally, malware detection based on dynamic features such as system call sequences and operations occupies with the help of sandbox and virtual machine. Although dynamic detectors achieve satisfactory performance, they remain unsolved problems. First, excessive manual efforts on the initialization of executable environment for each samples severely lowers the efficiency of the analysis. Second, sandbox reaches its limitation when analyzing large-scale and bulky samples, which costs excessive computational resources and time. A sandbox can only analyze one sample at the same time, which is not suitable for large-scale sample detection requirements in real environment. Currently, most security vendors and researchers prefer static feature analysis when detecting massive samples of malware, such as the file header [25], opcodes [28], CFG (Call Flow Graph) [17]. Malware detection based on static features is highly efficient and has low risk that will not have any impact on the physical environment.

Due to the limitation of dynamic analysis that mentioned above, we focus on Mining Trojan detection based on static features. Specifically, we convert a binary sample file into three static manifestations, including Format File (FMT),

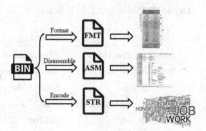

Fig. 1. Conversion of static files.

Assembly Sentence File (ASM), and String File (STR), which is illustrated in Fig. 1.

FMT is a special encoding used by the operating system to store information. Each type of information can be saved in one or more file formats on the computer and may have a different file extension which can help the application recognize the file format. For example, the JPEG file format in image files is only used to store static images, while HTML files can store formatted text. The general malware is often stored in the Windows executable file PE (Portable Executable) format or the Linux executable file ELF format. In this paper, we focus on PE files.

ASM can be exported by disassembling the machine code in the binary file, which can be implemented by public tools. In this paper, we use Objdump, a disassembler that can quickly interpret machine code to assembly code. Functions and call flows of the samples are relatively understandable in assembly code to some extend, though it is less readable compared with high-level language.

STR is a set of strings extracted from a binary sample. After encoding the machine code with ASCII, the continuous sequences that end with terminator '\0' are considered as stings and are extracted to construct STR. Theoretically, numerous features on natural language are included in STR such as function names, hard code data, input or output file, etc.

FMT, ASM and STR can be obtained from binary files with high efficiency, which is straightforward and explainable. Next, features are extracted from the above static files.

3.2 Multi-dimensional Static Feature Vector

We propose Multi-dimensional Static Feature Vector (MSFV) to represent Mining Trojan samples. MSFV is jointly constructed by the features that extracted from FMT, ASM and STR.

FMT Features. Take the PE file under the Windows OS as an example. PE files use a flat address space where all codes and data are merged together to form a large organizational structure. Commonly used DLL and EXE are both

Table 1. Selected FMT features

Num	Extracted from	Feature	Meaning
1	PE Header	NumberofSections	The number of sections
2		SizeOfOptionalHeader	Optional header size
3	Image Optional Header	SizeOfCode	Size of the code section
4		SizeOfInitializedData	Size of the initialized data section
5		BaseOfCode	Address of the beginning-of-code section
6		BaseOfData	Address of the beginning-of-data section
7		ImageBase	Preferred address of the image
8		SizeOfImage	Size of the image
9		SizeofStackReserve	Size of the stack to reserve
10		SizeofHeapReserve	Size of the local heap space to reserve
11	Section	text_Entropy	Information entropy of text, rdata, data section
12		rdata_Entropy	
13		data_Entropy	

PE files. The content of the file is divided into different sections, each section has its own attributes in the memory, such as whether the block is readable and writable, or read-only, etc. The fields in FMT are the most basic static information of the file, which reflect the overall structure of the file when it was created. Different files will also vary a lot in formatting information, which can distinguish the differences between files.

Numerous researches have demonstrated that malware and the benign ones vary a lot in file headers [8, 25]. We found that there are also big differences between the headers of the Mining Trojan and other samples. For example, the value of the *NumberOfSections* field of the *CoinMiner* mining family is probably 4, while the value of ImageBase in the Optional Header is much larger than that of other samples. Through the analysis of numerous Mining Trojans, we have extracted 13 features from FMT, they are shown in Table 1.

ASM Features. Disassembling and analyzing samples are very effective methods among malware detectors. Many researchers utilize the features of opcode to identify malware. However, most of the previous methods extract opcode features to tackle binary classification on malicious and non-malicious samples, which cannot deeply detect specific malicious types, especially Mining Trojan.

The mining function is the core part of the Mining Trojan. It is designed to satisfy verification conditions of cryptocurrency, which typically involves a very complex hash operation to achieve the proof of work (PoW). The PoW mechanism introduces scanning for a particular value, such as SHA-256, where

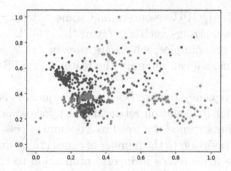

Fig. 2. The distribution of OpFings after dimension reduction.

a random hash starts with one or more zeros. Then as the number of zeros increases, the amount of work required to find the solution increases exponentially. PoW function can reflect the features of Mining Trojan samples to a large extent. Take the newly released Monero coin mining algorithm RandomX as an example. RandomX involves complex Blake2b, AES and other cryptographic algorithms with multiple internal loops. Therefore, RandomX requires a lot of jumps, arithmetic operations, and shifts. Although a normal program may have some complex encryption or hash functions, it does not introduce PoW mechanism, so its code logic will not be too complicated.

The opcodes of the sample performed fingerprint generation to mark the specificity of the mining function. We propose $OpFing$ based on the distributions of 49 most frequent opcodes, including data transfer instructions (MOV, LEA, PUSH, etc.), arithmetic operation instructions (ADD, SUB, MUL, etc.), logical operation instructions (XOR, AND, TEST, etc.) and so on. The $OpFing$ of a sample can be calculated as $OpFing = \{p_1, p_2, ..., p_n\}(p_i = \frac{o_i}{\sum_{j=0}^{49} o_j})$, where o_i is the number of $opcode_i$ in a sample.

We randomly select 1,000 Mining Trojans and 1,000 other samples. The distribution of their $OpFings$ is shown in Fig. 2. We argue that $OpFing$ can be employed as an effective metric to detect Mining Trojans. b

STR Features. In order to collect the mined cryptocurrency into the pocket, the programmer of the Mining Trojan often embeds some strings related to the Bitcoin, wallet address, and mining function in the Trojan. We conducted a static analysis of common Mining Trojan families, and found that there are some specific strings in each family. Take the XMRig Mining Trojan family as an example. XMRig is an open source, cross-platform Monero mining program active on the current Internet. Strings such as "xmrig", "monero", "mining" can be easily found in XMRig samples. In addition to the unique strings of each mining family, there are also some strings that appear frequently in all Mining Trojans. For example, in order to improve the efficiency of mining, Trojans may often request CPU/GPU resources and some external libraries to assist calculations. Therefore, strings such as "OpenCL", "GPU", "CUDA" etc. are often hard-coded in the samples, which are rare in other non-Mining Trojan samples. Based on this, we can quantify the features of STR by measuring the string frequency.

TF-IDF (Term Frequency-Inverse Document Frequency) is a commonly used weighting technique for information retrieval and information exploration. It is used to evaluate the importance of a word to a document set. The importance of a word increases in proportion to the number of times it appears in the document, but at the same time it decreases in inverse proportion to the frequency of its appearance in the corpus. In our work, we treat each string (s) as a word. The calculation of TF-IDF for s is as followed.

$$TF - IDF(s, d, D) = TF(s, d) \cdot IDF(s, D) \tag{1}$$

$$TF(s, d) = \frac{f_{s,d}}{\sum_{s' \in d} f_{s',d}} \tag{2}$$

$$IDF(s, D) = log \frac{|D|}{n_s} \tag{3}$$

where d is a STR file; D is all the STR files $f_{s,d}$ is the count of s in d; n_s is the number of STR files in which s appears and $|D|$ is the total number of files. By TF-IDF, strings in STR can be embedded in the vector.

MSFV can be obtained by combining the vectors obtained from the above three files like $M\vec{S}FV = \{V_{FMT}, \vec{V_{ASM}}, \vec{V_{STR}}\}$.

4   Miner-Killer System

In this section, we introduce the proposed Miner-Killer system for Miner Trojan detection. Demonstrated as Fig. 3, Miner-Killer consists of Preprocessing module, Extractor, Training module and Detection module.

Preprocessing. An original binary file (BIN) is transformed to FMT, ASM, STR with this module. Specifically, diverse tools are employed to jointly construct the above files. First, FMT information including headers, sections are extracted by PEiD, a static file analysis tool. Then, ASM file is obtained by disassembling BIN with Objdump. STR is generated by encoding the binary file with the corresponding relationship between ASCII code and machine code. Strings are truncated with the terminator '\0'. Specially, we discard the binaries cannot be parsed.

Extractor. MSFV of each sample is generated byExtractor. The extracted features for each file are introduced in detail in Sect. 3. Moreover, Extractor will label the extracted MSFV before training.

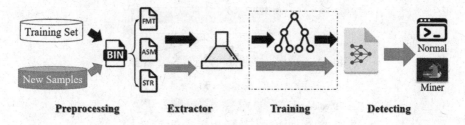

Fig. 3. Overview of Miner-Killer.

Algorithm 1. Framework of ensemble learning for our system.

Input:
    Training dataset $D = \{(x_1, y_1), (x_2, y_2), ..., (x_m, y_m)\}$;
    Base learners $\xi_1, \xi_2, ..., \xi_T$;
    Meta learner ξ;
Output:
    Ensemble Classifier H;
1: $Step1$;
2: **for** each $t \in [1, T]$ **do**
3:     $h_t = \xi_t(D)$;
4: **end for**
5: $Step2$;
6: **for** each $i \in [1, m]$ **do**
7:     $D_h = \{x'_i, y_i\}$, where $x'_i = \{h_1(x_i), h_2(x_i), ..., h_T(x_i)\}$
8: **end for**
9: $Step3$;
10: **return** $H = \xi(D_h)$;

Training. Inspired by the Ensemble Learning, we employ the multi-stacked classifiers to learn from the features from diverse files that extracted with different methods. The ensemble strategy is based on the stacking method. Stacking can combine multiple heterogeneous models and help finding the appropriate weight of each model. Algorithm 1 describes the framework of ensemble learning.

We consider CART (Classification and Regression Trees), RF (Random Forest), SVM (Support Vector Machines), XGBoost (eXtreme Gradient Boosting), kNN (k-Nearest Neighbor) as the base learners, while LR (Linear Regression) is considered as the meta learner. The stacking ensemble model is shown in Fig. 4.

Detecting. The detecting module is responsible for predicting samples in the real environment. After pre-processing and feature extraction, the samples to be detected are input into the detection module, which the well-trained stacking ensemble model is used to determine whether the sample is a Mining Trojan.

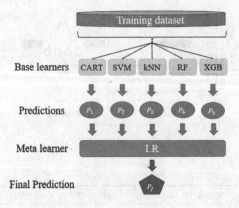

Fig. 4. Stacking ensemble model.

5   Experiments

5.1   Dataset

Comparison experiments are carefully designed to validate the rationality and effectiveness of our proposed methods. First, we introduce the public dataset used in the experiment and some evaluation standard calculation methods in the experiment. Then we introduce the baseline model for comparison and compare it with Miner-Killer. Finally, we compared the performance of Miner-Killer and some advanced methods.

DataCon2020-Malware. DataCon2020-Malware [19] is a public dataset provided by QiAnXin Technology Research Institute. The dataset consists of real-world network traffic that captured from Mining Trojan and the benign software. After data cleaning, samples with a size between 20 KB and 10 MB are extracted from them. Excessive similar samples are removed by code similarity analysis to the diversity of samples. To avoid running the sample, the MZ header, PE header, and import/export tables in PE files have been erased. Although the cleaned samples cannot be analyzed dynamically, the code instruction characteristics of the mining function still exist.

Win-Miner. Win-Miner is another dataset created by ourselves. We collect 3000 mining Trojans from VirusTotal [1], which is a famous website that provides free suspicious file analysis services. Moreover, we collected all DLL and EXE files in the system directories (System32, SysWOW64, SystemApps, Windows) in the Windows 10 pure system as negative samples and jointly construct Win-Miner.

DataCon2020-Malware contains 3887 mining Trojans as positive samples set, and the other 7760 as negative samples set. Win-Miner contains 3000 positive samples and 4983 negative samples.

Table 2. Comparison results of different features

Features	DataCon2020-Malware				Win-Miner			
	ACC	Precision	Recall	F1-score	ACC	Precision	Recall	F1-score
FTM-F	0.9498	0.9673	0.8874	0.9245	0.9404	0.9030	0.9761	0.9374
OpFing	0.7341	0.7328	0.7442	0.7410	0.7023	0.6938	0.7026	0.6997
TF-IDF	0.9167	0.7116	0.7699	0.7315	0.9082	0.8569	0.8804	0.8704
MSFV	**0.9778**	**0.9828**	**0.9774**	**0.9803**	**0.9953**	**0.9808**	**0.9892**	**0.9862**

5.2 Evaluation Metrics

In order to validate the quality of the results, the performance is evaluated using a confusion matrix. The symbols in the matrix can thus be identified:

- TP: True Positive FP: False Positive
- FN: False Negative TN: True Negative

We utilize Accuracy (ACC), Precision, Recall to select the appropriate model. They are defined as follows:

$$ACC = \frac{TP + TN}{TP + FP + FN + TN} \tag{4}$$

$$Precision = \frac{TP}{TP + FP} \tag{5}$$

$$Recall = \frac{TP}{TP + FN} \tag{6}$$

$$F1 - score = \frac{2 \times Precision \times Recall}{Precision + Recall} \tag{7}$$

5.3 Analysis of Our Proposed Features

In order to verify the effectiveness of the feature vector MSFV extracted from the Mining Trojan, we conduct experiment separately on three components of MSFV including FMT based features (FTM-F), ASM based features (OpFing) and STR based features (TF-IDF). Compatible steps are employed in each experiment during training and detection. Also, we evaluate the Miner-Killer with complete MSFV to validate the effectiveness. The experimental results are shown in Table 2.

We argue that when each feature is used for prediction separately, the metrics are effective but not sufficient to support real-world detection tasks. However, all metrics have improved significantly when combined into MSFV. Experimental results demonstrate the rationality of our proposed MSFV, which can jointly learn from different features and significantly improve the performance.

Table 3. Comparison results of Miner-Killer and Well-known AVs

Solution	DataCon2020-Malware		Win-Miner	
	TPR	FPR	TPR	FPR
AV-1 (offline)	0.9485	0.0	0.9526	0.0
AV-1 (online)	0.8110	0.0	0.9783	0.0
AV-2 (offline)	0.0136	0.0	0.8521	0.0
AV-2 (online)	0.0035	0.0	0.9054	0.0
AV-3 (offline)	0.1030	0.0	0.9206	0.0
AV-3 (online)	0.1030	0.0	0.9709	0.0
Miner-Killer	**0.9774**	**0.0104**	**0.9892**	**0.0124**

5.4 Compared with Well-Known AVs

Anti-virus (AV) software is now the most widely used computer protection software. In actual scenarios, AV is most likely to be used to defend against mining Trojans. In order to verify the effectiveness of Miner-Killer, we also employ several well-known AVs to scan DataCon2020-Malware and Win-Miner. Due to the interests of manufacturers and commercial competition, we do not announce the specific AV software chosen in the experiments and name them AV-1, AV-2 and AV-3 instead. We install the latest versions of these three AVs in three virtual machines with the same environment and configuration. Considering that the current mainstream AV software have online cloud scanning functions, we conduct online detection and offline detection for each AV. Moreover, our statistics on whether AV can detect the mining Trojan depends on further viewing the detailed report information of AV. If the report contains miner-related information, we consider it to be recognized as a mining Trojan. If the detection report of the positive sample identifies the mining Trojan as other malicious software such as RAT, Backdoor, etc., we also consider this detection to fail.

In real environment, users tend to pay more attention to the detection rate and false alarm rate, namely TPR, FPR, so we use these two metrics to evaluate the detection performance of AV. Their definitions are as follows (Table 3):

$$TPR = \frac{TP}{TP + FN} \qquad (8)$$

$$FPR = \frac{FP}{TN + FP} \qquad (9)$$

The detection results is shown in Table 4. It can be found that on the DataCon2020-Malware dataset, AV-1 performs the best. The TPR in offline detection is 0.8110, and TPR in the online detection is 0.9485, which is much higher than the other two AVs, but still inferior to the proposed Miner-Killer. For the other two AVs, both the offline detection rate and the online detection rate are far from enough. On the Win-Miner dataset, the three AVs perform

Table 4. Comparison results of Miner-Killer and other methods

System	DataCon2020-Malware			Win-Miner		
	ACC	Precision	Recall	ACC	Precision	Recall
MalConv	0.7810	0.7149	0.8026	0.8429	0.8041	0.8824
LZJD	0.5403	0.3203	0.9765	0.7269	0.4838	0.9765
Miner-Killer	**0.9778**	**0.9828**	**0.9774**	**0.9953**	**0.9808**	**0.9892**

well, but are still little behind Miner-Killer. The reason for such inefficiency on the Datacon2020-Malware dataset is that the mining Trojan samples in the DataCon2020-Malware dataset are not complete. Some PE headers and import and export tables are removed, which causes the signatures of the samples to be completely different from the original samples. The AV-2 and AV-3 detection principles may be based on hash matching, so they are completely invalid on the DataCon2020-Malware dataset. However, in actual situations, malicious samples can easily evade static detection by changing some strings or code structure. Therefore, although the method based entirely on hash matching is very accurate, it will cause a large number of false positives. Therefore, in the detection of mining Trojans, Miner-Killer's performance is superior than these 3 well-known AVs.

5.5 Compared with Other Methods

In order to verify the effectiveness of our proposed method, we compared two advanced methods in malware detection, namely MalConv [20] based on deep neural network and LZJD [21] based on byte sequence.

MalConv is a neural network model, it has access to the entire file which allows the model to detect the few informative features regardless of location. This solution avoids a number of the issues with the more common byte n-gram approach. It achieves consistent generalization across both test sets, despite the challenges of learning a sequence problem of unprecedented length.

LZJD (Lempel-Ziv Jaccard Distance) is a new distance metric which can measure the similarity between two arbitrary objects. The author uses raw bytes for Microsoft Windows files and Android applications, ASCII disassembly, and moderately compressed Android APKs. This comes with improved accuracy compared to NCD (Normalized Compression Distance).

We reproduced these two methods on the DataCon2020-Malware dataset and Win-Miner dataset, and the experimental results are shown in Table 4. It can be found that Miner-Killer performs much better than MalConv and LZJD.

6   Conclusion and Future Work

In this paper, we propose Miner-Killer to tackle the vacancy of Mining Trojan detection. We first carried out feature engineering based on static feature analysis, and proposed MSFV to represent the static features of a sample. The detection module is trained by the stacking ensemble models and applied to predict whether the new sample is a Mining Trojan. We verify the validity of our feature and model on two real datasets, and the performance is superior to well-known AVs and the state-of-the-art methods. In the future, we will continue to strengthen our detection model with the continuous evolution of Mining Trojans, and strive to apply the model to the detection of other types of malware.

Acknowledgment. This work was supported by the National Key R&D Program of China with No. 2018YFC0806900 and No. 2018YFB0805004, Beijing Municipal Science & Technology Commission with Project No. Z191100007119009, NSFC No.61902397, NSFC No. U2003111 and NSFC No. 61871378.

References

1. https://www.virustotal.com/gui/
2. Anderson, B., Quist, D., Neil, J., Storlie, C., Lane, T.: Graph-based malware detection using dynamic analysis. J. Comput. Virol. **7**(4), 247–258 (2011)
3. Anderson, B., Storlie, C., Lane, T.: Improving malware classification: bridging the static/dynamic gap. In: Proceedings of the 5th ACM Workshop on Security and Artificial Intelligence, pp. 3–14 (2012)
4. Bailey, M., Oberheide, J., Andersen, J., Mao, Z.M., Jahanian, F., Nazario, J.: Automated classification and analysis of internet malware. In: Kruegel, C., Lippmann, R., Clark, A. (eds.) RAID 2007. LNCS, vol. 4637, pp. 178–197. Springer, Heidelberg (2007). https://doi.org/10.1007/978-3-540-74320-0_10
5. Böhme, R., Christin, N., Edelman, B., Moore, T.: Bitcoin: economics, technology, and governance. J. Econ. Perspect. **29**(2), 213–38 (2015)
6. Carlin, D., Burgess, J., O'Kane, P., Sezer, S.: You could be mine (d): the rise of cryptojacking. IEEE Secur. Priv. **18**(2), 16–22 (2019)
7. Cesare, S., Xiang, Y., Zhou, W.: Control flow-based malware variantdetection. IEEE Trans. Dependable Secure Comput. **11**(4), 307–317 (2013)
8. David, B., Filiol, E., Gallienne, K.: Structural analysis of binary executable headers for malware detection optimization. J. Comput. Virol. Hacking Tech. **13**(2), 87–93 (2016). https://doi.org/10.1007/s11416-016-0274-2
9. Eskandari, S., Leoutsarakos, A., Mursch, T., Clark, J.: A first look at browser-based cryptojacking. In: 2018 IEEE European Symposium on Security and Privacy Workshops (EuroS&PW), pp. 58–66. IEEE (2018)
10. Grinberg, R.: Bitcoin: an innovative alternative digital currency. Hastings Sci. Tech. LJ **4**, 159 (2012)
11. Hong, G., et al.: How you get shot in the back: a systematical study about cryptojacking in the real world. In: Proceedings of the 2018 ACM SIGSAC Conference on Computer and Communications Security, pp. 1701–1713 (2018)
12. Idika, N., Mathur, A.P.: A survey of malware detection techniques. Purdue University **48**, 2007–2 (2007)
13. Jordaney, R., et al.: Transcend: detecting concept drift in malware classification models. In: 26th {USENIX} Security Symposium ({USENIX} Security 2017), pp. 625–642 (2017)

14. Kolosnjaji, B., Zarras, A., Webster, G., Eckert, C.: Deep learning for classification of malware system call sequences. In: Kang, B.H., Bai, Q. (eds.) AI 2016. LNCS (LNAI), vol. 9992, pp. 137–149. Springer, Cham (2016). https://doi.org/10.1007/978-3-319-50127-7_11

15. Kolter, J.Z., Maloof, M.A.: Learning to detect and classify malicious executables in the wild. J. Mach. Learn. Res. **7**(Dec), 2721–2744 (2006)

16. Lo, R.W., Levitt, K.N., Olsson, R.A.: MCF: a malicious code filter. Comput. Secur. **14**(6), 541–566 (1995)

17. Mariconti, E., Onwuzurike, L., Andriotis, P., De Cristofaro, E., Ross, G., Stringhini, G.: Mamadroid: detecting android malware by building Markov chains of behavioral models. arXiv preprint arXiv:1612.04433 (2016)

18. Microsoft 365 Defender Threat Intelligence Team: Threat actor leverages coin miner techniques to stay under the radar - here's how to spot them (2020). https://www.microsoft.com/security/blog/2020/11/30/

19. QiAnXin Technology Research Institute: Datacon 2020-malware (2020). https://datacon.qianxin.com/opendata/maliciouscode

20. Raff, E., Barker, J., Sylvester, J., Brandon, R., Catanzaro, B., Nicholas, C.K.: Malware detection by eating a whole EXE. In: The Workshops of the Thirty-Second AAAI Conference on Artificial Intelligence, New Orleans, Louisiana, USA, 2–7 February 2018. AAAI Workshops, vol. WS-18, pp. 268–276. AAAI Press (2018)

21. Raff, E., Nicholas, C.: An alternative to NCD for large sequences, Lempel-Ziv Jaccard distance. In: Proceedings of the 23rd ACM SIGKDD International Conference on Knowledge Discovery and Data Mining, pp. 1007–1015 (2017)

22. Rieck, K., Trinius, P., Willems, C., Holz, T.: Automatic analysis of malware behavior using machine learning. J. Comput. Secur. **19**(4), 639–668 (2011)

23. Rodriguez, J.D.P., Posegga, J.: Rapid: resource and API-based detection against in-browser miners. In: Proceedings of the 34th Annual Computer Security Applications Conference, pp. 313–326 (2018)

24. Santos, I., Devesa, J., Brezo, F., Nieves, J., Bringas, P.G.: OPEM: a static-dynamic approach for machine-learning-based malware detection. In: Herrero, A., et al. (eds.) International Joint Conference CISIS'12-ICEUTE 12-SOCO 12 Special Sessions, pp. 271–280. Springer, Heidelberg (2013). https://doi.org/10.1007/978-3-642-33018-6_28

25. Shafiq, M.Z., Tabish, S.M., Mirza, F., Farooq, M.: PE-miner: mining structural information to detect malicious executables in realtime. In: Kirda, E., Jha, S., Balzarotti, D. (eds.) RAID 2009. LNCS, vol. 5758, pp. 121–141. Springer, Heidelberg (2009). https://doi.org/10.1007/978-3-642-04342-0_7

26. Tencent Security Threat Intelligence Center: 2019 annual mining trojan report (2020). https://s.tencent.com/research/report/887.html

27. Zareh, A., Shahriari, H.R.: Botcointrap: detection of bitcoin miner botnet using host based approach. In: 2018 15th International ISC (Iranian Society of Cryptology) Conference on Information Security and Cryptology (ISCISC), pp. 1–6. IEEE (2018)

28. Zhang, J., Qin, Z., Yin, H., Ou, L., Xiao, S., Hu, Y.: Malware variant detection using opcode image recognition with small training sets. In: 2016 25th International Conference on Computer Communication and Networks (ICCCN), pp. 1–9. IEEE (2016)

Botnet Detection Based on Multilateral Attribute Graph

Hua Cheng[1] ⓘ, Yinda Shen[1] ⓘ, Tao Cheng[1] ⓘ, Yiquan Fang[2(✉)] ⓘ,
and Jianfan Ling[1] ⓘ

[1] College of Information Science and Engineering,
East China University of Science and Technology, Shanghai 200237, China
[2] Information Office, East China University of Science and Technology,
Shanghai 200237, China
fyq@ecust.edu.cn

Abstract. Botnets have become the infrastructure of cryptocurrency in recent years, but traditional graph-based detection methods ignore multiple flows and their features. We propose a botnet detection method (ME-LGCN) by node classification based on the fine-grained multilateral attribute graph (fMAG). Multiple flows and their features are appended on the simple graph of network topology as multilateral structures and attributes in fMAG. Latent Graph Convolutional Neural Network (Latent-GCN) is used for node classification, where multi-edge embedding learns the multilateral attributes as an interaction vector, direct on-vertex embedding extends node representation, and GCN aggregates information of neighborhoods. Experiments on real datasets show that ME-LGCN provides significant improvements compared to other methods with a more than 3% improvement in F1.

Keywords: Botnet · Latent Graphic Convolutional Neural Network (Latent-GCN) · Multilateral attribute graph

1 Introduction

Botnets have become serious threats on the Internet, especially to finance, education, Internet of Things (IoT), and etc. According to Eversec Lab, DDOS attacks of botnets in 2019 increased by 51.2% monthly compared with the last year, and attack methods are more diversified [1]. An effective botnet detection is an important research issue in cybersecurity.

Flow features such as ratio of packets sent and received, average bytes per second, etc. are analyzed in botnet detection [2,3]. However, these flow-based botnet detection methods ignore network topology and fail to exploit the features of communication.

The graph-based botnet detection methods mine the structure of botnets [4–7], but their topologies only contain the relative location of hosts without host or flow features [4,6]. For example, Zhou [8] used GCN to classify nodes, and optimized by adding convolutional layers, Chowdhury [4] identified bots in

© Springer Nature Switzerland AG 2021
W. Lu et al. (Eds.): SciSec 2021, LNCS 13005, pp. 66–76, 2021.
https://doi.org/10.1007/978-3-030-89137-4_5

graphs by clustering without communication features and got low identification accuracy.

By introducing flows and features, we achieve better descriptions of flows between hosts. Multilateral structures and features are introduced and attached to simple graphs to obtain a fine-grained multilateral attribute graph (fMAG).

Compared with GCN's isotropic aggregation of neighborhoods, multi-edge embedding is introduced for the purpose of selectively focusing on the neighborhoods. We propose MultiEdge-LatentGCN (ME-LGCN), a botnet detection method based on Latent-GCN which learns from fMAG of network topology and performs node classification for bots. Experiments show that the detection accuracy of ME-LGCN is better than other methods including GCN-based methods and flow features selecting is also important in modeling the fMAG.

2 Multilateral Attribute Graph of Botnet

2.1 Communication Features of Botnet

Botnet behaviors are different in flows and hosts features from the normal network applications. For example, standard deviation of the number of flow packets, average size of packets, and standard deviation of packet size in P2P botnets are obviously smaller than that of normal traffic [9].

(1) Flow features

Flow features reflect the interactive behaviors of hosts, including flow byte features (APL, TBT, DPL, and PV), flow packet features (IOPR), flow time features (BS, PS, PPS, and AIT), and flow behavior features (Dur and Proto), and their combinations. The combination of features provides a comprehensive description of flows. It is found that combination of APL (average payload packet length), IOPR (ratio between the number of outgoing packets and the number of incoming packets), BS (average bits per second), Dur (duration), and Proto (protocol) can achieve a high detection accuracy [10].

(2) Host features

Host features include host packet features (aps and apr), host byte features (abs, abr), and host behavior features (acd), and their combinations. The combination of aps (number of packets sent by the host), apr (number of packets received by the host), abs (number of bytes sent by the host), abr (number of bytes received by the host), and acd (average connection duration of the host) achieves a high accuracy of botnet detection in IoT [11].

2.2 Fine-Grained Multilateral Attribute Graph

Simple graphs are used in most traditional studies on botnet detection, which only contain the topology, with a unilateral edge between nodes and without any attributes on edges and nodes. There are limits in simple graph on: (1) simplify

the complex communications between hosts to uninformative edge where only
the structure of botnets is possessed. (2) simplify the multiple communications
between hosts to one edge. The simplifications ignore multiple interactions and
their features at different periods which are important features to classify bots
and normal hosts.

A fine-grained graph of network is modeled based on the simple graph with
multiple communications and their features. The fine-grained graph include multiple edges between nodes, and multiple edges and host attributes.

Definition 1. *(fMAG)*

$$G = (V, E, X, F)$$

*where V is the nodes set, each host is a node $v_i \in V$, E is the edges set, the nth
communication between host i and j is the edge $e_{i,j}^n \in E$, X and F are the nodes'
and edges' attributes sets.*

Definition 2. *(Node attribute vector)*

$$x_i = [q_1, q_2, q_3, \ldots, q_i]$$

$x_i \in X$ *is the attribute vector of node v_i, and q_i is a kind of host features, such
as byte feature abs.*

Definition 3. *(Edge attribute vector)*

$$f_{i,j}^n = [t_1, t_2, t_3, \ldots, t_i]$$

$f_{i,j}^n \in F$ *is the feature vector of edge $e_{i,j}^n$, and t_i is a kind of flow features, such as
byte feature APL. The matrix S_{ij} is defined as the multilateral attributes between
nodes, as in Fig. 1.*

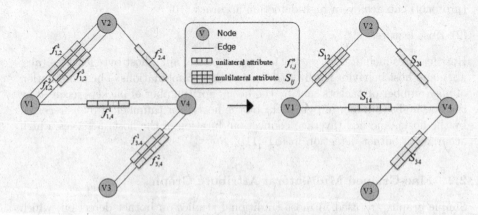

Fig. 1. Fine-grained multilateral attribute graph.

3   Botnet Detection Method Based on fMAG

We propose the botnet detection method ME-LGCN based on fMAG and Latent-GCN [12,13], where the interaction feature vector $\hat{w}_i$ of multilateral attributes is computed and concatenate with the node feature vector X_i to enrich representation of the neighborhoods.

GCN is a multilayer neural network that operates directly on a graph and induces embedding vectors of nodes based on properties of their neighborhoods. A node aggregates feature information from its topological neighborhoods in each convolutional layer. In this way, feature information propagates over network topology to node embedding, and then node embedding learned as such is used in classification tasks. GCN can capture information only about the first-order neighborhoods with one layer convolution. When multiple layers GCN are stacked, information about larger neighborhoods are integrated.

There are limits in GCN information propagation mechanism, which only relies on the aggregation of the first-order neighborhoods [12] and have no information of connected edges. Latent-GCN with multi-edge embedding (MEE) and direct on-vertex embedding (DVE) is introduced for fMAGs in botnet detection.

3.1   Multi-Edge Embedding (MEE)

The interaction matrix S_{ij} of fMAG is defined as the multilateral structure and edge attributes. It describes multiple communication behaviors between hosts and their interactive behavior features.

The core of fMAG is to extract the effective information of interaction matrix S_{ij} where several aggregation methods based on S_{ij} can be used, such as average aggregation, maximum aggregation, etc. However, these types of aggregations haven't learning mechanisms and cannot capture important details from the combination of features. Therefore, this paper adopts CNN-based multi-edge embedding to extract important features where CNN can automatically learn to extract edge attributes and perceive locally by multiple kernels.

Multi-edge embedding learns the latent representations w_{ij} of matrix S_{ij} in the form of an adjacency tensor by a CNN network, which represents the behaviors and weights between hosts. The latent representations are behavior features that can be extended to the representation of nodes through direct on-vertex embedding. Multi-edge embedding is defined as follows:

$$w_{ij} = \Gamma(S_{ij})$$

$\Gamma()$ is the CNN network, w_{ij} is the weights vector of the potential relations between v_i and v_j.

As shown in Fig. 2, the multilateral attribute $S_{ij} = [f_1, f_2, f_3, \ldots, f_k, \ldots, f_N]$, f_k represents the unilateral attributes composed of z ($z=5$) features. $f_k = [f_{k1}, f_{k2}, f_{k3}, f_{k4}, f_{k5}]$ is the vector of flow features APL, IOPR, BS, Dur, and Proto mentioned in 2.1.

w_{ij} is computed by multi-edge embedding:

1) A 1D convolution is adopted on a fMAG, with K kernels (size 3, stride 1) and z channels where z is the number of features of each edge.
2) A 1D max pooling is operated across the output of each kernel (shape of $K \times (\mid S_{ij} \mid - 2)$), and followed by an activation function $ReLU\ (x) = max\ (0,x)$.
3) The resulting layer of size K is followed by two fully connected layers of sizes $2L$ and L to obtain the desired embedding size. Activation functions (also $ReLU$) are employed after every fully connected layer, and dropout ($p = 0.2$) is applied to the second-to-last layer (of size $2L$). We defined $L=5$.
4) The interactive feature vector w_{ij} with $L=5$ of the edges in fMAG is obtained.

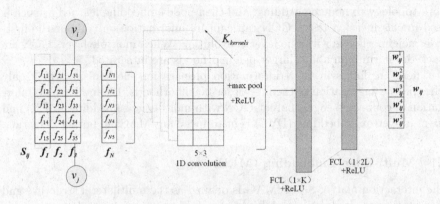

Fig. 2. Multi-Edge Embedding.

3.2 Direct On-Vertex Embedding(DVE)

The latent edge representation w_{ij} is considered as the behavior features of hosts which can effectively promote the botnet detection. In direct on-vertex embedding, w_{ij} is concatenated with the node representation to enrich nodes information in Latent-GCN.

　　MEE is performed on edges in the neighborhood N_i of node v_i. DVE performs an average pooling operation on w_{ij} to obtain the output vector $\hat{w}_i$. Concatenating $\hat{w}_i$ with the host feature vector X_i of node v_i to expand into a new feature vector X_i' [12,13], which is the new input of Latent-GCN, as shown in Fig. 3.

3.3 Latent-GCN

Latent-GCN employed a learning mechanism that transforms multi-edges populations into latent relations, serving as the input for R-GCN-like further propagation [12,13]. Different from the isotropic aggregation of GCN, Latent-GCN learns the latent representations w_{ij} to express the importance of relations between nodes, and selectively focuses on the neighborhoods by w_{ij}, which describes local features more accurately.

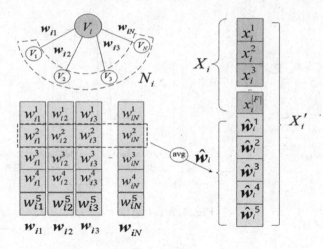

Fig. 3. Direct on-Vertex Embedding.

Latent-GCN propagation rules:

$$h_i^{l+1} = \sigma \left(\frac{1}{c_i} \sum_{r \in R} \lfloor w_{ii}^r h_i^l + \sum_{r \in R} w_{ij}^r h_j^l \rfloor W_r^l \right)$$

where

$$c_i = \sum_{r \in R} \left(w_{ii}^r + \sum_{j \in N_i} w_{ij}^r \right)$$

h_i^l is the representation of node v_i in layer l, N_i is the direct neighborhoods node set of v_i, R is the direct neighborhoods edge set of v_i, and r is edge in R.

w_{ij}^r is the weight of r to describe the relation information extracted from adjacent edges. w_{ii}^r is useless since self-connections don't exist in botnets. σ is the nonlinear activation function, and W_r^l is the parameter matrix.

3.4 Bot Detection Methods

ME-LGCN is shown in Fig. 4, including two convolutional layers in Latent-GCN. The first layer only contains information of the direct neighborhoods. After the second layer, each node will contain information about neighborhoods in its two-hop range. Dropout ($p=5$) is applied to the output of the first convolutional layer.

ME-LGCN method is defined as follows:

1. Analyze pcap files by Argus [14] into flows containing communication features sets T.

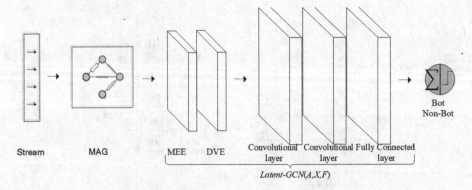

Fig. 4. ME-LGCN.

2. Calculate flow features {APL, IOPR, BS, Dur, Proto} and host features {aps, apr, abs, abr, acd} according to T.
3. Model fMAG as $G = (V,E,X,F)$ from hosts, communications, and features.
4. Input G into $LatentGCN(A,X,F)$ for the botnet detection model training.

Here, parameters in $LatentGCN(A,X,F)$ are as follows:

- The adjacency matrix A of fMAG to describe the topology.
- Node attributes matrix X, $x_i \in X$ (dimension is $N \times 5$, N is the number of nodes):

$$x_i = [q_{aps}, q_{apr}, q_{abs}, q_{abr}, q_{acd}]$$

where $q_{aps}, q_{apr}, q_{abs}, q_{abr}, q_{acd}$ are 5 host features of aps, apr, abs, abr, acd.
- Edge attributes matrix F, $f_{i,j} \in F$

$$f_{i,j} = [f_{i,j}^1, f_{i,j}^2, \ldots, f_{i,j}^n]$$
$$f_{i,j}^n = [t_{APL}, t_{IOPR}, t_{BS}, t_{Dur}, t_{Proto}]$$

Where $t_{APL}, t_{IOPR}, t_{BS}, t_{Dur}, t_{Proto}$ are 5 flow features APL, IOPR, BS, Dur and Proto.

The receptive field of GCN is proportional to the number of convolutional layers. Appropriately increasing the number of layers can enlarge the receptive field to obtain neighborhoods information in a larger range. However, too many convolutional layers in graph convolution will make the representation of nodes smooth and lack discrimination [15] in the aggregation operation. In the experiment of GCN [16], as the number of layers increases to more than 2, its detection performance decreases. All nodes eventually learn the same representation as the too many layers stacked in GCN. We use two convolutional layers in Latent-GCN here.

4   Experiments and Analysis

4.1   Datasets

We collect our sampling dataset by the sampling strategy that selects all bots in real datasets of CTU-Malware [17], ISCX [18], PeerRush [19], EnhancePeer-Hunter [20] since bots are scarce, and mixes bots with real backgrounding traffics. The type of bots includes IRC and P2P in real.

There are a large number of irrelevant nodes, whose degree is 1 and is isolated from graphs in backgrounding traffics. Such nodes will be filtered out in sampling datasets. For the reason of the limited number of bots, bots account for 3% in the sampling dataset.

For the dataset we use a fixed train/validation/test split scheme with ratios 70/10/20. Binary weighted cross-entropy loss function is adapted to the unbalanced dataset. All models were subjected to 10 training sessions with independent, random weight initialization, a learning rate of 0.005, weight decay of $5 \cdot 10^{-4}$. The resulting accuracy on the test sets are averaged.

Table 1. Real dataset sampling

Data set	Number of bot nodes	Number of backgrounding nodes	Ratio
CTU-Malware	104	3328	3.125%
ISCX	35	1120	3.125%
PeerRush	17	544	3.125%
EnhancePeerHunter	37	1184	3.125%
Total	193	6176	3.125%

4.2   Experiments and Discussions

(1) Algorithms comparison

The comparison experiments are based on four methods: Bot-DL [21], Graph-Cluster [4], Graph-ML [6], and Bot-GCN [8]. Bot-DL models bot features in individual network traffic by deep neural networks. Graph-Cluster detects bots by cluster method based on host features in graphs. Graph and machine learning are combined in Graph-ML to detect bots. Bot-GCN performs graph convolution modeling directly using topology.

Table 2. Algorithms comparison experiment

	Precision	Recall	F1
Bot-DL	91.6%	89.4%	0.905
Graph-Cluster	92.1%	90.7%	0.914
Graph-ML	89.6%	88.5%	0.890
Bot-GCN	93.5%	92.6%	0.931
ME-LGCN	95.8%	96.5%	0.961

In Table 2, ME-LGCN and Bot-GCN outperform other graph-based methods, including Graph-ML and Graph-Cluster which are learnt from graph features such as out-degree, in-degree, specific community structure and subgraphs. It shows that GCN and deep learning have better learning abilities in extracting graph features.

Bot-DL, as a flow-based detection method, is 6% lower on precision and recall than our method, since it only includes the flows interaction features and ignores its network topology.

Bot-GCN is 3% lower than ME-LGCN in F1 since Bot-GCN models the network as a simple graph without the communication features in its representation learning. While ME-LGCN promote the recognition accuracy for including flows and nodes features in fMAG, and enriching nodes representation in GCN.

(2) Ablation experiments
1) Ablation experiments on features
Due to the importance of communication features, our ablation experiments contain flow feature group (APL, IOPR, BS, Dur and Proto) or host feature group (aps, apr, abs, abr and ace). The results are shown in Table 3.

Table 3. Ablation experiments on features group

	Communication features	Precision	Recall	F1
1 Bot-GCN	No features	93.5%	92.6%	0.931
2 ME-LGCN_F	Flow features group	95.6%	96.4%	0.960
3 ME-LGCN_H	Host features group	93.8%	94.1%	0.939
4 ME-LGCN_FH	(Flow+Host) features group	95.8%	96.5%	0.961

It shows that flow feature group plays a crucial role in the whole group because flow features are more fine-grained than host features. Part of features of flows and hosts are similar, e.g. APL (flow), abs (host) and abr (host) are based on bytes, IOPR (flow), aps (host) and apr (host) are based on packets, Dur (flow) and acd (host) are based on behaviors. But flow features group includes more important time feature BS and behavior feature Proto. What's more, ME-LGCN_H outperforms Bot-GCN by adding hosts features.

2) Ablation experiments on flow features
Other ablation experiments focus on flow features, where excludes byte, packet, time or behavior feature respectively. The results are shown in Table 4.

Table 4. Ablation experiments on flow features

Features	Exclude	Precision	Recall	F1
IOPR, BS, Dur, Proto	APL	94.90%	95.60%	0.952
APL, BS, Dur, Proto	IOPR	95.30%	95.80%	0.956
APL, IOPR, Dur, Proto	BS	94.40%	94.20%	0.943
APL, IOPR, BS	Dur, Proto	94.70%	93.90%	0.943
APL, IOPR, BS, Dur, Proto		95.60%	96.40%	0.960

Features without BS or APL decreases 1–2% in F1. It shows that time (BS) and behavior (Dur and Proto) features are the most influential factors and have similar impacts on detection accuracies.

Time features BS (average bits per second) and Byte features APL (average payload packet length) reflect the similarity of network communications and payload of bots families effectively. The traffics of legitimate hosts are diverse and random in time distribution while bots tend to run in predefined actions resulting more uniform flows.

Features without Dur and Proto also decreases 1–2% in F1. Dur can distinguish the communication behaviors because most bots have one-way transient connections as the probe, followed by long-term communications. Proto can filter out a large amount of irrelevant traffic.

Packet features (IOPR) are less important, because bots can avoid detection by filling empty or garbage payload in packets.

5   Conclusion

In this paper, we propose a botnet detection method ME-LGCN based on fMAG and Latent-GCN, to address limitations of traditional detection models. We realize a fMAG of network that contains multilateral structure, edges and nodes features. And Latent-GCN is adopted to the fMAG for botnet detection where the communication information is learned by multi-edge embedding and enrich the representation of nodes in graph.

References

1. Freebuf Homepage. https://www.freebuf.com/company-information/225232.html. Accessed 13 May 2021
2. Alieyan, K., ALmomani, A., Manasrah, A., Kadhum, M.M.: A survey of botnet detection based on DNS. Neural Comput. Appl. **28**(7), 1541–1558 (2015). https://doi.org/10.1007/s00521-015-2128-0
3. Khanchi, S., Vahdat, A., Heywood, M.I., Nur Zincir-Heywood, A.: On botnet detection with genetic programming under streaming data label budgets and class imbalance. Swarm Evol. Comput. **39**, 120–140 (2018)
4. Chowdhury, S., et al.: Botnet detection using graph-based feature clustering. J. Big Data, **4**, 14 (2017)
5. Venkatesh, B., Choudhury, S.H., Nagaraja, S., Balakrishnan, N.: BotSpot: fast graph based identification of structured P2P bots. J. Comput. Virol. Hacking Tech. **11**(4), 247–261 (2015)
6. Daya, A. A., Salahuddin, M. A., Limam, N., etc.: A graph-based machine learning approach for bot detection. In: Dong, Y., et al. Symposium on Integrated Network and Service Management (IM) 2019, IFIP/IEEE, pp. 144–152. Arlington, VA, USA (2019)
7. Jaikumar, P., Kak, A.C.: A graph-theoretic framework for isolating botnets in a network. Secur. Commun. Netw. **8**, 2605–2623 (2015)

8. Zhou, J., Xu, Z., Rush, A.M., Yu, M.: Automating botnet detection with graph neural networks, arXiv preprint arXiv:2003.06344, https://arxiv.org/abs/2003.06344 (2020)

9. Xiaoli, L., Tang, G.: Covert P2P botnet detection based on traffic characteristics. Comput. Appl. Res. **30**(06), 1867–1870 (2013)

10. Beigi, E.B., Jazi, H.H., et al.: Towards effective feature selection in machine learning-based botnet detection approaches. In: Wang, C. et al. Conference on Communications and Network Security (CNS), IEEE, pp. 247–255. San Francisco, CA, USA (2014)

11. Protogerou, A., Papadopoulos, S., Drosou, A., Tzovaras, D., Refanidis, I.: A graph neural network method for distributed anomaly detection in IoT. Evol. Syst. (pre-publish) (2020)

12. Hermsen, F., Bloem, P., Jansen, F.: End-to-end learning from complex multigraphs with latent graph convolutional networks. arXiv preprint arXiv:1908.05365, https://arxiv.org/abs/1908.05365 (2019)

13. Vos, W.B.W.: End-to-end learning of latent edge weights for graph convolutional networks. University of Amsterdam, Amsterdam. https://esc.fnwi.uva.nl/thesis/centraal/files/f696360596.pdf. Accessed 23 Apr 2021

14. Argus Homepage, https://qosient.com/argus/gettingstarted.shtml. Accessed 11 May 2021

15. Bingbing, X., Keting, C., Junjie, H., et al.: Review of graph volume neural networks. Acta Computa Sinica **043**(005), 755–780 (2020)

16. Kipf, T.N., Welling, M.: Semi-supervised classification with graph convolutional networks, arXiv preprint arXiv:1609.0290, https://arxiv.org/abs/1609.02907 (2016)

17. Garcia, S., Grill, M., Stiborek, J., et al.: An empirical comparison of botnet detection methods. Comput. Secur. **45**, 100–123 (2014)

18. David, Z., Issa, T. et al.: Botnet detection based on traffic behavior analysis and flow intervals - sciencedirect. Comput. Secur. **39**(4), 2–16 (2013)

19. Babak, R., Roberto, P. et al.: PeerRush: mining for unwanted P2P traffic. J. Inf. Secur. Appl. **19**(3), 194–208 (2014)

20. Zhuang, D., Chang, J.M.: Enhanced PeerHunter: detecting peer-to-peer Botnets through network-flow level community behavior analysis. IEEE Trans. Inf. Forensics Secur. **14**(6), 1485–1500 (2018)

21. Pektas, A., Acarman, T.: Botnet detection based on network flow summary and deep learning. Int. J. Netw. Manage. **28**(6), e2039.1-e2039.15 (2018)

A New Method for Inferring Ground-Truth Labels and Malware Detector Effectiveness Metrics

John Charlton[1], Pang Du[2], and Shouhuai Xu[3(✉)]

[1] Department of Computer Science, University of Texas at San Antonio, San Antonio, USA
John.E.Charlton@gmail.com
[2] Department of Statistics, Virginia Tech, Blacksburg, USA
[3] Department of Computer Science, University of Colorado Colorado Springs, Colorado Springs, USA
sxu@uccs.edu

Abstract. In the context of malware detection, ground-truth labels of files are often difficult or costly to obtain; as a consequence, malware detector effectiveness metrics (e.g., false-positive and false-negative rates) are hard to measure. The unavailability of ground-truth labels also hinder the training of machine learning based malware detectors. These issues are often encountered by researchers and practitioners and force them to use various heuristics without justification. Therefore, seeking principled methods has become an important open problem. In this paper, we present a principled method for tackling the problem.

Keywords: Malware detection · Security metrics · Security measurement · Inference.

1 Introduction

Cybersecurity metrics is one of the most notoriously difficult open problems, despite the numerous efforts that have been made by the research community (see, e.g., [2–6,8,14,17,18,21–23,27]). At a high level, security metrics research can be divided into two categories: (i) *defining metrics* to measure what needs to be measured, which is still largely open [6,18]; (ii) *designing procedures* to measure what needs to be measured, namely the measurement of well-defined security metrics. This paper falls into the latter category (ii), by considering malware detection and the measurement of *ground-truth* labels for files and malware detector effectiveness metrics, such as false-positive and false-negative rates. This is an important problem because ground-truth labels of files (e.g., malicious or benign) are often assumed to be given and then leveraged for measuring malware detector effectiveness or training malware detectors.

Unfortunately, ground-truth labels are often difficult or costly to obtain. For a small set of files, we may use human experts to provide labels. However, perfect labels cannot be guaranteed because humans are error-prone and can make mistakes. For a large set of files, it is unrealistic for human experts to label them. Given this, one may resort to some third-party services. However, third-party service providers often leave the problem to

ⓒ Springer Nature Switzerland AG 2021
W. Lu et al. (Eds.): SciSec 2021, LNCS 13005, pp. 77–92, 2021.
https://doi.org/10.1007/978-3-030-89137-4_6

the end users. A typical scenario that is often encountered in the real world is the following: Third-party service providers, such as VirusTotal, provide labels of files given by a number of malware detectors, but these labels are in conflict with each other (i.e., a file is labeled by some detectors as malicious, but benign by others) [1,7,12,15,16,19,28]. This phenomenon is widely exhibited in the cybersecurity domain, including blacklists of malicious websites [10,13,20,24–26].

Without support of principled solutions, the challenge has forced researchers and practitioners to use various heuristics. Two popular heuristics are: Given a set of malware detectors, a file is treated as malicious as long as a certain threshold *number* vs. *fraction* (e.g., majority) of them label it as malicious [15,16,19]. These heuristics are troublesome because each malware detector has different capabilities in detecting malware. This calls for principled solutions and has motivated a few efforts.

Kantchelian et al. [12] use a *Bayesian* method to infer the ground-truth labels of files and malware detector effectiveness metrics, by making four *assumptions*: (i) a detector has an equal chance in mislabeling any benign file as malicious and an equal chance in mislabeling any malicious file as benign, which may not hold because a detector can be ·better at recognizing one kind of malware than another; (ii) detectors label files in an independent fashion, which may not hold when they use some common techniques; (iii) the percentage of malicious files is about 50%; (iv) detectors incur low false-positives and high false-negatives. The preceding (iii) and (iv) are associated with the prior distributions that are inherent to the Bayesian approach. Du et al. [7] use a *frequentist* approach to design statistical estimators to measure malware detectors' effectiveness metrics and the fraction of malicious files in a given set of files (but *not* the ground-truth labels), while only making the preceding assumptions (i) and (ii).

Charlton et al. [1] propose a new approach to measuring detectors' *relative accuracy* in the absence of ground-truth labels. The relative accuracy is measured with an *ordinal scale* [18], meaning that it only tells which detector is more accurate than which other detector, but not how much more accurate (i.e., detectors' absolute accuracy or effectiveness metrics remains unaddressed, so do the ground-truth labels). While heuristic in nature, this approach is attractive because it does *not* need any of the preceding assumptions (i)–(iv). This motivates us to explore how to turn the heuristic into a principled method for inferring ground-truth labels and detector effectiveness metrics.

Our Contributions. Our core contribution is to show that the *relative accuracy* approach [1] can be turned into a principled *weighted* majority voting method for inferring ground-truth labels and detector effectiveness metrics. The key idea is to treat an *enhanced* version of relative accuracy as a detector's voting weight, where the enhancement comes from the introduction of a *bellwether* detector whose effectiveness is known because it labels any file uniformly at random and independent of anything else. In the case of binary classification, it labels each file as malicious (benign) with a 0.5 probability, independent of anything else; this means that the bellwether detector has an *expected* true-positive rate, true-negative rate, and accuracy of 0.5 when the number of files is large enough. Intuitively, the bellwether detector serves as a *reference point* in the ordinal scale of relative accuracy because we know both its relative accuracy and absolute accuracy (i.e., 0.5 for the latter). This reference point offers a better scaling of relative accuracy than the counterpart in its absence. This improved scaling brings detectors' relative accuracy closer to their absolute accuracy, respectively. The weighted majority voting method, which is actually an iterative process, leads to the *inferred* ground-truth labels, which allows us to infer malware detector effectiveness metrics.

In order to understand *why* the proposed method works, we give an *algebraic* interpretation of relative accuracy (with or without employing the bellwether detector), by making connections to the well-known Principal Component Analysis (PCA). We show that the *similarity matrix* for describing the similarity between the labels given by malware detectors plays a role similar to that of the *correlation matrix* in PCA. A similarity matrix can be decomposed to a set of eigenvectors and eigenvalues; the eigenvectors represent the unit vectors describing an n-dimensional space with n being the number of detectors, and the eigenvalues provide a measurement of magnitude, or importance, associated with these vectors respectively. The larger the eigenvalue, the higher the importance of the detectors corresponding to it; the detectors corresponding to the higher ordered eigenvectors have higher relative accuracy and can be deemed as more trusted and given larger weights. In other words, detectors corresponding to the higher ordered eigenvectors and eigenvalues provide a more pivotal decision mathematically than the lower ordered ones. Because of this algebraic interpretation, we deem the relative accuracy approach an *algebraic* one, which is in contrast to *statistical* approaches [7, 12].

We validate the principled method (Algorithm 4) via synthetic data with known ground-truth labels and detector effectiveness metrics. Experimental results show it can accurately infer ground-truth labels and detector effectiveness metrics, especially so when eliminating the "poor" detectors with bellwether relative accuracy smaller than that of the bellwether detector. Then, we apply the method to analyze a real-world dataset, for which neither ground-truth labels nor detector effectiveness is known. We find that among other things, both the strategy of trading low false-positive for low false-negative and its opposite are widely employed by real-world malware detectors.

Related Work. This paper falls into the field of security metrics research. For the state-of-the-art security metrics research in a broader context, we refer to [2–6, 8, 14, 17, 18, 21–23, 27]. This paper deals with the measurement of well-defined metrics in the particular context of malware detection, namely: Given a number of malware detectors that have labeled a number of files, how can we infer the ground-truth labels of the files (i.e., malicious vs. benign) and malware detector effectiveness metrics? To tackle the problem, there are a number of heuristics [15, 16, 19, 28], but few principled solutions [7, 12] which make a number of assumptions as mentioned above. This study is inspired by the heuristic relative accuracy approach by [1], by making a solid step in turning the heuristic into a principled weighted majority voting method.

Paper Outline. Section 2 presents the problem. Section 3 revisits the notion of relative accuracy. Section 4 describes the methods used to tackle the problem. Section 5 applies the method to a real-world dataset. Section 6 concludes the paper with future directions.

2   Problem Statement

Suppose we are given a matrix $\mathbf{V} = (V_{ij})_{1 \leq i \leq n, 1 \leq j \leq m}$, where m is the number of files, n is the number of malware detectors denoted by $D_1, \ldots, D_n$, and

$$
V_{ij} = \begin{cases} 1 & \text{if detector } D_i \text{ labels file } j \text{ as malicious} \\ 0 & \text{if detector } D_i \text{ labels file } j \text{ as benign} \\ -1 & \text{if detector } D_i \text{ does not label file } j \text{ at all (which can happen in practice).} \end{cases}
$$

The problem is to infer (i) the ground-truth labels of the files (i.e., malicious vs. benign) and (ii) the detectors' effectiveness metrics in terms of the widely-used true-positive rate (TPR), true-negative rate (TNR) and accuracy (ACC) [18]. Let TP_i, TN_i, FP_i and FN_i respectively denote the number of true-positives, true-negatives, false-positives, and false-negatives associated with detector D_i. Recall that $\mathsf{TPR}_i = \mathsf{TP}_i/(\mathsf{TP}_i + \mathsf{FN}_i)$, $\mathsf{TNR}_i = \mathsf{TN}_i/(\mathsf{TN}_i + \mathsf{FP}_i)$ and $\mathsf{ACC}_i = (\mathsf{TP}_i + \mathsf{TN}_i)/(\mathsf{TP}_i + \mathsf{TN}_i + \mathsf{FP}_i + \mathsf{FN}_i)$ [18].

3   Relative Accuracy Revisited

A *weaker* variant of the preceding problem is to infer if D_i is *more accurate* than D_j. This variant is weaker because a solution to this problem is not guaranteed to solve the preceding problem. Nevertheless, this weaker problem leads to the notion of *relative accuracy*, or RA, on an *ordinal* scale, which is a discrete ordered set that permits comparisons between two measurements [18]. Let RA_i denote inferred relative accuracy of D_i. It is empirically shown $RA_i > RA_k$ means D_i is *more accurate* than D_k and $RA_i \neq \mathsf{ACC}_i$ [1].

3.1   Review of Previous Approach [1] to Computing Relative Accuracy

The known approach to computing relative accuracy is based on the following concepts with respect to matrix $\mathbf{V}$ [1]. In order to deal with the fact that some files may not be labelled by every detector, a *count matrix*, denoted by $\mathbf{C} = (C_{ik})_{1 \leq i, k \leq n}$, is defined to describe the number of files that are labelled by a pair of detectors D_i and D_k as follows:

$$
C_{ik} = C_{ki} = \sum_{\ell=1}^{m} \begin{cases} 1 & \text{if } V_{i\ell} \neq -1 \wedge V_{k\ell} \neq -1, \\ 0 & \text{if } V_{i\ell} = -1 \vee V_{k\ell} = -1. \end{cases}
$$

In order to measure the agreement between the labels given by a pair of detector, an *agreement matrix*, denoted by $\mathbf{A} = (A_{ik})_{1 \leq i, k \leq n}$, is defined to describe the number of files that are given the same label by detectors D_i and D_k as follows:

$$
A_{ik} = A_{ki} = \sum_{\ell=1}^{m} \begin{cases} 1 & \text{if } V_{i\ell} = V_{k\ell} \wedge V_{i\ell} \neq -1 \wedge V_{k\ell} \neq -1 \\ 0 & \text{if } V_{i\ell} \neq V_{k\ell} \vee V_{i\ell} = -1 \vee V_{k\ell} = -1. \end{cases}
$$

In order to measure the similarity between two detectors, a *similarity matrix*, denoted by $\mathbf{S} = (S_{ik})_{1 \leq i, k \leq n}$ where $S_{ik} = A_{ik}/C_{ik}$, is defined to describe the degree of agreement between detectors D_i and D_k. Note that $\mathbf{S}$ is a real, symmetric matrix. These lead to:

Algorithm 1. Known approach to computing relative accuracy [1]

Input: similarity matrix $\mathbf{S} = (S_{ik})_{1 \leq i, k \leq n}$; tolerable error threshold ϵ

Output: relative accuracy vector $\mathbf{RA} = (RA_1, \ldots, RA_n)^\mathsf{T}$

1: $\delta \leftarrow 2\epsilon$ {It suffice to initialize δ as any value that is greater than ϵ}
2: $\mathbf{RA} \leftarrow [1, \ldots, 1]_{1 \times n}^\mathsf{T}$ {Initiate relative accuracy vector $\mathbf{RA}$}
3: **while** $\delta > \epsilon$ **do**
4:    $\mathbf{NextRA} \leftarrow \mathbf{S} \times \mathbf{RA}$ {Multiply similarity matrix by current relative accuracy}
5:    $\mathbf{NextRA} \leftarrow \mathbf{NextRA} / \max(\mathbf{NextRA})$ {Normalize calculated relative accuracy with respect to the largest element in matrix $\mathbf{NextRA}$}
6:    $\delta \leftarrow \sum_{1 \leq i \leq n} |RA_i - \mathrm{NextRA}_i|$ {Calculate δ between the current and next $\mathbf{RA}$}
7:    $\mathbf{RA} \leftarrow \mathbf{NextRA}$
8: **end while**
9: Return $\mathbf{RA}$

Definition 1. (relative accuracy [1]**).** *The relative accuracy of detector D_i, denoted by RA_i where $1 \leq i \leq n$, is defined by a number in interval $[0, 1]$ such that $RA_i > RA_k$ means detector D_i is more accurate than detector D_k.*

Algorithm 1 [1] computes detectors' relative accuracy vector $\mathbf{RA} = (RA_1, \ldots, RA_n)$, by taking similarity matrix $\mathbf{S} = (S_{ik})_{1 \leq i, k \leq n}$ as input. The algorithm halts when $\delta < \epsilon$, where δ is the sum of the difference for all of the RA_i's between two consecutive iterations and ϵ is a given threshold. In each iteration of the algorithm, the following is conducted: multiply the current relative accuracy vector $\mathbf{RA}$ by $\mathbf{S}$ from the left-hand side (Step 4); scale the result by the largest value in the resulting matrix (Step 5); update $\mathbf{RA}$ for the next iteration (Steps 6–7).

3.2 New Approach to Computing Relative Accuracy and Deeper Analysis

Using synthetic data with known ground-truth information, Algorithm 1 is shown to assure $RA_i > RA_k$ when $\mathsf{ACC}_i > \mathsf{ACC}_k$ [1]. However, it is a heuristic because no explanation on *why it works* is given [1]. Our new approach starts with an observation. Let N_z be the normalization scalar at the z-th iteration in Algorithm 1 and $N_* = N_1 \times \ldots \times N_z$. By leveraging the associative property of scalar multiplication, we observe

$$\mathbf{RA} = \underbrace{\mathbf{S} \ldots (\mathbf{S}(\mathbf{S}(\mathbf{1})/N_1)/N_2) \ldots /N_z}_{z \text{ times}} = \underbrace{\mathbf{S} \ldots (\mathbf{S}(\mathbf{S}(\mathbf{1})))}_{z \text{ times}}/N_* = \mathbf{S}^z \mathbf{1}/N_*. \quad (1)$$

Since $\mathbf{S}$ is a real-valued symmetric matrix, it can undergo eigendecomposition, the eigenvalues are real, and the eigenvectors can be selected real and orthonormal [11]. Let $\lambda_1 \geq \lambda_2 \geq \ldots \geq \lambda_n \geq 0$ and $\mathbf{e}_1, \mathbf{e}_2, \ldots, \mathbf{e}_n$ be respectively the eigenvalues and eigenvectors of $\mathbf{S}$ [11]. The spectral decomposition of $\mathbf{S}$ is:

$$\mathbf{S} = \mathbf{U}\mathbf{D}\mathbf{U}^\mathsf{T} = \sum_{i=1}^{n} \lambda_i \mathbf{e}_i \mathbf{e}_i^\mathsf{T}, \quad (2)$$

where $\mathbf{U} = (\mathbf{e}_1, \ldots, \mathbf{e}_n)$ is an orthonormal matrix such that $\mathbf{U}^\mathsf{T}\mathbf{U} = \mathbf{U}\mathbf{U}^\mathsf{T} = \mathbf{I}$, $\mathbf{I}$ being the identity matrix, and $\mathbf{D} = \mathrm{diag}(\lambda_1, \ldots, \lambda_n)$[11]. Denote by $\mathbf{D}^z =$

diag$(\lambda_1^z, \ldots, \lambda_n^z)$. By combining (1) and (2), we have

$$N_* \mathbf{RA} = \mathbf{S}^z \mathbf{1} = (\mathbf{UDU}^\mathsf{T})^z \mathbf{1} = \mathbf{UD}^z \mathbf{U}^\mathsf{T} \mathbf{1} = \left(\sum_{i=1}^n \lambda_i^z \mathbf{e}_i \mathbf{e}_i^\mathsf{T} \right) \mathbf{1} = \sum_{i=1}^n \lambda_i^z \mathbf{e}_i (\mathbf{e}_i^\mathsf{T} \mathbf{1}).$$

$$(3)$$

By replacing $\mathbf{U} \times \mathbf{D}^z \times \mathbf{U}^T$ for $\mathbf{S}^z$ in Eq. (1), we rewrite Algorithm 1 as Algorithm 2.

Algorithm 2. New approach to computing relative accuracy using eigenvalues

---

Input: similarity matrix $\mathbf{S} = (S_{ik})_{1 \leq i,k \leq n}$; tolerable error threshold ϵ
Output: relative accuracy vector $\mathbf{RA} = (RA_1, \ldots, RA_n)^\mathsf{T}$

1: $\delta \leftarrow 2\epsilon$ {It suffices to initialize δ as any value that is greater than ϵ}
2: $c \leftarrow 1$ {Set initial step}
3: $(\mathbf{U}, \mathbf{D}) \leftarrow (eigenvector(\mathbf{S}), eigenvalue(\mathbf{S}))$ {Eigendecomposition}
4: $\mathbf{CurrentRA} \leftarrow \mathbf{U} \times \mathbf{D}^c \times \mathbf{U}^\mathsf{T} / \max(\mathbf{U} \times \mathbf{D}^c \times \mathbf{U}^\mathsf{T})$ {Calculate initial $\mathbf{RA}$ and normalize}
5: **while** $\delta > \epsilon$ **do**
6:     $\mathbf{NextRA} \leftarrow (\mathbf{U} \times \mathbf{D}^c \times \mathbf{U}^\mathsf{T}) / \max(\mathbf{U} \times \mathbf{D}^c \times \mathbf{U}^\mathsf{T})$ {Update $\mathbf{RA}$ and normalize}
7:     $\delta \leftarrow \sum_{1 \leq i \leq n} |\mathbf{NextRA}_i - \mathbf{CurrentRA}_i|$ {Calculate δ between two consecutive $\mathbf{RA}$'s.}
8:     $c \leftarrow c + 1$ {Iterate step}
9:     $\mathbf{CurrentRA} \leftarrow \mathbf{NextRA}$ {Assign new value}
10: **end while**
11: Return $\mathbf{CurrentRA}$ {$\mathbf{RA} \leftarrow \mathbf{CurrentRA}$}

Algorithm 2 has two advantages: (i) We can rigorously prove Algorithm 2, and therefore Algorithm 1, converges; this is assured by Theorem 1. (ii) Algorithm 2 permits an *algebraic* interpretation of relative accuracy. Details follow.

Theorem 1. *Algorithm 2 always converges, meaning error $\delta \leq \epsilon$ eventually.*

Proof. The z-th iteration of the loop leads to vector $\mathbf{RA}_z \leftarrow \mathbf{U} \times \mathbf{D}^z \times \mathbf{U}^\mathsf{T} / \max(\mathbf{U} \times \mathbf{D}^z \times \mathbf{U}^\mathsf{T})$. By leveraging the aforementioned $\mathbf{U} \times \mathbf{U}^T = \mathbf{U} \times \mathbf{U}^{-1} = \mathbf{I}$, we obtain

$$
\begin{aligned}
\mathbf{RA}_z &= \frac{\mathbf{U} \times \mathbf{D}^z \times \mathbf{U}^\mathsf{T}}{\max(\mathbf{U} \times \mathbf{D}^z \times \mathbf{U}^\mathsf{T})} = \frac{\mathbf{U} \times \mathbf{D}_1 \times \mathbf{D}_2 \times \cdots \times \mathbf{D}_z \times \mathbf{U}^\mathsf{T}}{\max(\mathbf{U} \times \mathbf{D}_1 \times \mathbf{D}_2 \times \cdots \times \mathbf{D}_z \times \mathbf{U}^\mathsf{T})} \\
&= \frac{\mathbf{U} \times \mathbf{D}_1 \times (\mathbf{U}^\mathsf{T} \times \mathbf{U}) \times \mathbf{D}_2 \times (\mathbf{U}^\mathsf{T} \times \mathbf{U}) \ldots \mathbf{D}_z \times \mathbf{U}^\mathsf{T}}{\max(\mathbf{U} \times \mathbf{D}_1 \times (\mathbf{U}^\mathsf{T} \times \mathbf{U}) \times \mathbf{D}_2 \times (\mathbf{U}^\mathsf{T} \times \mathbf{U}) \ldots \mathbf{D}_z \times \mathbf{U}^\mathsf{T}}) \\
&= \frac{(\mathbf{U} \times \mathbf{D}_1 \times \mathbf{U}^\mathsf{T}) \times (\mathbf{U} \times \mathbf{D}_2 \times \mathbf{U}^\mathsf{T}) \ldots (\mathbf{U} \times \mathbf{D}_z \times \mathbf{U}^\mathsf{T})}{\max((\mathbf{U} \times \mathbf{D}_1 \times \mathbf{U}^\mathsf{T}) \times (\mathbf{U} \times \mathbf{D}_2 \times \mathbf{U}^\mathsf{T}) \ldots (\mathbf{U} \times \mathbf{D}_z \times \mathbf{U}^\mathsf{T}}) \\
&= \frac{(\mathbf{U} \times \mathbf{D} \times \mathbf{U}^\mathsf{T})_1 \times (\mathbf{U} \times \mathbf{D} \times \mathbf{U}^\mathsf{T})_2 \ldots (\mathbf{U} \times \mathbf{D} \times \mathbf{U}^\mathsf{T})_z}{\max((\mathbf{U} \times \mathbf{D} \times \mathbf{U}^\mathsf{T})_1 \times (\mathbf{U} \times \mathbf{D} \times \mathbf{U}^\mathsf{T})_2 \ldots (\mathbf{U} \times \mathbf{D} \times \mathbf{U}^\mathsf{T})_z)} \\
&= \frac{(\mathbf{U} \times \mathbf{D} \times \mathbf{U}^\mathsf{T})^z}{\max((\mathbf{U} \times \mathbf{D} \times \mathbf{U}^\mathsf{T})^z)} = \frac{(\mathbf{U} \times \mathbf{D} \times \mathbf{U}^\mathsf{T})^z}{(\max(\mathbf{U} \times \mathbf{D} \times \mathbf{U}^\mathsf{T}))^z}.
\end{aligned}
$$

Let $\mathbf{Y} = \mathbf{U} \times \mathbf{D} \times \mathbf{U}^\mathsf{T}$, y be an arbitrary element of $\mathbf{Y}$, and $y^* = \max(\mathbf{Y})$ being the maximum element. Then, $\forall y \in \mathbf{Y}$, $y \in (0, 1)$, $\max(\mathbf{Y}^x) = (\max(\mathbf{Y}))^x$, and $y \leq y^*$. Thus,

$$\lim_{z \to +\infty} \frac{y^z}{(y^*)^z} = \begin{cases} 1 & \text{if } y = \max(\mathbf{Y}) \\ 0 & \text{if } y < \max(\mathbf{Y}) \end{cases}$$

assures that the difference δ between two consecutive iterations monotonically decreases, namely $\delta \leq \epsilon$ eventually and the algorithm halts. $\qquad\square$

An Algebraic Interpretations of Relative Accuracy. Algorithm 2 permits an algebraic interpretation of relative accuracy. Consider a data matrix $\mathbf{V} = (V_{ij})_{1 \leq i \leq n, 1 \leq j \leq m}$, where the i-th row represents the i-th variable and each column is a vector of observed values for the n variables. Let $\bar{V}_i = \sum_{j=1}^m V_{ij}/m$ and $\sigma_i^2 = \sum_{j=1}^m (V_{ij} - \bar{V}_i)^2/(m-1)$ be respectively the sample mean and sample variance of the i-th row, or variable V_i. The sample correlation between variables V_i and V_k is $R_{ik} = \{(n-1)\sigma_i\sigma_k\}^{-1} \sum_{j=1}^m (V_{ij} - \bar{V}_j)(V_{kj} - \bar{V}_j)$. In PCA [9], the sample correlation matrix is $\mathbf{R} = (R_{ik})_{1 \leq i,k \leq n}$. Let $\gamma_1 \geq \gamma_2 \geq \ldots, \geq \gamma_n \geq 0$ and $\mathbf{f}_1, \mathbf{f}_2, \ldots, \mathbf{f}_n$ with $\mathbf{f}_i = (f_{i1}, \ldots, f_{im})^\mathsf{T}$ be respectively the eigenvalues and eigenvectors of the correlation matrix $\mathbf{R}$. The spectral decomposition of $\mathbf{R}$ is $\mathbf{R} = \sum_{i=1}^n \gamma_i \mathbf{f}_i \mathbf{f}_i^\mathsf{T}$, where $\mathbf{f}_i$ is the weight vector for the i-th *principal component* defined as $Z_i = \sum_{j=1}^m f_{ij} V_j$, which is a linear combination of the original (column) variables $V_1, \ldots, V_n$. Due to the orthogonality between the $\mathbf{f}_i$'s, the principal components, namely the Z_i's are uncorrelated with each other, meaning that their pairwise correlations are all zeros. Recall that $V_i = (V_{i1}, \ldots, V_{im})$ represents an observation. Imagine that we plot the n observations (i.e., $V_1, \ldots, V_n$) in the n-dimensional space such that each dimension representing one V_i for $1 \leq i \leq n$. Then, the first principal component weight vector $\mathbf{f}_1$ represents the direction where these n observations exhibit the most variation (i.e., having the widest spread); the second principal component weight vector $\mathbf{f}_2$ is orthogonal to $\mathbf{f}_1$ and represents the direction of the most variation among all the directions that are perpendicular to $\mathbf{f}_1$; the third principal component weight vector $\mathbf{f}_3$ is orthogonal to both $\mathbf{f}_1$ and $\mathbf{f}_2$ and represents the direction of the most variation among all the directions that are perpendicular to both $\mathbf{f}_1$ and $\mathbf{f}_2$.

The relative accuracy measure groups detectors according to the magnitudes of the corresponding entries in the vector $\mathbf{RA}$. Note that if $\lambda_i > \lambda_j$, then as z increases the gap between λ_i^z and λ_j^z will become increasingly larger. At some point, we will have $\lambda_i^z \gg \lambda_j^z$. These λ values are the elements of the diagonal matrix $\mathbf{D}$ from Equation (3). Due to the uniqueness of eigenvalues, we observe strict ordering $\lambda_1 > \lambda_2 > \lambda_3 > \ldots \geq 0$. The iterations in Algorithm 2 increase z, meaning that at some point we would observe $\lambda_1^z \gg \lambda_2^z \gg \lambda_2^z \gg \ldots \geq 0$. When Algorithm 2 converges, the highest value entries in relative accuracy vector $\mathbf{RA}$, according to Eq. (3), correspond to $\lambda_1^z \mathbf{e}_1 (\mathbf{e}_1^\mathsf{T} \mathbf{1})$; that is, the highest value entries in the eigenvector $\mathbf{e}_1$ determine the directions of $\mathbf{e}_1$ in the n-dimensional space, with each dimension representing a detector. Similarly, the second group of detectors identified by the relative accuracy would match up with the highest entries in the second eigenvector $\mathbf{e}_2$ of the similarity matrix $\mathbf{S}$. Just like that an entry R_{jl} of the correlation matrix $\mathbf{R}$ in PCA represents how similar two variables V_j and V_l co-vary with each other, an entry S_{ik} of similarity matrix $\mathbf{S}$ represents how similar two detectors D_i and D_k label files. Therefore, while the ordered eigenvectors of $\mathbf{R}$ in PCA represent the ordered directions where the variables $\{V_1, \ldots, V_n\}$ have the most covariance, the ordered eigenvectors of $\mathbf{S}$ represent the ordered directions where detectors $\{D_1, \ldots, D_n\}$ make the most similar decisions. This means that the clustering yielded by the relative magnitudes of entries in vector $\mathbf{RA}$ is indeed meaningful.

Remark. The preceding algebraic interpretation is sound when "good" detectors are not overwhelmed by "poor" detectors, namely when the average ground-truth accuracy (ACC) of each detector involved is greater than 50%. Otherwise, the algebraic meaning behind the algorithm would be inverted, and we'd be calculating which detectors that make the most similar, but incorrect, decisions. This inspires us to propose the idea of leveraging a bellwether detector to recognize/filter the "poor" detectors. Details follow.

3.3   Enhancing Algorithm 2 with a Bellwether Reference Detector

Intuitively, the normalization in Algorithm 2 (Step 6) assures that the most accurate detector would have the highest relative accuracy 1, meaning that each detector has a relative accuracy falling into $[0, 1]$. We observe that if we know the absolute effectiveness of a reference detector, we can make a better use of the relative accuracy because we can see the distance between the reference detector's relative accuracy to its absolute accuracy. This motivates us to introduce a *bellwether* detector, so called in reference to herd animals, where the bellwether member of the flock acts as an indicator and predictor into the behavior of the other members. For our purposes, the bellwether detector is a new artificial detector with known absolute effectiveness which can be derived from the fact that it uniformly labels files at random, independent of anything else. In the case of binary classification, the bellwether detector labels each file as malicious (benign) with a 0.5 probability, independent of anything else. This means that the bellwether detector has an *expected* TPR = TNR = ACC = 0.5 when the number of files is large enough.

Recall that $\mathbf{Y} = \mathbf{U} \times \mathbf{D} \times \mathbf{U}^\mathsf{T}$ and the relative accuracy in the z-th iteration is $\mathbf{Y}^z/(y^*)^z$ where $y^* = \max(\mathbf{Y})$ is the maximum element in $\mathbf{Y}$ (Theorem 1). It is evident that RA_i is proportional to both its initial value and y^*, making it a geometric series if the iterations were infinite. This means that it's possible to scale $\mathbf{RA}$ *without* iterations while maintaining the geometric relationship between the entries, by leveraging a single entry of known value (i.e., $\text{ACC}_{bellwether} = 0.5$), which is the role of the bellwether detector. The preceding discussion leads to Algorithm 3, which produces an improved relative accuracy, denoted by *bellwether accuracy* or $\mathbf{BA_i}$, for detector i.

In Algorithm 3, we use the eigenvectors and eigenvalues to calculate an initial relative accuracy vector with the bellwether detector (Step 2). The relative accuracy of the bellwether detector, where $BA_{bellwether} = BA_{n+1}$, is subtracted from each entry of $\mathbf{BA}$ (Step 3). This has the effect of transforming the values of $\mathbf{BA}$ so that $BA_{bellwether}$ lies on point 0. The entries of $\mathbf{BA}$ are normalized to the range $(-0.5, 0.5)$ and then transformed to $(0, 1)$, which sets $BA_{bellwether} = 0.5$ and distributes the rest of the values according to their geometric relationship. Due to the distribution of this geometric series and the fixed location of the bellwether detector in the array, the results are the same for the first, second, or z-th iteration. This eliminates the need for iterations.

Another potential property of Algorithm 3 is: It may be universally true that $|BA_i - \text{ACC}_i| \leq |RA_i - \text{ACC}_i|$, meaning that BA_i is a better approximation of ACC_i than

---

Algorithm 3. Computing relative accuracy using eigenvalues and a bellwether detector

Input: similarity matrix $\mathbf{S} = (S_{ik})_{1 \leq i,k \leq n+1}$ with D_{n+1} being the bellwether detector;
Output: bellwether accuracy vector $\mathbf{BA_{n+1}} = (BA_1, \ldots, BA_n, 0.5)^{\mathsf{T}}$

1: $(\mathbf{U}, \mathbf{D}) \leftarrow (eigenvector(\mathbf{S}), eigenvalue(\mathbf{S}))$ {Eigendecomposition}
2: $\mathbf{BA} \leftarrow \mathbf{U} \times \mathbf{D} \times \mathbf{U}^{\mathsf{T}} / \max(\mathbf{U} \times \mathbf{D} \times \mathbf{U}^{\mathsf{T}})$ {Calculate $\mathbf{BA}$}
3: $\mathbf{BA} \leftarrow \mathbf{BA} - \mathbf{BA_{n+1}}$ {Making bellwether-based adjustment}
4: $\mathbf{BA} \leftarrow \mathbf{BA}/(2 \times |\max(\mathbf{BA})|) + 0.5$ {Normalizing $(-0.5, 0.5)$ and transforming to $(0, 1)$}

5: Return $\mathbf{BA}$

RA_i does. Although we cannot prove this rigorously at the time of writing, we do find empirical evidence using synthetic data with known ground-truth information in **Experiments 1–10**, as shown in Fig. 1.

4   Inferring Ground-Truth Labels and Effectiveness Metrics

Method. Consider $\mathbf{V} = (V_{ij})_{1 \leq i \leq \eta, 1 \leq j \leq m}$ and $\mathbf{BA} = (BA_1, \ldots, BA_\eta)$ as input, where η is the number of detectors that will participate in the process of inferring ground-truth labels and detector effectiveness metrics. In the recommended use case, we only use detectors with a bellwether relative accuracy higher than that of the bellwether detector's, namely $BA_i > BA_{bellwether} = 0.5$ for any $1 \leq i \leq \eta$; in this case we have $1 \leq \eta \leq n$. It is possible for $\eta = n+1$, with D_{n+1} being the bellwether detector; that is, all of the detectors (including the bellwether detector) participate in the process of inference. In practice it would not be a good idea to include $BA_{bellwether}$ as part of the input because of its random nature (i.e., it is a known source of noise and adds no useful information). Even if included, it should not be involved in any useful computation (e.g., voting, if applicable). Other variants are possible, for example using detectors with bellwether relative accuracy *significantly* higher than $BA_{bellwether} = 0.5$.

Given the input mentioned above, now we design a novel method, Algorithm 4, to infer the ground-truth labels, denoted by $(\text{malign}_1, \ldots, \text{malign}_m)$, and detector effectiveness metrics TPR_i', TNR_i' and ACC_i' for $1 \leq i \leq \eta$. At the core of the algorithm is *weighted majority voting*, where weights are iteratively derived from $\mathbf{BA}$. Specifically, the initial $\mathbf{BA}$ is used to weigh individual detector's votes, providing a detector of a higher BA_i with a larger vote weight. The weighted voting leads to malicious or benign labels of files. The updated labels are used to update effectiveness metrics $\mathbf{TPR'}$, $\mathbf{TNR'}$ and $\mathbf{ACC'}$, which in turn are used to update the detectors' weights. The algorithm halts when the inferred $\mathbf{ACC}$ between two consecutive iterations is below a threshold ϵ. Its computational complexity depends on the number of iterations, for which are are unable to give an explicit estimation at this point; in each iteration, the computational complexity is $\mathcal{O}(m\eta)$. In our experiments presented later, we will empirically measure the actual computational complexity.

Designing Experiment with Synthetic Data to Validate the Method. In order to generate synthetic data with known ground-truth labels and detector effectiveness, we consider TPR and TNR, which are often interpreted as probabilities in practice. We gener-

---

Algorithm 4. Inferring ground-truth labels and effectiveness metrics

---

Input: Detector labelling results $\mathbf{V} = (V_{ij})_{1 \le i \le \eta, 1 \le j \le m}$; bellwether-incurred accuracy vector $\mathbf{BA} = (BA_1, \ldots, BA_\eta)^\mathsf{T}$; tolerable error threshold ϵ

Output: Inferred ground-truth labels $(\mathsf{Malign}_1, \ldots, \mathsf{Malign}_m)$ and detectors' effectiveness metrics $\mathbf{TPR'} = (\mathsf{TPR'_1}, \ldots, \mathsf{TPR'_\eta})^\mathsf{T}$, $\mathbf{TNR'} = (\mathsf{TNR'_1}, \ldots, \mathsf{TNR'_\eta})^\mathsf{T}$, $\mathbf{ACC'} = (\mathsf{ACC'_1}, \ldots, \mathsf{ACC'_\eta})^\mathsf{T}$;

1: $\delta \leftarrow 2\epsilon$ {It suffices to initialize δ as any value that is greater than ϵ}
2: $\mathbf{ACC'} \leftarrow \mathbf{BA}$ {Initiate accuracy vector as $\mathbf{BA}$}
3: **while** $\delta > \epsilon$ **do**
4: 　$\mathbf{TN}, \mathbf{TP}, \mathbf{FN}, \mathbf{FP} \leftarrow (0, \ldots, 0)^\mathsf{T}_{1 \times \eta}$ {Initialize $\mathsf{TN}_i = \mathsf{TP}_i = \mathsf{FN}_i = \mathsf{FP}_i = 0$ for $1 \le i \le \eta$}
5: 　**for** $j := 1$ **to** m **do**
6: 　　$\mathsf{MalignWeight} \leftarrow 0$;　$\mathsf{BenignWeight} \leftarrow 0$;　{Initialize weights as 0}
7: 　　**for** $i := 1$ **to** η **do**
8: 　　　**if** $V_{ij} = 1$ **then**
9: 　　　　$\mathsf{MalignWeight} \leftarrow \mathsf{MalignWeight} + \mathsf{ACC'_i}$ {Count detector i's vote for malicious}
10: 　　　**else**
11: 　　　　$\mathsf{BenignWeight} \leftarrow \mathsf{BenignWeight} + \mathsf{ACC'_i}$ {Count detector i's vote for benign}
12: 　　　**end if**
13: 　　**end for**
14: 　　**if** $\mathsf{MalignWeight} > \frac{\mathsf{MalignWeight}+\mathsf{BenignWeight}}{2}$ **then**
15: 　　　$\mathsf{Malign}_j \leftarrow 1$ {If majority of weighted votes are malicious, label file j as malicious}
16: 　　**else**
17: 　　　$\mathsf{Malign}_j \leftarrow 0$
18: 　　**end if**
19: 　　**for** $i := 1$ **to** η **do**
20: 　　　**if** $\mathsf{Malign}_j = 0$ **then**
21: 　　　　**if** $V_{ij} = 1$ **then**
22: 　　　　　$\mathsf{FP}_i \leftarrow \mathsf{FP}_i + 1$ {file j is a false-positive by detector i}
23: 　　　　**else if** $V_{ij} = 0$ **then**
24: 　　　　　$\mathsf{TN}_i \leftarrow \mathsf{TN}_i + 1$ {file j is a true-negative by detector i}
25: 　　　　**end if**
26: 　　　**else**
27: 　　　　**if** $V_{ij} = 1$ **then**
28: 　　　　　$\mathsf{TP}_i \leftarrow \mathsf{TP}_i + 1$ {file j is a true-positive by detector i}
29: 　　　　**else if** $V_{ij} = 0$ **then**
30: 　　　　　$\mathsf{FN}_i \leftarrow \mathsf{FN}_i + 1$ {file j is a false-negative by detector i}
31: 　　　　**end if**
32: 　　　**end if**
33: 　　**end for**
34: 　**end for**
35: 　$\delta \leftarrow \sum_{i=1}^{\eta} |\mathsf{ACC'_i} - \frac{\mathsf{TN}_i+\mathsf{TP}_i}{\mathsf{TN}_i+\mathsf{TP}_i+\mathsf{FN}_i+\mathsf{FP}_i}|$ {Changes in ACC between this and last iterations}
36: 　**for** $i := 1$ **to** η **do**
37: 　　$\mathsf{ACC'_i} \leftarrow \frac{\mathsf{TN}_i+\mathsf{TP}_i}{\mathsf{TN}_i+\mathsf{TP}_i+\mathsf{FN}_i+\mathsf{FP}_i}$,　$\mathsf{TPR'_i} \leftarrow \frac{\mathsf{TP}_i}{\mathsf{TP}_i+\mathsf{FN}_i}$,　$\mathsf{TNR'_i} \leftarrow \frac{\mathsf{TN}_i}{\mathsf{TN}_i+\mathsf{FP}_i}$
38: 　**end for**
39: 　$\mathbf{Malign} \leftarrow (\mathsf{Malign}_1, \ldots, \mathsf{Malign}_m)$; $\mathbf{ACC'} \leftarrow (\mathsf{ACC'_1}, \ldots, \mathsf{ACC'_\eta})^\mathsf{T}$; $\mathbf{TPR'} \leftarrow (\mathsf{TPR'_1}, \ldots, \mathsf{TPR'_\eta})^\mathsf{T}$; $\mathbf{TNR'} \leftarrow (\mathsf{TNR'_1}, \ldots, \mathsf{TNR'_\eta})^\mathsf{T}$
40: **end while**
41: Return inferred ground-truth labels $\mathbf{Malign}$ and $\mathbf{TPR'}$, $\mathbf{TNR'}$ and $\mathbf{ACC'}$

---

ate three synthetic datasets, denoted by **D1**, **D2** and **D3**. Each dataset contains one million example files, but different ratios of malicious vs. benign entries: (i) **D1** contains 300,000 malicious files and 700,000 benign files; (ii) **D2** contains 500,000 malicious files and 500,000 benign files; and (iii) **D3** contains 700,000 malicious files and 300,000 benign files. This is to show that the algorithms are equally applicable to various ratios. Note that no actual files are generated because we only need their ground-truth labels and their labels given by the detectors. For a detector, we generate its label on a file according to the detector's TPR and TNR, as follows. If the ground-truth label of the file is malicious (i.e., malign), then the detector labels it as 1 (malicious) with probability TPR and 0 (benign) with probability $1 - $ TPR; if the ground truth label of the file is benign, then the detector labels it as 0 with probability TNR and labels it as 1 with probability $1 - $ TNR. Given the labels, the accuracy ACC of a detector can be computed as described in Sect. 2. We apply Algorithm 3 to the synthetic datasets **D1-D3** as well as the detectors' labels on these files to derive the detectors' relative accuracy (i.e., relative accuracy with the bellwether detector **BA**), and then apply Algorithm 4 with the **BA** to derive their inferred TPR', TNR' and ACC'. Finally, we compare these inferred metrics to their ground-truth counterparts TPR, TNR and ACC to validate the method.

We conduct 10 experiments, denoted by **Experiments 1–10**. For purposes of robustness, the experiments consider detectors with varying ACC's. The 10 experiments are: **(1)** 50 detectors with varying ground-truth ACC: 10 detectors with ACC $\in [0.85, 0.95]$, 10 with ACC $\in [0.75, 0.85]$, 10 with ACC $\in [0.7, 0.8]$, and 20 with ACC $\in [0.65, 0.75]$. **(2)** 50 detectors: 10 detectors with ACC $\in [0.9, 1]$; 10 with ACC $\in [0.85, 0.95]$; 10 with ACC $\in [0.8, 0.9]$; 20 with ACC $\in [0.75, 0.85]$. **(3)** 50 detectors with ACC $\in [0.9, 1]$. **(4)** 90 detectors: 50 with ACC $\in [0.9, 1]$, 10 with ACC $\in [0.85, 0.95]$, 10 with ACC $\in [0.8, 0.9]$, 10 with ACC $\in [0.75, 0.85]$, and 10 with ACC $\in [0.35, 0.45]$. **(5)** 50 detectors: 10 detectors with ACC $\in [0.9, 1]$, 10 with ACC $\in [0.85, 0.95]$, 10 with ACC $\in [0.8, 0.9]$, 10 with ACC $\in [0.75, 0.85]$, and 10 with ACC $\in [0.35, 0.45]$. **(6)** 50 detectors: 40 detectors with ACC $\in [0.9, 1]$ and 10 with ACC $\in [0.35, 0.45]$. **(7)** 50 detectors: 30 detectors with ACC $\in [0.9, 1]$ and 20 with ACC $\in [0.35, 0.45]$. **(8)** 50 detectors with 25 detectors with ACC $\in [0.9, 1]$ and 25 detectors with ACC $\in [0.35, 0.45]$. **(9)** 50 detectors with 20 detectors with ACC $\in [0.9, 1]$ and 30 detectors with ACC $\in [0.35, 0.45]$. **(10)** 50 detectors with 10 detectors with ACC $\in [0.9, 1]$ and 40 detectors with ACC $\in [0.35, 0.45]$.

Experimental Results. The computational complexity of Algorithm 4 is $O(\eta m)$ for each iteration when $\delta > \epsilon$, where $\eta << m$. Unfortunately, we cannot estimate how many iterations it will take before reaching $\delta < \epsilon$ at the time of writing.

For each experiment and each detector D_i, there are four sets of values: the ground-truth effectiveness metrics TPR_i, TNR_i, and ACC_i, where TPR_i and TNR_i are the input for generating synthetic data for detector D_i and ACC_i is derived from them as mentioned above; the relative accuracy RA_i (Algorithm 1); the bellwether relative accuracy BA_i (Algorithm 3); and the inferred effectiveness metrics TPR'_i, TNR'_i, and ACC'_i (Algorithm 4). Owing to space limit, we only present the experimental results on ACC'_i, while noting that the results on TPR'_i and TNR'_i exhibit similar characteristics. Moreover, we only present the experimental results with **D1**, because the results with **D2** and **D3** are almost the same as that of **D1**.

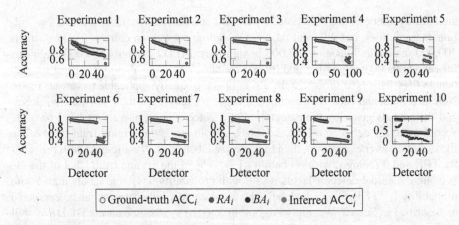

Fig. 1. Results of **Experiments 1–10** with synthetic dataset **D1**: ground-truth ACC_i (which is, when invisible, hidden behind the inferred ACC_i' curve), relative accuracy (RA_i, which is, when invisible, hidden behind the inferred ACC_i' curve), bellwether relative accuracy (BA_i, which is, when invisible, hidden behind the inferred ACC_i' curve), and inferred accuracy ACC_i' (y-axis) of detector i (x-axis), in the descending order of ACC.

Figure 1 plots the experimental results with dataset **D1**. We make the following observations. First, we observe $RA_i \neq ACC_i$ and $BA_i \neq ACC_i$, which is expected and highlights the necessity of Algorithm 4. Nevertheless, we observe that $|ACC_i - BA_i| \leq |ACC_i - RA_i|$ holds for every i in the experiments, meaning that bellwether relative accuracy improves upon the relative accuracy. Second, we observe the inferred $ACC_i' \approx ACC_i$ in most cases. In **Experiments 1–9**, we observe $\max_i(|ACC_i - ACC_i'|) = 2 \times 10^{-6}$; in **Experiment 10**, we observe a higher error, with $\max_i(|ACC_i - ACC_i'|) \approx 0.04$ and average error 0.012 (among all detectors), due to the fact that there are only 10 good detectors with ACC $\in [0.9, 1]$ but 40 poor detectors with ACC $\in [0.35, 0.45]$. This confirms the usefulness of Algorithm 4. Third, we select detectors with $BA_i > 0.5$ and pass them to Algorithm 4 (which corresponds to the recommended use case mentioned above), also in **Experiments 1–10**. We contrast this result with what is plotted in Fig. 1, which uses all of the detectors (rather than a selection of them). Owing to space limit, we only report that **Experiments 1–3** do not differ in these two settings because no detectors have $BA_i \leq 0.5$; ACC_i' in **Experiments 4–9** are improved and match ACC_i exactly; ACC_i' in **Experiment 10** is most improved, with the largest error being $\max_i(|ACC_i' - ACC_i|) \approx 0.04$. In each of the 10 experiments, we highlight that at most 2 (out of 1 million) files are mislabelled, leading to negligible TNR_i' and TPR_i'. This highlights the usefulness of using the bellwether detector to filter out detectors with $BA_i \leq 0.5$. Fourth, the order-preserving property that $ACC_i > ACC_j$ implies $ACC_i' > ACC_j'$ is preserved when detectors with $BA_i \leq 0.5$ are eliminated but not before they are eliminated. This further highlights the importance of filtering out detectors with $BA_i \leq 0.5$.

In order to show that Algorithm 4 outperforms the heuristic of unweighted majority voting, we also conduct **Experiments 1–10** with the latter. By contrasting the results, we observe that unweighted majority voting, while performing moderately well in

Experiments 1–7 with a maximum number of mislabeled files being 17, performs poorly in **Experiments 8–10** where poor detectors begin to outnumber good detectors, with 4,350, 17,450, and 441,500 files mislabeled, respectively. This reiterates the advantage of the recommended use case of the principled Algorithm 4 (i.e., filtering out detectors with $BA_i \leq 0.5$) over the heuristic of unweighted majority voting.

Insight 1. *Algorithm 4 is a principled method for inferring ground-truth labels and detector effectiveness, especially when eliminating the detectors whose $BA_i \leq 0.5$. It also substantially outperforms the unweighted majority voting heuristic.*

5 Applying the Method to Real-World Dataset

Now we apply the method to a real-world dataset collected from VirusTotal, with $n = 62$ detectors and $m = 10,738,585$ files. Each file is labeled as malicious (1) or benign (0), but not every file is labeled by every detector. The dataset is succinctly represented by matrix $\mathbf{V} = (V_{ij})_{n \times m}$, which leads to similarity matrix $\mathbf{S}$, and the bellwether relative accuracy vector $\mathbf{BA}$ according to Algorithm 3. We conduct two experiments with Algorithm 4: the first experiment corresponds to the recommended use case of only using detectors with $BA_i > 0.5$; the second experiment uses all of the 62 detectors together with the bellwether detector which is always given voting weight 0 (i.e., $\eta = 63$), while aiming to draw more insights. We observe that in the aforementioned experiments, with an input of $m = 10,738,585$ files and $\eta \leq 63$ detectors, Algorithm 4 took on the order of tens of minutes to complete each iteration, with a maximum number of 8 iterations.

In the first experiment, we observe 56 (out of the 62) detectors have $BA_i > 0.5$. Algorithm 4 outputs $7,408,449$ files as malicious and the TPR'_i, TNR'_i and ACC'_i's for the 56 detectors. We observe 22 (out of the 56) detectors have $\text{TNR}'_i > \text{TPR}'_i$ (i.e., they prefer low false-positives to low false-negatives) and the other 34 have $\text{TNR}'_i < \text{TPR}'_i$ (i.e., these detectors prefer the opposite). This suggests that a majority of the good detectors prefer low false-negatives to low false-positives; this is consistent with a finding reported in [7]. Treating the inferred labels as ground-truth (as validated in Sect. 4), we can test the heuristic unweighted majority voting, which has to use all of the detectors because it cannot distinguish which detectors are more accurate than others. We find that the unweighted majority voting method only labels $6,021,073$ (out of the $7,408,449$ malicious) files as malicious, meaning high false-negatives.

For the second experiment, Fig. 2 plots the bellwether relative accuracy BA_i and the inferred ACC'_i, TPR'_i and TNR'_i for detectors $1 \leq i \leq 62$, in descending order respective of ACC'_i, with $BA_{bellwether} = 0.5$ as the reference line; note that $\text{TPR}'_{bellwether} = 0.506$, $\text{TNR}'_{bellwether} = 0.504$, $\text{ACC}'_{bellwether} = 0.505$ are not plotted. We make the following observations. First, four detectors $i \in \{59, 60, 61, 62\}$ have $BA_i \approx 0$, $\text{TPR}'_i \approx 0$, $\text{TNR}'_i \approx 0$, and $\text{ACC}'_i \approx 0$, meaning they are not reliable. Looking into the data we find that they only labeled $52, 51, 37, 1$ files, respectively. Second, detectors D_5 and D_{37} have $BA_5 = 0.256$ but $\text{ACC}'_5 = 0.92$ and $BA_{37} = 0.515$ but $\text{ACC}'_{37} = 0.83$. This does not contradict with anything discussed above, because it can be explained by the fact that D_5 labels about 33% of the files and D_{37} labels

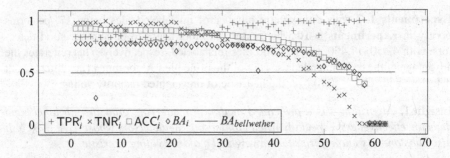

Fig. 2. Plots of bellwether relative accuracy BA_i, and inferred TPR'_i, TNR'_i and ACC'_i (the y-axis) for detectors $1 \leq i \leq 62$ (the x-axis), with $BA_{bellwether} = 0.5$ being the reference line.

about 69%. Scaling BA_5 and BA_{37} proportional to the number of files they label would rectify this phenomenon and place the values where expected in **BA**, namely $BA_5 = 0.256/0.33 = 0.775$ and $BA_{37} = 0.515/0.69 = 0.746$. Nevertheless, this does highlight that $BA_i > BA_k$ does not necessarily imply $\mathsf{ACC}'_i > \mathsf{ACC}'_k$ when D_i and D_k label significantly different sets of files, which is inherent to the definition of similarity because C_{ik} applies to the *union* of the two sets of files that are labeled by D_i and D_k, whereas A_{ik} applies to the *intersection* of the two sets. In the full version of the paper we will investigate whether requiring that all detectors label the *same* set of files would make our method even more robust. Third, treating as the ground-truth the outcome in the first experiment (with detectors of $BA_i > 0.5$), the TPR'_i, TNR'_i and ACC'_i's of the detectors that are common to these two experiments are largely consistent, indicating that individual detector metrics are consistent during the recovery process. Fourth, 22 detectors have $\mathsf{TNR}'_i > \mathsf{TPR}'_i$ (i.e., they prefer low false-positives to low false-negatives) and the remainder show the opposite. This is consistent with what is observed in the first experiment mentioned above.

Insight 2. *The principled weighted majority voting method is significant more accurate than the unweighted majority voting heuristic. Most detectors prefer low false-negatives to low false-positives.*

6   Conclusion

We have presented a principled weighted majority voting method for inferring ground-truth labels of files and malware detector effectiveness metrics, taking as input the (conflicting) labels given by a set of malware detectors on a set of files. The proposed method is supported by an algebraic interpretation of the notion of relative accuracy introduced in [1]. Another key idea is to introduce the notion of bellwether detector for serving as a reference to eliminate the detectors that perform worse than random labeling of files. We empirically validate the method by using synthetic data with known ground-truth information. We apply the method to a real-world dataset collected from VirusTotal.

The present paper makes a solid step towards characterizing the proposed method, but there are some outstanding open problems: Can "$BA_i > BA_j$ implying $\mathsf{ACC}_i > $

ACC_j" be rigorously proven? Can the error bounds on $|ACC_i - ACC'_i|$ be rigorously characterized? Can the idea of eliminating detectors with $BA_i \leq 0.5$ be rigorously justified? If any of the above is not universally true, what is the necessary and sufficient condition under which it is true?

Acknowledgement. We thank the reviewers for their useful comments. This work was supported in part by NSF Grant #2122631 (#1814825) and by a Grant from the State of Colorado.

References

1. Charlton, J., Du, P., Cho, J.H., Xu, S.: Measuring relative accuracy of malware detectors in the absence of ground truth. In: Proceedings IEEE MILCOM, pp. 450–455 (2018)
2. Chen, H., Cho, J., Xu, S.: Quantifying the security effectiveness of firewalls and dmzs. In: Proceedings HoTSoS 2018, pp. 9:1–9:11 (2018)
3. Chen, H., Cho, J., Xu, S.: Quantifying the security effectiveness of network diversity. In: Proceedings HoTSoS 2018, p. 24:1 (2018)
4. Cheng, Y., Deng, J., Li, J., DeLoach, S., Singhal, A., Ou, X.: Metrics of security. In: Cyber Defense and Situational Awareness, pp. 263–295 (2014)
5. Cho, J., Hurley, P., Xu, S.: Metrics and measurement of trustworthy systems. In: IEEE Military Communication Conference (MILCOM 2016) (2016)
6. Cho, J., Xu, S., Hurley, P., Mackay, M., Benjamin, T., Beaumont, M.: Stram: measuring the trustworthiness of computer-based systems. ACM Comput. Surv. **51**(6), 128:1–128:47 (2019)
7. Du, P., Sun, Z., Chen, H., Cho, J.H., Xu, S.: Statistical estimation of malware detection metrics in the absence of ground truth. IEEE T-IFS **13**(12), 2965–2980 (2018)
8. Homer, J., et al.: Aggregating vulnerability metrics in enterprise networks using attack graphs. J. Comput. Secur. **21**(4), 561–597 (2013)
9. Hotelling, H.: Analysis of a complex of statistical variables into principal components. J. Educ. Psychol. **24**(6), 417 (1933)
10. Invernizzi, L., Benvenuti, S., Cova, M., Comparetti, P.M., Kruegel, C., Vigna, G.: Evilseed: a guided approach to finding malicious web pages. In: IEEE Symposium on Security and Privacy, pp. 428–442 (2012)
11. Johnson, C.R., Horn, R.A.: Matrix Analysis. Cambridge University Press, Cambridge (1985)
12. Kantchelian, A., et al.: Better malware ground truth: techniques for weighting anti-virus vendor labels. In: Proceedings 2015 ACM Workshop on Artificial Intelligence and Security, pp. 45–56 (2015)
13. Kührer, M., Rossow, C., Holz, T.: Paint it black: evaluating the effectiveness of malware blacklists. In: Proceedings Research in Attacks, Intrusions and Defenses (RAID 2014), pp. 1–21 (2014)
14. Mireles, J., Ficke, E., Cho, J., Hurley, P., Xu, S.: Metrics towards measuring cyber agility. IEEE T-IFS **14**(12), 3217–3232 (2019)
15. Mohaisen, A., Alrawi, O.: Av-meter: an evaluation of antivirus scans and labels. In: Proceedings DIMVA, pp. 112–131 (2014)
16. Morales, J., Xu, S., Sandhu, R.: Analyzing malware detection efficiency with multiple anti-malware programs. In: Proceedings CyberSecurity (2012)
17. Noel, S., Jajodia, S.: A suite of metrics for network attack graph analytics. In: Network Security Metrics, pp. 141–176. Springer, Cham (2017). https://doi.org/10.1007/978-3-319-66505-4_7

18. Pendleton, M., Garcia-Lebron, R., Cho, J., Xu, S.: A survey on systems security metrics. ACM Comput. Surv. **49**(4), 62:1–62:35 (2016)
19. Perdisci, R., ManChon, U.: Vamo: Towards a fully automated malware clustering validity analysis. In: Proceedings. ACSAC, pp. 329–338 (2012)
20. Pritom, M., Schweitzer, K., Bateman, R., Xu, M., Xu, S.: Data-driven characterization and detection of COVID-19 themed malicious websites. In: IEEE ISI 2020 (2020)
21. Ramos, A., Lazar, M., Filho, R.H., Rodrigues, J.J.P.C.: Model-based quantitative network security metrics: a survey. IEEE Commun. Surv. Tutorials **19**(4), 2704–2734 (2017)
22. Wang, L., Jajodia, S., Singhal, A.: Network Security Metrics. Springer, Cham (2017). https://doi.org/10.1007/978-3-319-66505-4
23. Wang, L., Jajodia, S., Singhal, A., Cheng, P., Noel, S.: K-zero day safety: a network security metric for measuring the risk of unknown vulnerabilities. IEEE TDSC **11**(1), 30–44 (2014)
24. Xu, L., Zhan, Z., Xu, S., Ye, K.: Cross-layer detection of malicious websites. In: ACM CODASPY, pp. 141–152 (2013)
25. Xu, L., Zhan, Z., Xu, S., Ye, K.: An evasion and counter-evasion study in malicious websites detection. In: IEEE CNS, pp. 265–273 (2014)
26. Zhang, J., Durumeric, Z., Bailey, M., Liu, M., Karir, M.: On the mismanagement and maliciousness of networks. In: Proceedings NDSS 2014 (2014)
27. Zhang, M., Wang, L., Jajodia, S., Singhal, A., Albanese, M.: Network diversity: a security metric for evaluating the resilience of networks against zero-day attacks. IEEE Trans. Inf. Forensics Secur. **11**(5), 1071–1086 (2016)
28. Zhu, S., et al.: Measuring and modeling the label dynamics of online anti-malware engines. In: 29th USENIX Security Symposium, USENIX Security 2020, 12–14, August 2020, pp. 2361–2378 (2020)

Machine Learning for Cybersecurity

Protecting Data Privacy in Federated Learning Combining Differential Privacy and Weak Encryption

Chuanyin Wang[1,2], Cunqing Ma[1], Min Li[1,2(✉)], Neng Gao[1], Yifei Zhang[1], and Zhuoxiang Shen[1,2]

[1] State Key Laboratory of Information Security, Institute of Information Engineering, Chinese Academy of Sciences, Beijing, China
{wangchuanyin,macunqing,minli,gaoneng,zhangyifei,shenzhuoxiang}@iie.ac.cn
[2] School of Cyber Security, University of Chinese Academy of Sciences, Beijing, China

Abstract. As a typical application of decentralization, federated learning prevents privacy leakage of crowdsourcing data for various training tasks. Instead of transmitting actual data, federated learning only updates model parameters of server by learning multiple sub-models from clients. However, these parameters may be leaked during transmission and further used by attackers to restore client data. Existing technologies used to protect parameters from privacy leakage do not achieve the sufficient protection of parameter information. In this paper, we propose a novel and efficient privacy protection method, which perturbs the privacy information contained in the parameters and completes its ciphertext representation in transmission. Regarding to the perturbation part, differential privacy is utilized to perturb the real parameters, which can minimize the privacy information contained in the parameters. To further camouflage the parameters, the weak encryption keeps the ciphertext form of the parameters as they are transmitted from the client to the server. As a result, neither the server nor any middle attacker can obtain the real information of the parameter directly. The experiments show that our method effectively resists attacks from both malicious clients and malicious server.

Keywords: Federated learning · Privacy · Differential privacy · Weak encryption.

1 Introduction

With the rapid development of deep learning, a large amount of data collected from users are used to train the models to improve their accuracy. However, once those data are illegally obtained by attackers in data collection or similar scenarios, it will cause privacy disclosure. To solve this problem, the researchers have proposed a decentralized training and learning framework named federated learning [1]. As shown in Fig. 1, federated learning conducts decentralized

© Springer Nature Switzerland AG 2021
W. Lu et al. (Eds.): SciSec 2021, LNCS 13005, pp. 95–109, 2021.
https://doi.org/10.1007/978-3-030-89137-4_7

model training in many clients. Then it aggregates these local parameters into server's global model. The training data is distributed in each client, which greatly reduces the storage burden of the centralized server. At the same time, it only transmits the parameters or the global model between the clients and the server rather than the whole training data, which avoids the privacy leakage caused by the direct flow of private data between users and data collectors. With its unique advantages, it has become the focus of researchers in recent years [2,3].

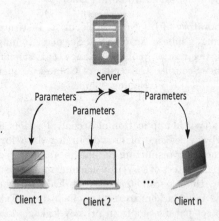

Fig. 1. Federated Learning

Unfortunately, the ability of the training model to remember the characteristics of the data will still lead to the malicious use of the parameters passed in the federated learning. It is possible to obtain relevant privacy features by deep analyzing the parameters. Generative Adversarial Network (GAN) [11] is one of the prevalent frameworks for adversarial training, which can generate related privacy features according to the parameters obtained [4]. As a result, external attackers and malicious server are able to use GAN to perform many illegal actions based on these parameters [5,6]. Furthermore, parameters can be obtained from clients. Therefore, privacy leakage lead federated learning to be vulnerable in many parts.

To address these issues, a large number of excellent researches, such as Secure Multi-party Computation (SMC), homomorphic encryption, differential privacy and so on, are used for federal learning. As a security protocol, SMC [7] is mainly used for secure aggregation, which can prevent malicious server attacks. However, this method involves a great quantity computational overhead. Another technology is homomorphic encryption utilized to encrypt the transmitted parameters [8], which does not suit all clients because the server must rely on a non-colluding external participant for encryption or decryption. Differential privacy [9] is an important data privacy protection technology in recent years. The intermediate parameters can be added with noise according to the differential privacy mechanism, such as Laplace mechanism [29], which reduces the risk of privacy leakage. Although the parameters are handled in the above several ways, privacy features can still be obtained from intermediate parameters in clients or server. In [10], the update parameters are processed in a non-informative way, which prevents the attackers from obtaining the residual characteristics of the training parameters. However, this method has a big drawback. If there is a malicious client, the parameters information will be obtained without any processing, which will result in the same degree of privacy disclosure compared with no privacy protection. We realize that when a malicious client participates in the training normally, it is very difficult for an honest client to detect malicious operations performed on them by a malicious client. Therefore, this paper tries to resist attacks from malicious clients, servers and third-party attackers on the premise of ensuring the accuracy of training tasks.

In this paper, we propose a privacy-preserving solution that perturbs the privacy features and guarantees the parameters shown in ciphertext. Resisting malicious clients is a key step in this scheme, which is realized by parameter perturbation. In this step, we use differential privacy to confuse the update parameters of each client to reduce the attack efficiency of the attacker and prevent malicious clients from obtaining private information of real parameters. However, differential privacy only is not enough to resist attacks from malicious servers and external attackers. As it happens, weak encryption used in our solution works well with differential privacy. In line with our design, we process the update parameters with weak encryption to realize the ciphertext representation of the parameters, which have been kept non-informative form during the parameters' communication and aggregation. When the global parameters are passed back to the client for next iteration, the server decrypts the global parameters with all clients. Then the updated parameters are re-encrypted and sent back to the server after it completes the training. In the case of eliminating the data privacy features contained in the update parameters, the accuracy of the training task will not be lost in the whole process of encryption and decryption. The entire solution effectively reduces not only the risk of internal attacks, but also more comprehensively resists external attacks.

Our main contributions are as follows:

- We have shown that the existing protection methods cannot fully protect users' private information in federated learning during iterating global models;
- We have proposed a novel and efficient federated learning scheme combining differential privacy and weak encryption, which achieves high security of client-to-server parameters and low-risk of server-to-client parameters;
- Experimental result shows that our scheme obtains the best protection of data privacy under existing methods and achieves the best trade-off between security and effectiveness.

2   Related Work and Background

The feature of federal learning is that the client continuously updates the parameters and the server aggregates the parameters. Researchers have proposed many ways to aggregate parameters on the server, such as federated averaging (FedAvg) [27] and federated stochastic variance reduced gradient (FSVRG) [28]. In the rest of this paper, we use FedAvg as parameters aggregation method. This part introduces the threats faced by the implementation of federal learning and related privacy protection technologies.

2.1   Privacy Threats in Federated Learning

Membership Inference Attacks. The purpose of member inference attack [12] is to determine whether the information obtained is in the dataset used to train the model. An attacker can train a predictive model to predict the user's identity attributes through this attack. In [13], this type of attack uses the intermediate updates of federated learning to infer the members with 99% accuracy. In [15], the author proposed the mGAN-AI framework, in which the malicious server can infer user-level privacy information without interfering the overall training. This will cause serious privacy leakage for users whose membership is sensitive, such as patients.

Reconstruction Attacks. The attacker can successfully reconstruct the data from other clients according to the intermediate updates because the neural network has the property of remembering the training data. This kind of attack is mainly divided into external attack and more serious internal attack. The internal attack includes client-based reconstruction attacks and server-based reconstruction attacks. 1)Client-based reconstruction attacks are embodied in [4] and [14], which reconstruct private data of clients through global models and parameters. At the same time, we can realize that it is difficult for the server to distinguish or find the existence of malicious clients in the case of equal contributions from clients, which makes this kind of attacks easier. 2)Server-based reconstruction attacks use the technology in [5] to directly obtain the updated parameters of the client and complete the reconstruction attacks.

2.2   Relevant Privacy Protection Technology

According to the latest technology in federated learning, there are mainly two protection methods: one is the clients preprocesses the training data; the other is the researchers use the encryption protocol or noise-adding operation which is most suitable for federated learning to realize the non-operable information representation of update parameters.

Secure Multi-party Computation(SMC). This technique, which achieve specific purpose privacy protection through complex computing protocols, was put into practical application soon after it was proposed [16]. In addition, the widespread use of neural networks attracts a large number of researchers to use

SMC in this field because of its demand for big data [17–19]. In [18], the author combines secret sharing, secret key negotiation, pseudo-random generator, digital signature and other related cryptographic algorithms to realize the safe transmission of parameters. The server obtains the aggregate parameters instead of the intermediate update parameters of each client. However, the global parameters aggregated by the server are sent back to the clients in plaintext, which still has the risk of privacy leakage. Furthermore, it will bring a lot of computational and communication overhead before and after the implementation of the relevant security protocols.

Differential Privacy(DP). As a widely used privacy protection technology, DP proposes an effective scheme for the protection of personal privacy attributes [20]. Due to its strong theoretical support, a large number of researchers have proposed to use DP for privacy protection in federated learning [21–23]. In [9], the author proposed a detailed scheme which protect update parameters. After the parameters of each client are passed to the server for aggregation, they add a certain amount of noise for the aggregated parameters. This ensures that the parameters transmitted in the communication are not true values, which confuses the authenticity of the parameters. However, only using differential privacy fails to protect the privacy of client and server under federated learning. Therefore, some researchers combine differential privacy and homomorphic encryption in [19]. Unfortunately, this combination brings a lot of computational overhead.

GAN and Other Technologies. Under normal operation, the client is difficult to find out whether there are other malicious clients in federated learning. This makes it hard to use the defense methods to resist malicious clients. Therefore, some researchers use GAN to generate fake training data in honest clients [24]. In this solution, the fake data generated by GAN reduce the attribute characteristics perceived by the human eye, which reduce the risk of data leakage of clients. But the accuracy of the learning model is greatly reduced by this method, which reflects that the balance of utility and privacy does not work well. In order to minimize the risk of data being reconstructed, the author in [10] proposed a method of non-informative parameters, which ensures that the parameters are presented in the correct form only on the client side. Compared to the approach based on differential privacy, this not only is a low-cost and safe method, but also removes all residual features. However, when existing malicious clients, the intermediate parameters that sever transmits to clients will be completely exposed to the attacker.

3   Preliminaries

3.1   Related Technologies

Differential Privacy [30]. A mechanism A is a random function that satisfies ϵ-differential privacy(ϵ-DP), if for any neighboring datasets D_1 and D_2 differing on at most one element, and for any $M \subset \text{Range}(A)$,

$$Pr\left[A\left(D_1\right) \in M\right] \leq e^\epsilon Pr\left[A\left(D_2\right) \in M\right] \tag{1}$$

where ϵ denotes the privacy budget which represents the level at which data privacy is protected. Generally speaking, the level of privacy protection is inversely proportional to accuracy.

Laplace Mechanism [29]. Given random function f, f' is a function that satisfies ϵ-differential privacy(ϵ-DP) with respect to f. The Laplace mechanism is defined as:

$$f'(D) = f(D) + Lap\left(\frac{\Delta f}{\epsilon}\right) \tag{2}$$

where Δf denotes the sensitivity which defined as the maximum of $\|f(D_1) - f(D_2)\|$ for neighboring datasets D_1 and D_2, $Lap\left(\frac{\Delta f}{\epsilon}\right)$ denotes samples from the Laplace distribution. In our paper, function f computes the model parameters for each client.

3.2 Threat Model

The two threats involved in this paper come from malicious clients [4] and malicious servers [15]. Both obtain parameters information of clients without intervening model training. In the end, these attackers reconstruct or infer user data based on GAN network.

In federated learning, all participants have a common learning goal. They understand the type and label of neural network architecture. For the attack model proposed in [4], there are two participants, A (attacker) and V (victim), and they have labels $[a, b]$ and $[b, c]$ respectively. During the entire federated training, both participants participate in the training normally, and the attacker's operations cannot be found on other clients. The attack process is roughly as follows: first, the victim V trains the network and transmits the trained parameters to the server; second, the attacker A downloads the parameters from the server to the local and uses the obtained parameters to update his GAN network. According to the GAN network, A generates the data of the sample of the victim V with label a and label it as c. In the process of the overall iteration, the attacker continuously optimizes the GAN network and generates enough samples for the victim to be labeled a. The server-side attack is faster. It directly obtains the parameters of other clients and performs GAN training.

4 Methodology

In this section, we propose an efficient and privacy-preserving solution in federated learning. As Fig. 2 shows, our defense mechanism mainly includes parameter perturbation and weak encryption in addition to local training and parameter aggregation in clients and server respectively.

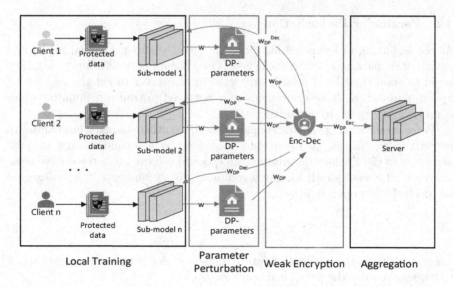

Fig. 2. The overview of DP-based parameter perturbation and update parameters weak encryption in federated learning

4.1   Overview

Encryption technologies, such as homomorphic encryption, are the widely utilized to protect the privacy of data in parameter aggregation of federated learning. Unfortunately, the generation of secret keys and both encryption and decryption will greatly increase computational overhead. To overcome this challenge, we use a novel parameter processing way named weak encryption to achieve non-informative update parameters, which ensure that the update parameters will not be obtained by external attackers and malicious servers in the form of plaintext. In addition, we exploit differential privacy to further obfuscation parameters which can defend against malicious or compromised clients. The combination of the two-step operation can realize the defense of both malicious server and clients.

As shown in the Fig. 2, the server and clients need to conduct several iterations to complete the training of the global model, and one iteration represents an epoch. For one epoch, every client obtains the update parameters of local model w by training their sub-model with local private data. To achieve the goal of privacy-preserving, users utilize differential privacy to blind the parameters w to w_{DP} firstly. Furthermore, they encrypt parameters w_{DP} to w_{DP}^{Enc}. After all clients complete the local training and the transmission of parameters, server aggregates the parameters in the form of w_{DP}^{Enc} which do not need to decrypt. Ultimately, server decrypts the global parameters to w_{DP}^{Dec}. If the test accuracy does not reach the set threshold, the server passes the decrypted global parameters back to the client for the next iteration.

4.2 Parameter Perturbation

At the beginning of federated learning, the server shares the global model and initialization parameters with each client. Once clients get that information, they begin to train their local models and wait for the server to get the request for update parameters. Note that clients may not need to transmit update parameters for every epoch in our setting.

Before transmitting the update parameters, we utilize Laplace mechanism to perturb them, that is, all parameters are added by a certain amount of noise according to the Laplace distribution. In order to achieve more reasonable noise addition, all clients jointly choose a common privacy budget ϵ. Clients execute the perturbation operation by

$$w_{dp} = w + Lap\left(\frac{\Delta f}{\epsilon}\right) \tag{3}$$

where w denotes the original update parameters, Δf denotes the global sensitivity, w_{dp} denotes the perturbed parameters.

4.3 Weak Encryption

Considering the risks posed by servers and third-party attackers, the parameters are further encrypted in this article. As the privacy of data increasingly vital, various encryption technologies are constantly being proposed to achieve privacy-preserving. Homomorphic encryption is a definitely excellent way in the field of machine learning. But practical application of encryption has huge limitations due to computational and communication overhead. In particular, federated learning, which requires learning at the edge of the client and cannot provide good computing power, makes traditional encryption more difficult to implement. To address this problem, we propose a more efficient and secure method.

According to the characteristics of federated learning, as long as the intermediate parameters are not doped with the distribution information of clients' data during the transmission process, it is difficult for an attacker to obtain clients' data information based on the parameters. In [10], the author proposed a new method, which maximizes the parameter entropy distribution. So, we utilize it to realize the weak encryption for our method.

Due to the algorithm settings of FedAvg, the following assumptions are made: K clients train the sub-models, a centralized server performs t-round parameter aggregation, and the global weight is w_t in round t. Therefore, the encrypted form of the intermediate parameter can be expressed as the formula (4).

$$w_{t+1}^{k,Enc} = w_{t+1}^k \cdot LocalUpdate(k, w_t)^{-1} \cdot H(shape(); \alpha, \beta) \tag{4}$$

where w_{t+1}^k denotes the weight of client k in round $t+1$, $w_{t+1}^{k,Enc}$ denotes the weight after encryption, $LocalUpdate(k, w_t)^{-1}$ denotes local learning method of client's model, such as stochastic gradient descent, $H(shape(); \alpha, \beta)$ denotes matrix of non-informative numbers, following the uniform probability distribution bounded by α and β, whose dimensionality corresponds to that of the matrix of parameters w_{t+1}^k.

The information exploited to encrypt the update parameters can only be available locally. First, the updated weight w_{t+1} is multiplied by the (pseudo-) inverse matrix of the return value of the update method, which completes the preliminary non-informative update parameters. Furthermore, the preliminary non-informative update parameters need to be multiplied by $H()$, which can not only restore the matrix shape of the update parameters but also maximize the non-informative extent of the update parameters, to ensure that the parameters are aggregated accurately on the server.

After the two processes mentioned above, the update parameters are passed to the server. And the server aggregates the parameters without decryption. Then, the server decrypts the global parameters to update global model and do the next iteration. The formula for decryption is as follows.

$$w_{t+1}^{Dec} = w_{t+1}^{Enc} - \sum_{k \in S_t} \frac{n_k}{n}(w_{t+1}^k \cdot LocalUpdate(k, w_t)^{-1} \cdot w_{t+1}^{k,Enc} - w_{t+1}^k) \quad (5)$$

where w_{t+1}^{Dec} denotes the global parameters after decryption, n denotes the total amount of data, n_k denotes the number of samples that the user k has. Importantly, the decryption, which is equivalent to the inverse operation of encryption, requires the participation of all clients. They decrypt their own parts based on local weight and model function information they have, that is, each client subtracts the offset generated by the encryption on the client.

The above works complete the encryption of the clients' local update parameters and the decryption of the server's global parameters. Because clients cannot know whether the server is honest or not, the parameters cannot be decrypted and must be accurately aggregated in server. According to this demand, the parameters are integrated in the encrypted state and expressed as the following form.

$$w_{t+1}^{Enc} = \sum_{k=1}^{K} \frac{n_k}{n} w_{t+1}^k \cdot LocalUpdate(k, w_t)^{-1} \cdot H(shape(); \alpha, \beta) \quad (6)$$

where w_{t+1}^{Enc} denotes global parameters that keep the encrypted state. It can be seen from the formula that there is no difference between the aggregation parameters in the encrypted state and the decrypted state except numerically.

In summary, weak encryption completes the encryption of the local parameters, the parameters aggregation in the encryption state and the decryption of the global parameters for the next iteration. Algorithm 1 is our overall implementation process.

In Algorithm 1, the first step is to determine the initial weight of the input and the number of clients. The $C \cdot K$ in the second row represents that clients are drawn in a certain proportion to update the parameters in each iteration, which can save time and converge faster. Note that C denotes the proportion of the

---

Algorithm 1. Privacy-protected in Federated Learning

Require: Initial weight w_0, total clients K
1: **for** *each round* $t = 1, 2, \ldots$ **do**
2:     $M \leftarrow max(C \cdot K, 1)$
3:     $S_t \leftarrow (random\ set\ of\ M\ clients)$
4:     **for** *each client* $k \in S_t$ **do**
5:         $w_{t+1}^k = LocalUpdate(k, w_t)$
6:         $w_{dp,t+1}^k = w_{t+1}^k + Lap\left(\frac{\Delta f}{\epsilon}\right)$
7:         $w_{t+1}^{k,Enc} \leftarrow w_{dp,t+1}^k$
8:     **end for**
9:     $w_{t+1}^{Enc} = \sum_{k \in S_t} \frac{n_k}{n} w_{t+1}^{k,Enc}$
10:    $w_{t+1}^{Dec} \leftarrow w_{t+1}^{Enc}$
11: **end for**

---

number of clients participating in each iteration to the total number of clients. For the attacker, this step reduces the attack frequency to a certain extent. In line 5–7, after each client updates the parameters, they undergo parameter perturbation and weak encryption before uploading. In line 9, the server aggregates the clients' encryption parameters obtained in each round under encryption. Finally, in line 10, all clients decrypt the global parameters, which can update the global model and prepare for the next iteration.

5   Experiments

In order to verify our hypothesis, we will conduct experiments from the following aspects. We first implement multiple attacks which can reconstruct the data of other clients through the parameters in reality and prove the superiority of our scheme. Then, in order to further verify the feasibility of this scheme, we compare the computational cost with the previous scheme. Finally, we evaluate the model accuracy of our solution and show that we have a good trade-off between accuracy and utility. In addition, all our experiments are carried out on MNIST dataset using CNN architecture.

5.1   Defensive Performance

According to the threat model in Sect. 3.2, our goal is to recuperate as much data information as possible according to the updated parameters. We use this configuration, which uses CNN to act on MNIST dataset on common FedAvg, to recover training samples identified by labels. MNIST dataset contains 60,000 training samples and 10,000 test samples, and 10 categories. According to the data format, the federated learning we designed has 11 clients, including 10 normal clients and 1 malicious client. Note that each honest client has a category of data, but the malicious client does not own any other clients' data, which can guarantee the authenticity of reconstruction experiment results.

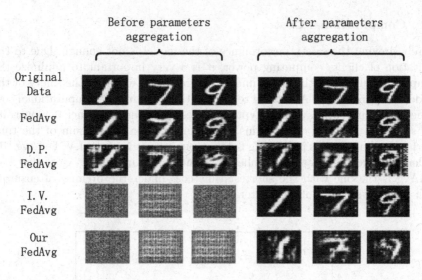

Fig. 3. Reconstructing data before and after parameters aggregation. We use the federated learning algorithm implemented by FedAvg on the MNIST dataset. The images labeled FedAvg are the result of reconstruction without any privacy protection. The images labeled as D.P FedAvg are reconstructed based on differential privacy. The images labeled I.V. FedAvg represent the result of reconstruction based on non-informative parameters. The images labeled as Our FedAvg are reconstructed based on our method.

After our continuous experimental verification, the experimental results are shown in Fig. 3. The attack experiments are carried out before and after parameters aggregation. Furthermore, each part conducts four different types of reconstruction experiments, including common FedAvg (FedAvg), FedAvg based on differential privacy (D.P. FedAvg [9]), FedAvg based on non-informative parameters(I.V. FedAvg [10]), and FedAvg based on the protection method proposed in this paper. For the attack before parameters aggregation, we conclude that our FedAvg and I.V. FedAvg , which have not been reconstructed any available data, achieve the maximum degree of privacy protection. At the same time, malicious reconstructed of data in our FedAvg and D.P. FedAvg are the worst and it is difficult to distinguish the authenticity of the reconstruction content in the attack after parameters aggregation. In the whole parameters iteration using our scheme, the attacker cannot obtain the user's exact privacy information.

Furthermore, [19] has given a detailed theoretical proof that DP provides privacy-preserving, that is, malicious clients cannot obtain any information from honest clients under the condition of enough privacy budget. To sum up, our solution can provide the best privacy protection in the existing way.

5.2   Computational Cost

Merely proving the safety performance of the model is not enough. Due to the limitation of clients computing power, it is a very important to minimize the computational cost of the client under the premise of ensuring the safety of the model and parameters. According to our solution, the mainly computational cost comes from encryption and decryption stages. In order to further demonstrate the superiority of our scheme, this experiment compares the sum of the time overhead of parameters processing between our scheme and the I.V. FedAvg [10] under the condition that the number of parameters is increasing. Note that I.V. FedAvg is the one with the shortest time cost under the premise of ensuring high-strength security of parameters.

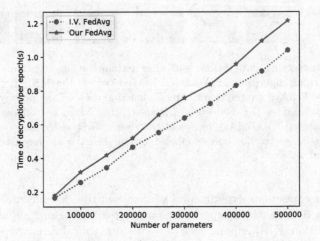

Fig. 4. The time cost of parameters processing in I.V. FedAvg and our scheme.

As shown in Fig. 4, the two curves indicate the time cost by the two schemes in the encryption and decryption stage as the number of parameters increases. Although the time cost of both schemes is increasing, the increase of this change is very small compared with the increase of parameter. In addition, the time difference between our scheme and the I.V. FedAvg in time cost is very small under the same setting, which is just a constant level difference. Therefore, combining the results of this experiment and the analysis in 5.1 shows that our scheme has obtained a higher intensity of privacy protection on the basis of a small increase in computational cost. In contrast, our scheme is more secure and more suitable for multi-client scenarios.

5.3   Accuracy

In the research of this article, the accuracy of the model is the most critical index when privacy is effectively protected. At the same time, the impact of different privacy budget on accuracy and the loss of accuracy caused by privacy budget are key issues. To explain these problems, this experiment analyzes the impact of privacy budget on accuracy under different numbers of clients and the difference of accuracy in the same number of clients between using differential privacy and not using differential privacy.

As shown in Fig. 5(a), the privacy budget is directly proportional to the accuracy rate in the case of the same number of clients. At the same time, the number of clients is directly proportional to the accuracy rate under the same privacy budget. The accuracy of the model has reached 97.8% when the privacy budget and the number of clients are taken as 10 and 100 respectively. In Fig. 5(b), the loss of accuracy is very small under different privacy budget. Furthermore, if we want to obtain a higher model accuracy rate in the case of a low privacy budget, we can increase the number of clients to achieve the goal according to the conclusion in Fig. 5(a). Therefore, the scheme proposed in this paper effectively realizes the trade-off between effectiveness and privacy.

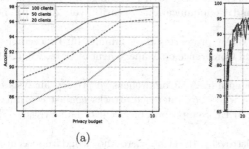
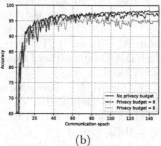

(a)   (b)

Fig. 5. Accuracy. (a)The accuracy in different privacy budget. (b)The accuracy difference between using differential privacy and not using differential privacy.

6   Conclusion and Future Work

Although federated learning, a decentralized application, guarantees the localization of data, it cannot deal with the problem of privacy leakage caused by parameters during the communication between the client and the server. Aiming at the privacy threat of its parameters, we utilize parameters perturbation and weak encryption to protect the parameters passed in the entire model learning. Weak encryption is more efficient than traditional encryption to realize the noninformative representation of the parameters. In addition, differential privacy further balances privacy and effectiveness. Finally, experiments show that our solution not only effectively resists attacks from malicious servers and external attackers, but also effectively reduces the risk of privacy leakage caused by malicious clients. Furthermore, the accuracy of the model in our solution can be adjusted to maximize the accuracy of the model without any noise. Generally, the attacker can only obtain part of the parameter information of the participant. However, it is possible to reconstruct some private information when the attacker obtains the model update parameters of all rounds of participants. For future work, we would like to further enhance our defense performance with low overhead by performing more complex mathematical operations.

References

1. McMahan, B., Moore, E., Ramage, D., et al.: Communication-efficient learning of deep networks from decentralized data. In: Artificial Intelligence and Statistics, pp. 1273–1282. PMLR (2017)
2. Ammad-Ud-Din, M., Ivannikova, E., Khan, S.A., et al.: Federated collaborative filtering for privacy-preserving personalized recommendation system. arXiv preprint arXiv:1901.09888 (2019)
3. Hard, A., Rao, K., Mathews, R., et al.: Federated learning for mobile keyboard prediction. arXiv preprint arXiv:1811.03604 (2018)
4. Hitaj, B., Ateniese, G., Perez-Cruz, F.: Deep models under the GAN: information leakage from collaborative deep learning. In: Proceedings of the. ACM SIGSAC Conference on Computer and Communications Security, vol. 2017, pp. 603–618 (2017)
5. Agrawal, R., Srikant, R.: Privacy-preserving data mining. In: Proceedings of the ACM SIGMOD International Conference on Management of Data, vol. (2000), pp. 439–450 (2000)
6. Nasr, M., Shokri, R., Houmansadr, A.: Comprehensive privacy analysis of deep learning: Passive and active white-box inference attacks against centralized and federated learning. In: 2019 IEEE Symposium on Security and Privacy (SP), pp. 739–753. IEEE (2019)
7. Ishai, Y., Kushilevitz, E., Ostrovsky, R., et al.: Zero-knowledge from secure multiparty computation. In: Proceedings of the Thirty-Ninth Annual ACM Symposium on Theory of Computing, pp. 21–30 (2007)
8. Aono, Y., Hayashi, T., Trieu Phong, L., et al. Scalable and secure logistic regression via homomorphic encryption. In: Proceedings of the Sixth ACM Conference on Data and Application Security and Privacy, pp. 142–144 (2016)
9. Geyer, R.C., Klein, T., Nabi, M.: Differentially private federated learning: a client level perspective. arXiv preprint arXiv:1712.07557 (2017)
10. Li, Q., Zhu, W., Wu, C., et al.: InvisibleFL: federated learning over non-informative intermediate updates against multimedia privacy leakages. In: Proceedings of the 28th ACM International Conference on Multimedia, pp. 753–762 (2020)
11. Goodfellow, I., Pouget-Abadie, J., Mirza, M., et al.: Generative adversarial nets. Adv. Neural Inf. Process. Syst. **27**, 2672–2680 (2014)
12. Truex, S., Liu, L., Gursoy, M.E., et al.: Demystifying membership inference attacks in machine learning as a service. IEEE Trans. Serv. Comput. (2019)
13. Melis, L., Song, C., De Cristofaro, E., et al.: Exploiting unintended feature leakage in collaborative learning. In: 2019 IEEE Symposium on Security and Privacy (SP), pp. 691–706. IEEE (2019)

14. Bhowmick, A., Duchi, J., Freudiger, J., et al.: Protection against reconstruction and its applications in private federated learning. arXiv preprint arXiv:1812.00984 (2018)

15. Wang, Z., Song, M., Zhang, Z., et al.: Beyond inferring class representatives: user-level privacy leakage from federated learning. In: IEEE INFOCOM 2019-IEEE Conference on Computer Communications, pp. 2512–2520. IEEE (2019)

16. Canetti, R., Feige, U., Goldreich, O., et al.: Adaptively secure multi-party computation. In: Proceedings of the Twenty-Eighth aannual ACM Symposium on Theory of Computing, pp. 639–648 (1996)

17. Du, W., Han, Y.S., Chen, S.: Privacy-preserving multivariate statistical analysis: Linear regression and classification. In: Proceedings of the 2004 SIAM International Conference on Data Mining. Society for Industrial and Applied Mathematics, pp. 222–233 (2004)

18. Bonawitz, K., Ivanov, V., Kreuter, B., et al.: Practical secure aggregation for privacy-preserving machine learning. In: Proceedings of the. ACM SIGSAC Conference on Computer and Communications Security, vol. 2017, pp. 1175–1191 (2017)

19. Hao, M., Li, H., Xu, G., et al.: Towards efficient and privacy-preserving federated deep learning. In: ICC 2019–2019 IEEE International Conference on Communications (ICC), pp. 1–6. IEEE (2019)

20. van Tilborg, H.C.A., Jajodia, S. (eds.): Encyclopedia of Cryptography and Security. Springer, Boston, MA (2011). https://doi.org/10.1007/978-1-4419-5906-5

21. Augenstein, S., McMahan, H.B., Ramage, D., et al.: Generative models for effective ml on private, decentralized datasets. arXiv preprint arXiv:1911.06679 (2019)

22. Zhu, T., Philip, S.Y.: Applying differential privacy mechanism in artificial intelligence. In: 2019 IEEE 39th International Conference on Distributed Computing Systems (ICDCS), pp. 1601–1609. IEEE (2019)

23. Xie, L., Lin, K., Wang, S., et al.: Differentially private generative adversarial network. arXiv preprint arXiv:1802.06739 (2018)

24. Luo, X., Zhu, X.: Exploiting defenses against GAN-based feature inference attacks in federated learning. arXiv preprint arXiv:2004.12571 (2020)

25. Choi, Y., Choi, M., Kim, M., et al.: Stargan: Unified generative adversarial networks for multi-domain image-to-image translation. In: Proceedings of the IEEE Conference on Computer Vision and Pattern Recognition, pp. 8789–8797 (2018)

26. Zhu, J.Y., Park, T., Isola, P., et al.: Unpaired image-to-image translation using cycle-consistent adversarial networks. In: Proceedings of the IEEE International Conference on Computer Vision, pp. 2223–2232 (2017)

27. Lim, W.Y.B., Luong, N.C., Hoang, D.T., et al.: Federated learning in mobile edge networks: a comprehensive survey. IEEE Commun. Surv Tutorials (2020)

28. Konečný, J., McMahan, B., Ramage, D.: Federated optimization: Distributed optimization beyond the datacenter. arXiv preprint arXiv:1511.03575 (2015)

29. Dwork, C., McSherry, F., Nissim, K., Smith, A.: Calibrating noise to sensitivity in private data analysis. In: Halevi, S., Rabin, T. (eds.) TCC 2006. LNCS, vol. 3876, pp. 265–284. Springer, Heidelberg (2006). https://doi.org/10.1007/11681878_14

30. Dwork, C.: Differential privacy: a survey of results. In: Agrawal, M., Du, D., Duan, Z., Li, A. (eds.) TAMC 2008. LNCS, vol. 4978, pp. 1–19. Springer, Heidelberg (2008). https://doi.org/10.1007/978-3-540-79228-4_1

Using Chinese Natural Language to Configure Authorization Policies in Attribute-Based Access Control System

Zhuoxiang Shen[1,2], Neng Gao[1], Zeyi Liu[3(✉)], Min Li[1,2], and Chuanyin Wang[1,2]

[1] State Key Laboratory of Information Security, Institute of Information Engineering, Chinese Academy of Sciences, Beijing, China
{shenzhuoxiang,gaoneng,minli,wangchuanyin}@iie.ac.cn
[2] School of Cyber Security, University of Chinese Academy of Sciences, Beijing, China
[3] Institute of Information Engineering, Chinese Academy of Sciences, Beijing, China
liuzeyi@iie.ac.cn

Abstract. In recent years, attribute-based access control (ABAC) is more and more popular because of its flexibility and fine-grained data management. However, manually configuring authorization policies in ABAC system is a time-consuming, labor-intensive, and tedious work. Many researchers explore the ways of automatically configuring authorization policies by parsing requirement specifications that are expressed in natural language. Previous works only focus on English and ignore the semantics of comparative relationship. In this paper, we propose a method based on Chinese including procedures of key words extraction, tag alignment and expression transformation. It can parse Chinese sentence into constraint expressions and authorization sign, by which ABAC system is able to configure authorization policies automatically. Our evaluation results show that it has good performance not only in the independent tests on each procedure but also in the systematic tests on the whole method.

Keywords: Attribute-based access control · Authorization policy · Natural language · Chinese.

1 Introduction

In recent years, attribute-based access control (ABAC) is more and more popular because of its flexibility and fine-grained data management. It has good application potential in the scenarios of big data and distributed system [5,6]. ABAC is a kind of access control model where the authorization decisions are made based on a set of attributes [14]. An attribute is an entity's property, which can be expressed as (name, value) pair. Usually, ABAC system administrator use tags to represent attributes, and will give various people and data different tags according to their attributes.

Even though ABAC is a promising access control model, it still relies on dozens of authorization policies defined by humans. However, in real-world scenario, most of organizations only have high-level requirement specifications that

© Springer Nature Switzerland AG 2021
W. Lu et al. (Eds.): SciSec 2021, LNCS 13005, pp. 110–125, 2021.
https://doi.org/10.1007/978-3-030-89137-4_8

are expressed in natural language. ABAC system administrator must comprehend the specifications in advance, and then manually configure authorization policies in system. If we consider this behavior on the scale of big data, manual configuration is a time-consuming, labor-intensive, and tedious work. It is better for the administrators that machines can comprehend the human-written specifications, and automatically configure authorization policies in ABAC system.

Some researches have been done to explore the ways of transforming natural language into authorization policies directly [11–16,18], but there are two main problems in these existing methods. The first problem is that almost all these studies are based on English text. As the language that has the largest number of users in the world, Chinese has been hardly paid any attention to. Researches on Chinese are very different from those on English. They have their own grammar and linguistic features. Word segmentation is a main difference. There is no space in Chinese characters, which suggests that the accuracy of segmentation will impact on the effectiveness of whole method.

The other problem is that existing studies often ignore the semantics of comparative relationship, which is usually used in people's daily life. Take the Chinese sentence[1] *group leader above staff can access salary form*, which means that the staff whose position is higher than group leader can access salary form, as an example. The authorized people not only include group leaders but may also refer to department directors and organization bosses. Those previous studies cannot comprehend complete semantics of this sentence because they often ignore the word *above*.

To tackle these problems, in this paper, we propose a method including procedures of key words extraction, tag alignment and expression transformation. It can parse Chinese sentence into constraint expressions and authorization sign, by which ABAC system is able to configure authorization policies automatically. We firstly extract all key words in the sentence that is useful to make certain of authorization policy. These key words are not well-organized and need to be further processed by tag alignment. Then we can obtain a sequence composed of function words and tags. By a set of pre-defined parsing rules, we can parse this sequence to constraint expressions. Constraint expressions tell ABAC system what authorization subjects are and what authorization objects are. Note that there is a special key word called negative word. The default authorization sign is *permit*, but if we identify any negative word in sentence, we will flip it to *deny*. With authorization subjects, authorization objects and authorization sign, ABAC system could automatically configure authorization policies. We conduct experiments on procedures of our method individually and systematically. Our method shows good performance not only in the independent tests on each procedure but also in the systematic tests on the whole method.

This paper makes the following main contributions:

– We propose a method including procedures of key words extraction, tag alignment and expression transformation. In this method, we try to dig out

---

[1] Since we deal with Chinese text, all examples of sentence obey Chinese grammar rules. The words shown in all examples are directly translated from Chinese.

sentence semantics deeply, especially logical and comparative relationship in the sentence.
- We come up with an approach that focuses on Chinese grammar and its linguistic features, which has not received much attention by previous work.
- We perform experiments to show the effectiveness and efficiency of the proposed approach. Our evaluation results show that it has good performance not only in the independent tests on each procedure but also in the systematic tests on the whole method.

The rest of the paper is organized as follows: We start with related work in Sect. 2. In Sect. 3, we present our approach in detail. The experiments and results are illustrated in Sect. 4. Finally, the conclusion and future work will be described in Sect. 5.

2   Related Work

There are some of representative works to extract authorization policies from natural language text. Xiao et al. [18] were the first to automatically configure authorization policies from requirement specification. They defined 4 patterns to locate relevant sentences and extracted entities by heuristics based on the same set of patterns. Slankas et al. [15] proposed a machine learning based approach called Access Control Relation Extraction (ACRE). They used bootstrapping skill to extract entities according to patterns obtained from dependency tree of sentences. They also extended ACRE by evaluating the approach in larger datasets [16]. Narouei et al. [12,13] automatically identified predicate-argument structure (PAS) based on semantic role labeling (SRL), and then used a set of pre-defined rules to extract authorization policies. They also proposed a method based on deep recurrent neural network that uses pre-trained word embeddings to identify content of authorization policies [11].

Extracting useful information from natural language text is also active in other cybersecurity researches. Chen et al. [4] tried to find logical vulnerabilities in payment syndication services only by the development documentation without any program analysis. They use finite state machine (FSM) to construct payment model by analyzing development documentation using dependency parsing. And then they observe whether some security-related parameters are visible to satisfy some security requirements by FSM. Five new critical vulnerabilities are discovered by their approach. Story et al. [17] proposed a method, which compares the practices described in privacy policy documentation to the practices performed by smartphone apps to detect non-compliance with laws, by classifying privacy practice statements based on a data type, party, and modality.

3   Methodology

In this section, we will specifically describe how our approach works. We firstly give an overview of our method with an example. After that, we will introduce the key procedures in detail including key words extraction, tag alignment and expression transformation, which will be explained in Sects. 3.2, 3.3 and 3.4 respectively.

3.1 Overview

Before an administrator configures any authorization policy, what one thing must have been done is to mark the persons and data defined in access control system as various tags according to their function and purpose. Tag is used to describe a group of entities that have common features and attributes, which are defined as a triplet ($\langle type \rangle, \langle name \rangle, \langle value \rangle$). For example, if we want to refer to all persons whose age is 16, the tag can be set to ($num, age, 16$). The formal definition of tag will be introduced in Sect. 3.2. How to mark and manage these tags is not our research focus. We suppose the administrator has correctly marked them. In the next procedure, we will use tag to refer to a group of entities.

We observe that any authorization policy has similar pattern. That is *who can (or cannot) access what*. There are three elements in this pattern, which are authorization subject, authorization object and authorization sign. We simply call them subject, object and sign respectively. Subject indicates who access data, while object is used to describe what data are accessed by people. Sign shows if subject is permitted to access object. A policy has two possible signs. These are *permit* and *deny*. Our objective is to dig out the three elements from input sentence to facilitate access control system to configure policies automatically. Subject and object are described by constraint expression about tag, and we obtain authorization sign by identifying if negative word is existed in the sentence.

When an input sentence comes, the first thing we need to do is to extract all key words that is useful to make certain of three elements in policy. These key words include name and value of tag, and some function words that represent logical or comparative relationship between tags. For example, in Fig. 1, *secretary* is a tag value that defined in tag name *job*, while *privilege level* and *security level* are tag names, which define values including A, B, C, D and E. A is the highest level while E is the lowest one. The function word *above* indicates what we refer to about privilege level is not only B level but all levels greater than B, like A level in this example. The function word *and* represents a logical relationship, which suggests leaders can access data, and at the same time, those secretaries whose privilege level is greater than B are also able to access data. These function words play a significant role in generating constraint expression correctly. Note that there is another kind of function word which is not shown in the example. That is negative word. The default authorization sign is *permit*, but if we identify any negative word, such as *not, forbid*, we will flip the sign to *deny*. The detail method of key words extraction will be illustrated in Sect. 3.2.

After key words extraction, we can obtain a sequence of key words. However, these key words should be well-organized to reflect complete semantics. We need to classify all tag values into the tag name that they belong to, and then we can get a complete triplet of tag. That process is called tag alignment. For example,

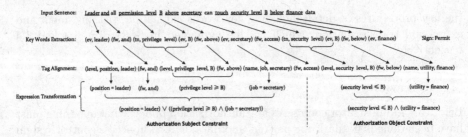

Fig. 1. An overview of our method with a specific example.

in Fig. 1, we have two tag values B, but B is defined in not only *privilege level* but also *security level*. A method should be designed to make certain of what tag names they need to be aligned with. We use the nearest search algorithm to align multi-defined values. We require the input sentence should explicitly express the tag name for multi-defined values, otherwise the sentence is ambiguous, and we will raise an exception. Note that for those values that have only one definition, we can align them directly with no explicit tag name because the alignment is unique. In Sect. 3.3, we will go into detail of tag alignment.

Once all tag values are aligned with their corresponding tag name, we can obtain a sequence that has well-organized semantics, which is composed of function words and triplets of tag. Next, we should transform the sequence semantics to constraint expression according to a set of parsing rules. These parsing rules are pre-defined in Appendix A. As shown in Fig. 1, the function word *access* is a boundary of sequence, and the left side describes authorization subject while the right side characterizes authorization object. As a result, the left part and right part are transformed to constraint expression of subject and object respectively. We will fully illustrate how a constraint expression is represented and transformed in Sect. 3.4.

3.2   Key Words Extraction

Before we start to go into detail, we firstly need to formally define tag, function word, and key word.

Definition 1 (Tag). *The tag $t \in T$ is used to describe a group of entities, which is a triplet, and $T \subseteq TC \times TN \times TV$, where*

- *TC is set of value types, $TC = \{name, level, num, time\}$.*
- *TN is set of tag names.*
- *TV is set of all values defined in tag names.*

In Definition 1, there are four types in TC, which are name type, level type, number type and time type. Name type and level type are very similar. They mean that their value is a string, and all values are finite and discrete. In other words, they define *enumeration values*. The only difference between name type and level type is that the values of level type have comparative relationship, which means we can compare these values, but name type doesn't have this feature. For example, *security level* has five values A, B, C, D and E. A is the highest level while E is the lowest one. Apparently, these values have comparative relationship. However, if we consider *department*, we could get technical department, business department, legal department and so on. Those values are independent, and we can't say business department is greater than technical department. Number type and time type mean their values are number and time respectively. Different from enumeration values, number and time are infinite and continuous. We cannot list them one by one, so we also call them *non-enumeration values*.

Definition 2 (Function Word). *The function word is the word that describes logical or comparative relationship between tags. The set of all function words are marked as FW.*

Definition 3 (Key Word). *The key word $k \in K$ is a 2-tuple, and $K \subseteq KC \times KW$, where*

- *KC is set of word classes, $KC = \{tn, ev, nev, fw\}$.*
- *KW is set of all useful words, $KW = TN \cup TV \cup FW$.*

In KC, ev and nev represent enumeration value and non-enumeration value respectively, which were illustrated before. The tn refer to tag name, and fw means function word. These words of the four classes are what we want to extract in the sentence. To extract key words, we firstly need to segment the sentence to individual words. Different from English, there is no space in Chinese characters. That's why word segmentation is very important for Chinese. Considering there are a large parts of domain terms and special expression in the sentence, which could be defined by administrator, we prepare a special-words database to improve accuracy of segmentation and identification. The database includes all pre-defined words such as tag names, enumeration values and function words.

However, even though we have the database of special words, we cannot list all values of time and number. To avoid them being segmented by mistake, we firstly use regular expression to match them. Then we add them into the database. We also parse them to analyze their formatted values. With this special-words database, we can cut the sentence more accurately.

What we must consider is that different people have various language customs. Synonym is very common in language use. To improve robustness, our goal is to identify not only the words in the database, but also their synonym. Word embedding [9,10] is a good way to quantitatively evaluate semantics similarity between words by mapping the word into a multi-dimensional vector and calculating the distance between them. In this paper, we use pre-trained Chinese word vector [8] to map words. However, there are two problems to be solved.

- **Out-of-Vocabulary (OOV).** As we mentioned before, special-words database has a large parts of domain terms and special expression, which are probably not in pre-trained word vector list, i.e., we may not find a vector to map those words. To the end, we need to continue segmentation of these words until all their slices have corresponding vector. We calculate vector of this kind of words as average of all their slices' vector. For example, the word *business consultant* is not in pre-trained word vector list, but *business* and *consultant* are. As a result, the vector of *business consultant* is calculated by the average vector of *business* and *consultant*.

- **Phrase-to-Word.** By having special-words database, those domain terms and special expression will not be segmented by mistake. However, this is inapplicable to their synonyms. In other words, synonyms in the input sentence could still be segmented to phrases. So, we need to deal with the problem of phrase-to-word matching. The key problem is to distinguish if a sentence word is independent or a part of phrase. In this paper, we use two-round identification. The first round is to identify independent words and get rid of all irrelevant words. Each word in the sentence will be calculated the similarity with all words in the database, and we can get the top similarity and its corresponding word in the database. If the similarity is high enough, i.e. greater than *one_round_threshold_high*, to guarantee the sentence word can exactly match a database word, we think the word in sentence is independent and we can directly match it. We also observe if the similarity is lower than *one_round_threshold_low*. If so, we will directly get rid of the sentence word because we regard it as irrelevant word. However, there are many words whose similarities are between these two thresholds. As a result, we need the second-round identification. We try to combine adjacent words into phrase as much as possible until the similarity of phrase prepares to decrease. If the final similarity is greater than *two_round_threshold*, we can match the phrase to the corresponding word in database. Usually *two_round_threshold* should be relatively smaller than *one_round_threshold_high* because the similarity of phrase matching is often lower than that of word matching.

We can finally get a sequence of key words. Note that there is a special key word called negative word. If negative word in the sequence, we will delete it and flip the authorization sign to *deny*. The whole algorithm of key words extraction is illustrated in Appendix B.

3.3   Tag Alignment

Key words should be well-organized to completely represent semantics of tags. The problem is that we need to align tag values with the tag name that they belong to. For some tag values defined only in one tag name, we can directly align them with no ambiguity. If a tag value is multi-defined, we require the input sentence should explicitly express its tag name. It is our observation that the tag value is usually very close to its tag name in the sentence. There is a good chance that the nearest tag name that the value is defined in is the correct alignment. So, we choose the nearest search algorithm to align those multi-defined tag values. The algorithm is described in Appendix C.

3.4   Expression Transformation

Our final goal is to make certain of authorization subject and object by extracting tags in the input sentence. A good way to describe them is constraint expression. To the end, we try to develop a special parser to analyze tag sequence according to a set of parsing rules pre-defined in Appendix A, and automatically transform it into constraint expression. Note that these rules have priority, which means that a rule can be processed only after all previous rules have been processed. We observe that the function word *(fw, access)* is a boundary word. The left part of sentence is used to describe subject, while the right part characterizes object. So, with the function word *(fw, access)*, the left part and right part of sentence are processed separately. Constraint expression is a logical expression, which is represented by a binary tree. The bottom-up strategy is adopted to generate constraint expression. It means that we construct the whole binary tree via obtaining the subtrees step by step. The detail algorithm is described in Appendix D.

4   Experiments

4.1   Experiment Settings

- *Groundtruth Dataset.* To model different language customs, we collect 150 sentences from 15 people. We manually extract their key words and align them. We also manually mark their constraint expressions and authorization signs. As a result, any item of groundtruth dataset includes six elements which are input sentence, key words sequence, tag sequence, subject constraint expression, object constraint expression and authorization sign.
- *Parameters.* In our experiments, we set *one_round_threshold_high* to 0.85, and *one_round_threshold_low*, *two_round_threshold* to 0.4, 0.7 respectively.
- *Implementation.* We use *jieba* [3], a famous Chinese word segmentor, to segment the input sentence. For the pre-trained Chinese word vector, we choose *baidubaike* [1] as the corpus, which can be regarded as Chinese Wikipedia. The corpus of *baidubaike* has more than 630,000 Chinese words. With such a large vocabulary, we believe it can relieve the OOV problem to the most extent. We measure the words similarity by cosine distance between vectors using the tool of *gensim* [2]. All the methods are implemented in Python 3.7.

4.2   Metrics

Since our method is made up of key words extraction, tag alignment and expression transformation, we will test the three components individually. We will also have systematic evaluations on the whole method. For key words extraction and tag alignment, these procedures' result is a sequence. We use precision, recall and F1-score to analyze their performance, which are defined as follows:

$$Precision = \frac{TP}{TP + FP}$$

$$Recall = \frac{TP}{TP + FN}$$

$$F1 = \frac{2 * Precision * Recall}{Precision + Recall}$$

where true positive (TP) means the number of sequence elements that are correctly identified, false positive (FP) means the number of sequence elements that are misidentified, false negative (FN) is the number of correct sequence elements that are not identified.

The result of expression transformation is a binary tree. Our idea is that we measure similarity between groundtruth binary tree and the one obtained from algorithm to model the accuracy of transformation. However, it's very time-consuming to directly compare tree-structured data similarity [19]. But we note that the result is a binary tree, we can uniquely transform a binary tree to a sequence via post-order traversal without any loss of structure information. Then the problem of tree-structured data similarity is changed to that of sequence similarity. Edit distance is a generally accepted way to measure sequence similarity. In this paper, we use Levenshtein distance [7] to model the accuracy of expression transformation. The Levenshtein distance between two sequences is the minimum number of edit operations, including insertions, deletions and substitutions, required to change one sequence into the other. Obviously, the maximum Levenshtein distance between two sequences is the maximum length of them. Thus, we can model expression transformation accuracy as follows:

$$Acc = 1 - \frac{ld}{maxlength}$$

where ld is Levenshtein distance between the sequences from algorithm result and its groundtruth, $maxlength$ is the maximum length of them.

4.3   Evaluations on Key Words Extraction and Tag Alignment

In this section, we will test the performance of key words extraction and tag alignment independently. Note that in real-world scenario, the results of key words extraction procedure will affect tag alignment because the procedure of tag alignment needs to accept the results of key words extraction. However, since we are doing independent test now, in order to control variable, we use groundtruth of key words sequence for evaluating tag alignment.

Firstly, we want to evaluate their average performance over all test samples. Table 1 lists experiment results. The average F1-score of key words extraction is 96.57%, while that of tag alignment is 98.60%. These results indicate that key words extraction and tag alignment have good overall performance.

We also want to investigate deeply in each sample. Figure 2 shows samples distribution about precision, recall, and F1-score, which are illustrated by normalized histograms. In Fig. 2a, we know that 83.33% of samples whose F1-score is greater than 90% in key words extraction. Figure 2b shows that in the experiment of tag alignment, 91.33% of samples' F1-score is over 90%. That means most of samples can get good results.

Table 1. The average performance of key words extraction and tag alignment over all test samples.

	TP	FP	FN	Precision(%)	Recall(%)	F1-score(%)
Key words Extraction	1015	39	33	96.30	96.85	96.57
Tag alignment	879	5	20	99.43	97.78	98.60

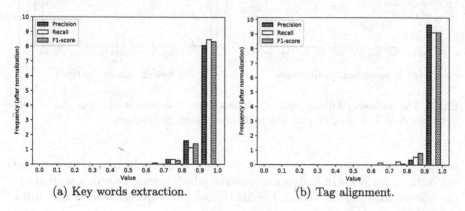

(a) Key words extraction.   (b) Tag alignment.

Fig. 2. The normalized histograms of samples about precision, recall, and F1-score to show samples distribution.

4.4 Evaluations on Expression Transformation

In this section, we are going to independently test the performance of expression transformation. In order to control variable, we also use groundtruth of tag sequence to evaluate expression transformation. For the average performance, we find that subject constraint transformation can get 97.24% accuracy, while object constraint transformation can get 99.22% accuracy. Generally, if we regard overall accuracy of constraint expression transformation as the mean value of two accuracies just mentioned, we can get 98.23% overall transformation accuracy.

We also want to investigate samples distribution about transformation accuracies of subject constraint and object constraint. In Fig. 3a, we can see that 86.67% of samples get accuracy over 90% for subject constraint transformation, and if we focus on transformation of object constraint, 96.00% of samples can get accuracy over 90%. It indicates that expression transformation performs well not only overall but individually.

4.5 Systematic Evaluations

The previous sections focus on independent test, which means we only test one procedure's performance per experiment. However, in real-world scenario, the three procedures will be integrated into a system, and their results will influence each other. Therefore, we are also interested in the system's overall performance.

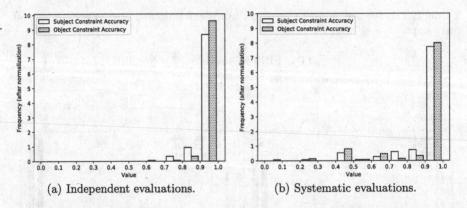

(a) Independent evaluations.   (b) Systematic evaluations.

Fig. 3. The normalized histograms of samples about transformation accuracies of subject constraint and object constraint to show samples distribution.

In this section, we are going to have systematic evaluations to observe how well our method performs in real-world scenario, which means we give a sentence to the system, and directly obtain the final constraint expressions and the authorization sign.

According to our evaluations, we get 92.16% accuracy of subject constraint transformation, and 90.85% accuracy of object constraint transformation on average. We calculate overall accuracy of constraint expression transformation by mean value of these two accuracies, which is 91.51%. Likewise, samples distribution is illustrated in Fig. 3b, which shows that 77.33% of samples get accuracy over 90% for subject constraint transformation, and for object constraint transformation, 80.00% of samples can get accuracy over 90%. Note that the results of systematic evaluations are a little worse than that of independent test. This is because the results of systematic evaluations incorporate all errors from the system's three procedures. Even so, it still performs well in real-world scenario.

Next, we want to test accuracy of authorization signs. In our evaluations, 94.67% of authorization signs are correctly identified. We also test average time for processing each sentence, which is about 0.114 s per sentence. It means our method's cost is very low.

5   Conclusion and Future Work

In this paper, we try to use Chinese sentence to tell ABAC system how to configure authorization policies automatically. Our approach includes procedures of key words extraction, tag alignment and expression transformation. Synonym is very common in language use because different people have various language customs. We use word embedding to quantitatively measure the similarity between words by vector distance. We also provide our own solutions to two practical problems of OOV and Phrase-to-Word. Finally, we can get subject constraint expression, object constraint expression, and authorization sign. With these three necessary elements, ABAC system is able to configure authorization policies automatically.

However, there are still some limitations in our scheme. Though the sentence in requirement specification is relatively standard, the rule-based method is difficult to deal with highly abstract sentences. Ellipsis and implication are common in daily language use, but they are too vague to be recognized by machines. Ambiguity is also a problem. We believe that state-of-the-art machine learning models can relieve these problems, but the effectiveness of these models is highly dependent on a large amount of high-quality labeled data. Collecting such domain-specific labeled data is not easy. Semi-supervised learning and Generative Adversarial Networks could be promising choices, but we still need to examine their feasibility.

A   Parsing Rules for Tag Sequence

Note that these parsing rules have priority. The first rule has the highest priority, while the last one has the lowest priority. To describe the rules exactly, we directly express them as Chinese.

$$(time, n, v_1)(fw, 到)(time, n, v_2) \rightarrow ((n \geq v_1) \wedge (n \leq v_2))$$
$$(num, n, v_1)(fw, 到)(num, n, v_2) \rightarrow ((n \geq v_1) \wedge (n \leq v_2))$$
$$(fw, 晚于)(time, n, v) \rightarrow (n \geq v)$$
$$(fw, 早于)(time, n, v) \rightarrow (n \leq v)$$
$$(time, n, v)(fw, 以后) \rightarrow (n \geq v)$$
$$(time, n, v)(fw, 以前) \rightarrow (n \leq v)$$
$$(fw, 大于)(level \vee num, n, v) \rightarrow (n \geq v)$$
$$(fw, 小于)(level \vee num, n, v) \rightarrow (n \leq v)$$
$$(level \vee num, n, v)(fw, 以上) \rightarrow (n \geq v)$$
$$(level \vee num, n, v)(fw, 以下) \rightarrow (n \leq v)$$
$$(name \vee level \vee num \vee time, n, v) \rightarrow (n = v)$$
$$(< expr\,1 >)(< expr\,2 >) \rightarrow ((< expr\,1 >) \wedge (< expr\,2 >))$$
$$(< expr\,1 >)(fw, 和)(< expr\,2 >) \rightarrow ((< expr\,1 >) \vee (< expr\,2 >))$$

where $< expr\,n >$ represents constraint expression.

B   Algorithm for Key Words Extraction

Algorithm 1. Key Words Extraction

Input: the input sentence *stce*, the pre-trained Chinese word vector list *wv*, the special-words database *swd*.

Output: the key words sequence *kwseq*, the authorization sign *sign*.

```
 1 time_num_words ← match_time_and_num_by_regular_expression(stce)
 2 time_num_values ← parse_time_and_num_to_formatted_value(time_num_words)
 3 for each w ∈ swd do
 4     swd_vector[w] ← GetOOVVector(w)
 5 end for
 6 s ← Segmentor().add_words(swd + time_num_words)
 7 kwseq ← s.cut(stce), i ← 0, sign ← permit
 8 for each w ∈ kwseq do
 9     if w ∈ time_num_words then
10         w.replace_to((nev, time_num_values[w]))
11     else
12         w_vec ← GetOOVVector(w)
13         (top_similarity, top_word) ← find_most_similar_word(w_vec, swd_vector)
14         if top_similarity ≥ one_round_threshold_high then
15             w.replace_to((get_word_class_in_KC(top_word), top_word))
16         else if top_similarity ≤ one_round_threshold_low then
17             w.delete()
18         end if
19     end if
20 end for
21 while i < length(kwseq) do
22     if type(kwseq[i]) is not the 2-tuple of key words then
23         prev_similarity ← 0, j ← i
24         while (type(kwseq[j]) is not the 2-tuple of key words) and (j < length(kwseq)) do
25             phrase ← combine words from index i to index j
26             w_vec ← GetOOVVector(phrase)
27             (top_similarity, top_word) ← find_most_similar_word(w_vec, swd_vector)
28             if top_similarity ≥ prev_similarity then
29                 prev_similarity ← top_similarity, prev_word ← top_word, j ← j + 1
30             else
31                 break
32             end if
33         end while
34         if prev_similarity ≥ two_round_threshold then
35             replace words from i to j - 1 into (get_word_class_in_KC(prev_word), prev_word)
36         else
37             delete kwseq[i], i ← i - 1
38         end if
39     end if
40     i ← i + 1
41 end while
42 if (fw, deny) ∈ kwseq then
43     delete (fw, deny), sign ← deny
44 end if
45
46 function GETOOVVECTOR(word)
47     if word ∈ wv then
48         return wv[word]
49     else
50         word_list ← Segmentor().cut(word)
51         initialize average_vector to empty vector
52         for each w ∈ word_list do
53             if w ∉ wv then
54                 average_vector += wv[ws] for each ws ∈ w.cut_to_character_list()
55             else
56                 average_vector += wv[w]
57             end if
58         end for
59         return average_vector
60     end if
61 end function
```

C   Algorithm for Tag Alignment

Algorithm 2. Tag Alignment

Input: the key words sequence *kwseq*.
Output: the sequence *tagseq* including only function words and triplets of tag.

```
 1  initialize tagseq to empty array
 2  for each (kc, kw) ∈ kwseq do
 3      if (kc = ev) and (kw is only defined in tn_match) then
 4          tc_match ← find_type_in_TC(tn_match)
 5          tagseq.insert_at_end((tc_match, tn_match, kw))
 6      else if kc = fw then
 7          tagseq.insert_at_end((kc, kw))
 8      else if (kc = ev) or (kc = nev) then
 9          idx ← kwseq.index((kc, kw)), left ← idx - 1, right ← idx + 1, flag ← False
10          while (left ≥ 0) or (right < length(kwseq)) do
11              if left ≥ 0 then
12                  if (kwseq[left].kc = tn) and (kw is defined in kwseq[left].kw) then
13                      tc_match ← find_type_in_TC(kwseq[left].kw)
14                      tagseq.insert_at_end((tc, kwseq[left].kw, kw))
15                      flag ← True, break
16                  end if
17                  left ← left - 1
18              end if
19              if right < length(kwseq) then
20                  if (kwseq[right].kc = tn) and (kw is defined in kwseq[right].kw) then
21                      tc_match ← find_type_in_TC(kwseq[right].kw)
22                      tagseq.insert_at_end((tc, kwseq[right].kw, kw))
23                      flag ← True, break
24                  end if
25                  right ← right + 1
26              end if
27          end while
28          if flag = False then
29              raise Exception("Sentence is ambiguous")
30          end if
31      end if
32  end for
```

D   Algorithm for Expression Transformation

Algorithm 3. Expression Transformation

Input: *tagseq* obtained from Algorithm 2 output, the pre-defined parsing rules *rules_list*.
Output: the subject constraint expression *sub_expr*, the object constraint expression *obj_expr*.

```
 1  (sub_expr, obj_expr) ← tagseq.split_by((fw, access))
 2  for each r ∈ rules_list do
 3      if sub_expr[i..j] can match r then
 4          expr_t ← generate expression subtree according to r
 5          replace sub_expr[i..j] to expr_t
 6      end if
 7      if obj_expr[m..n] can match r then
 8          expr_t ← generate expression subtree according to r
 9          replace obj_expr[m..n] to expr_t
10      end if
11  end for
```

References

1. Baidubaike corpus. https://github.com/Embedding/Chinese-Word-Vectors
2. Gensim. https://radimrehurek.com/gensim/
3. Jieba. https://github.com/fxsjy/jieba/
4. Chen, Y., et al.: Devils in the guidance: predicting logic vulnerabilities in payment syndication services through automated documentation analysis. In: 28th {USENIX} Security Symposium ({USENIX} Security 2019), pp. 747–764 (2019)
5. Fedrecheski, G., De Biase, L.C.C., Calcina-Ccori, P.C., Zuffo, M.K.: Attribute-based access control for the swarm with distributed policy management. IEEE Trans. Consum. Electron. **65**(1), 90–98 (2018)
6. Hu, V.C., et al.: Guide to attribute based access control (abac) definition and considerations (draft). NIST Spec. Publ. **800**(162), 1–54 (2013)
7. Levenshtein, V.I.: Binary codes capable of correcting deletions, insertions, and reversals. In: Soviet Physics Doklady, vol. 10, pp. 707–710. Soviet Union (1966)
8. Li, S., Zhao, Z., Hu, R., Li, W., Liu, T., Du, X.: Analogical reasoning on chinese morphological and semantic relations. In: Proceedings of the 56th Annual Meeting of the Association for Computational Linguistics (Short Papers), vol. 2, pp. 138–143. Association for Computational Linguistics (2018). http://aclweb.org/anthology/P18-2023
9. Mikolov, T., Chen, K., Corrado, G., Dean, J.: Efficient estimation of word representations in vector space. arXiv preprint arXiv:1301.3781 (2013)
10. Mikolov, T., Sutskever, I., Chen, K., Corrado, G., Dean, J.: Distributed representations of words and phrases and their compositionality. arXiv preprint arXiv:1310.4546 (2013)
11. Narouei, M., Khanpour, H., Takabi, H., Parde, N., Nielsen, R.: Towards a top-down policy engineering framework for attribute-based access control. In: Proceedings of the 22nd ACM on Symposium on Access Control Models and Technologies, pp. 103–114 (2017)
12. Narouei, M., Takabi, H.: Automatic top-down role engineering framework using natural language processing techniques. In: Akram, R.N., Jajodia, S. (eds.) WISTP 2015. LNCS, vol. 9311, pp. 137–152. Springer, Cham (2015). https://doi.org/10.1007/978-3-319-24018-3_9
13. Narouei, M., Takabi, H.: Towards an automatic top-down role engineering approach using natural language processing techniques. In: Proceedings of the 20th ACM Symposium on Access Control Models and Technologies, pp. 157–160 (2015)
14. Narouei, M., Takabi, H., Nielsen, R.: Automatic extraction of access control policies from natural language documents. IEEE Trans. Dependable Secure Comput. **17**(3), 506–517 (2018)
15. Slankas, J., Williams, L.: Access control policy extraction from unconstrained natural language text. In: 2013 International Conference on Social Computing, pp. 435–440. IEEE (2013)
16. Slankas, J., Xiao, X., Williams, L., Xie, T.: Relation extraction for inferring access control rules from natural language artifacts. In: Proceedings of the 30th Annual Computer Security Applications Conference, pp. 366–375 (2014)
17. Story, P., et al.: Natural language processing for mobile app privacy compliance. In: AAAI Spring Symposium on Privacy-Enhancing Artificial Intelligence and Language Technologies (2019)

18. Xiao, X., Paradkar, A., Thummalapenta, S., Xie, T.: Automated extraction of security policies from natural-language software documents. In: Proceedings of the ACM SIGSOFT 20th International Symposium on the Foundations of Software Engineering, pp. 1–11 (2012)
19. Yang, R., Kalnis, P., Tung, A.K.: Similarity evaluation on tree-structured data. In: Proceedings of the 2005 ACM SIGMOD International Conference on Management of Data, pp. 754–765 (2005)

A Data-Free Approach for Targeted Universal Adversarial Perturbation

Xiaoyu Wang[1(✉)], Tao Bai[1,2], and Jun Zhao[1,2]

[1] Xi'an Jiaotong University, Xi'an, China
wxystudio@stu.xjtu.edu.cn
[2] Nanyang Technological University, Jurong West, Singapore
{bait0002,JunZhao}@ntu.edu.sg

Abstract. The existence of adversarial example problem puts forward high demand on the robustness of neural network. This paper proposes a universal adversarial perturbation(UAP) attack method in data-free scenario, which can realize targeted attack to any class specified by the attacker. We design a unique loss function to balance the purpose of perturbing model and targeting label. As far as we know, our method is the first UAP attack method that can achieve targeted attack in data-free scenario. Especially, in federated learning a malicious user can fool other users' model without being noticed. We hope our attack method can inspire more researchers in the community, and enable them to better understand and defend against UAP attacks.

Keywords: Universal adversarial perturbation · Data free · Federated learning

1 Introduction

In the last few years, the vulnerability of deep neural network has received tremendous attention from academia. many studies [6,12] show that neural network can be affected by adversarial example attack. Training with the model under attack, attacker obtains a small perturbation which can't be recognized by human(which is usually limited to $-10 \sim 10$ pixel values). The attacker adds the unrecognizable perturbation to one natural image so that the model recognizes this image incorrectly.

But there are some drawbacks in adversarial example attack. Each perturbation only corresponds to one specific sample, which is cumbersome in launching attack. For this reason, universal adversarial perturbation [15] is proposed. Compared with traditional adversarial example attack, it does not generate a corresponding perturbation for each data, but creates a universal perturbation for all data in the whole dataset. The targeted UAP attack can make the data misclassified by the model into a specific category.

Supported by organization Nanyang Technological University.

W. Lu et al. (Eds.): SciSec 2021, LNCS 13005, pp. 126–138, 2021.
https://doi.org/10.1007/978-3-030-89137-4_9

What's not good enough is that, the above attacks totally rely on the attacker mastering the real dataset. In reality, this condition is very harsh. Therefore, some researchers proposed data-free attack, which uses membership-inference data [20], GAN-generation data [21], or creates data from Gaussian distribution [16,17] to replace the original training dataset. For this kind of attack, the attacker doesn't need to have access to real data so that can launch attack more conveniently.

However, we found that none of the above methods can achieve targeted UAP attack in data-free scenario. In reality the attacker not only can't get in touch with the real training data, but also want to launch targeted attack. For example, in an autonomous driving scenario, it will be more threatening to confuse a model to recognize the "stop" road sign as "acceleration", than only regard it as "slow down". Based on the above analysis, this kind of attack is of great practical significance.

In this paper we introduce a more dangerous scenario. In 2016, Google[14] introduce federated learning, which can launch a cloud platform for distributedly training neural network with multiple users. It has two obvious advantages:

1. It can make use of all users' data to train a general model. Some people who are lack of data can train a model by crowd sourcing.
2. Users can deal with their own data locally without uploading their own data to the platform, which avoids some privacy issues.

In the federated learning scenario, each user possesses one portion of data. If a malicious user want to launch UAP attack to global model or even target one specific label, he will face the problem of data insufficiency. In this typical environment, previous UAP attack methods will fail.

For the above reasons, In this paper we propose a new universal adversarial perturbation attack method. Our method can achieve targeted attack in data-free scenario, and we have done experiments to verify in natural and man-made scenes, which proves our work is of great practical significance Fig. 1.

In summary, our contribution is:

1. We propose a new universal adversarial attack method. As far as we know, we are the first to propose a targeted attack method in data-free scenario. Especially It can seriously threaten the security of federated learning.
2. We design a unique loss function for our attack, which combines the purpose of perturbing the model prediction and making it move towards one specific label.
3. We do experiments to verify the feasibility of our attack method on a variety of computer vision application scenarios, including natural scene and autonomous driving, especially in federated learning.

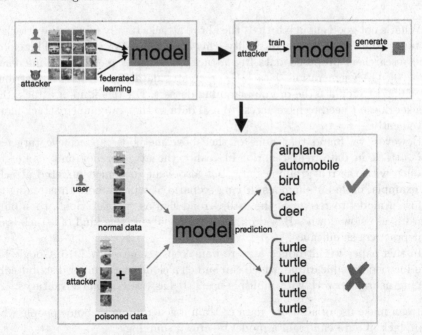

Fig. 1. This is the main process of targeted UAP attack launched in federated learning scenario. All users train a global model and a malicious user has access to the model, then uses it to generate a small perturbation. After adding the perturbation to natural image, the prediction of model will be totally wrong. The single perturbation is applicable to all the data in dataset, so we call it universal adversarial perturbation(UAP). In this figure we target all the perturbed images into "turtle" class.

2   Related Work

Moosavi-Dezfooli *et al.* [15] proposed universal adversarial perturbation and did experiments on classification task. However, their attack cannot target a specific label, and the attackers need to have the original training data of the model. The subsequent UAP attacks are generally divided into two directions, targeted and untargeted attacks. We mainly introduce targeted attacks here. Poursaeed *et al.* [19] introduced a GAN-based method [5] to launch UAP attacks. Brown *et al.* [2] demonstrated that they can use adversarial patch to create UAP, but the visual effect of their attack is so obvious that human can easily distinguish the attacked data. Hirano *et al.* [8] showed that an improved version of FGSM [13] can realize the targeted UAP attack. Benz *et al.* [1] proposed a double targeted attack method which can make model recognize one specific class data as another. Finlayson *et al.* [4] adopted UAP attack to medical images, so that a kind of cancerous cell can be identified incorrectly.

But the above methods both require the attacker have the training dataset of the model they want to attack. In reality, this prerequisite is very harsh. Zhang *et al.* [23] applied a completely unrelated dataset to be treated as proxy data to generate targeted UAP. Mopuri *et al.* [17] randomly selected samples from Gaussian distribution and a special loss can be used to amplify the output of each layer of the model, thereby changing the final prediction result. Later they [16] sampled from the Gaussian distribution as proxy data and used a special loss function to make the output of each layer artificially amplified, which makes the final prediction result incorrect. In the end Mopuri *et al.* [20] concluded to use membership inference method [22] to infer the training dataset, and the inferred data is used to replace the original data for training, finally the UAP perturbation is obtained. Sam *et al.* [21] analyzed a new data-free UAP generation framework based on the linearity assumption.

However, we claim that the above research has obvious limitations. Among them, the UAP attack method used in the data-free scenario cannot achieve targeted attack, which is very important for attacker. Therefore, we propose an attack method that can be used in data-free scenario and can realize a targeted attack. After that, we do experiments to verify our idea on a variety of tasks.

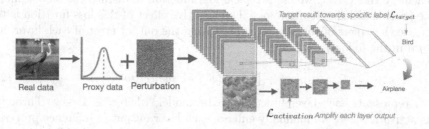

Fig. 2. This is the basic framework of our attack method. To achieve the goal of targeted attack in data-free scenario, we design two key loss functions. The first is activation loss. It artificially amplifies the output of each layer in the model and finally corrupts the model prediction. The second is target loss, because we want the prediction to be specific to one label as much as possible, we add a CrossEntropy loss to manually guide the direction of optimization. Finally our attack can make the model prediction to target one specific label.

3   Our Approach

3.1   Universal Adversarial Attack

In universal adversarial training, considering a neural network model f, attacker often initialize a restricted perturbation (e.g., $-10 \sim 10$ pixels), which is unrecognized by human. Then the perturbation is trained with some well-designed algorithms, until being added to one image can be predicted as a wrong category. In the theoretical framework, UAP attack can be understood as follow:

$$f(x) \neq f(x + \delta) \text{ subject to } \delta \in \Delta \tag{1}$$

f(x) is the model we want to attack, x is the image which will be classified. δ represents the perturbation, and Δ controls the pixel range of the perturbation, which is usually $[-10, 10]$ pixels. To achieve this object, the common method is to manually control the direction of optimization. In the neural network-based model attack, researchers usually adjust optimization process by defining the optimization method and loss function.

3.2 Data-Free Targeted UAP

In traditional UAP attack, the disturbed prediction label is not regular, which is not practical to attacker in reality. We design a loss function to balance the purpose of perturbing model prediction and targeting one label, which is divided into activation Loss and target loss. The details are shown in the Fig. 2.

Activation Loss. In the data-free scenario, we sample data from the Gaussian distribution as proxy data to train a pertuabation. Our goal is adding the perturbation to the real data and confuse the model to output a wrong prediction. To achieve this target, we use a typical loss function to disturb the model inference process called activation loss. The intuitive effect of this loss function is to increase the power of the attack by increasing the output error of each layer, as shown in the following formula:

$$\mathcal{L}_{activation} = - \prod_{i=1}^{n} l_i(x + \delta) \ subject \ to \ \delta \in \Delta \tag{2}$$

l_i represents each layer function in the model, where $i \in 1 \sim n$. Through this activation loss, we manually enlarge each layer output in inference process, which causes seriously influence to final prediction of the model. But there is a side effect that we can't know what direction do we push the optimization forward. So we design a target loss to constrain the uncertainty.

Target Loss. The targeted attack needs to design a loss function so that the prediction result is given into a specified category by the model. The training goal can be expressed as follow:

$$f(x + \delta) = y_i, f(x) = y_j, y_i \neq y_j, y_i, y_j \in Y \tag{3}$$

where y_i and y_j are different labels, Y is the set of labels.

In order to achieve this goal, we use a CrossEntropy loss function to manually "push" the prediction result forward to specific label:

$$\mathcal{L}_{target} = -log \frac{exp(y_{target})}{\Sigma_{j=1}^{n} exp(y_j)} \tag{4}$$

where the y_{target} is the specific label which attacker want to target.

3.3   Update Perturbation

Finally we combine the above two loss functions to achieve our attack, which is a targeted universal adversarial perturbation attack in data-free scenario. In every training epoch, we update the perturbation by Backpropagation with the model parameter fixed. Finally we can attach this obtained perturbation to any data we want to attack.

3.4   Algorithm

Algorithm 1. data-free targeted UAP

Input:

the adversary of pixel δ, the initial perturbation δ_0, the targeted model f, the proxy data d_i sampled from Gaussian distribution $N(\mu, \sigma^2)$ per epoch, the training epoch time E, the output after activation of each layer l_j

Output:

the final result δ

Train:

  for epoch i in range(E):
  $\qquad input \leftarrow d_i, \delta_i$
  $\qquad output \leftarrow f(d_i + \delta_i)$
  $\qquad \mathcal{L}_{activation} \leftarrow = \prod_{j=1}^{n} l_j(x + \delta)$
  $\qquad \mathcal{L}_{target} \leftarrow CrossEntropy(output, target)$
  $\qquad \mathcal{L}_{total} \leftarrow \mathcal{L}_{activation} + \mathcal{L}_{target}$
  $\qquad \delta_i \leftarrow \delta_i + \frac{\partial \mathcal{F}}{\partial \delta_i}(\mathcal{L}_{activation} + \mathcal{L}_{target})$
  $\qquad \delta_i = clip(\delta_i)$
  $\qquad \delta_{i+1} = \delta_i$
  end for

---

4   Federated Learning

In 2016, McMahan *et al.* [14] proposed the federated learning, a distributed training method for neural network model. In this scenario, all users train with their own data locally and then update the parameters to global model, which not only avoids revealing private data but also obtains a more powerful model.

4.1   Difficulties in UAP Attack

But there are lots of privacy issues in federated learning. The Basic reason is all users have access to the global model, which will reveal much information about the training data. When a malicious user camouflages in ordinary users and joins the training process, he can generate a perturbation to confuse the global model. But there are some difficulties. The first is the attacker only has a part of data. In the worst case, he will only have access to one category data. The second is that if the attacker want to launch UAP attack to one target label, but he possibly has not ever seen data in this category. The above difficulties highly hinders people implement UAP attack in federated learning scenario.

4.2   Threaten to Model

Our attack method brings too much threaten to federated learning. Note that in usual federated learning process, all users only have a part of data(in our experiment, data is manually separated into multiple sets). Sometimes the attacker even doesn't have the specific category's data he want to attack. So when the malicious user want to launch a UAP attack targeting one label, it is hard to use previous UAP attack method. Our data-free targeted UAP attack method is a perfect solution to this problem. We verify the practicability of our idea in the experiment.

5   Experimental Results

5.1   Experiment Setup

We do experiments on dataset CIFAR 10 [11], GTSRB [9] and CIFAR 100. CIFAR 10 is a classification dataset containing 60000 32x32 images in 10 classes, with 6000 images per class. CIFAR 100 is just like the CIFAR-10, except it has 100 classes containing 600 images each. The 100 classes in the CIFAR-100 are grouped into 20 superclasses. Each image comes with a "fine" label and a "coarse" label. The GTSRB dataset is prepared for single-image, multi-class classification problem in autonomous driving. It consists of more than 40 classes traffic signs and more than 50,000 images in total. Each of images is of different views and illumination. After experimental verification, we confirm that our algorithm can achieve targeted UAP in data-free scenario. As far as we know, we are the first researchers to achieve this attack.

Our experiment includes multiple backbones, from resnet18 [7] to resnet152. The initial model was pretrained on Imagenet [3], and then we trained on the relative dataset. The optimizer we use is Adam [10], and the training framework is pytorch [18].

5.2   Metrics

We use fooling rate as the standard metrics to evaluate our attack success rate. We define the total number of data in the dataset as M. After adding the created perturbation to the data, the number of data which is labeled as targeted label is m. Then we can calculate the fooling rate is m/M.

Note that there exists some data which is previously labeled as targeted data, but we don't excluded them. Because there are also some data which is labeled as targeted category before, while is not labeled as targeted category after being perturbed. We refer to previous research about this topic and they all ignore this condition. So our metrics makes sense.

5.3   Classification Result

The classification results on various datasets are in Table 1 and Table 2, which is consistent with our analysis. With the model gets deeper, it contains more information of the real dataset, so we can extract more unrecognized feature from the model. When we add the perturbation to original image, the deeper model will be more likely to be confused.

Table 1. Classification fooling rate in CIFAR 10 and GTSRB

Fooling Rate \ Model Dataset	Resnet18	Resnet34	Resnet152
CIFAR 10	68.4 %	71.1 %	72.3 %
GTSRB	61.2 %	63.1 %	64.2 %

CIFAR100. In CIFAR100, due to the limited space we only show 7 categories attack result.

Table 2. Classification fooling rate CIFAR100. Due to the limitation of space, we only list 7 coarse classes result.

Fooling Rate \ Class Model	Fish	Flowers	Food Containers	Fruit&Vegetables	Insects	People	Trees
Resnet18	51.1 %	54.3 %	46.2 %	71.2 %	68.1 %	40.1 %	59.1 %
Resnet34	50.4 %	58.2 %	46.7 %	73.1 %	69.4 %	40.2 %	57.3 %
Resnet152	52.8 %	59.1 %	49.3 %	74.7 %	72.1 %	44.1 %	62.1 %

CIFAR10. In CIFAR 10, we present the total fooling rate over 9 categories(one label left for targeted label) in Table 1.

| airplane | mobile | cat | deer | dog | frog | horse | ship | truck |
| bird | bird | bird | bird | bird | bird | bird | bird | bird |

Fig. 3. This is the attack result on CIFAR 10 dataset. All the other 9 categories data perturbed are classified as bird.

GTSRB. In GTSRB, we choose 10 non-digit labels for training, because we think digit label have more correlation than non-digit label, which will be more easy to launch UAP attack. The non-digit label can completely remove the influence of correlation.

sign 1   sign 2   sign 3   sign 4   sign 5   sign 6   sign 7   sign 8   sign 9

number number number number number number number number number

Fig. 4. This is the attack result on GTSRB dataset. In this dataset there exist 42 categories, where has 10 digit classes and others are non-digit classes. We consider all the digit classes as one class. We choose 11 non-digit classes to attack because we think the inter-digit classes attack will be more easy, which can't demonstrate the power of our attack method. Finally the non-digit class data all be classified as numbers.

Fig. 5. This is the attack result on CIFAR10 dataset.

Fig. 6. This is the attack result on GTSRB dataset.

Fig. 7. The sample previously labeled as others but classified as "bird"

5.4 Transferability

We find that the UAP attack has transferability, which means the UAP generated from one model can fool another model probably. This phenomenon shows the essence of UAP is some real features of natural things but can't be recognized by human. The attacker can use one proxy model to create UAP then attack the real application model. As Table 3 shows, we find that the UAP trained on deeper model is more likely to attack the shallower model. We think the reason is the same as the principle of ResNet. [7] It can be considered that the deeper model contains the whole feature and information in shallower model. It is equal to use deeper model to "inference" the shallower model. The experimental result is perfectly in line with our expectations.

Table 3. Transferability across three model type. The trained model is the user model trained with original dataset, the attack model is the attacker want to fool

Fooling Rate Attack Model Trained Model	Resnet18	Resnet34	Resnet152
Resnet18	-	42.3 %	26.2 %
Resnet34	43.1 %	-	36.7 %
Resnet152	32.8 %	39.1 %	-

5.5   Federated Learning

We launch the federated learning experiment in i.i.d (independent and identically distributed) environment. The data is split into 5 parts and each user possess one. We choose one user as attacker. After training a global model the malicious user starts an UAP attack.

We show the baseline of federated learning training result and the attack fooling rate as follows:

Table 4. This is the federated learning result. Accuracy denotes the baseline model accuracy of federated learning. Fooling rate represents the attack precision when a malicious user want to launch our unique UAP attack to the global model.

Dataset	Accuracy	Fooling rate
MNIST	97.1%	81.2%
CIFAR10	92.3%	72.1%
GTSRB	93.6%	62.5%

Note that both the accuracy and fooling rate are a little worse than normal training. Because the parameter lost in federated learning algorithm and communication, we can only get a lower performance model. But we can verify our method is suitable for federated learning environment, bringing high risk to user security.

6   Discussion

6.1   Defense of UAP Attack

As we know, the UAP attack is essentially utilizing some unrecognized feature in natural things, so the direct way to defense UAP attack is to repeatedly train the model with real data that added perturbation. But this is not feasible in reality. Because the users can't train the model iteratively while using it. Due to the limited space, we do not give the corresponding experimental results here. We hope the community can find an effective solution to this problem.

6.2 Federated Learning Data Distribution

In this article we separate data into independent identically distribution, which is reasonable. In traditional federated learning scenario, researchers often split dataset into i.i.d and non-i.i.d. Usually the classification result will be worse in non-i.i.d than result in i.i.d. We ignore the non-i.i.d environment because of the diversity of data volume in each category. Suppose the extreme case where no data sample is in one category or all the data are in one category, the fooling rate will be much different in such two case. So we launch the federated learning experiment in i.i.d scenario.

7 Conclusion

In this article, we implement a data-free UAP attack method that can target a specific label in data-free scenario. As far as we know, we are the first researchers to achieve it. and we claim our method will bring much threaten to federated learning when a user is malicious. In the future work, there are still some problems to be solved, such as the theoretical explanation of adversarial examples, how to effectively defend against adversarial examples and how to use adversarial examples to help us understand biological computer vision.

Acknowledgement. This paper is supported by 1) Singapore Ministry of Education Academic Research Fund Tier 1 RG128/18, Tier 1 RG115/19, Tier 1 RT07/19, Tier 1 RT01/19, Tier 1 RG24/20, and Tier 2 MOE2019-T2-1-176, 2) NTU-WASP Joint Project, 3) Singapore NRF National Satellite of Excellence, Design Science and Technology for Secure Critical Infrastructure NSoE DeST-SCI2019-0012, 4) AI Singapore (AISG) 100 Experiments (100E) programme, and 5) NTU Project for Large Vertical Take-Off & Landing (VTOL) Research Platform.

References

1. Benz, P., Zhang, C., Imtiaz, T., Kweon, I.S.: Double targeted universal adversarial perturbations. In: Proceedings of the Asian Conference on Computer Vision (2020)
2. Brown, T.B., Mané, D., Roy, A., Abadi, M., Gilmer, J.: Adversarial patch. arXiv preprint arXiv:1712.09665 (2017)
3. Deng, J., Dong, W., Socher, R., Li, L.J., Li, K., Fei-Fei, L.: Imagenet: a large-scale hierarchical image database. In: 2009 IEEE Conference on Computer Vision and Pattern Recognition, pp. 248–255. IEEE (2009)
4. Finlayson, S.G., Bowers, J.D., Ito, J., Zittrain, J.L., Beam, A.L., Kohane, I.S.: Adversarial attacks on medical machine learning. Science **363**(6433), 1287–1289 (2019)

5. Goodfellow, I., et al.: Generative adversarial nets. Adv. Neural Inf. Process. Syst. **27**, 2672–2680 (2014)
6. Goodfellow, I.J., Shlens, J., Szegedy, C.: Explaining and harnessing adversarial examples. arXiv preprint arXiv:1412.6572 (2014)
7. He, K., Zhang, X., Ren, S., Sun, J.: Deep residual learning for image recognition. In: Proceedings of the IEEE Conference on Computer Vision and Pattern Recognition, pp. 770–778 (2016)
8. Hirano, H., Takemoto, K.: Simple iterative method for generating targeted universal adversarial perturbations. arXiv preprint arXiv:1911.06502 (2019)
9. Houben, S., Stallkamp, J., Salmen, J., Schlipsing, M., Igel, C.: Detection of traffic signs in real-world images: the German traffic sign detection benchmark. In: International Joint Conference on Neural Networks, vol. 1288 (2013)
10. Kingma, D.P., Ba, J.: Adam: a method for stochastic optimization. arXiv preprint arXiv:1412.6980 (2014)
11. Krizhevsky, A., Hinton, G., et al.: Learning multiple layers of features from tiny images (2009)
12. Kurakin, A., Goodfellow, I., Bengio, S.: Adversarial examples in the physical world. arXiv preprint arXiv:1607.02533 (2016)
13. Madry, A., Makelov, A., Schmidt, L., Tsipras, D., Vladu, A.: Towards deep learning models resistant to adversarial attacks. arXiv preprint arXiv:1706.06083 (2017)
14. McMahan, B., Moore, E., Ramage, D., Hampson, S., y Arcas, B.A.: Communication-efficient learning of deep networks from decentralized data. In: Artificial Intelligence and Statistics, pp. 1273–1282. PMLR (2017)
15. Moosavi-Dezfooli, S.M., Fawzi, A., Fawzi, O., Frossard, P.: Universal adversarial perturbations. In: Proceedings of the IEEE Conference on Computer Vision and Pattern Recognition, pp. 1765–1773 (2017)
16. Mopuri, K.R., Ganeshan, A., Babu, R.V.: Generalizable data-free objective for crafting universal adversarial perturbations. IEEE Trans. Pattern Anal. Mach. Intell. **41**(10), 2452–2465 (2018)
17. Mopuri, K.R., Garg, U., Babu, R.V.: Fast feature fool: a data independent approach to universal adversarial perturbations. arXiv preprint arXiv:1707.05572 (2017)
18. Paszke, A., et al.: Pytorch: an imperative style, high-performance deep learning library. In: Advances in Neural Information Processing Systems, pp. 8026–8037 (2019)
19. Poursaeed, O., Katsman, I., Gao, B., Belongie, S.: Generative adversarial perturbations. In: Proceedings of the IEEE Conference on Computer Vision and Pattern Recognition, pp. 4422–4431 (2018)
20. Reddy Mopuri, K., Krishna Uppala, P., Venkatesh Babu, R.: Ask, acquire, and attack: data-free uap generation using class impressions. In: Proceedings of the European Conference on Computer Vision (ECCV), pp. 19–34 (2018)
21. Sam, D.B., Sudharsan, K., Radhakrishnan, V.B., et al.: Crafting data-free universal adversaries with dilate loss (2019)
22. Shokri, R., Stronati, M., Song, C., Shmatikov, V.: Membership inference attacks against machine learning models. In: 2017 IEEE Symposium on Security and Privacy (SP), pp. 3–18. IEEE (2017)
23. Zhang, C., Benz, P., Imtiaz, T., Kweon, I.S.: Understanding adversarial examples from the mutual influence of images and perturbations. In: Proceedings of the IEEE/CVF Conference on Computer Vision and Pattern Recognition, pp. 14521–14530 (2020)

Caps-LSTM: A Novel Hierarchical Encrypted VPN Network Traffic Identification Using CapsNet and LSTM

Jiyue Tang[1,2], Le Yang[1,2], Song Liu[1(✉)], Wenmao Liu[3], Meng Wang[3], Chonghua Wang[4], Bo Jiang[1,2], and Zhigang Lu[1,2]

[1] Institute of Information Engineering, Chinese Academy of Sciences, Beijing, China
{tangjiyue,yangle,liusong1106,jiangbo,luzhigang}@iie.ac.cn
[2] School of Cyber Security, University of Chinese Academy of Sciences, Beijing, China
[3] Innovation Center of NSFOCUS Inc., Beijing, China
{liuwenmao,wangmeng7}@nsfocus.com
[4] China Industrial Control Systems Cyber Emergency Response Team, Beijing, China
chonghuaw@live.com

Abstract. At present, encryption technologies are widely applied in the network, providing a lot of opportunities for attackers to hide their command and control activities, and thus encrypted traffic detection technology is one of the important means to prevent malicious attacks in advance. The existing methods based on machine learning cannot get rid of the artificial dependence of feature selection. Moreover, deep learning methods ignore the hierarchical characteristics of traffic. Therefore, we propose a novel deep neural network that combines CapsNet and LSTM to implement a hierarchical encrypted traffic recognition model, Caps-LSTM, which splits the traffic twice and classifies the encrypted traffic hierarchically based on the temporal and spatial characteristics, where CapsNet learns the lower spatial characteristics of the traffic and LSTM learns the upper temporal characteristics of the traffic. Finally, the softmax classifier is used to achieve effective detection of encrypted traffic services and specific application categories. Compared with the existing advanced methods based on the common data set ISCX VPN-nonVPN, the experimental results show that Caps-LSTM is more effective.

Keywords: Encrypted traffic recognition · Deep neural network · Capsule neural networks · Long short term memory networks

---

This research is supported by National Key Research and Development Program of China (No.2019QY1300), and CCF-NSFOCUS Kun-Peng Scientific Research Foundation (No.2020010), Youth Innovation Promotion Association CAS (No.2021156), the Strategic Priority Research Program of Chinese Academy of Sciences (No.XDC02040100) and National Natural Science Foundation of China (No.61802404). This work is also supported by the Program of Key Laboratory of Network Assessment Technology, the Chinese Academy of Sciences, Program of Beijing Key Laboratory of Network Security and Protection Technology.

W. Lu et al. (Eds.): SciSec 2021, LNCS 13005, pp. 139–153, 2021.
https://doi.org/10.1007/978-3-030-89137-4_10

1 Introduction

Many malicious behaviors take advantage of the encryption protocol to camouflage. The encrypted communication traffic is no longer expressed in plain text, so it cannot be effectively detected by traditional methods [1]. Currently, encrypted traffic classification is the focus of network behavior analysis, network planning and construction, network anomaly detection research, and is one of the key technologies to ensure the quality of service (QoS).

Traffic detection technologies can be roughly divided into four categories: port-based identification methods, identification methods based on deep packet inspection (DPI), methods based on machine learning and methods based on deep learning [2]. Currently, the port number can no longer be used as a unique identifier to accurately identify traffic. DPI-based methods are more mainstream, and their core task is to match characteristic codes [3]. However, the widespread use of data encryption and protocol encapsulation technologies makes this method no longer suitable for traffic detection. The method based on machine learning has high accuracy and is also suitable for encrypted traffic. Nevertheless, the classification effect directly depends on the quality of manually extracted features, which requires rich prior knowledge and is not suitable for the real environment of massive traffic [4].

Among many detection technologies against unknown threats and attacks, the recognition technology based on deep learning becomes more important and practical [5]. In order to automatically learn different features for classification, most of current methods are still based on the CNN model, but these deep learning methods lose a lot of valuable information due to the pooling layer operation, such as the relative position between features, the relationship between the part of the feature and the whole, and so on. Whereas, CapsNet adopts the form of "routing-by-agreement", which makes the neurons in one layer only pay attention to the most active feature selector in the local pool and ignore other selectors with little correlation through the weight matrix. And considering attributes of features, including many different kinds of instantiation parameters, such as size, direction, position, shape, etc., the input and output of neurons use vectors instead of scalars of traditional neurons. In addition, our method also combines the long-short term memory network (LSTM) to jointly learn spatio-temporal characteristics of the flow.

Caps-LSTM, a novel encrypted traffic detection model based on the capsule neural network (CapsNet) and LSTM, is proposed in this paper. It splits the traffic twice, so that the continuous traffic in the original real environment can be converted into discrete flow and the noise can be reduced. CapsNet is used to process the original traffic in an image manner to extract underlying spatial characteristics of the traffic [6]. Moreover, LSTM is used to extract upper time series features of the flow to further complete the autonomous learning of spatio-temporal features. The experimental results show that when the model is applied to the data set ISCX VPN-nonVPN, the classification effect is better than existing state-of-the-art approaches, indicating that our model is more competitive.

The main innovations of this paper are summarized as follows:

- Caps-LSTM, a hierarchical encrypted traffic recognition model based on deep learning, is proposed. It combines CapsNet and LSTM to automatically extract spatio-temporal characteristics of traffic according to the packet and flow level.
- The continuous traffic in the real environment is divided twice, anonymized and cleaned. The traffic is split twice in the form of flow and session respectively, and the maximum number of packets in the session is set to continuously segment the session to increase the weight of the effective session.
- The whole method is end-to-end, which means that only the original traffic data is input, and the intermediate process does not require manual feature extraction, which eliminates the dependence on manpower to a certain extent. And the problem of data imbalance can be addressed, that is, actual samples of each category are randomly selected according to the proportion of the number of samples of each category in the classification task.
- This model is applied to the public ISCX VPN-nonVPN data set, so that all state-of-the-art methods for experimenting on this data set are comparable to each other. Essentially, the focus of the research is to come up with better models to tackle difficult problems, rather than targeting fixed data sets.

The remainder of this paper is structured as follows. Section 2 introduces related work. Section 3 elaborates on the proposed model. Section 4 is the experimental analysis and comparison. Section 5 summarizes.

2 Related Work

According to different objects, encryption traffic identification methods can be roughly divided into four categories: port-based methods, DPI-based methods, machine learning-based methods, and deep learning-based methods. In general, the first three categories are viewed as traditional identification methods.

2.1 Traditional Encrypted Traffic Identification Methods

The most common port-based traffic identification method is used to detect and map the matching port number rules on the corresponding network protocols or network applications [7]. However, in order to bypass firewalls or intrusion detection systems, many applications generally adopt port masquerading technology and network address translation protocol, which makes the port number no longer a unique identifier for identifying traffic. An experimental research conducted by Moore et al. find that the accuracy rate is less than 70% by using the list published by the official IANA to classify network traffic [8]. Madhukar et al. verify through experiments that 30%–70% of the collected traffic cannot be correctly identified using the port-based method alone [9]. In short, the port-based recognition technology is simple to implement, but the accuracy of identification is reduced and the detection of protocols is very limited, which cannot meet the needs of today's encrypted traffic detection.

In order to improve the accuracy of protocol recognition, methods based on DPI are developed. The core part of DPI technologies is to match the feature fields in the application layer to classify applications [10,11]. Subhabrata Sen et al. compile the characteristics of five protocols, convert Gnutella, Edonkey, Directconnect, BitTorrent and Kazaa, into regular expressions, and propose a method to accurately identify P2P traffic by using application-layer protocols [12]. DPI-based detection methods have high accuracy and fast computing speed. However, the unique identification of each type of traffic needs to be obtained through expert analysis, and only existing flow types can be identified. Due to the extensive use of data encryption and protocol encapsulation technologies, the method of decomposing data packets for characteristic code matching can no longer be applied to the identification and classification of encrypted traffic.

The flow-based feature classification method based on machine learning generally extracts flow characteristics by manual design [13]. For example, characteristics such as the duration of each flow, the number of flow bytes per second and the median value of the flow size are fed into the classifier and trained through classification algorithms to complete the classification task. Similarly, when using packet characteristics to perform categorizing tasks, most researchers select features including the total number of packets, the length of packets, the interval time between packet arrivals, and so on. Zander et al. establish the model by combining an unsupervised Bayesian classifier and EM method, and apply it to eight common network flow protocols, with an average recognition accuracy of over 80% [14,15]. Although the identification method based on machine learning will not trigger off privacy leakage and can identify various encryption protocols in network communication, the classification effect largely depends on the quality of features extracted manually.

2.2 Encrypted Traffic Identification Methods Based on Deep Learning

By inputting raw data and hierarchical learning, advanced feature data can be automatically captured for further classification and other tasks, thereby mitigating the dependency issue of artificially designed features.

Wang et al. use SAE to construct a model for the classification task of network traffic [16]. In order to improve the defects of manual feature extraction, Lottfollahi et al. propose a two-layer convolutional neural network model to achieve the function of automatically extracting features [17]. Lopez et al. propose a method combining CNN and RNN models for traffic classification, but it still has the defect of manually extracting features [18]. Although papers continue to put forward encrypted traffic detection technologies based on deep learning, most of these methods still use the CNN model. CNN accumulates feature sets in each subsequent layer to better solve the image classification problem, but due to the pooling operation, most of the valid information, such as the relative spatial location between these features, is lost. Considering the above limitations, we propose a novel encrypted traffic detection technology.

3 The Proposed Model

The hierarchical encrypted traffic recognition model based on CapsNet and LSTM is elaborated in this section, which contains three modules: the original flow conversion module, the layered training module based on CapsNet and LSTM, and the final recognition module of encrypted flow. Figure 1 presents a high-level overview of our approach.

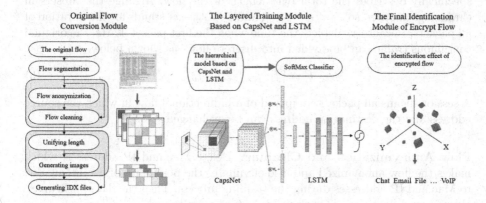

Fig. 1. Overall frame diagram of Caps-LSTM.

3.1 Original Flow Conversion Module

In the data preprocessing stage, in order to improve the universal applicability of the model, the original traffic is processed into a canonical form for unified input. The specific process can be roughly divided into four steps: flow-based splitting, flow anonymization and cleaning, session-based splitting and normalizing input.

Flow-Based Splitting. The first segmentation of traffic is to convert the entire original continuous traffic in the real environment into discrete flows. To be specific, the original traffic is separated into a variety of data packets according to five-tuple information (source IP address, source port, destination IP address, destination port, transport layer protocol), and all data packets with the same five-tuple information are assembled into a discrete flow. The original traffic T is expressed as a set as shown in (1):

$$T = \{t_1, t_2, \ldots, t_{|T|}\}$$
$$t_n = (g_n, l_n, x_n), n = 1, 2, \ldots, |T|, l_n \in (\mathbf{0}, +\infty), x_n \in [\mathbf{0}, +\infty) \tag{1}$$

where t_n is the nth data packet in the original continuous traffic, g_n represents the five-tuple of t_n, l_n denotes the byte length of t_n, and x_n is the start time of the nth data packet. The original traffic is segmented for the first time based on the flow. First, it is divided into multiple subsets P_n, indicating that the original traffic is composed of multiple data packets, and then multiple data packets are aggregated into a flow f_0 according to the same five-tuple information, which is expressed as follows:

$$P_n = \{t_1 = (g_1, l_1, x_1), \ldots, t_m = (g_m, l_m, x_m)\}$$
$$f_0 = (g, l, x, x_0)$$
(2)

where m serves as the number of data packets contained in P_n. $g = g_1 = \cdots = g_m$ represents that these m data packets have the same five-tuple, and $l = \sum_1^m l_n$ specifically describes the total byte length of the flow. Arrange the subsets in chronological order, so $x_1 < \cdots < x_m$, and $x = x_m - x_1$ stands for the duration of all packets. Because x_0 depicts the time when the first packet starts, the original continuous traffic can be divided into discrete flows as shown below.

$$F = \{f_1, f_2, f_3, \ldots, f_m\}$$
(3)

A session means all packets composed of a bidirectional flow in which the source address and the destination address can be exchanged.

Flow Anonymization and Cleaning. Delete Mac and IP addresses, which makes the flow anonymized and also eliminates the possibility of overfitting due to Mac and IP addresses during the training process. Then the data packets are cleaned, and data packets with valid content are retained.

Session-Based Splitting. The session is continuously segmented by setting the maximum number of packets in the session to split the large-size data packet of data transmission into several small-size data packets to reduce noise and dilute irrelevant sessions. The way to set the maximum number of packets in a session is to obtain the difference between the total byte length of a sample and the fixed byte length of the file header, and then obtain the ratio of the difference to the minimum packet byte length after MAC and IP addresses are deleted. In order to avoid the confusion of segmentation, the maximum number of packets is set to the largest even value that does not exceed this integer ratio.

Normalizing Input. Inspired by the processing method of the MNIST data set, the flow is processed into images by uniformly processing the flow into a certain byte, such as 784 bytes [19]. If it is greater than 784 bytes, the excess part of the file is cut off; if it is less than 784 bytes, add 0x00 to the blank at the end. It is further converted into a 28×28 matrix, and finally compressed into an IDX file. By further processing the flow image into a matrix form of a specific size, it is converted into the standard input format of commonly used deep neural networks, which improves the universality of the model.

3.2   Hierarchical Training Model Based on CapsNet and LSTM

CapsNet. Compared with other neural networks, CapsNet is unique in that it uses vectorized capsules instead of traditional scalar neurons [20]. In particular, the length of the output vector encodes the detection probability of the feature, and the direction of the vector encodes the state of the feature. CNN methods extract many spatial correlations by using continuous convolutional layers or maximum pooling layers, which lose valuable information. For example, the relative spatial relationship between encoded features is not considered. However, CapsNet adopts the form of "dynamic routing", through the weight matrix, so that neurons in one layer only pay attention to the most active feature selector in the local pool, and ignore other selectors with small relevance.

The way CapsNet learns spatial features is as follows. Specifically, the first convolutional layer selects ReLU as the activation function in CapsNet, and the latter two layers use a novel nonlinear squashing activation function for the vector form of the capsule, as shown below:

$$v_j = \frac{\| s_j \|^2}{1 + \| s_j \|^2} \frac{s_j}{\| s_j \|} \tag{4}$$

$$\widehat{u}_{j|i} = W_{ij} u_i \tag{5}$$

$$s_j = \sum_i c_{ij} \widehat{u}_{j|i} \tag{6}$$

$$c_{ij} = \frac{exp(b_{ij})}{\sum_k exp(b_{ik})} \tag{7}$$

$$b_{ij} = b_{ij} + \widehat{u}_{j|i} \cdot v_j \tag{8}$$

where v_j is the output vector of capsule j, and s_j is the input vector. The compression operation ensures that the length of the vector is within the range of $(0, 1)$. $\widehat{u}_{j|i}$ is the input vector of the advanced capsule j. In order to obtain the spatial relationship between local features and high-level features of the network-level traffic state extracted by the PrimaryCaps layer, the affine transformation can be performed by multiplying the local feature u_i of the primary capsule i by the weight matrix W_{ij}. For DigitCaps, the input s_j of the advanced capsule j is the weighted sum of all input vectors $\widehat{u}_{j|i}$ from primary capsules in this layer. c_{ij} is the coupling coefficient determined by the iterative operation of the dynamic routing algorithm. For each primary capsule i in the PrimaryCaps layer, use the softmax function to sum the coupling coefficient c_{ij} of all its advanced capsules j to 1. The routing logic b_{ij} stands for the logarithmic prior probability of coupling between the primary capsule i and the advanced capsule j. In the iterative process, the routing logic b_{ij} is updated by using the dot product of the input and output of capsule j.

LSTM. When the sequence is too long, the hidden layer vector of RNN can no longer remember the information long ago, so LSTM is adopted to learn temporal features. The LSTM architecture has a basic unit called a memory

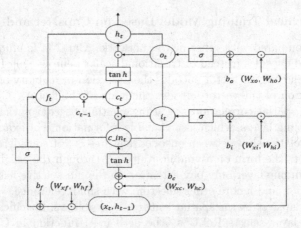

Fig. 2. Schematic diagram of LSTM neurons.

block in its hidden layer, which mainly introduces forget gates, input gates and output gates [21]. Indeed, the internal structure of a neuron is shown in Fig. 2.

The input is x_t and h_{t-1}, where h_{t-1} is the hidden layer state at the previous moment. Forget gate f_t, input gate i_t, output gate o_t and unit state gate c_t are newly introduced variables of the LSTM model. c_in_t represents the update status at time t. W_{*f}, W_{*i}, W_{*o}, W_{*c}, b_f, b_i, b_o, b_c are their respective weights and variable deviations. x_t and h_t are the input and final output of the memory cell at time t, respectively. The calculation formula of each variable is as follows:

$$f_t = sigm(W_{xf}x_t + W_{hf}h_{t-1} + b_f) \tag{9}$$

$$i_t = sigm(W_{xi}x_t + W_{hi}h_{t-1} + b_i) \tag{10}$$

$$o_t = sigm(W_{xo}x_t + W_{ho}h_{t-1} + b_o) \tag{11}$$

$$c\_in_t = tanh(W_{xc}x_t + W_{hc}h_{t-1} + b_c) \tag{12}$$

$$c_t = f_tc_{t-1} + i_tc\_in_t \tag{13}$$

$$h_t = o_ttanh(c_t) \tag{14}$$

It can be noted that each of the three gates of LSTM is a combination of a sigmoid neural network layer and element-wise multiplication.

The Core of Caps-LSTM. As depicted in Fig. 3, the processed 28×28 flow matrix is fed into the ReLU Conv1 layer, called the first convolutional layer, which is the frequently-used convolutional layer. Convolution operation is carried out with convolution kernels of 9×9 in size, in which 256 convolution kernels with a selected step size of 1 is used to generate 256 characteristic matrices, all of which is 20×20. The second layer is the PrimaryCaps layer, which is the main part of the CapsNet network. As the input information layer of the capsule, scalars transmitted by the first convolutional layer are converted into vectors,

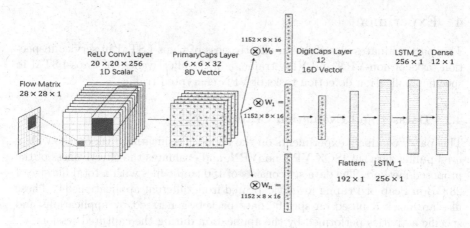

Fig. 3. Schematic diagram of Caps-LSTM core module.

which not only contain the size of the feature, but also consider attributes of the feature. The capsule information unit to which each vector belongs contains 8 ordinary convolution units. The length of the vector is expressed as the probability of the category of the original traffic, and the direction of the vector is expressed as characteristic attributes of the original traffic. Then input the 8-dimensional vector into the LSTM module as a 192×1 matrix, and finally output 12 categories. The specific parameter settings are shown in Table 1.

Table 1. Parameter settings of Caps-LSTM core module.

Layer name	Operation	Input size	Filter	Stride	Output size
ReLU Conv1	Convolution	28×28	9×9	1	$20 \times 20 \times 256$
PrimaryCap_conv2d	Convolution	$20 \times 20 \times 256$	9×9	2	$6 \times 6 \times 256$
PrimaryCap_reshape	Reshape	$6 \times 6 \times 256$	9×9	2	$1152 \times 8 \times 1$
PrimaryCap_squash	Lambda	$1152 \times 8 \times 1$	9×9	2	$1152 \times 8 \times 1$
DigitCaps	CapsuleLayer	$1152 \times 8 \times 1$	—	—	$12 \times 16 \times 1$
Flatten_1	Flatten	$12 \times 16 \times 1$	—	—	192×1
LSTM_1	LSTM	192×1	—	—	256×1
LSTM_2	LSTM	256×1	—	—	256×1
Dense	Dense	256×1	—	—	12×1

3.3 The Final Identification Module of Encrypted Flow

In the final identification module of encrypted flow, the encrypted flow after data preprocessing is sent to the trained model in the previous module, and then the acquired spatiotemporal features are used for classification using the softmax classifier to complete the efficient detection task of services and specific application categories.

4   Experiment

This part evaluates classification effectiveness of Caps-LSTM in service inspection tasks of non-VPN and VPN traffic, and the effectiveness of Caps-LSTM in specific application detection tasks of VPN encrypted traffic.

4.1   Dataset and Evaluation Criteria

This paper conducts experiments on the traffic classification task on the widely used public data set ISCX VPN-nonVPN, and evaluates the effectiveness of the proposed method. The data set consists of 150 traffic files with a total file size of 28 GB in Pcap or Pcapng format captured from different applications [4]. These files are marked based on specific data packets generated by applications and specific activities performed by the application during the captured session.

Accuracy, Precision, Recall and F-measure are four evaluation indicators that are widely used in statistical classification [22]. As shown in (15–18), we use the aforementioned accuracy-related metrics to evaluate the classification effect of the classifier.

$$Accuracy = \frac{TP + TN}{TP + FP + FN + TN} \tag{15}$$

$$Precision = \frac{TP}{TP + FP} \tag{16}$$

$$Recall = \frac{TP}{TP + FN} \tag{17}$$

$$F_1 = \frac{2 \times precision \times recall}{precsion + recall} \tag{18}$$

4.2   Data Preprocessing

After the first segmentation of traffic based on flow, more than half of the data packets in the 12 service categories are less than 0.5 KB in size. In order to tackle the above problems, the second segmentation of flow based on the session is performed, and the main large-size flow packets that mainly affect the classification effect are split into continuous small-size files to achieve the effect of noise reduction.

In order to solve the problem of data imbalance, we randomly sample the actual samples of each category according to the proportion of the number of samples of each category in the classification task. To be specific, in order to ensure the diversity of experimental samples and reduce the experimental error, after the input of the data set is unified and standardized, the overall sample number is set to be no more than 60000, in which the actual sample number of different applications is randomly selected according to the proportion of each type of total samples in each service. Table 2 counts the total number of experimental samples of various types of applications for non-encrypted traffic and encrypted traffic corresponding to nonVPN and VPN in the public data set ISCX VPN-nonVPN, and the service category to which they belong.

Table 2. The service category of the specific application in ISCX VPN-nonVPN and the total number of samples.

Serices	Applications	Total number of sessions
Chat	AIM Facebook Hangouts ICQ Skype	15200
Email	Email Gmail	10150
File	Ftps Scp Sftp Skype	60000
P2P	Torrent	7565
Streaming	Facebook Hangouts Netflix Skype Spotify Vimeo YouTube	47368
VoIP	Facebook Hangouts Skype Voipbuster	60000
VPN_Chat	AIM Facebook Hangouts ICQ Skype	8816
VPN_Email	Email	1582
VPN_File	Ftps Stsflp Skype	24265
VPN_P2P	Bittorrent	26688
VPN_Streaming	Facebook Netsfllix Spotify Vimeo YouTube	60000
VPN_VoIP	Hangouts Skype Voipbuster	60000

5   Experimental Results

5.1   Encrypted Traffic Service Identification Effect Evaluation

We make use of 76327 files in the data set in the above preprocessing process for experiments. The experimental results are shown in Table 3, where Support represents the number of files in each category. It can be seen that the precision and recall of the 12 classification results are all over 97%, and even those values of more than half of the categories exceed 99%.

Table 3. The recognition effect of encrypted traffic services.

Categories	Pre	Rec	F_1	Support
Chat	0.9797	0.9855	0.9826	3040
Email	0.9831	0.9724	0.9777	2030
File	0.9998	0.9997	0.9997	12000
P2P	0.994	0.9914	0.9927	1513
Streaming	0.998	0.9986	0.9983	9474
VoIP	0.9993	0.9997	0.9995	12000
VPN_Chat	0.9847	0.9836	0.9841	1763
VPN_Email	0.9937	0.9968	0.9953	316
VPN_File	0.9946	0.9957	0.9952	4853
VPN_P2P	0.9998	0.9991	0.9994	5338
VPN_Streaming	0.9998	0.9999	0.9999	12000
VPN_VoIP	0.9999	0.9998	0.9998	12000
Total value	0.9975	0.9975	0.9975	76327
Accuracy	0.9975			

Table 4. The recognition effect of encrypted traffic applications.

Categories	Pre	Rec	F_1	Support
VPN_Hangouts	0.9962	0.9981	0.9972	13996
VPN_Netflix	0.9987	0.9982	0.9984	10893
VPN_Skype	0.9974	0.9959	0.9966	10739
VPN_Vemo	0.9978	0.996	0.9969	4013
VPN_VoipBuster	0.9997	0.9999	0.9998	9323
Total value	0.9978	0.9978	0.9978	48964
Accuracy	0.9978			

The confusion matrix of the encrypted traffic service identification result is shown in Fig. 4a. The abscissa represents the actual service category, and the ordinate represents the predicted service category. It can be seen that almost all

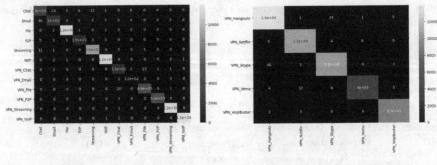

(a) Identify service categories.   (b) Identify specific applications.

Fig. 4. Row-normalized confusion matrices using Caps-LSTM.

service categories are correctly identified, indicating that the Caps-LSTM model is highly efficient in the task of identifying encrypted traffic services.

Compared with other methods that are commonly used in experiments on the data set ISCX VPV-nonVPN, as depicted in Table 4, it is obvious from the comparison results that the model presented in this paper is more accurate when applied to encrypted traffic service classification tasks, pointing out that the model is more competitive.

Table 5. Comparison of Caps-LSTM and other methods in encrypted traffic service classification task.

References	Methods	Packet forms	Precision	Recall	F_1
Ref. [17]	Decision tree	Session	0.75	0.75	0.75
	Random forests	Session	0.80	0.80	0.80
	SAE	Deep packet	0.92	0.92	0.92
	1DCNN	Deep packet	0.93	0.94	0.93
Ref. [23]	1DCNN	Session	0.85	0.86	0.86
Ref. [24]	CNN-LSTM	Deep packet	0.91	0.91	0.91
This paper	Caps-LSTM	Session packet	**0.9939**	**0.9975**	**0.9975**

5.2 Encrypted Traffic Application Identification Effect Evaluation

VPN data packets are selected in this experiment to complete the classification task of specific applications of encryption traffic. Similar to the previous section, 48964 files are selected to identify encrypted traffic applications. The effect is shown in Table 5, which clearly demonstrates that the precision, recall, F1 and accuracy of the classification result are all 0.9978.

The confusion matrix of encrypted traffic application recognition results is shown in Fig. 4b. Obviously, similar to the above encrypted traffic service identification task, the number of misclassified samples is very small, almost negligible.

Table 6. Comparison of Caps-LSTM and other methods in encrypted traffic application classification task.

References	Tasks	Methods	Packet forms	Precision	Recall	F1
Ref. [17]	All applications	Naive Bayes	Session	0.34	0.4	0.37
	All applications	Decision tree	Session	0.90	0.90	0.90
	All applications	Random forests	Session	0.90	0.91	0.90
	All applications	Logistic regression	Session	0.91	0.91	0.91
	All applications	SAE	Deep packet	0.95	0.96	0.95
Ref. [25]	All applications	CNN	Deep Packet	0.973	0.973	0.973
This paper	VPN applications	Caps-LSTM	Session packet	**0.998**	**0.9978**	**0.9978**

As depicted in Table 6, we compare Caps-LSTM with other methods, where our model performs more detailed classification tasks, identifying applications in VPN instead of all applications, so our sample size is smaller. As a consequence, the experimental results of Caps-LSTM are numerically higher than other methods, which means that the proposed model is more efficient in the application classification of encrypted traffic.

Similarly, compare the experimental results of SAE, CNN and Caps-LSTM models that are also based on the ISCX VPN-nonVPN data set for encrypted traffic service identification tasks. As shown in Fig. 5, it can be seen that when Caps-LSTM performs encrypted traffic identification tasks, the overall results of precision and recall are higher, indicating that the Caps-LSTM model is more competitive.

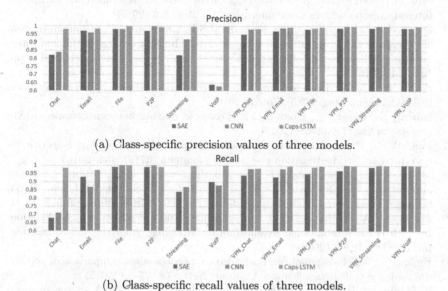

(a) Class-specific precision values of three models.

(b) Class-specific recall values of three models.

Fig. 5. Comparisons of SAE, CNN and Caps-LSTM when applied in the encrypted traffic service classification task.

6   Conclusion

Considering that network traffic identification technology runs through all the main links of network security protection, a novel encrypted traffic identification method with hierarchical learning of spatiotemporal characteristics is proposed. In other words, CapsNet learns the spatial characteristics of the lower layer of network traffic, not only converts the original real traffic into an image matrix to automatically learn features, but also considers specific feature attributes, using vectors instead of scalars. LSTM fully autonomously learns the upper-layer temporal characteristics between traffic, which may be ignored by humans, in order to classify encrypted traffic more comprehensively and accurately. The Caps-LSTM model performs traffic anonymization in the data preprocessing part, and performs secondary segmentation of traffic based on flow and session respectively to achieve noise reduction processing. Experimental results show that when Caps-LSTM is applied to the public data set ISCX VPN-nonVP N, the proposed method performs better than the existing advanced methods in terms of accuracy, precision, recall and F_1, and is more competitive.

References

1. Velan, P., Čermák, M., Čeleda, P., Drašar, M.: A survey of methods for encrypted traffic classification and analysis. Int. J. Netw. Manage. **25**(5), 355–374 (2015)
2. Biersack, E., Callegari, C., Matijasevic, M., et al.: Data traffic monitoring and analysis. Lect. Notes Comput. Sci. **5**(23), 12561–12570 (2013)
3. Sherry, J., Lan, C., Popa, R.A., Ratnasamy, S.: Blindbox: deep packet inspection over encrypted traffic. In: Proceedings of the 2015 ACM Conference on Special Interest Group on Data Communication, pp. 213–226 (2015)
4. Draper-Gil, G., Lashkari, A.H., Mamun, M.S.I., Ghorbani, A.A.: Characterization of encrypted and vpn traffic using time-related. In: Proceedings of the 2nd International Conference on Information Systems Security and Privacy (ICISSP), pp. 407–414 (2016)
5. Rezaei, S., Liu, X.: Deep learning for encrypted traffic classification: an overview. IEEE Commun. Mag. **57**(5), 76–81 (2019)
6. Sabour, S., Frosst, N., Hinton, G.E. Dynamic routing between capsules. arXiv preprint arXiv:1710.09829 (2017)
7. Pan, W.B., Cheng, G., Guo, X.J., Huang, S.X.: Review and perspective on encrypted traffic identification research. J. Commun. **37**(9), 154 (2016)
8. Moore, A.W., Papagiannaki, K.: Toward the accurate identification of network applications. In: Dovrolis, C. (ed.) PAM 2005. LNCS, vol. 3431, pp. 41–54. Springer, Heidelberg (2005). https://doi.org/10.1007/978-3-540-31966-5_4
9. Madhukar, A., Williamson, C.: A longitudinal study of p2p traffic classification. In: 14th IEEE International Symposium on Modeling, Analysis, and Simulation, pp. 179–188. IEEE (2006)
10. Bujlow, T., Carela-Español, V., Barlet-Ros, P.: Independent comparison of popular dpi tools for traffic classification. Comput. Netw. **76**, 75–89 (2015)
11. El-Maghraby, R.T., Abd Elazim, N.M., Bahaa-Eldin, A.M.: A survey on deep packet inspection. In: 2017 12th International Conference on Computer Engineering and Systems (ICCES), pp. 188–197. IEEE (2017)

12. Sen, S., Spatscheck, O., Wang, D.: Accurate, scalable in-network identification of p2p traffic using application signatures. In: Proceedings of the 13th International Conference on World Wide Web, pp. 512–521 (2004)

13. Anderson, B., McGrew, D.: Machine learning for encrypted malware traffic classification: accounting for noisy labels and non-stationarity. In: Proceedings of the 23rd ACM SIGKDD International Conference on Knowledge Discovery and Data Mining, pp. 1723–1732 (2017)

14. Zander, S., Nguyen, T., Armitage, G.: Automated traffic classification and application identification using machine learning. In: The IEEE Conference on Local Computer Networks 30th Anniversary (LCN 2005), pp. 250–257. IEEE (2005)

15. Zander, S., Nguyen, T., Armitage, G.: Self-learning IP traffic classification based on statistical flow characteristics. In: Dovrolis, C. (ed.) PAM 2005. LNCS, vol. 3431, pp. 325–328. Springer, Heidelberg (2005). https://doi.org/10.1007/978-3-540-31966-5_26

16. Wang, Z.: The applications of deep learning on traffic identification. BlackHat USA **24**(11), 1–10 (2015)

17. Lotfollahi, M., Jafari Siavoshani, M., Shirali Hossein Zade, R., Saberian, M.: Deep packet: a novel approach for encrypted traffic classification using deep learning. Soft Comput. **24**(3), 1999–2012 (2019). https://doi.org/10.1007/s00500-019-04030-2

18. Lopez-Martin, M., Carro, B., Sanchez-Esguevillas, A., Lloret, J.: Network traffic classifier with convolutional and recurrent neural networks for internet of things. IEEE Access **5**, 18042–18050 (2017)

19. Yong Zhang, X., Chen, L.J., Wang, X., Guo, D.: Network intrusion detection: based on deep hierarchical network and original flow data. IEEE Access **7**, 37004–37016 (2019)

20. Cui, S., Jiang, B., Cai, Z., Lu, Z., Liu, S., Liu, J.: A session-packets-based encrypted traffic classification using capsule neural networks. In: 2019 IEEE 21st International Conference on High Performance Computing and Communications; IEEE 17th International Conference on Smart City; IEEE 5th International Conference on Data Science and Systems (HPCC/SmartCity/DSS), pp. 429–436. IEEE (2019)

21. Gers, F.A., Schmidhuber, J., Cummins, F.: Learning to forget: continual prediction with lstm (1999)

22. Powers, D.M.W.: Evaluation: from precision, recall and f-measure to roc, informedness, markedness and correlation. arXiv preprint arXiv:2010.16061 (2020)

23. Wang, W., Zhu, M., Wang, J., Zeng, X., Yang, Z.: End-to-end encrypted traffic classification with one-dimensional convolution neural networks. In: 2017 IEEE International Conference on Intelligence and Security Informatics (ISI), pp. 43–48. IEEE (2017)

24. Zou, Z., Ge, J., Zheng, H., Wu, Y., Han, C., Yao, Z.: Encrypted traffic classification with a convolutional long short-term memory neural network. In: 2018 IEEE 20th International Conference on High Performance Computing and Communications, IEEE 16th International Conference on Smart City, IEEE 4th International Conference on Data Science and Systems (HPCC/SmartCity/DSS), pp. 329–334. IEEE (2018)

25. Zhiyong, B., Zhou, B., Cheng, P., Zhang, K., Ling, Z.-H.: Encrypted network traffic classification using deep and parallel network-in-network models. IEEE Access **8**, 132950–132959 (2020)

Multi-granularity Mobile Encrypted Traffic Classification Based on Fusion Features

Hui Zhang[1,2,3], Gaopeng Gou[2], Gang Xiong[2(✉)], Chang Liu[2], Yuewen Tan[1,2], and Ke Ye[4]

[1] School of Cyber Security, University of Chinese Academy of Sciences, Beijing, China
[2] Institute of Information Engineering, Chinese Academy of Sciences, Beijing, China
{zhanghui,gougaopeng,xionggang,liuchang,tanyuewen}@iie.ac.cn
[3] National Computer Network Emergency Response Technical Team/Coordination Center of China, Beijing, China
[4] School of Computer Science and Technology, Beijing Institute of Technology, Beijing, China
yeke@bit.edu.cn

Abstract. The prosperity and development of mobile network makes mobile applications inseparable from people's life. Although the encryption of mobile communication traffic protects the privacy of users to a certain extent, it also brings great challenges to network management and supervision. At present, many researches use machine learning or deep learning to classify encrypted traffic, but most of them only focus on single granularity classification task. Moreover, the method of multi granularity classification is more artificial, which cannot fully mine the effective information of multi granularity encrypted traffic classification. In this paper, we propose fusion feature based model, an end-to-end framework, which can automatically generate distinguishing fingerprints at three different granularities: app, in-app activity, and app-activity. Specifically, we use 1D-CNN to extract the spatial characteristics of the first packet payloads, and bidirectional LSTM to learn the timing characteristics of the packet length sequences and the packet direction sequences. Extensive experiments based on real-world encrypted mobile traffic show that, the proposed model achieves the best results in the multi-granularity classification task of mobile encrypted traffic, compared with the four state-of-the-art methods. Our work can provide an effective solution for the hierarchical and refined management of mobile networks.

Keywords: Encrypted traffic · Traffic classification · Mobile applications · Activity · Multi-granularity · Deep learning

---

This work was partially supported by the National Key Special Project of China (Grant No. 2020YFB1820105).

W. Lu et al. (Eds.): SciSec 2021, LNCS 13005, pp. 154–170, 2021.
https://doi.org/10.1007/978-3-030-89137-4_11

1   Introduction

In recent years, with the development and popularization of the mobile Internet, mobile devices such as smart phones have been increasingly used in people's daily work and life. While the mobile network brings convenience to people, it also poses the threat of privacy information leakage. To this end, the researchers proposed the SSL/TLS encryption protocols [9,12] to protect users' personal information and network behaviors. However, for network administrators, they will face more severe challenges. Traditional traffic analysis techniques, such as port-based [6,24,37] and deep packet inspection based methods [4,11,16], are no longer applicable. Network traffic classification is the key of network behavior analysis and network anomaly detection. It is also the prerequisite and foundation for improving network management, improving service quality (QoS), and monitoring application security [27]. In recent years, encrypted traffic classification problem has attracted wide attention of academia and industry [7,25,32,33,39].

Current research in the field of mobile encrypted traffic classification mainly focuses on two levels: **one is the classification of mobile encrypted applications**, that is, the encrypted traffic generated from specific applications (such as Skype, YouTube, Hangouts, etc.) or application types (such as FTP, P2P, etc.) are identified [2,3,22,26]. The main solution of current researches includes the selection and optimization of classification features [26,30,31] and the application of models, such as machine learning or deep learning models [1,3,30,31]. **The second is the activity-level classification within the encrypted applications**, that is, based on the known application types, the internal user behaviors [8,15,19,21,33] are refined classification. The former pays more attention to activity classification within instant messaging applications. These researches on user activity classification techniques aim to arouse people's attention to the protection of mobile application communication privacy [19], and are also the basis for further research on recommendation algorithms [14] and user portraits [38].

The existing mobile encryption traffic classification methods have two main deficiencies: First, the classification method is usually applicable to a single granularity (either at the app level or at the in-app activity level), and cannot be applied well to multi-granularity classification task of mobile encrypted traffic. Meanwhile, the multi-granularity method like ActiveTracker model [19] has special requirements for the duration of a single activity, which directly leads to the deterioration of the generality of the model. In addition, for the refined granularity, such as in-app activity classification, the current state-of-the-art methods adopt feature engineering combined with machine learning technology. The time cost of manually designing features is high, and it is very dependent on personal experience and professional knowledge [21].

In this paper, we propose a fusion feature based (FFB) model for multi-granularity mobile encrypted traffic classification, including the app classification, in-app activity classification, and app-activity classification. FFB model fully extracts effective features from the packet level and flow level information, so as to fully learn the temporal and spatial attributes of mobile encrypted traffic. Specifically, at the data packet level, 1D-CNN is used to automatically extract the spatial characteristics of the payload of the first data packet; at the flow level, we consider the directional sequence feature of the data packet, and the latter two sequence features are automatically learned through the bidirectional LSTM. The FFB model provides a better way to achieve hierarchical and refined classification of mobile networks. We evaluate the FFB model and four state-of-the-art methods on a real-world mobile application encrypted traffic dataset. The experimental results show that our FFB model outperforms four advanced methods in multi-granularity classification tasks.

The main contributions of this article are summarized as follows:

1. We provide a fusion feature based method for multi-granularity mobile encrypted traffic classification. We apply the representation learning ideas of the deep learning model to the problem of refined classification of mobile encrypted traffic, which can automatically extract key information from the encrypted original information and generate distinguishing fingerprints at three different granularities: app, in-app activity, and app-activity.
2. We integrate packet payloads and flow information to increase the discrimination of classification. Specifically, 1D-CNN is used to automatically extract the spatial characteristics of the first packet payload, and bidirectional LSTM is used to automatically learn the timing characteristics of the packet length sequence and the packet direction sequence. The valuable information jointly extracted from multiple feature views can generate multi-granularity and multi-level distinguishing fingerprints.
3. Evaluated on the real-world encrypted network traffic collected from volunteers, we conduct extensive experiments and achieve the excellent recognition results. The results show that our FFB model outperforms the four advanced in multi-granularity mobile encrypted traffic classification tasks.

The rest of this article is organized as follows. Section 2 summarizes the related work. Section 3 introduces FFB model in detail. Section 4 introduces our data collection method, evaluates our solution through a large number of experiments, and compares and analyzes with four baseline methods. Finally, we summarize our paper in Sect. 5.

2   Related Work

2.1   Internet Encrypted Traffic Classification

The focus of Internet encrypted traffic classification is to distinguish the different protocol types and service types carried by encrypted traffic. An early popular research method is to generate service signatures from the payload of SSL/TLS, and then divide network traffic into different applications and services [17]. Later, Anderson et al. [5] and Mamun et al. [23] applied machine learning methods to encrypted traffic classification, and both used the statistical characteristics of data packets or data streams to construct fingerprints. Wang et al. [34] tried for the first time to apply the deep neural network commonly used in the field of image recognition to encrypted traffic recognition, and proposed an end-to-end traffic classification method that extracts the first 784 bytes of a flow or session, and then uses one-dimensional convolution for processing. Deep Fingerprinting (DF) [29], uses a deep learning classifier based on CNNs to achieve over 0.9 for both precision and recall in the open world. Since CNN cannot effectively use the timing relationship between messages, some scholars have proposed a deep learning method for encrypted traffic classification using LSTM [35] and the HAN model, which led to research combining CNN, LSTM and other commonly used deep learning models [22, 26, 29].

2.2 Mobile Application Traffic Classification

With the widespread use of smart phones, the identification of traffic generated by mobile applications has become a recent research hotspot. Taylor et al. [30] proposed a method called AppScanner. They divided the traffic into upstream, downstream and complete flows, and extracted 18 statistical features from each flow, a total of 54 features were used as a feature set. Considering the time series relationship of encrypted traffic, Korczyński et al. [18] proposed to use the message type in the encrypted traffic as the state, and construct a first-order homogeneous Markov state transition matrix as the application fingerprint. Shen et al. [28] clustered the length of the certificate and the length of the first data packet under the second-order Markov model to improve the classification performance. Liu et al. [20] proposed a data packet length sequence classification method FS-Net based on the GRU model, which further improved the classification effect. In terms of in-app activity recognition, Conti et al. [8] are interested in the extent to which external attackers can identify specific operations performed by users on their mobile applications, and designed a way to hierarchize behavioral traffic. Clustering, followed by a fingerprint construction method that uses central flow to characterize the original flow. Fu et al. [13] developed a system called CUMMA to classify the service usage of mobile messaging applications by jointly modeling user activity patterns, network traffic characteristics, and temporal dependencies. Li et al. [19] proposed an attack model called ActiveTracker based on the deep neural network model, which can reveal the finegrained trajectory of the user's mobile application usage from the sniffed encrypted Internet traffic. However, the model assumes that a activity should last at least 15 s. This constraint reduces the generality of the model.

3   Fusion Feature Based Model

Figure 1 shows the overall structure of our proposed multi-granularity mobile encryption traffic identification FFB model. The model includes preprocessing stage, feature extraction stage, training and recognition stage.

To start with, we extract the stream's payload and packet size sequence from the pcap file. Next, we use some deep learning methods to extract features from the preprocessed data. Finally, we train the model and complete the recognition task.

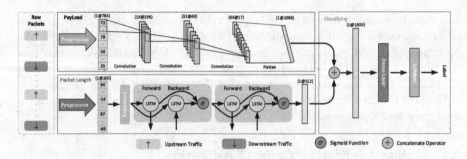

Fig. 1. Overview of the proposed FFB model

3.1 Data Preprocessing

We identify applications based on TLS and UDP streams, and each stream is uniquely characterized by 5-tuple information (SrcIP, SrcPort, DstIP, DstPort, IP protocol). We use the tshark tool to split the captured pcap file, obtain the packet length sequence of the stream and the transport layer load, and save these data in the pkl file.

Packet Length Sequence. Since the MTU of the capture network card is 1500, the value range of the single value of the packet length sequence we captured is [−1500, 1500], where a negative value indicates the incoming direction, and a positive value indicates the outgoing direction. In our method, we record the packet length sequence of the first 200 packets of each stream, and fill it with 0 if it is less than 200, and finally form a 1×200 one-dimensional vector.

Transport Layer Payload. In the preprocessing stage, we use the extended query fields "tcp.payload" and "udp.payload" of the tshark tool to extract the transport layer load of each packet (this model is mainly for TLStraffic classification, so it is discarded IP headers and other strong feature information that may make the network excessively dependent). In our method, we extract the first 784 bytes of the transport layer payload (whether encrypted or not) from a stream, and fill the bytes less than 784 with 0, and finally form a 1×784 one-dimensional vector.

3.2 Feature Extraction

The FFB model combines the characteristics of the transport layer payload and the data packet length sequence. Among them, 1D-CNN is used on the payload and the bidirectional LSTM is used on the data packet length sequence.

Transport Layer Payload Characteristics. Krizhevsky et al. won the Large-scale Visual Recognition Challenge (ILSVRC) in 2012, which greatly promoted the wide application of CNNs in the field of image classification. Yoon Kim [36] used 1D-CNN to learn the features of sentence classification and achieved good results. In view of the fact that network traffic can essentially be regarded as a one-dimensional byte stream organized in a hierarchical structure, inspired by the above work, we use 1D-CNN to process the payload information of the first data packet.

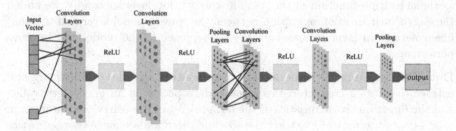

Fig. 2. A basic architecture of CNN

A typical CNN model structure is shown in Fig. 2. In each CNN-layer, 1D forward propagationis express as follows:

$$x_k^{(l)} = b_k^{(l)} + \sum_{i=1}^{N_{l-1}} conv1D(w_{i,k}^{(l-1)}, s_i^{(l-1)}) \tag{1}$$

$$y_k^{(l)} = f(x_k^{(l)}) \tag{2}$$

$$E_p = \sum_{i=1}^{N_{l-1}} (y_i^{(l)} - t_i^p)^2 \tag{3}$$

where $x_{i,j}^{(l)}$ is defined as the input feature map, $b_k^{(l)}$ is defined as the bias of the kth neuron at the layer l, $s_i^{(l-1)}$ is the output of the ith neuron at layer l-1, $w_{i,k}^{(l-1)}$ is the kernel from the ith neuron at layer l-1 to the kth neuron at layer l. $conv1D()$ is used to perform 1D convolution without zero-padding, f() is the activation function, E_p is the mean-squared error(MSE).

Backpropagation to calculate residuals:

$$\frac{\partial E}{\partial w_{i,k}^{(l-1)}} = \frac{\partial E}{\partial x_k'} y_i^{(l-1)} \tag{4}$$

$$\frac{\partial E}{\partial b_k^{(l)}} = \frac{\partial E}{\partial x_k'} \tag{5}$$

$$\frac{\partial E}{\partial s_k^{(l)}} = \sum_{i=1}^{N_{l+1}} \frac{\partial E}{\partial x_i^{(l+1)}} \frac{\partial x_{k=1}^{(l+1)}}{\partial s_i^{(l)}} \tag{6}$$

In the CNN model actually selected, we use a three-layer convolutional neural network, the number of convolution kernels used in each layer is [16, 32, 64], and the size of the convolution kernel is [8, 8, 7]. Each convolutional layer module includes a one-dimensional convolutional layer, a nonlinear activation layer, a one-dimensional convolutional layer, a nonlinear activation layer, and a pooling layer from beginning to end. In this model, we use the ReLU activation function as the activation function of the nonlinear activation layer. Secondly, we added the BatchNormalization operation between the convolutional layer and the non-linear activation layer to speed up the convergence of the model and improve performance.

Data Packet Length Sequence Characteristics. In order to fully learn and extract the timing characteristics of each data packet in an encrypted traffic, and the direction characteristics of the data packet in the behavioral interaction process, we automatically extract the size and direction sequence characteristics of the data packet through the bidirectional LSTM. Long short-term memory (LSTM) represents a popular variant of recurrent neural networks, which can model "long-term dependencies" and is easy to train. Previously, it has achieved excellent results in the fields of speech recognition and natural language processing. The field of encrypted traffic identification has also been used more and more widely.

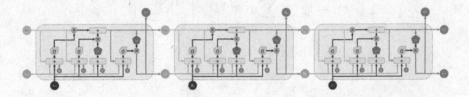

Fig. 3. A basic architecture of LSTM

A typical LSTM model structure is shown in Fig. 3. The calculation formulas of the three core gate functions—Input gate, Forgotten gate and Output gate are as follows:

$$i^{(i)} = \sigma(W_{ix}x^{(t)} + W_{ih}h^{(t-1)} + b_i) \tag{7}$$

$$f^{(t)} = \sigma(W_{fx}x^{(t)} + W_{fh}h^{(t-1)} + b_f) \tag{8}$$

$$o^{(t)} = \sigma(W_{ox}x^{(t)} + W_{oh}h^{(t-1)} + b_o) \tag{9}$$

First, we map the value range of the packet length sequence feature from [−1500, 1500] to [0, 3000], and then call embedding to perform a 128-dimensional embedded representation of each value. This vector incorporates the context of the relevant packet length information. After that, we input its embedded representation into the two-way LSTM network and extract feature information from it.

3.3 Training and Recognition

We concatenate two different abstract features together to obtain a 1600-length real number vector, then input it to the last fully connected layer, and then connect it to a fully connected layer with K neurons and use softmax as its nonlinearity Activation function, where K is the number of mobile application activity that need to be classified. Two different abstract features jointly optimize the same category of targets, jointly calculate multiple types of cross-entropy loss, and update the parameters of the two neural networks through the backpropagation algorithm.

Overfitting is a common problem in deep learning. We choose to use Batch-Norm and Dropout operations in the network to reduce overfitting. Dropout is usually set to discard 10% neuron information, and for the penultimate fully connected layer, we choose to discard 50% neuron information to enhance its robustness.

In summary, our FFB model learns the payload characteristics of the first packet through CNN, and learns the joint timing characteristics of the packet size sequence and the packet direction sequence through Bidirectional LSTM.

4 Evaluation

4.1 Data Set

We recruited some volunteers and collected APP activity data sets that encrypted Internet traffic through smartphones. These volunteers use specially configured mobile phones (Xiaomi MI 5s Plus, google pixel 5, iPhone 6s) to run various APPs and complete various practical functions. The smartphones are connected to Wi-Fi access points (APs) operated by desktop computers.), run the sniffing tool WireShark on the desktop, which is used to grab the data packet information of the smartphone from the AP. In the specific operation link, volunteers will repeatedly start the application to perform a certain activity within a period of time, and at the same time record the start time and end time of the activity, and the activity label. Then, an interval of 20s starts the next application activity traffic labeling. In the end, we will get a activity time relationship table (start time, end time, activity label) and a pcap file of the application, and divide the data packet into several activity data packets according to the activity schedule, and finally form our application activity traffic data set. We can automatically mark multiple batches for the above operations, and constantly equalize the samples.

We are particularly interested in social apps and selected five popular apps that are currently the most widely used: Hangouts, Messenger, QQ, Signal and WeChat. We focus on 7 types of in-app activity, including: message (sending short messages), picture (sending pictures), file (transmitting files), video (transmitting video), videocall (video call), voicecall (voice call), location (shared geographic location), see Table 2.

Table 1. Statistics of the collected internet traffic

Class	App	Activity	Records	Packets	Traffic(Mb)
0	signal	location	2252	149084	78.0
1	signal	voicecall	3034	318051	54.7
2	signal	msg	985	58725	15.2
3	wechat	pic	1093	55252	43.5
4	qq	voicecall	1524	228970	41.9
5	wechat	file	1221	327423	293.4
6	messenger	pic	782	107327	74.4
7	wechat	msg	3697	80422	40.1
8	messenger	location	1073	49696	22.7
9	wechat	location	5641	84303	23.0
10	qq	videocall	1387	676790	485.9
11	wechat	voicecall	12836	853274	109.1
12	qq	msg	1854	43737	13.8
13	wechat	video	1407	148995	122.2
14	qq	video	703	54278	45.1
15	hangouts	pic	1000	775195	882.3
16	hangouts	videocall	1169	613825	544.5
17	qq	file	1569	547889	531.2
18	messenger	msg	1177	108017	44.7
19	hangouts	msg	331	54549	10.1

Table 2. Interested apps and activity types

	Msg	Pic	File	Video	Videocall	Voicecall	Location
Hangouts	✓	✓			✓		
Messenger	✓	✓					✓
QQ	✓		✓	✓	✓	✓	
Signal	✓					✓	✓
Wechat	✓	✓	✓	✓		✓	✓

In order to ensure the effect of deep learning, we preprocessed the original data and filtered out repeated Acks packets, retransmitted packets, and behavioral data streams with a packet length of 7 or less. This is because 7 is the length of the shortest "complete" stream, that is, the stream containing TCP handshake (three packets) and HTTP request, response and confirmation (four packets). Table 1 shows the statistics of the collected internet traffic.

4.2   Evaluation Index

In order to effectively evaluate the performance of FFB, this article first introduces some basic indicators: true positive (TP), false negative (FN), true negative (TN) and false positive (FP). TP is the amount of traffic categorized as app i (activity i or app-activity i) that completely belongs to app i (activity i or app-activity i). FN is the traffic categorized as app i (activity i or app-activity i), which is completely the amount of app j (activity j or app-activity j). TN is the amount of traffic classified as app j (activity j or app-activity j), which completely belongs to the amount of app i (activity i or app-activity i). FP is the amount of traffic classified as app j (activity j or app-activity j) that completely belongs to app j (activity j or app-activity j).

In the training phase, the Accuracy (ACC) is used to indicate the improvement of the model identification ability, and the accuracy rate is the proportion of all the correct sample sizes to the training data during the iterative training.

In the test phase, Precision (P) that shows how many flows predicted to app i (activity i or app-activity i) are actual app i (activity i or app-activity i), Recall (R) that shows the percentage of flows that are correctly predicted versus all flows that belong to app i (activity i or app-activity i), and F1 is used to comprehensively evaluate the classification accuracy of HTTPS traffic. To evaluate our method on all 5 apps, 7 in-app activity and 20 app-activity, we introduced six overall indicators, called macro precision, macro recall, macro F1 (representing the average value of P, R, and F1 respectively), and weighted precision, weightedrecall, weighted F1 (representing the weighted average value of P, R, and F1 respectively).

4.3   Comparison Methods

Some state-of-the-art methods are summarized as comparison methods as follows:

1. **AppScanner** [30] divides an encrypted network traffic into bursts according to the duration of the activity, and generates application fingerprints based on the statistical characteristics of the bursts, thereby realizing automatic real-time identification of Android applications.
2. **Deep Fingerprinting** [29] (DF) is a new website fingerprint attack model for Tor. It uses a type of deep learning called Convolutional Neural Network (CNN) and focuses on two defense methods, WTF-PAD and Walkie-Talkie. Experiments prove that the DF attack model is very effective.
3. **FS-Net** [20] is an end-to-end classification model based on recurrent neural networks and an autoencoder both traffic classification and packet feature mining, which learns representative features from the raw flows, and then classifies them in a unified framework.
4. **ActiveTracker** [19] is a new type of sniffing attack based on a deep neural network (DNN) that can reveal the fine-grained trajectory of user's mobile app usage from a sniffed encrypted Internet traffic stream, which considered to be the latest solution for in-app activity recognition.

4.4   MainParameters

In summary, the main parameters of FFB model are described in Table 3, 4 and 5.

Table 3. Main parameters of CNN Layer

CNN Layer	Filter num	Kernel size	Strides	Output Shape
Input				(None, 784, 1)
1D_conv1	16	8	1	(None, 784, 16)
1D_pooling1		8	4	(None, 196, 16)
1D_conv2	32	8	1	(None, 196, 32)
1D_pooling2		8	4	(None, 49, 32)
1D_conv3	64	8	1	(None, 49, 64)
1D_pooling3		7	3	(None, 17, 64)
Flatten				(None, 1088)

Table 4. Main parameters of LSTM Layer

LSTM Layer	Units	Emb size	Output shape
Input			(None, 200)
Embedding		64	(None, 200, 64)
Bidirectional1	128		(None, 200, 256)
Bidirectional2	256		(None, 512)

Table 5. Main parameters of FC Layer

FC Layer	Units	Output shape
Concatentate		(None, 1600)
Dense1	256	(None, 256)
Softmax	20	(None, 20)

4.5 Comparative Experiment

Performance of App Recognition. First of all, we compare FFB model and baseline methods on app recognition, that focuses on identifying apps from the mobile encrypted traffic without considering the activities.

Figure 4 shows the experimental results in terms of accuracy, recall and F1-score.

In the APP recognition task, each classifier has achieved good results, and the recognition macro F1 for each APP is greater than 93.5%. Our FFB model achieves the highest performance in accuracy, recall and F1. Macro precision, macro recall and macro F1 are all higher than 99%; weighted precision, weighted recall and weighted F1 are respectively 99.38%, 99.37% and 99.38%. Among the four baseline methods, FS-Net has the best recognition effect on apps, with macro F1 of 99.06%. ActiveTracker's macro F1 is 93.56%, that is the lowest among the baseline methods. But in general, the five methods are all effective at the granularity of app recognition.

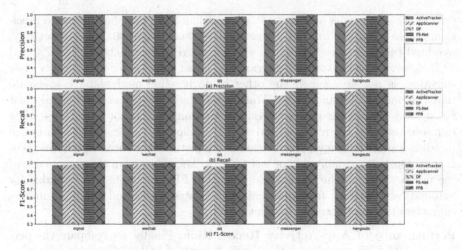

Fig. 4. Performance of app classification

Performance of In-App Activity Recognition. Next, we compared the performance of FFB model and the baseline method in-app activity recognition. The goal of this task is to identify specific activity within the application from encrypted traffic. As mentioned in Sect. 4.1 above, we focus on 7 types of activity in our experiments.

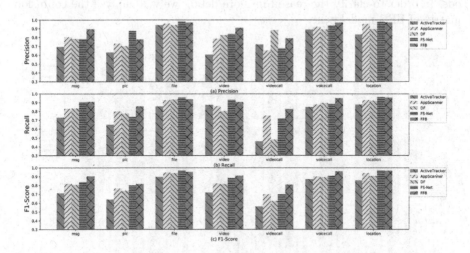

Fig. 5. Performance of in-app activity classification

From the experimental results in Fig. 5, it can be clearly seen that the advantages of FFB model in the granularity of activity recognition have begun to appear. The performance of the five methods is still the best, and the F1 of each of the seven types of activity is greater than 81%. Specifically, macro precision, macro recall and macro F1 were 89.64%, 90.53% and 90.05%, respectively; weighted precision, weighted recall and weighted F1 were 92.87%, 92.67% and 92.75%, respectively. ActiveTracker, as the latest solution for app activity classification, is not as good as the other three baseline methods. We speculate that this may be because ActiveTracker assumes that the activity should last for at least 15 s. In the process of data collection, we did not have this restriction, but imitated the real user activity. The following actions, such as message (sending a short message), picture (sending a picture) and location (sharing geographic location), usually do not last for 15 s. Therefore, from the perspective of the practicability of the classification method, FFB model is more suitable for automatically learning from real mobile encrypted traffic and obtaining unique characteristics generated by different activity.

Performance of App-Activity Recognition. Finally, we compare the performance of FFB model and the baseline method in identifying app-activity. This is the most difficult task because it needs to identify the combination of applications and activity at the finest level of granularity.

As shown in the experimental results shown in Fig. 6, our proposed model once again achieved the highest accuracy, recall and F1 for almost all app-activity categories. The macro F1 and weighted F1 of FFB model are 86.267% and 92.09%, respectively. There are three types of app-activity that have relatively low recognition effects, namely QQ-voicecall (class 4), QQ-videocall (class 10) and Hangouts-msg (class 19), but this phenomenon is common in all five methods. In order to clarify the reason in more detail, we will analyze the confusion matrix of FFB model next.

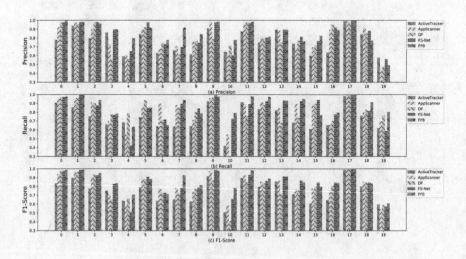

Fig. 6. Performance of app-activity classification

4.6   Confusion Matrix

We draw the confusion matrices of FFB model on three level classification tasks, they are app recognition, in-app activity recognition, and app-activity recognition as illustrated in Fig. 7. As shown in Fig. 7a, we noticed that with the exception of QQ, most applications can be correctly identified. 2% of the traffic generated by QQ was misclassified as traffic generated by Wechat. In terms of in-app activity classification, by analyzing the confusion matrix shown in Fig. 7b, it can be found that 14% of the traffic generated by the videocall activity was incorrectly classified as the traffic generated by the voicecall activity. 8.5% of the traffic generated by picture sending activity is incorrectly classified as the traffic generated by the message sending activity, while 5.7% and 5.6% is respectively misclassified as traffic generated by videocall activity and location activity.

To find out the reason for the misclassification, we further analyzed the confusion matrix shown in Fig. 7c. Most misclassifications occur in the activity of recognizing voice calls, video calls, and sending short messages. Specifically, most misclassifications occur in recognizing QQ-voicecall (class 4), QQ-videocall (class 10), and Hangouts-msg (Class 19). One possible explanation is that in the same application, the behavior of voice calls and video calls is very similar, and there are challenges in distinguishing the two behaviors of sending pictures and sending messages.

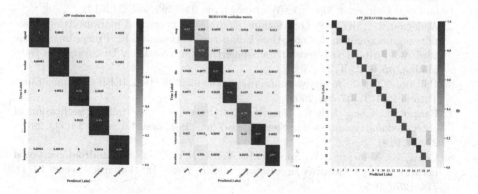

Fig. 7. Confusion matrix of FFB model

5   Conclusion

In this paper, we propose fusion feature based (FFB) model, an end-to-end framework that can automatically classify multi-granularity mobile encrypted traffic. We intergrate packet level and flow level information to increase the discrimination of refined classification of mobile encrypted traffic. We use 1D-CNN to extract the spatial characteristics of the payload of the first packet, and bidirectional LSTM to learn the timing characteristics of the packet length sequence and the packet direction sequence, which can automatically generate distinguishing fingerprints at three different granularities: app, in-app activity, and app-activity. Extensive experiments based on real-world encrypted mobile traffic show that, the proposed FFB model achieves the best results in the multi-granularity classification task of mobile encrypted traffic compared with the four comparison methods. Our work is very helpful for the hierarchical and refined management of mobile networks.

Acknowledgements. This work was partially supported by the National Key Special Project of China (Grant No. 2020YFB1820105).

References

1. Aceto, G., Ciuonzo, D., Montieri, A., Pescapé, A.: Mobile encrypted traffic classification using deep learning. In: 2018 Network Traffic Measurement and Analysis Conference (TMA), pp. 1–8. IEEE (2018)
2. Aceto, G., Ciuonzo, D., Montieri, A., Pescapé, A.: Multi-classification approaches for classifying mobile app traffic. J. Netw. Comput. Appl. **103**, 131–145 (2018)
3. Aceto, G., Ciuonzo, D., Montieri, A., Pescapé, A.: Mobile encrypted traffic classification using deep learning: Experimental evaluation, lessons learned, and challenges. IEEE Trans. Netw. Serv. Manage. **16**(2), 445–458 (2019)
4. Alcock, S., Nelson, R.: Measuring the accuracy of open-source payload-based traffic classifiers using popular internet applications. In: 38th Annual IEEE Conference on Local Computer Networks-Workshops, pp. 956–963. IEEE (2013)
5. Anderson, B., McGrew, D.: Machine learning for encrypted malware traffic classification: accounting for noisy labels and non-stationarity. In: Proceedings of the 23rd ACM SIGKDD International Conference on Knowledge Discovery and Data Mining, pp. 1723–1732 (2017)
6. Callado, A., et al.: A survey on internet traffic identification. IEEE Commun. Surv. Tutorials **11**(3), 37–52 (2009)
7. Casino, F., Choo, K.K.R., Patsakis, C.: Hedge: efficient traffic classification of encrypted and compressed packets. IEEE Trans. Inf. Forensics Secur. **14**(11), 2916–2926 (2019)
8. Conti, M., Mancini, L.V., Spolaor, R., Verde, N.V.: Analyzing android encrypted network traffic to identify user actions. IEEE Trans. Inf. Forensics Secur. **11**(1), 114–125 (2015)
9. Dierks, T., Rescorla, E.: The transport layer security (tls) protocol version 1.2 (2008)
10. Dubin, R., Dvir, A., Pele, O., Hadar, O.: I know what you saw last minute–encrypted http adaptive video streaming title classification. IEEE Trans. Inf. Forensics Secur. **12**(12), 3039–3049 (2017)
11. Finsterbusch, M., Richter, C., Rocha, E., Muller, J.A., Hanssgen, K.: A survey of payload-based traffic classification approaches. IEEE Commun. Surv. Tutorials **16**(2), 1135–1156 (2013)
12. Freier, A., Karlton, P., Kocher, P.: The secure sockets layer (SSL) protocol version 3.0. Tech. rep., RFC 6101 (2011)
13. Fu, Y., Xiong, H., Lu, X., Yang, J., Chen, C.: Service usage classification with encrypted internet traffic in mobile messaging apps. IEEE Trans. Mob. Comput. **15**(11), 2851–2864 (2016)

14. Gong, S.: A collaborative filtering recommendation algorithm based on user clustering and item clustering. J. Softw. **5**(7), 745–752 (2010)
15. Hou, C., Shi, J., Kang, C., Cao, Z., Gang, X.: Classifying user activities in the encrypted wechat traffic. In: 2018 IEEE 37th International Performance Computing and Communications Conference (IPCCC), pp. 1–8. IEEE (2018)
16. Jamdagni, A., Tan, Z., He, X., Nanda, P., Liu, R.P.: Repids: a multi tier real-time payload-based intrusion detection system. Comput. Netw. **57**(3), 811–824 (2013)
17. Kim, S.M., Goo, Y.H., Kim, M.S., Choi, S.G., Choi, M.J.: A method for service identification of SSL/TLS encrypted traffic with the relation of session ID and server IP. In: 2015 17th Asia-Pacific Network Operations and Management Symposium (APNOMS), pp. 487–490. IEEE (2015)
18. Korczyński, M., Duda, A.: Markov chain fingerprinting to classify encrypted traffic. In: IEEE INFOCOM 2014-IEEE Conference on Computer Communications, pp. 781–789. IEEE (2014)
19. Li, D., Li, W., Wang, X., Nguyen, C.T., Lu, S.: App trajectory recognition over encrypted internet traffic based on deep neural network. Comput. Netw. **179**, 107372 (2020)
20. Liu, C., He, L., Xiong, G., Cao, Z., Li, Z.: Fs-net: a flow sequence network for encrypted traffic classification. In: IEEE INFOCOM 2019-IEEE Conference on Computer Communications, pp. 1171–1179. IEEE (2019)
21. Liu, J., Fu, Y., Ming, J., Ren, Y., Sun, L., Xiong, H.: Effective and real-time in-app activity analysis in encrypted internet traffic streams. In: Proceedings of the 23rd ACM SIGKDD International Conference on Knowledge Discovery and Data Mining, pp. 335–344 (2017)
22. Lotfollahi, M., Siavoshani, M.J., Zade, R.S.H., Saberian, M.: Deep packet: a novel approach for encrypted traffic classification using deep learning. Soft Comput. **24**(3), 1999–2012 (2020)
23. Mamun, M.S.I., Ghorbani, A.A., Stakhanova, N.: An entropy based encrypted traffic classifier. In: Qing, S., Okamoto, E., Kim, K., Liu, D. (eds.) ICICS 2015. LNCS, vol. 9543, pp. 282–294. Springer, Cham (2016). https://doi.org/10.1007/978-3-319-29814-6_23
24. McPherson, J., Ma, K.L., Krystosk, P., Bartoletti, T., Christensen, M.: Portvis: a tool for port-based detection of security events. In: Proceedings of the 2004 ACM Workshop on Visualization and Data Mining for Computer Security, pp. 73–81 (2004)
25. Niu, W., Zhuo, Z., Zhang, X., Du, X., Yang, G., Guizani, M.: A heuristic statistical testing based approach for encrypted network traffic identification. IEEE Trans. Veh. Technol. **68**(4), 3843–3853 (2019)
26. Rezaei, S., Kroencke, B., Liu, X.: Large-scale mobile app identification using deep learning. IEEE Access **8**, 348–362 (2019)
27. Roughan, M., Sen, S., Spatscheck, O., Duffield, N.: Class-of-service mapping for QoS: a statistical signature-based approach to IP traffic classification. In: Proceedings of the 4th ACM SIGCOMM Conference on Internet Measurement, pp. 135–148 (2004)
28. Shen, M., Wei, M., Zhu, L., Wang, M., Li, F.: Certificate-aware encrypted traffic classification using second-order Markov chain. In: 2016 IEEE/ACM 24th International Symposium on Quality of Service (IWQoS), pp. 1–10. IEEE (2016)
29. Sirinam, P., Imani, M., Juarez, M., Wright, M.: Deep fingerprinting: undermining website fingerprinting defenses with deep learning. In: Proceedings of the 2018 ACM SIGSAC Conference on Computer and Communications Security, pp. 1928–1943 (2018)

30. Taylor, V.F., Spolaor, R., Conti, M., Martinovic, I.: Appscanner: automatic fingerprinting of smartphone apps from encrypted network traffic. In: 2016 IEEE European Symposium on Security and Privacy (EuroS&P), pp. 439–454. IEEE (2016)

31. Taylor, V.F., Spolaor, R., Conti, M., Martinovic, I.: Robust smartphone app identification via encrypted network traffic analysis. IEEE Trans. Inf. Forensics Secur. **13**(1), 63–78 (2017)

32. Wang, C., et al.: Fingerprinting encrypted voice traffic on smart speakers with deep learning. In: Proceedings of the 13th ACM Conference on Security and Privacy in Wireless and Mobile Networks, pp. 254–265 (2020)

33. Wang, J., Cao, Z., Kang, C., Xiong, G.: User behavior classification in encrypted cloud camera traffic. In: 2019 IEEE Global Communications Conference (GLOBE-COM), pp. 1–6. IEEE (2019)

34. Wang, W., Zhu, M., Wang, J., Zeng, X., Yang, Z.: End-to-end encrypted traffic classification with one-dimensional convolution neural networks. In: 2017 IEEE International Conference on Intelligence and Security Informatics (ISI), pp. 43–48. IEEE (2017)

35. Yao, H., Liu, C., Zhang, P., Wu, S., Jiang, C., Yu, S.: Identification of encrypted traffic through attention mechanism based long short term memory. IEEE Trans. Big Data (2019)

36. Yoon, K.: Convolutional neural networks for sentence classification. arXiv (2014)

37. Yoon, S.H., Park, J.W., Park, J.S., Oh, Y.S., Kim, M.S.: Internet application traffic classification using fixed IP-port. In: Hong, C.S., Tonouchi, T., Ma, Y., Chao, C.S. (eds.) APNOMS 2009. LNCS, vol. 5787, pp. 21–30. Springer, Heidelberg (2009). https://doi.org/10.1007/978-3-642-04492-2_3

38. Yu, C., Tian, X., Guo, Y.: Research on user portrait based on behavior-content fusion model. Libr. Inf. Work **62**(13), 54–63 (2018)

39. Zhang, H., Papadopoulos, C., Massey, D.: Detecting encrypted botnet traffic. In: 2013 Proceedings IEEE INFOCOM, pp. 3453–1358. IEEE (2013)

Stochastic Simulation Techniques for Inference and Sensitivity Analysis of Bayesian Attack Graphs

Isaac Matthews$^{(\boxtimes)}$ ⓘ, Sadegh Soudjani ⓘ, and Aad van Moorsel ⓘ

School of Computing, Newcastle University, Newcastle upon Tyne, UK
I.J.Matthews2@newcastle.ac.uk

Abstract. A vulnerability scan combined with information about a computer network can be used to create an attack graph, a model of how the elements of a network could be used in an attack to reach specific states or goals in the network. These graphs can be understood probabilistically by turning them into Bayesian attack graphs (BAGs), making it possible to quantitatively analyse the security of large networks. In the event of an attack, probabilities on the graph change depending on the evidence discovered (e.g., by an intrusion detection system or knowledge of a host's activity). Since such scenarios are difficult to solve through direct computation, we discuss three stochastic simulation techniques for updating the probabilities dynamically based on the evidence and compare their speed and accuracy. From our experiments we conclude that likelihood weighting is most efficient for most uses. We also consider sensitivity analysis of BAGs, to identify the most critical nodes for protection of the network and solve the uncertainty problem for the assignment of priors to nodes. Since sensitivity analysis can easily become computationally expensive, we present and demonstrate an efficient sensitivity analysis approach that exploits a quantitative relation with stochastic inference.

Keywords: Bayesian attack graph · Vulnerability scan · Stochastic simulation · Intrusion detection · Network security · Probabilistic model

1 Introduction

Attack graphs are models of how vulnerabilities can be exploited to attack a network. They are directed graphs that demonstrate how multiple vulnerabilities and system configurations can be leveraged during a single attack in order to reach states in the network that were previously inaccessible to the attacker. An example of such a state is root privilege on a database that contains sensitive information. Attack graphs can be generated by performing a vulnerability scan of a network using a tool like OpenVAS [7] or Nessus [20], and then processing the results with an attack graph generator. For this paper, we use MulVAL [16] as it is open source and is used by the majority of the literature on attack graphs.

© Springer Nature Switzerland AG 2021
W. Lu et al. (Eds.): SciSec 2021, LNCS 13005, pp. 171–186, 2021.
https://doi.org/10.1007/978-3-030-89137-4_12

Attack graphs can be combined with Bayesian networks (BNs) to allow for a probabilistic analysis of the security of a network [3,8,12]. This combination is known as a Bayesian Attack Graph (BAG). These BAGs are generated by incorporating likelihood information for vulnerabilities into the original attack graph. One method of constructing BAGs is to acquire information on each vulnerability that is present in the graph from a vulnerability repository like the National Vulnerability Database. The Common Vulnerability Scoring System (CVSS) [4] vector that is in the database contains information, e.g., on the attack complexity for exploiting a vulnerability and the availability of an exploit [4], which can be used in various ways to estimate the likelihood that the vulnerability will be exploited [2,5,9].

BAGs are particularly promising as a dynamic risk assessment tool where an administrator models new security controls and their effects on a network. A network's most likely attack paths and most vulnerable hosts can be dynamically analysed, and this can be updated dependent on information from an intrusion detection system [18].

Well-defined (i.e., acyclic) BAGs can be solved using computational techniques that are well-known from the theory of BNs [13]. In recent work systematic approaches have also been proposed for BAGs that have loops and cycles, e.g., [10]. However, direct computational approaches become prohibitively slow if the number of nodes in the BAG is large, and can have large space requirements due to an increase in the size of the cliques in the graphs and their probability tables [13]. Therefore, it becomes important to consider stochastic simulation techniques.

In this paper, we focus on performing inference and sensitivity analysis on BAGs using stochastic simulation. We do this for dynamic scenarios that do not lend themselves for exact computation, namely scenarios that include observed evidence in the BAGs. We discuss how any evidence or alterations to the network can be included in the BAG analysis. That is, we create a dynamic model of the security of the network that can be used to deduce an attacker's most likely next move and their route thus far, as well as quantitatively evaluate and compare the effectiveness of different security controls and changes to the network.

While inference for BAGs using stochastic simulation has been explored by others [1,14], there has to date not been a comparison of different techniques' performances on BAGs. In this paper we employ three stochastic simulations techniques, probabilistic logic sampling (PLS), likelihood weighting (LW), and backward simulation (BS). We evaluate the performance of these techniques in their speed and accuracy as well as how they perform with different quantities of evidence to be included in the graph and different sizes of graph.

The primary outcome of our work is a recommendation of the most efficient simulation technique to use for inference in attack graphs. The recommendation is to use likelihood weighting, which performs well for both low and high evidence scenarios. Moreover, we establish a quantitative relation between stochastic inference and sensitivity analysis of BAGs. We discuss how the methods for including evidence in the graphs can also be used to measure the graphs sensitivity to each vulnerability in the network, and develop a fast approach to calculate these sensitivities without requiring many simulations or any analysis of distributions.

The rest of this paper is organised as follows. Section 2 describes the formalism for BAGs that is used throughout the paper and introduces the running example along with the motivation for the work. Section 3 introduces and discusses the three sampling techniques that are implemented and their accuracy. Section 4 then evaluates the performances of these techniques with regard to accuracy, amount of evidence and size of the graph. Section 5 introduces our measure of sensitivity and its importance. Finally Sect. 6 compares this work with the current literature available and Sect. 7 presents our conclusions.

2   Bayesian Attack Graphs

We consider a small enterprise network as a standard example used in the literature [8, 10, 17] to motivate the use of BAGs and demonstrate the sampling techniques discussed in this paper.

2.1   Motivating Example

The architecture of the small enterprise network can be seen in Fig. 1. In this scenario, the network administrator wants to protect the database server on the internal network from being accessed and the data being exfiltrated. The internal network with the database server can be accessed via the internal firewall one of two ways, either from the web server or from one of the workstations (grouped together and treated as one host for simplicity). Both of these routes require access to the demilitarized zone subnet (DMZ), which can be accessed by the internet through the external firewall.

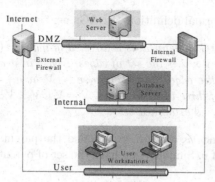

Fig. 1. Example of a small enterprise network architecture.

We then run a vulnerability scan on the network, which discovers a vulnerability on each of the hosts. On the database server, there is a MySQL vulnerability, the web server has a vulnerability in Apache, and the workstations have an

Internet Explorer vulnerability. With this vulnerability scan, we can generate an attack graph, for instance using the tools provided in MulVAL [16]. The attack graph represents how the vulnerabilities can be used in conjunction with one another to reach a high enough privilege on the database server to access the data.

2.2 Bayesian Attack Graphs

Figure 2 shows the resulting BAG from running a scan on the network presented in Fig. 1. For clarity, the nodes have been coloured to show which of the hosts in the architecture they correspond to. Nodes that have multiple colours are related to a transition between two hosts (from the colour on the left to the colour on the right). Node 0 in white colour is not related to any host on the network but represents an attack from the internet. Node 1 is deemed the goal node as it represents the primary state that the attacker must not reach, or else the data in the database becomes accessible to them. In general the goal node or nodes is the collection of nodes that allow the attacker to achieve something that the network administrator is trying to prevent.

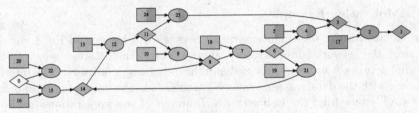

Fig. 2. The BAG of the small enterprise network presented in Fig. 1.

We provide the formal definition of BAGs next.

Definition 1. *A BAG is defined as a directed graph $\mathcal{G} = (\mathcal{V}, \mathcal{E})$, where $\mathcal{V}$ is the set of nodes and $\mathcal{E} \subset \mathcal{V} \times \mathcal{V}$ is the set of edges. Nodes in $\mathcal{V}$ are connected by edges from $\mathcal{E}$. We denote the edge connecting $v_i, v_j \in \mathcal{V}$ by $e_{ij} = (v_i, v_j)$. The set of nodes is comprised of three types of nodes, $\mathcal{V} = V_l \cup V_a \cup V_o$, representing LEAF, AND and OR nodes, as explained below.*

For any $v, v' \in \mathcal{V}$ and $(v, v') \in \mathcal{E}$, v is called the parent node of v' and v' is called a child node of v. Similarly, we have the set of parent nodes $pa(v') := \{v \in \mathcal{V} \mid (v, v') \in \mathcal{E}\}$.

The three types of nodes are as follows, first introduced in informal terms, then formally within the context of BAGs:

- V_l is the set of LEAF nodes in the graph, nodes that have no parent. They represent network configurations, the existence of vulnerablities or running services, and different conditions in the network, for example network connection information in the form of HACLs (host access control lists).

- V_a are the AND nodes, which have requisite conditions *all* of which must be satisfied in order to be accessed (an AND nodes parents have a conjunctive relationship). An example of an AND node would be the remote exploitation of a vulnerability, given that the vulnerability exists and the attacker has access to a host that is allowed access to the machine the vulnerability is located on. An AND node could also represent a movement between hosts if there are the fulfilled requirements of a configuration node for access between the machines and the attacker has access to one of them already.
- V_o are the OR nodes, which have requisite conditions of which *at least one* must be satisfied in order to be accessed (an OR node's parents have a disjunctive relationship). These nodes represent micro-states within the network that encode information about an attacker's location and privilege in the system. For example, if a machine has several vulnerabilities that could be exploited to achieve privilege escalation on that machine then exploiting any of those vulnerabilities would grant the attacker access to the state of higher privilege on the host. The overall macro-state of the attacker, being their privilege on each host and their access to and between each of the hosts, would be an enumeration of all the OR nodes that had been accessed.

As indicated in Fig. 2, the LEAF nodes are drawn as rectangles on the graph, the AND nodes are ellipses and the OR nodes are diamonds.

Suppose a local probability function $p : \mathcal{V} \to [0, 1]$ is given. Any BAG $\mathcal{G} = (\mathcal{V}, \mathcal{E})$ as in Definition 1 with local probability function $p : \mathcal{V} \to [0, 1]$ can be translated into a BN, which is denoted by the tuple $\mathcal{B} = (\mathcal{V}, \mathcal{E}, \mathcal{T})$. Let us consider the set of nodes $\mathcal{V} = \{1, 2, \ldots, n\}$ and associate a Boolean random variable X_k to each node $k \in \mathcal{V}$. The set $\mathcal{T}$ is a collection of probability tables that are constructed as follows. For all $k \in V_l$,

$$\text{Prob}(X_k = 1) = p(k) \quad \text{and} \quad \text{Prob}(X_k = 0) = 1 - p(k). \tag{1}$$

For $k \in V_a$, let $pa(k) = \mathbf{1}$ indicate that all the parent variables of the node k are equal to one. Then,

$$\begin{cases} \text{Prob}(X_k = 1|pa(k) = \mathbf{1}) = p(k), & \text{Prob}(X_k = 1|pa(k) \neq \mathbf{1}) = 0, \\ \text{Prob}(X_k = 0|pa(k) = \mathbf{1}) = 1 - p(k), & \text{Prob}(X_k = 0|pa(k) \neq \mathbf{1}) = 1. \end{cases} \tag{2}$$

For $k \in V_o$, let $pa(k) = \mathbf{0}$ indicate that all the parent variables of the node k are equal to zero. Then,

$$\text{Prob}(X_k = 1|pa(k) = \mathbf{0}) = 0, \quad \text{Prob}(X_k = 1|pa(k) \neq \mathbf{0}) = p(k), \tag{3}$$

and $\text{Prob}(X_k = 0|pa(k))$ is the complement of above probabilities.

Remark 1. Note that here we use the AND/OR formalism for BAGs [15] having three types of nodes, but another common formalism is the plain BAG [19] that has only one type of nodes.

In the work [10] the relation between the two formalisms is demonstrated, including how to transform one form to the other, and as such this paper is relevant to both types of BAGs.

2.3   Problem Statement

Problem 1. (Access Probabilities). Consider an attack graph $(\mathcal{V}, \mathcal{E})$ with local probability function $p : \mathcal{V} \rightarrow [0, 1]$. Compute $\text{Prob}(X_k = 1)$ for any $k \in \mathcal{V}$. This quantity is called the *access probability* of the node k and is simply denoted by $P(X_k)$. It will give the likelihood that an attacker will reach node k in an attack and will depend on the local probability function p and the structure of the attack graph.

Problem 2. (Inference). Suppose some evidence of an attack is known in the form of $\mathcal{Z} = \mathbf{z}$, where $\mathcal{Z} \subset \mathcal{V}$ is the set of random variables associated to the nodes for which we have the respective evidence values $\mathbf{z}$. Compute the likelihood that the attacker gain access to node $k \in \mathcal{V}$ given such an evidence: $P(X_k | \mathcal{Z} = \mathbf{z})$.

Problem 3. (Sensitivity Analysis). The local probability function $p : \mathcal{V} \rightarrow [0, 1]$ is often estimated based on prior knowledge or data on the network. Compute the sensitivity of access probabilities $P(X_k)$ and conditional probabilities $P(X_k | \mathcal{Z} = \mathbf{z})$ to the values $p(v)$ for any $v \in \mathcal{V}$. If $p(v)$ has a distribution, compute an interval for these quantities with a confidence bound.

We provide stochastic simulation techniques to answer Problems 1 and 2 in Sect. 3, and present a novel solution to Problem 3 in Sect. 5.

3   Sampling Techniques

3.1   Generating Samples

Using the BAG formalism defined in Sect. 2.2 a single attack can be modelled as the array of LEAF nodes. The value of the local probabilities correspond to 'achieving' something in an attack, such that if the node is given the value 1 then the exploit has worked or a condition has been met. Similarly, if the value is 0 then an exploit or condition has failed. The reach of the attack can then be calculated. In this way, after sampling the nodes a state on the graph is either accessible or inaccessible. With the example of Fig. 2, a single attack configuration would equate to all the rectangular LEAF nodes being set as y or n. States of the rest of the nodes are then obtained from combining this with samples from the local probability functions. The attackers' ability to reach an important state, e.g., corresponding to the ability to execute code on the database server at node 1, becomes either y or n.

We prepare the graph by assigning the LEAF nodes a series of prior distributions based upon factors like the ease of exploitation of a vulnerability. We then sample from the LEAF nodes and the local probability functions to create a single simulation of the entire graph.

3.2   Probabilistic Logic Sampling

For our attack graphs, probabilistic logic sampling (PLS) is performed by first sampling a configuration of LEAF nodes. A random number is generated between 0 and 1, if the number generated is less than the prior probability assigned to the LEAF node then the node is assigned a 1 (or y), if it is greater then the node is set at 0 (n). This is repeated for all LEAF nodes to create the configuration. When the configuration has been generated it can be used to prescribe states to the rest of the nodes in the graph. These states are then recorded as an array of 1s and 0s. This process is then repeated until N_s configurations have been generated and evaluated. The recorded arrays can be used to estimate the probability distributions of the nodes in the graph, with $\frac{N(X=1)}{N_s}$ being the estimated probability that an attacker will gain access to a particular node:

$$P(X) \approx \left(\frac{N(X = 1)}{N_s}, \frac{N(X = 0)}{N_s} \right) \tag{4}$$

The simplest way to include evidence with this technique is by discarding any samples that do not conform to the evidence provided. As such one is left with a subset of the original N_s simulations and can calculate the new probabilities in a similar way to Eq. (4).

In order to estimate the probability distribution of the kth variable with regard to the new evidence, $P(X_k | \mathcal{Z} = z)$, using N_s samples with PLS we use Algorithm 1 modified from [13]. Here $\mathcal{Z}$ is the variables or nodes that we have evidence for, $sp(X_k)$ is the state space of variable X_k, and $\mathbf{z}$ is the evidence that has been provided for these nodes. This would be in the form of a list of nodes that we know have been accessed created by an intrusion detection system, or a list of nodes that we are modelling as not accessed if we are comparing different security controls and their affect on the network.

Input: Set of nodes $\mathcal{V} = \{1, 2, \ldots, n\}$, local probabilities $p : \mathcal{V} \to [0, 1]$, number
of simulations N_s, evidence $\mathcal{Z} = \mathbf{z}$
Output: Conditional likelihoods $P(X_k | \mathcal{Z} = \mathbf{z})$ for all $k \in \mathcal{V}$
1. Let $(X_1, \ldots, X_n)$ be the associated Boolean random variables.
2. Initialise $N(X_k = x_k) = 0$ for all $x_k \in \{0, 1\}$ and all $k \in \mathcal{V}$.
3. **for** $j = 1$ *to* N_s :
   a) **for** $i = 1$ *to* n :
      Sample a state x_i for X_i using $P(X_i | pa(X_i) = \pi)$, where π is the
      configuration sampled for $pa(X_i)$
   b) If $\mathbf{x} = (x_1, \ldots, x_n)$ is consistent with $\mathbf{z}$, then
   $N(X_k = x_k) := N(X_k = x_k) + 1$ for all $k \in \mathcal{V}$, where x_k is the sampled
   state for X_k
   return $Prob(X_k = x_k | z) \approx \dfrac{N(X_k = x_k)}{\sum_{x \in sp(X_k)} N(X_k = x)}$

Algorithm 1: Performing PLS to approximate a distribution given some evidence.

3.3   Likelihood Weighting

Likelihood weighting (LW) is a method to deal with the problems of PLS for dealing with evidence, namely the inefficiency of generating samples that will be discarded if they conflict with evidence. Instead, for LW, only non-evidence variables are sampled from and as such no simulations are discarded. However this approach causes sampled variables to ignore evidence that is not present in their ancestors, and so an extra weighting has to be introduced. This weighting is equivalent to the probability a certain state will arise given the evidence provided.

Essentially we want to sample from the following distribution,

$$
\begin{aligned}
P(\mathcal{V}, \mathbf{z}) = \prod_{X \in \mathcal{V} \backslash \mathcal{Z}} P(X | pa(X)', pa(X)'' = \mathbf{z}) \\
\times \prod_{X \in \mathcal{Z}} P(X = e | pa(X)', pa(X)'' = \mathbf{z})
\end{aligned}
\tag{5}
$$

where $pa(X)''$ are parent nodes that have been instantiated by evidence, and $pa(X)'$ have not. By fixing the evidence variables then taking the sample, we instead are using

$$
P_s(\mathcal{V}, \mathbf{z}) = \prod_{X \in \mathcal{V} \backslash \mathcal{Z}} P(X | pa(X)', pa(X)'' = \mathbf{z})
\tag{6}
$$

So to rectify this we weigh each sample taken using

$$
w(\mathbf{x}, \mathbf{z}) = \prod_{Z \in \mathcal{Z}} P(Z = z | pa(X) = \pi)
\tag{7}
$$

where π is the configuration of the parents specified by $\mathbf{x}$ and $\mathbf{z}$. In order to estimate $P(X_k | \mathcal{Z} = z)$ using N_s samples, we use Algorithm 2 as defined in [13].

This is an improvement on PLS as it removes the inefficiency of discarding evidence, instead requiring the calculation of a weight for each simulation. A large number of samples may still be required, however, if the evidence provided is unlikely and therefore the difference between Eqs. 5 and 6 is large. This means the weighting would in general be very small and as such reaching an amount of error that is not too large may require a large computational time.

3.4   Backward Simulation

The final technique is based on the Backward Simulation (BS) method devised by Fung and Del Favero [6]. The primary difference between this and other techniques is that simulation runs originate at the known evidence and the simulation is run backwards. Once this process has terminated the remaining nodes are forward sampled in the standard way. The reason for this is to rectify the slow convergence caused by unlikely evidence.

Input: Set of nodes $\mathcal{V} = \{1, 2, \ldots, n\}$, local probabilities $p : \mathcal{V} \rightarrow [0, 1]$, number
       of simulations N_s, evidence $\mathcal{Z} = \mathbf{z}$
Output: Conditional likelihoods $P(X_k | \mathcal{Z} = \mathbf{z})$ for all $k \in \mathcal{V}$
1. Let $(X_1, \ldots, X_n)$ be the associated Boolean random variables.
2. **for** $j = 1$ *to* N_s :
   a) $w := 1$
   b) **for** $i = 1$ *to* n :
       - Let $\mathbf{x}'$ be the configuration of $(X_1, \ldots, X_{i-1})$ specified by $\mathbf{e}$ and
        previous samples
       - **if** $X_i \notin \mathcal{Z}$:
         Sample a state x_i for X_i using $P(X_i | pa(X_i) = \pi)$, where $pa(X_i) = \pi$
         is consistent with $\mathbf{x}'$
       else:
         $w := w \cdot P(X_i = z_i | pa(X_i) = \pi)$, where $pa(X_i) = \pi$ is consistent
         with $\mathbf{x}'$
   c) $N(X_k = x_k) := N(X_k = x_k) + w$, where x_k is the sampled state for X_k
return $P(X_k = x_k | \mathbf{z}) \approx \frac{N(X_k = x_k)}{\sum_{x \in sp(X_k)} N(X_k = x)}$

Algorithm 2: Performing likelihood weighting to approximate a distribution given some evidence

The backward sampling procedure begins at an evidence node and samples for the parents of the node using the distribution

$$P_s(pa(X_i)') = \frac{P(X_i | pa(X_i)' pa(X_i)'')}{Norm(i)}, i \in \mathcal{V}_b, \tag{8}$$

where $pa(X_i)'$ are the uninstantiated parents of X_i and $pa(X_i)''$ are the instantiated parents. The normalising constant $Norm(i)$ is calculated as

$$Norm(i) = \sum_{y \in XP(pa(X_i)')} P(X_i | y, X_{pa(X_i)''}). \tag{9}$$

with $XP(pa(X_i)')$ as the set of all possible cases for the uninstantiated parents of node X_i. Once all the ancestors of evidence nodes have been sampled, the forward sweep samples the remaining nodes as

$$P_s(X_i) = P(X_i | pa(X_i)), \quad \text{for all } i \in \mathcal{V}_f. \tag{10}$$

The weight for the simulation can be computed as the product of the normalisation constants along with the likelihood of nodes that were set by backwards sampling but were not sampled from themselves

$$w(\mathbf{x}, \mathbf{z}) = \prod_{i \in \mathcal{V} \setminus \mathcal{V}_s} P(X_i | pa(X_i)) \prod_{j \in \mathcal{V}_b} Norm(j). \tag{11}$$

As a form of likelihood weighting, BS is designed to cope better with very low-likelihood evidence. A large part of the computational cost of the algorithm comes from the calculation of the normalisation constants, which grows exponentially with the number of predecessor nodes. We would expect this technique to perform similarly to likelihood weighting for few evidence nodes but be an improvement when there are many nodes, as is demonstrated in the paper presenting the technique [6]. However the structure of the graph is of great importance and as such it is difficult to know beforehand which of the techniques will perform better for the application of BAGs.

3.5   Confidence Bounds

Since all these techniques are sampling from the same distribution once the corrective factors are applied, the standard error can be calculated in a similar way for each. As each simulation is random and independent from other simulations, it can be shown using the central limit theorem that

$$\sigma_{p(x)} = \sqrt{\frac{P(x)(1 - P(x))}{N_s}}. \tag{12}$$

4   Comparison

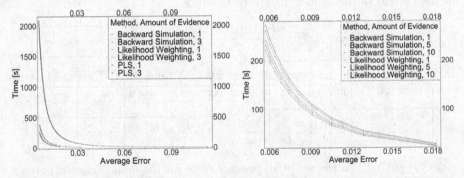

Fig. 3. Time against average node error for all three techniques.   **Fig. 4.** Time against average node error for BS and LW.

For the comparison of these techniques, each is first run on a 200 node attack graph from a small enterprise network with varying amounts of evidence. Figure 3 shows the increase in time (in wall clock seconds) required for improving the accuracy of results for situations when one and three evidence nodes have been included (the average time over thirty runs has been plotted; the error bars are too small to be drawn for this graph). As can be seen even with just one piece of evidence PLS performed poorly compared to the other methods, with three evidence nodes taking considerable amounts of time and runs with more than three evidence nodes timing out. The other two methods are run with five and ten evidence nodes provided, and the results for this can be seen in Fig. 4, again with the average result over thirty runs plotted. The minimum and maximum values are shown by the transparent ribbon. While these results are close, interestingly LW does outperform BS at higher quantities of evidence.

Figure 5 shows the convergence of each technique on a probability for one of the goals in the network, with the ribbon showing the error of the estimate. LW and BS converge equally quickly with three pieces of evidence but BS does converge faster when only one evidence is used.

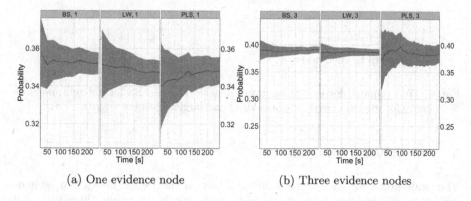

(a) One evidence node   (b) Three evidence nodes

Fig. 5. Convergence of goal node probability for all three techniques.

The techniques are also run across graph sizes of 100 nodes to 1500, again with 30 runs per graph size, with 1, 5 and 10 evidence nodes used. The results of these runs are shown in Fig. 6a with the points showing the average run time and the ribbon showing the maximum and minimum of the runs. PLS runs slightly worse than the other two techniques for one evidence node but performs very poorly for the other evidence levels so is omitted from the graphs for clarity. The stopping criteria for a run is an error of ± 0.02 per node.

BS performs best with one evidence node, and gives similar results for both 5 and 10 pieces of evidence. LW performs about as well at all evidence levels for graphs below 1000 nodes, but performs best with 10 evidence nodes for graphs larger than 1000.

Next the stopping criteria is relaxed to an error of ± 0.04 per node and the runs are repeated in a similar manner to Fig. 6a but up to graphs of 5000 nodes to investigate the scalability of the techniques. According to our industrial partner, as well as our own experience, graphs of this size correspond to large enterprise networks. For even larger networks, for example a 5G mobile network, the error can be further increased to improve scaling. These runs are plotted in Fig. 6b where it can be seen that LW out performs BS for all evidence levels at the larger graph sizes.

Given these results, likelihood weighting is the best technique for belief updating in BAGs as it not only performs slightly better overall across different evidence levels and graph sizes but also is easier to implement than backward simulation. Probabilistic logic sampling should only be used if no evidence is expected most of the time.

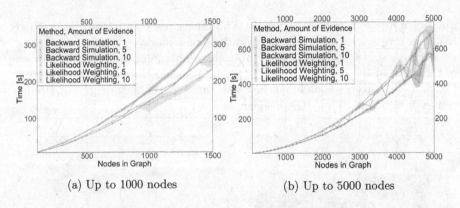

(a) Up to 1000 nodes   (b) Up to 5000 nodes

Fig. 6. Time required for increasing graph sizes for LW and BS for different amounts of evidence for medium sized networks *(left)* and larger networks *(right)*.

5   Sensitivity Analysis

The prior probabilities for the vulnerabilities on the LEAF nodes can be generated via different methods of varying complexity. For example Doynikova and Kotenko [3] use various parts of the CVSS vector and Cheng et al. [2] model the relationships of parts of the metrics to give them different weights and improve the accuracy of the probabilities. All these techniques however draw from the data available for a vulnerability which is often incomplete and quickly becomes outdated. Sensitivity analysis is important for the overall analysis of BAGs as it considers the impact of the original assignment of the probability.

To evaluate the sensitivity of the graph to the LEAF nodes, each node can be assigned a uniform probability distribution in turn rather than a single probability. A distribution can be generated for one or several goal nodes in the network with respect to each LEAF node; this is done by sampling from the LEAF nodes' uniform distribution, then generating a sample of the entire network as before. The change in the probability density of the access probability of the goal node in the network from Fig. 2 is shown in Fig. 7. The wider the distribution the more sensitive the goal node is to the probability applied at the LEAF node, if the LEAF node probability does not affect the goal node at all the probability density would be entirely concentrated at the goal probability value that is calculated when there are only single values for all LEAF nodes.

As such, the network is more sensitive to changes at node 17 or 16, whereas nodes 5 and 10 do not have much of an effect on the goal probability as shown by their narrow probability densities. This type of sensitivity analysis has been performed by others, as discussed in Sect. 6, however, in what follows we propose an alternative technique that requires much less computation and gives more usable results.

Theorem 1. *In any BAG, access probability of any node $P(X_k = x_k)$ is a polynomial function of the local probabilities $p(v)$, $v \in \mathcal{V}$. Moreover, for any*

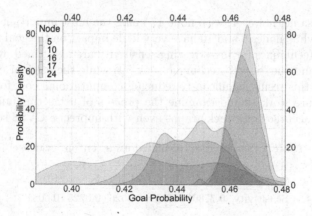

Fig. 7. Probability density of goal node when a uniform distribution is used for various leaf nodes, demonstrating their sensitivity.

$v \in \mathcal{V}$, $P(X_k = x_k)$ *is a linear function of* $p(v)$ *if* $p(v')$ *is fixed for all* $v' \neq v$. *The sensitivity of* $P(X_k = x_k)$ *with respect to any local probability* $p(v)$ *is*

$$\left| \frac{\partial}{\partial p(v)} P(X_k = x_k) \right| = |P(X_k = x_k | v = 1) - P(X_k = x_k | v = 0)|, \qquad (13)$$

which is always in the interval $[0, 1]$. *More generally, for any evidence* $\mathcal{Z} = z$,

$$\left| \frac{\partial}{\partial p(v)} P(X_k = x_k | \mathcal{Z} = z) \right|$$
$$= |P(X_k = x_k | \mathcal{Z} = z, v = 1) - P(X_k = x_k | \mathcal{Z} = z, v = 0)|. \qquad (14)$$

Both sensitivities in (13)–(14) *can be estimated using the efficient simulation techniques presented in this paper.*

Proof. The proof is inductive by sequentially conditioning the access probability on the LEAF nodes. The access probability $P(X_k = x_k)$ can be written as

$$P(X_k = x_k) = P(X_k = x_k | v = 0)P(v = 0) + P(X_k = x_k | v = 1)P(v = 1)$$
$$= P(X_k = x_k | v = 0)(1 - p(v)) + P(X_k = x_k | v = 1)p(v). \qquad (15)$$

Note that $P(X_k = x_k | v = 0)$ and $P(X_k = x_k | v = 0)$ are independent from $p(v)$. This gives linear dependency to $p(v)$ and makes $P(X_k = x_k)$ a polynomial function of all local probabilities. Moreover, the sensitivity with respect to $p(v)$ is: Sensitivity $= |P(X_k = x_k | v = 1) - P(X_k = x_k | v = 0)|$.

The sensitivities calculated in this manner are shown in Table 1, and using this sensitivity value allows quick evaluation of the importance of each node without the extensive computation or the required analysis of the probability distribution that is necessary to generate and interpret Fig. 7. The information remains the same, however, with node 17 being the most important followed by 16 then 24, while nodes 5 and 10 have very little impact on the goal node probability. Both techniques for investigating sensitivity are also timed, with a ±0.02 node error, and the 'on/off' technique took 59s while the original method took 1581s. With this result significantly reducing computational cost for sensitivity analysis, future work should examine the process of using this information to improve the accuracy of attack graphs even with imprecise CVSS scores.

Table 1. Sensitivities calculated using 'on/off' evidence.

Leaf Node	17	16	24	5	10
Sensitivity	0.7780	0.4388	0.3526	0.0225	0.0081

6   Related Work

One example of stochastic simulation techniques for attack graphs is by Noel and Jajodia [14]. They use PLS to compare different security fixes for a network. However this is performed by hand and as such it cannot be generally applied. Their use case compares several security controls that could be added to the network. This is achieved by examining the resulting distributions estimated when the changes are applied to the graph, in a manner similar to that shown in Fig. 7 as a sensitivity analysis. As discussed in Sect. 5, this requires more computation and also requires analysis of the resulting distributions. Baiardi and Sgandurra use Monte Carlo simulations in their Haruspex tool [1]. This tool is a fully featured program that uses attack graphs and threat agents to model security. It is an application for this type of graph, incorporating many different elements, but does not analyse different methods for simulation.

Muñoz-González et al. [11] present an exact method for inference in BAGs using the junction tree algorithm. This method is attractive due to its exact nature, but unfortunately is very limited in its application due to how it scales. This is caused by the requirement for tables to be generated based on the cliques created to start the calculations, and for large graphs these tables can become extremely large. It is better to have a trade-off in the accuracy of the method to reduce the space required, to allow scalability for the large graphs that are expected from enterprise networks. They go on to present an approximate technique in [12] using loopy belief propagation. The results of this scale well, linearly with respect to the number of nodes, while achieving a reasonable level of accuracy. The drawback to using this method, unlike stochastic simulation, is that there is no guarantee of convergence to the correct value.

7   Conclusion

In this paper we have presented and compared three stochastic simulation techniques that can be generally applied to inference of any BAG. We conclude that for most purposes the likelihood weighting process is the most efficient simulation technique to analyse an attack graph for any amount of evidence. We also provide a method to compute sensitivity, which does not require any complex analysis of distributions or prior sampling of node distributions. This can be used both as remediation for the high uncertainty in LEAF node prior probabilities, and as an easy prioritisation of vulnerabilities in light of their importance to a series of goal nodes.

References

1. Baiardi, F., Sgandurra, D.: Assessing ICT risk through a Monte Carlo method. Environ. Syst. Decis. **33**(4), 486–499 (2013). https://doi.org/10.1007/s10669-013-9463-4
2. Cheng, P., Wang, L., Jajodia, S., Singhal, A.: Refining CVSS-based network security metrics by examining the base scores. In: Network Security Metrics, pp. 25–52. Springer, Cham (2017). https://doi.org/10.1007/978-3-319-66505-4_2
3. Doynikova, E., Kotenko, I.: Enhancement of probabilistic attack graphs for accurate cyber security monitoring. In: IEEE SmartWorld/SCALCOM/UIC/ATC/CBDCom/IOP/SCI, pp. 1–6 (2017)
4. FIRST: Common vulnerability scoring system v3.1: Specification document (2019). https://www.first.org/cvss/v3.1/specification-document
5. Frigault, M., Wang, L., Jajodia, S., Singhal, A.: Measuring the overall network security by combining CVSS scores based on attack graphs and Bayesian networks. In: Network Security Metrics, pp. 1–23. Springer, Cham (2017). https://doi.org/10.1007/978-3-319-66505-4_1
6. Fung, R., Del Favero, B.: Backward simulation in Bayesian networks. In: Uncertainty Proceedings 1994, pp. 227–234. Elsevier (1994)
7. Greenbone: OpenVAS (2006). https://www.openvas.org/
8. Homer, J., et al.: Aggregating vulnerability metrics in enterprise networks using attack graphs. J. Comput. Secur. **21**(4), 561–597 (2013)
9. Keramati, M., Keramati, M.: Novel security metrics for ranking vulnerabilities in computer networks. In: 7th IST, pp. 883–888 (2014)
10. Matthews, I., Mace, J., Soudjani, S., van Moorsel, A.: Cyclic bayesian attack graphs: a systematic computational approach. In: IEEE 19th TrustCom (2020). https://doi.org/10.1109/TrustCom50675.2020.00030
11. Muñoz-González, L., Sgandurra, D., Barrere, M., Lupu, E.: Exact inference techniques for the analysis of Bayesian attack graphs. IEEE Trans. Dependable Secure Comput. **16**, 231–244 (2016)
12. Muñoz-González, L., Sgandurra, D., Paudice, A., Lupu, E.C.: Efficient attack graph analysis through approximate inference. CoRR abs/1606.07025 (2017)
13. Nielsen, T.D., Jensen, F.V.: Bayesian Networks and Decision Graphs. Springer, Heidelberg (2009). https://doi.org/10.1007/978-0-387-68282-2
14. Noel, S., Jajodia, S., Wang, L., Singhal, A.: Measuring security risk of networks using attack graphs. Int. J. Next-Gener. Comput. **1**(1), 135–147 (2010)
15. Ou, X., Boyer, W.F., McQueen, M.A.: A scalable approach to attack graph generation. In: 13th ACM CCS, pp. 336–345. ACM, New York (2006)
16. Ou, X., Govindavajhala, S., Appel, A.W.: MulVAL: a logic-based network security analyzer. In: Proceedings of the 14th Conference on USENIX Security Symposium, SSYM'05, vol. 14, p. 8. USENIX Association, Berkeley (2005)

17. Ou, X., Singhal, A.: Attack graph techniques. In: Ou, X., Singhal, A. (eds.) Quantitative Security Risk Assessment of Enterprise Networks. Springer Briefs in Computer Science, pp. 5–8. Springer, New York (2011). https://doi.org/10.1007/978-1-4614-1860-3_2
18. Poolsappasit, N., Dewri, R., Ray, I.: Dynamic security risk management using Bayesian attack graphs. IEEE Trans. Dependable Secure Comput. **9**(1), 61–74 (2012)
19. Swiler, L.P., Phillips, C., Ellis, D., Chakerian, S.: Computer-attack graph generation tool. In: Proceedings DARPA Information Survivability Conference and Exposition II. DISCEX'01, vol. 2, pp. 307–321 (2001)
20. Tenable: Nessus vulnerability scanner (1998). https://www.tenable.com/products/nessus/nessus-professional/

Simulations of Event-Based Cyber Dynamics via Adversarial Machine Learning

Zhaofeng Liu[1]([✉]), Yinchong Wang[1], Huashan Chen[2], and Wenlian Lu[1,3]

[1] Fudan University, NO. 220 Handan Road, Shanghai, China
wenlian@fudan.edu.cn
[2] University of Texas at San Antonio, San Antonio, TX 78249, USA
huashan.chen@utsa.edu
[3] Shanghai Key Laboratory for Contemporary Applied Mathematics,
Shanghai 200433, China

Abstract. In this paper, we apply cybersecurity dynamics theory into practical scenarios. We use machine learning models as detection tools of intrusion detection systems and consider cyber attacks against node computers as well as adversarial attacks against machine learning models. We pay our attention to two problems. The first problem is when the network is attacked, how we can observe the states of the network and estimate its equilibrium with a lower cost. We apply an event-based observation and estimation method combined with machine learning-based intrusion detection systems. The second problem is to control the cost and the convergence speed of cybersecurity dynamics when it is under attack. An event-based control method and machine learning-based intrusion detection systems are put into use in this scenario. We simulate both scenarios and analyze the dynamics' behaviors under an adversarial attack against the machine learning models on intrusion detection systems.

Keywords: Cybersecurity dynamics · Intrusion detection systems · Machine learning

1 Introduction

1.1 Research Background

Cybersecurity dynamics [23,24] is a new conception that concentrates on systematically understanding, characterizing, and quantifying cybersecurity from a holistic perspective. It aims to characterize how the attack-defense interactions govern the evolution of the global cybersecurity state [23] and how the resulting characteristics can be applied to guide cyber defense operations (see, for example, [14]).

W. Lu et al. (Eds.): SciSec 2021, LNCS 13005, pp. 187–201, 2021.
https://doi.org/10.1007/978-3-030-89137-4_13

Intrusion detection systems (IDS) [5] play a core role in cybersecurity. They have important functions such as monitoring hosts and networks, analyzing computer system behaviors, generating alarms, and responding to suspicious behaviors. They always act as an important part of reactive defense.

In this paper, we use machine learning models for host-based intrusion detection. We focus on log-based intrusion detection [18], where the IDS find anomalies in the log files so as to detect the malicious process and clean up the malware infecting the host. Due to the outstanding performance of machine learning technology in text analysis tasks, a variety of machine learning models have been used in the IDS to analyze the log text. However, the machine learning model itself can be the target of adversarial attacks and thus affects the performance of IDS [3,4]. A typical example is the *label reverse poisoning attack* [4], which reverses the labels of samples in the training data set and thus does harm to the machine learning model.

This paper will study the label reverse poisoning attack on various machine learning models and investigate its impact on cybersecurity dynamics.

1.2 Basic Concept

In the paper, we mainly talk about the *preventive and reactive cyber defense dynamics*:

$$\frac{di_v(t)}{dt} = f_v(i) = -\beta_v i_v(t) + \left[1 - (1 - \alpha_v)\prod_{u \in N_v}(1 - \gamma_{uv}i_u(t))\right](1 - i_v(t)). \tag{1}$$

There are two kinds of attacks in the dynamics: pull-based cyber attack and push-based cyber attack [27]. The attack-defense interaction takes place over an attack-defense graph structure $G = (V, E)$, where V is the vertex set representing computers and $(u, v) \in E$ means computer u can wage push-based attacks against computer v directly (i.e., the communication from u to v is allowed by the security policy). α_v is the probability that the node v is compromised by a pull-based attack. β_v is the probability that the compromised node v is recovered to safety. γ_{uv} indicates the probability that the compromised node u successfully infects secure node v. If the parameters are the same for all $v \in V$, we call the network node homogeneity. Otherwise the network is node heterogeneity. It is worth mentioning that in scenario 1 we consider node homogeneity network, that is, for any v, $\alpha_v = \alpha$, $\beta_v = \beta$ and $\gamma_{uv} = \gamma$. So the dynamics in scenario 1 is:

$$\frac{di_v(t)}{dt} = f_v(i) = -\beta i_v(t) + \left[1 - (1 - \alpha)\prod_{u \in N_v}(1 - \gamma i_u(t))\right](1 - i_v(t)). \tag{2}$$

While in scenario 2, since the pull-based attack has been removed by pre-control step, we don't consider its impact on dynamics. So the dynamics becomes:

$$\frac{di_v(t)}{dt} = f_v(i) = -\beta_v i_v(t) + \left[1 - \prod_{u \in N_v}(1 - \gamma_{uv}i_u(t))\right](1 - i_v(t)). \tag{3}$$

Note that the attacker refers to the person who launches the cyber attack while the adversary refers to the adversarial opponent of machine learning model. They are not necessarily the same one.

Notations are listed in Table 1.

1.3 Paper Outline

In Sect. 2, we elaborate the settings of our experiment. It includes the data set we use, the involving machine learning models, the type of cyber attacks and the performance of each machine learning model under the attacks. In Sect. 3, we introduce our first scenario about detecting the nodes of networks through machine learning and the accuracy of our observation. In Sect. 4, we explain our second scenario in which we combine an event-based method for the control tasks of cybersecurity with machine learning model. Besides, we study the performance of the method with each model under the same attack strength. In Sect. 5, we conclude this paper and propose some future research direction.

Table 1. Notations used throughout the paper

Notation	Description
$G = (V, E), A$	The attack-defense graph structure with adjacency $A = [a_{vu}]_{n \times n}$ where $a_{vu} = 1$ if and only if $(u, v) \in E$
$\lambda_{A,1}$	The maximum Eigenvalues of Adjacency matrix A
α_v	The probability that a secure computer is compromised by a pull-based attack.
β_v	The probability that a secure computer becomes compromised because a push-based attack
γ_{uv}	The probability that a compromised computer wages a successful push-based attack
$i_v(t), i(t)$	The probability is in the compromised state $i(t) = [i_1(t), \dots, i_n(t)]$
$\widehat{i_v(t)}, \widehat{s_v(t)}$	The probability that node v is in the compromised (secure) state at time t estimated from the sampling states

2 Machine Learning Model Deployment: Anomaly Detection Task Based on Text Classification

2.1 Experiment Settings

In this paper, we consider three types of machines learning models: SVM (Support Vector Machine), MLP (Multi Layer Perception) and CNN (Convolutional Neural Network).

All the three models have good performances in text analysis tasks. For CNN, we use GloVe algorithm [17] as the word-embedding method. The input feature map has 300 dimensions for each character. At the same time, the first 200 characters of each HTTP request sample are intercepted and used as the sample input. If the sample length is less than 200 characters, we use zero padding to supplement it. After three convolutional layers, we use ReLU function, maximum pooling and dropout. We set dropout rate as 0.5. The structure is shown in Fig. 1.

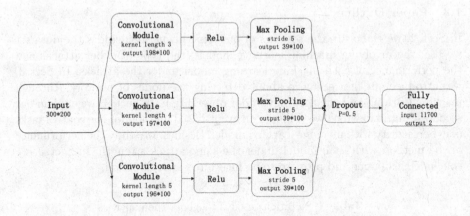

Fig. 1. The structure of CNN we used in this paper

For SVM and MLP, because the number of their layer is small, the dimension of the word-embedding used in GloVe algorithm (300*200 = 60000) is so high that the models in training process converge very difficultly. As an alternative, we choose TF-IDF feature vector representation [22], which achieves excellent performance in SVM and MLP. This method takes the first 500 dimensions of characters that appear most frequently in the vocabulary to construct the feature vector of the sample. That is to say, every feature vector is of 500 dimensions.

We use the CSIC2010 data set [6]. It is commonly used in the field of cyber-security research. The data set is publicly provided by the Spanish National Research Council (CSIC) and can be obtained at the official website of CSIC at https://www.isi.csic.es/dataset. This data set is widely used in the research of intrusion detection systems based on text classification and has produced many research results [20,21]. The abnormal (positive) request samples in this data set contain a variety of HTTP attacks, such as SQL injection attacks [2], buffer overflow attacks [7,16], private information collection [1,10], etc. Figure 2 shows a sample of an abnormal HTTP request in the CSIC2010 data set.

The CSIC2010 data set contains three txt text files: normalTrafficTraining.txt, normal-TrafficTest.txt and anomalousTrafficTest.txt. These three files have a total of 97,065 HTTP requests (including GET, POST and PUT). The first two files have a total of 72,000 normal HTTP requests, and the third file has 25065 abnormal requests. We analyze the HTTP sentence part of the requests in the three files and label the abnormal request as 1 (positive) and the normal request as −1 (negative) as the simulation data set of this paper.

The adversarial attack considered in this paper is the *label reverse poisoning attack* (i.e., reversing the labels of samples in training sets), which requires the adversary to manipulate the labels of the training set samples before the training process of the machine learning classifier. The attack intensity is represented by the proportion of label-reversed samples of all the sample.

2.2   The Performance of Each Model Under Adversarial Attacks

We test the performance of each model under attacks of different intensities. The models' performances are their accuracy on detecting malicious HTTP requests. As this paper mainly focuses on the ability of machine learning models on detecting positive samples under adversarial attacks, only the positive samples are screened for testing. That is to say, negative samples are not included in the test set. The accuracy formula is $Accuracy = \frac{TN+TP}{AllSamples}$. Notice that when there is no negative sample in test set, accuracy is equivalent to recall rate $Recall = \frac{TP}{TP+FN}$.

```
GET http://localhost:8080/tienda1/publico/anadir.jsp?id=2&nombre=Jam%F3n+Ib%E9rico&precio=85&cantidad=
%27%38+DROP+TABLE+usuarios%3B+SELECT+*+FROM+datos+WHERE+nombre+LIKE+%27%25&81=A%F1adir+al+carrito HTTP/1.1
User-Agent: Mozilla/5.0 (compatible; Konqueror/3.5; Linux) KHTML/3.5.8 (like Gecko)
Pragma: no-cache
Cache-control: no-cache
Accept: text/xml,application/xml,application/xhtml+xml,text/html;q=0.9,text/plain;q=0.8,image/png,*/*;q=0.5
Accept-Encoding: x-gzip, x-deflate, gzip, deflate
Accept-Charset: utf-8, utf-8;q=0.5, *;q=0.5
Accept-Language: en
Host: localhost:8080
Cookie: JSESSIONID=B92A8B48B9008CD29F622A994E8F658D
Connection: close
```

Fig. 2. An abnormal HTTP request sample in the CSIC2010 data set. This is a malicious request with an attack, and the highlighted part is related to SQL injection attack [9]

As shown in [11], when the intensity of the poisoning attack is approaching or exceeding 50%, the model's classification recall rate will face a 'cliff-like' fall down to below 0.5. In addition, theoretically, the effect of the label reverse poisoning attack after the attack intensity exceeding 50% will be centrosymmetric to a certain extent with the corresponding effect of the attack intensity less than 50%. Therefore, we only consider the outcome when the attack intensity is no more than 50%. The attack intensity gradually increases in the step length of 10%, and the recall rate of each model under adversarial attacks is shown in Table 2.

Table 2. Recall rates of different models under different attack intensity

	0	10%	20%	30%	40%
SVM	0.906	0.899	0.898	0.891	0.865
MLP	0.912	0.911	0.910	0.884	0.822
CNN	0.919	0.897	0.876	0.829	0.779

We can see from Table 2 that although the recall rate of the CNN model is the highest when there is no adversarial attack, when the attack intensity increases to 20% or above, the CNN model will suffer more damage than the other two models, with the recall rate showing a greater decline. So if we already know the existence of adversary, we should choose a more robust model like SVM and MLP to prevent the effectiveness of the machine learning model from being excessively impaired when it is attacked by an adversary.

3   Scenario 1: Observe the States of Network Nodes Through Machine Learning

In this scenario, we focus on a possible application of machine learning models in IDS. The IDS preliminarily observes the (sampling) state of the network nodes through the machine learning model, as shown in Fig. 3. The network in this scenario is node homogeneity (i.e., the parameters are node-independent). The details of scenario 1 are listed in Table 7.

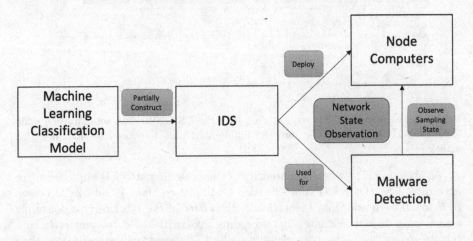

Fig. 3. Structure of scenario 1

3.1   Scenario Description

First, the node (i.e., computer) receives HTTP requests from other nodes in the network, some of which may contain malicious inputs. Once the malicious HTTP request is parsed, the attacker can obtain remote access to the compromised computer and further launch the same network attack on the neighbor nodes of the infected nodes [8]. For simplicity, we assume that the attacker cannot damage the log files in the compromised computers, including operating system logs, application logs, and system access logs that record HTTP requests.

The computers in the network do not use anti-malware tools, but reset the system for recovery (i.e., returning to the secure state). Since the computer cannot accurately determine its security state (i.e., whether is compromised or not), it must be reset at every point in time. In order to maintain computer's normal operation, we assume that the computer only reset a certain part of its own system at one time. Since each time the reset part may not cover the location of the malware, the computer is recovered to a secure state at a certain probability. We assume that the probability is a fixed value and denote it by β.

The IDS adopts a two-layer architecture to observe the sampling states of computers: in the first layer, the trained machine learning classifier model will quickly screen all kinds of log information of the node, and submit the detected suspected abnormal fragments to the next layer. In the second layer, an abnormal analysis tool with high resource consumption (such as processor computing resources or time resources) will further analyze all suspected abnormal fragments detected in the first layer, and accurately determine whether the corresponding fragments are abnormal. If the judgement is abnormal, the sampling state of the node will be recorded as '1' (compromised), otherwise it will be recorded as '0' (secure). Under this two-layer architecture, the observation results will only have FN (False Negative) and no FP (False Positive), and the sum of FN and recall rate is equal to 1.

3.2 Scenario Task: Estimate the Equilibrium of Cybersecurity Dynamics

In this scenario, it is necessary to estimate the equilibrium of cybersecurity dynamics in the network system through observations.

To reduce the observation cost, an event-based method [13] is used to estimate the equilibrium state of cybersecurity dynamics. We can see the setting of the scenario totally fits into the conditions of using the method. In the simulation, we use Gnutella network. This is a directed graph with $|V| = 8717$, $|E| = 31525$, maximal node in-degree 64 and $\lambda_{A,1} = 45.6167$ (Maximum eigenvalue). The other model parameters are set as: $\alpha = 0.2329$, $\beta = 0.6432$, $\gamma = 0.1712$, which means $i_v(t)$ converges to the unique nonzero equilibrium. We deploy aforementioned three machine learning models on IDS (SVM, MLP and CNN) and compare their estimations of equilibrium with the real state in network. Consider the mean of $\frac{1}{n}\sum_{v \in V} \frac{i_v(t) - \widehat{i_v(t)}}{i_v(t)}$ when $t \in [1300, 1500]$ and denote it by r. According to [13], the FN rate of IDS should be approximately equal to r. That is, the sum of the recall rate of model and r should be approximately equal to 1. We verified this in simulation according to the classification recall rate in Table 2. Table 3 shows the details.

Table 3. Recall rate $\mathcal{R}$ and estimation deviation r

	SVM	MLP	CNN
$\mathcal{R}$	0.906	0.912	0.919
r	0.081	0.076	0.069
$\mathcal{R}+r$	0.987	0.988	0.988

We can see that all the models satisfy $\mathcal{R} + r \approx 1$. So we can use $i_v(t) \approx \frac{\widehat{i_v(t)}}{\mathcal{R}}$ to correct our observation.

3.3 Scenario Variable: The Deployed Machine Learning Model is Under Adversarial Attack

Then we consider the adversarial attacks on machine learning models. The classification ability of models will decline when they are under attacks. As a result, the detection effect deteriorates to a certain extent. Therefore we need to consider the attack's effect on the equilibrium estimated by IDS. Suppose the attack reduces the recall rate of the model from $\mathcal{R}$ to $\mathcal{R}'$. Then the real equilibrium will be underestimated by approximately $r \approx 1 - \mathbb{R}'$. Denote the estimation of equilibrium under attack by $\widehat{i_v(t)}'$, then we have $\widehat{i_v(t)}' \approx \mathcal{R}' \times i_v(t)$. If we aren't aware of the attack and correct the result with previous recall rate $\mathcal{R}$, then the corrected result $\frac{\widehat{i_v(t)}'}{\mathcal{R}} \approx \frac{\mathcal{R}'}{\mathcal{R}} \times i_v(t) \leq i_v(t)$ is still underestimated. The formula above tells us that the ratio $\frac{\mathcal{R}'}{\mathcal{R}}$ determines the deviation rate between the true value and estimated value of equilibrium. So we call the index $1 - \frac{\mathcal{R}'}{\mathcal{R}}$ as *adversarial attack deviation rate*. Table 4 shows the deviation rates of different models under different attack intensity.

Table 4. Adversarial attack deviation rate

	0	10%	20%	30%	40%	50%
SVM	0	0.008	0.009	0.017	0.045	0.437
MLP	0	0.001	0.002	0.031	0.099	0.479
CNN	0	0.024	0.047	0.098	0.152	0.431

We can see under any intensity below 50%, the deviation rate of CNN is the highest, which means if we know the existence of adversary, we should deploy more robust classification and appropriately overestimate the equilibrium to reduce the deviation between the estimation and the true value.

4 Scenario 2: Using Machine Learning to Assist in Removing Malware

In this scenario, we use machine learning models to detect intrusions, lock the location of suspicious malware, and prepare for removal operations, as shown in Fig. 4. The network in this scenario is heterogeneous (i.e., the parameters are nodes-dependent). The details of scenario 2 are listed in Table 7.

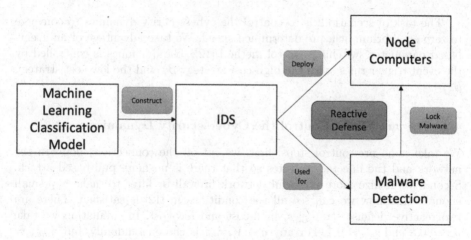

Fig. 4. Structure of scenario 2

4.1 Scenario Description

First, the node computer receives HTTP requests from other nodes in the network, some of which may contain malicious shellcode involving DoS (i.e., denial-of-service) attacks. Once the malicious HTTP request is parsed, the attacker can obtain the remote access to the compromised computer and execute the malicious code, which locks some important software systems of the compromised computer to deny access and attacks the neighbors of the compromised computer later [15,25,26]. For simplicity, we assume that adversary cannot damage the log files in the compromised computer, including operating system logs, application logs, and system access logs that record HTTP requests.

With regard to reactive defense, the node computers have two kinds of strategies.

- Low-cost reactive defense strategy: the machine learning based IDS quickly analyze the various log files, lock the location of suspicious malware, and then clean-up the malware without downtime (for eliminating false positive errors). The clearing success rate is modest, which is denoted by ϱ_-. As shown above, the probability that IDS can identify the malware is $\mathcal{R}$. Therefore, the probability that IDS identify and clear a malware is $\beta_- = \mathcal{R} \times \varrho_-$.
- High-cost reactive defense strategy: the machine learning based IDS quickly analyze the various log files, lock the location of suspicious malware, suspend certain services of the computer, and reset the relevant part of computer. It can remove malware with higher success rate, which is denoted by ϱ_+. Therefore the probability that IDS identify and clear a malware is $\beta_+ = \mathcal{R} \times \varrho_+$.

It is notable that DoS attack will explicitly damage the operation of the node computer, so the sampling state of the node can be accurately observed.

The task of scenario 2 is to control the cybersecurity dynamics to converge to zero equilibrium at a pre-determined speed. We take advantage of an event-based parameter switching control method [12]. The dynamics is controlled by the event trigger rules, with the high-cost strategy β_+ and the low-cost strategy β_-.

4.2   Scenario Task: Control the Cybersecurity Dynamics

We take some pre-control steps: first, we cut off the connections between the network and the infected websites so that there is no more pull-based attack. Second, we utilize more powerful network firewall or filter to make γ_{uv} small enough. And now we can see all the conditions in [12] is satisfied. There are two reactive defense strategies, high-cost and low-cost. In simulation we take $\varrho_+ = 0.8$ and $\varrho_- = 0.1$. For any $v \in V$, γ_{vu} is chosen randomly, but $\gamma_{max} = 0.017$. So the dynamics can converge to zero no matter the control is β_+ or β_-. Now we simulate under an event-based parameter switching method that controls the cybersecurity dynamics (3) on network where an machine learning model (SVM, MLP or CNN) are deployed on nodes. Consider the deviation between the mean of exponential convergence speed index $\mathcal{S}(t) = -\frac{1}{\Delta t} \ln \frac{i(t+\Delta t)}{i(t)}$ and criterion function's exponential speed index $\iota = 0.5$ when $t \in [0, 500]$. We calculate the index $\frac{|\mathcal{S}-\iota|}{\iota}$. And we also need to pay attention to control cost index $\frac{1}{n} \sum_{v \in V} \frac{T_+^v}{T_+^v + T_-^v}$. The threshold of exponential speed index and cost control index are 10% and 0.8 respectively.

The simulation results verify the effectiveness and efficiency of event-based parameter switching methods under each machine learning classifier model. The details are shown in Table 5.

Table 5. Control cost and converge speed deviation

	SVM	MLP	CNN
Control cost	0.66	0.66	0.65
Convergence speed deviation	7.85%	7.39%	7.56%

4.3   Scenario Variable: The Deployed Machine Learning Model Is Under Adversarial Attack

Now we examine how event-based parameter switching control of cybersecurity dynamics will be affected by adversarial attacks. When the adversary launches 40% poisoning attack, the corresponding event-based parameter switching control results are shown in Table 6.

Table 6. The effect under attack

	SVM	MLP	CNN
Control cost	0.67	0.70	Failure
Convergence speed deviation	8.77%	9.73%	

We note that the effectiveness of CNN-based IDS gets the most serious impairment. Under the low-cost control strategy, we have

$$\beta_- = \mathcal{R} \times \varrho_- < \lambda_{A,1} \times \gamma_{\max}. \tag{4}$$

It means that under 40% poisoning attack, the dynamics derived from the CNN-based IDS doesn't have the ability to converge to zero equilibrium. The theorem 1 proves that under conditions in (4), there will be Zeno behavior. It results in the failure of the event-based control method.

Theorem 1. *For any $v \in V$, if the low-cost control of the event-based Parameter Switching Method (the trigger rule is defined above) doesn't possess the ability to make the dynamics converge to zero, then the dynamics under control will cause Zeno behavior.*

Proof. We use the same notations as those in [12]. For any node $v \in V$, denote $i_v^\star$ by the dynamics' equilibrium under low-cost reactive defense strategy β_-. As the condition assumes, $i_v^\star \neq 0$. According to Sard lemma [19, 27], the measurement of the parameter regime where the dynamics converges polynomially is zero, so it can't be selected in practice. As a result, without the loss of generality, we can always assume that the dynamics converges exponentially in the parameter regime corresponding to low-cost reactive defense strategy β_-.

It is noted that the criterion functions in event-based parameter switching method

$$\begin{cases} \varphi_{up}(t) &= \mathrm{e}^{-\iota t}, \forall t \geq 0, \\ \varphi_{low}(t) &= L \times \mathrm{e}^{-\iota t}, \forall t \geq 0 \end{cases}$$

converge to zero exponentially. Where L is a positive constant, $0 \leq L \leq 1$. So when the dynamics fully evolved under the control of parameter switching, it has $\varphi_{low}(t) \leq i_v(t) \leq \varphi_{up}(t) \leq i_v^\star$. We consider the behavior of $i_v(t)$ when t is large enough. In the case of ignoring a constant coefficient, we still write $e^{-t\mathcal{S}_-^v(t)}$ as the convergence speed of the dynamics when the parameter $\beta_v = \beta_-$. Note that β_v will switch to low-cost setting β_- after $m_v(\tau_k^v) = \varphi_{low}(\tau_k^v)$.

After fully evolving, $i_v(t)$ tends to increase to the equilibrium point $i_v^\star$, while the upper criterion function $\varphi_{up}(t)$ converges to zero. Then we have

$$\varphi_{up}(\tau_k^v) - \varphi_{low}(\tau_k^v) \geq [i_v^\star - \varphi_{low}(\tau_k^v)][1 - e^{-(t_{k+1}^v - \tau_k^v)\mathcal{S}_-^v(t_{k+1}^v)}].$$

From above, we can get

$$t_{k+1}^v - \tau_k^v \leq -\frac{ln[1 - \frac{(1-L)e^{-\iota\tau_k^v}}{i_v^* - \varphi_{low}(\tau_k^v)}]}{\mathcal{S}_-^v(t_{k+1}^v)}. \tag{5}$$

As shown in [12], $t \to +\infty$ implies $k \to +\infty$ for both $\{t_k^v\}$ and $\{\tau_k^v\}$ (i.e., there are infinitely many parameter switching events)

Evidently, the right hand side of the inequality (5) converges to zero as $t \to +\infty$. It shows that $t_{k+1}^v - \tau_k^v$ has no positive lower bound. That is to say, the dynamics under control of event-based parameter switching method will cause Zeno behavior, which results in the failure of the present control method.   □

In addition, it should be noted that if the criterion functions in the event-based parameter switching method

$$\begin{cases} \varphi_{up}(t) &= e^{-\iota t}, \forall t \geq 0, \\ \varphi_{low}(t) &= L * e^{-\iota t}, \forall t \geq 0 \end{cases}$$

converge too fast, that is, the exponential convergence rate index ι in the criterion functions is defined too large, then when the machine learning models are under fierce adversarial attacks, there may be cases that even if the high-cost reactive defense strategy has maintained for a long time, the dynamics still cannot reach the target convergence speed. It also leads to the failure of the event-based parameter switching method.

If we already know the existence of adversary and the type of the possible attack, then from the above simulation and discussion, we can summarize some feasible plans for the event-based parameter switching method to deal with potential adversarial attacks against machine learning classifier models:

- Choose to deploy a more robust machine learning classifier model (which may sacrifice a small amount of classification recall rate when there is no adversarial attack).
- If the reactive defense strategy can no longer converge the dynamics to the zero equilibrium point under the adversarial attack, further control can be used to reduce the push-based attack success rate γ_{max} or to strengthen the reactive defense strategy (which may increase cost expenses, such as processor computing resources or time resources, or shutdown operations that affect the stable operation of the system).
- If the dynamics cannot reach the target convergence speed under adversarial attack, the target value needs to be lowered as appropriate to deal with the destruction of the adversarial attack.

Table 7. Details of two cybersecurity dynamics simulation scenarios

	Scenario 1	Scenario 2
Types of Nodes	Node homogeneity	Node heterogeneity
Types of malicious HTTP request	Malicious code snippets used to gain remote access	Malicious code snippets involved in DoS attacks used to gain remote access
Types of cyber attack	Trojan attack	DoS attack
The purpose of the cyber attack	Steal private data and send the same attack to neighbor nodes of the compromised node	Lock some important software systems of the node computer and attack neighbors
Scenario task	Estimation of equilibrium of cybersecurity dynamics	Control of cybersecurity dynamics
Intrusion detection systems architecture	Two-tier architecture: machine learning classifier model and anti-malware analysis module	Two-tier architecture: machine learning classifier model and anti-malware analysis module
Purpose of intrusion detection systems	Malware detection, to preliminarily observe the sampling states of network nodes	Malware detection and removal
Reactive defense	Reset and restore part of the system	Low-cost strategy: IDS + non-stop use of anti-malware tools
		High-cost strategy: IDS + shutdown reset and restore
Whether the sampling states of network nodes can be accurately observed	Can not be observed accurately	Can be observed accurately
Types of adversarial attacks	Poisoning attack	Poisoning attack
The effect of adversarial attacks	Estimation is lower than the true value after correction	May cause the parameter switching control method to fail

5   Conclusion

In this paper, we simulate the event-based methods for cybersecurity dynamics. We consider two practical scenarios where the defender employs machine learning methods for intrusion detection, which however may be the target of adversarial attacks. In the first scenario, we use an event-based method to reduce the cost of monitoring the network's security status. We study the deviation between our observation and the real situation when the machine learning models are under different intensities of adversarial attacks. It shows that although CNN gets the best performance when the network is safe, it is the most vulnerable model when an adversary exists. In addition, if we know the machine learning model is under attack, we should appropriately adjust our observations. In the second scenario, we apply an event-based parameter switching control method to reduce the cost of cleaning up the whole network at a target speed. We study the performance of our control method when the machine learning models are under adversarial attacks. We prove that when the poisoning attack is intensive enough, the control method can no longer converge the network to zero equilibrium and there will be Zeno behavior in the dynamics. That is the main finding of our paper.

There are still many open questions for future research, such as: How to apply the cybersecurity dynamics theory into other practical scenarios? How will the event-based methods perform in the new scenarios? Besides, how will the dynamics behave when the model is under different kinds of adversarial attacks?

References

1. Al-Bataineh, A., White, G.: Analysis and detection of malicious data exfiltration in web traffic. In: 2012 7th International Conference on Malicious and Unwanted Software, pp. 26–31. IEEE (2012)
2. Anley, C.: Advanced SQL injection in SQL server applications (2002)
3. Biggio, B., et al.: Security evaluation of support vector machines in adversarial environments. In: Ma, Y., Guo, G. (eds.) Support Vector Machines Applications, pp. 105–153. Springer, Cham (2014). https://doi.org/10.1007/978-3-319-02300-7_4
4. Biggio, B., Nelson, B., Laskov, P.: Poisoning attacks against support vector machines. arXiv preprint arXiv:1206.6389 (2012)
5. Denning, D.E.: An intrusion-detection model. IEEE Trans. Softw. Eng. 2, 222–232 (1987)
6. Giménez, C.T., Villegas, A.P., Marañón, G.Á.: Http data set CSIC 2010. Information Security Institute of CSIC (Spanish Research National Council) (2010)
7. Gupta, S.: Buffer overflow attack. IOSR J. Comput. Eng. 1(1), 10–23 (2012)
8. Halfond, W.G., Viegas, J., Orso, A., et al.: A classification of SQL-injection attacks and countermeasures. In: Proceedings of the IEEE International Symposium on Secure Software Engineering, vol. 1, pp. 13–15. IEEE (2006)
9. Ito, M., Iyatomi, H.: Web application firewall using character-level convolutional neural network. In: 2018 IEEE 14th International Colloquium on Signal Processing & Its Applications (CSPA), pp. 103–106. IEEE (2018)
10. Liu, Y., Corbett, C., Chiang, K., Archibald, R., Mukherjee, B., Ghosal, D.: Detecting sensitive data exfiltration by an insider attack. In: Proceedings of the 4th Annual Workshop on Cyber Security and Information Intelligence Research: Developing Strategies to Meet the Cyber Security and Information Intelligence Challenges Ahead, pp. 1–3 (2008)
11. Liu, Z., Jia, Z., Lu, W.: Security comparison of machine learning models facing different attack targets. In: Liu, F., Xu, J., Xu, S., Yung, M. (eds.) SciSec 2019. LNCS, vol. 11933, pp. 77–91. Springer, Cham (2019). https://doi.org/10.1007/978-3-030-34637-9_6
12. Liu, Z., Lu, W., Lang, Y.: An event-based parameter switching method for controlling cybersecurity dynamics. arXiv preprint arXiv:2104.13339 (2021)
13. Liu, Z., Zheng, R., Lu, W., Xu, S.: Using event-based method to estimate cybersecurity equilibrium. IEEE/CAA J. Automatica Sinica 8(2), 455–467 (2020)

14. Lu, W., Xu, S., Yi, X.: Optimizing active cyber defense. In: Das, S.K., Nita-Rotaru, C., Kantarcioglu, M. (eds.) GameSec 2013. LNCS, vol. 8252, pp. 206–225. Springer, Cham (2013). https://doi.org/10.1007/978-3-319-02786-9_13

15. Mahadev Kumar, V., Kumar, K.: Classification of DDOS attack tools and its handling techniques and strategy at application layer. 2016 2nd International Conference on Advances in Computing, Communication, & Automation (ICACCA) (Fall), pp. 1–6 (2016)

16. Papernot, N., McDaniel, P., Goodfellow, I.: Transferability in machine learning: from phenomena to black-box attacks using adversarial samples. arXiv preprint arXiv:1605.07277 (2016)

17. Pennington, J., Socher, R., Manning, C.: GloVe: global vectors for word representation. In: Proceedings of the 2014 Conference on Empirical Methods in Natural Language Processing (EMNLP), pp. 1532–1543. Association for Computational Linguistics (2014)

18. Raut, U.K.: Log based intrusion detection system. IOSR J. Comput. Eng. **20**(5), 15–22 (2018)

19. Sard, A.: The measure of the critical values of differentiable maps. Bull. Am. Math. Soc. **48**(12), 883–890 (1942)

20. Tekerek, A.: A novel architecture for web-based attack detection using convolutional neural network. Comput. Secur. **100**, 102096 (2021)

21. Torrano-Giménez, C., Perez-Villegas, A., Alvarez Maranón, G.: An anomaly-based approach for intrusion detection in web traffic (2010)

22. Wang, J., Zhou, Z., Chen, J.: Evaluating CNN and LSTM for web attack detection. In: Proceedings of the 2018 10th International Conference on Machine Learning and Computing, pp. 283–287 (2018)

23. Xu, S.: Cybersecurity dynamics. In: Proceedings of the 2014 Symposium and Bootcamp on the Science of Security, pp. 1–2 (2014)

24. Xu, S.: Cybersecurity dynamics: a foundation for the science of cybersecurity. In: Wang, C., Lu, Z. (eds.) Proactive and Dynamic Network Defense, vol. 31, pp. 1–31. Springer, Heidelberg (2019). https://doi.org/10.1007/978-3-030-10597-6_1

25. Zargar, S.T., Joshi, J., Tipper, D.: A survey of defense mechanisms against distributed denial of service (DDOS) flooding attacks. IEEE Commun. Surv. Tutor. **15**(4), 2046–2069 (2013)

26. Zebari, R.R., Zeebaree, S.R., Jacksi, K.: Impact analysis of HTTP and SYN flood DDOS attacks on apache 2 and IIS 10.0 web servers. In: 2018 International Conference on Advanced Science and Engineering (ICOASE), pp. 156–161. IEEE (2018)

27. Zheng, R., Lu, W., Xu, S.: Preventive and reactive cyber defense dynamics is globally stable. IEEE Trans. Netw. Sci. Eng. **5**(2), 156–170 (2017)

Dynamics, Network and Inference

Dismantling Interdependent Networks Based on Supra-Laplacian Energy

Wei Lin[1], Shuming Zhou[2,3]($\boxtimes$), Min Li[2,3], and Gaolin Chen[2,3]

[1] Concord University College, Fujian Normal University,
Fuzhou, Fujian 350117, People's Republic of China
[2] College of Mathematics and Informatics, Fujian Normal University,
Fuzhou, Fujian 350117, People's Republic of China
zhoushuming@fjnu.edu.cn
[3] Center for Applied Mathematics of Fujian Province (Fujian Normal University),
Fuzhou, Fujian 350117, People's Republic of China

Abstract. The vulnerability of complex networks is critical in the evaluation of robustness, especially attack resistance. The vulnerability of complex networks reflects the ability of network decomposition after deleting some key nodes, which is related to the collective influence maximization problem. Based on Supra-Laplacian energy, we propose a greedy algorithm (SLE) for interdependent networks to select a set of influential nodes with minimal coupling effect to maximize the collective influence. Compared with monolayer network, SLE algorithm is sensitive in interdependent networks in terms of connected component number, size of giant component, shortest distance and so on.

Keywords: Interdependent network · Laplacian energy ·
Supra-Laplacian matrix · Network vulnerability

1 Introduction

The research on network vulnerability and the related assessment methods have become the current research hotspot of complex networks [1], transportation network [2], water footprint network [3], familial language network [4] and more. If a small fraction of influential nodes in the network are attacked or fail, the cascade effect will spread to the entire network and finally lead to network paralysis. Therefore, identifying the key nodes in the network is critical for analyzing the vulnerability of the network, preventing network cascading failure and proposing effective recovery strategies.

In the real world, many kinds of interactions between individuals exist in the complex system. If we regard the multiple interaction ways simply as the edges in the monolayer network, our analysis of the complex system will be biased. In fact, complex system is composed of multiple networks with different structures and functions, which becomes the hot spot in network science [5].

W. Lu et al. (Eds.): SciSec 2021, LNCS 13005, pp. 205–213, 2021.
https://doi.org/10.1007/978-3-030-89137-4_14

Multilayer networks can be divided into three categories such as interdependent networks, multiplex networks and time-dependent networks [6]. This paper focuses on interdependent network with multi-dependence relation which is defined that a node is interdependent on several nodes on another layer. The feature that distinguishes multilayer network from monolayer network is the interaction, or coupling, between the different layers. Coupling in cross layers can significantly affect the cascade failure, so that interdependent network deserves more attention than monolayer network.

Laplacian energy is a measure to determine the structural information of a graph and can also be used to measure the importance of nodes [7–10], and improve network robustness [11]. The relative descend of Laplacian energy in the network due to the vanish of nodes in the network indicates the importance of nodes in the whole network. The importance of a node is determined by the change in Laplacian energy after the node is deleted. Besides, Laplacian energy has lower complexity than others except degree centrality. The contribution of this paper is to exploirt Supra-Laplacian energy to evaluate the coupling effect within the nodes to maximize the collective influence in interdependent networks. Furthermore, we evaluate the performance of our approach in both the monolayer and interdependent networks in terms of connected component number, size of giant component, shortest distance and so on.

The remainder of the paper is organized as follows. Section 2 introduces Laplacian energy of interdependent networks. Based on the coupling mechanism between nodes, the greedy algorithm is suggested in Sect. 3. In Sect. 4, we compare the proposed method with other centrality metrics in interdependent network. Section 5 concludes the paper.

2   Laplacian Energy of Interdependent Networks

Table 1. Important variables used in the context

Variables	Descriptions
m	Number of layers in interdependent network M
n	Number of nodes in M
Y_i	The ith layer of M
A	Supra-adjacency matrix
L	Supra-Laplacian matrix
D	Degree matrix

Take a two-layer interdependent network M with n nodes in each layer. Nodes from one layer randomly depend on a number of nodes in a different layer. This structure between the network layers is often called mesostructure. Similar to adjacency matrix for monolayer networks, some matrices such as

Supra-adjacency matrix can be used to study multilayer networks [12]. The Supra-adjacency matrix A of the interdependent network M is denoted by

$$A = A_Y + A_C = \begin{pmatrix} A_{Y_1} & 0 \\ 0 & A_{Y_2} \end{pmatrix} + \begin{pmatrix} 0 & A_C \\ A_C^T & 0 \end{pmatrix},$$

where A_{Y_i} $(i = 1, 2)$ is the $n \times n$ adjacency matrix of ith layer network and the connections between Y_1 and Y_2 are characterized by $n \times n$ adjacency matrix A_C (Table 1).

Further, we denote the Supra-Laplacian matrix of the interdependent network by

$$\begin{aligned} L &= L_Y + L_C \\ &= [D_Y - A_Y] + [D_C - A_C] \\ &= \begin{pmatrix} L_{Y_1} & 0 \\ 0 & L_{Y_2} \end{pmatrix} + \begin{pmatrix} D_1 & -A_C \\ -A_C^T & D_2 \end{pmatrix}, \end{aligned}$$

where $D_1 = diag(A_C 1_n)$, $D_2 = diag(A_C^T 1_n)$, and the Laplacian matrix of ith layer network is denoted L_{Y_i} $(i = 1, 2)$.

Definition 1. *If G is a graph of n vertices, and $\lambda_1, \lambda_2, \ldots, \lambda_n$ are the eigenvalues of its Laplacian matrix. The Laplacian energy of G is defined as the following invariant:*

$$E(G) = \sum_{i=1}^{n} \lambda_i^2.$$

In the following, we first define Laplacian centrality for a node in interdependent network M. In order to better reflect the structure of the interdependent network, the overlapping degree k_i^M of node v_i in the interdependent network is divided into two parts: d_i^Y represents the degree of node v_i in Y_i and the rest is d_i^C, i.e., $k_i^M = d_i^Y + d_i^C$.

Theorem 2.1. *For a two-layer interdependent network with N nodes, Supra-Laplacian energy of M*

$$E(M) = \sum_{i=1}^{N} (k_i^M)^2 + \sum_{i=1}^{N} k_i^M,$$

where k_i^M represents the overlapping degree of node v_i in M.

Theorem 2.2. *For a two-layer interdependent network with N nodes, Supra-Laplacian centrality of v_i is*

$$E_M(v_0) = (k_0^M)^2 + k_0^M + 2 \sum_{i \in N^M(v_0)} (k_i^M),$$

where k_i^M represents the overlapping degree of node v_i in M, and $N^M(v_0)$ denotes the neighborhood of vertex v_0.

Corollary 2.1. *For a two-layer interdependent network with N nodes, the Supra-Laplacian energy of edge e_{ij},*

$$E_M(e_{ij}) = 2(k_i^M + k_j^M),$$

where k_i^M represents the overlapping degree of node v_i in M.

Based on the Supra-Laplacian energy, we propose a greed algorithm to find a group of nodes to dismantle the network, whose advantages will be shown in Sect. 4.

3   Collective Influence Maximizing Algorithm

Coupling relationships play a connecting role in interdependent networks. Therefore, coupling should also be considered in the process of mining key nodes. The collective influence of nodes is not simply equal to the sum of the influences of individual nodes. Because the connections between the faulty nodes do not participate in fault propagation, the internal connections of the faulty node group are too dense, which reduces the ability of propagation and diffusion. We use the Supra-Laplacian energy of the edges to measure the coupling influence. According to the analysis above, to maximize the collective influence is actually to minimize $\sum_{i,j \in S} E_M(e_{ij})$, i.e.,

$$\Delta E(S) = \sum_{i \in S} E_M(v_i) - \sum_{i,j \in S} E_M(e_{ij}), \tag{1}$$

where $\sum_{i \in S} E_M(v_i)$ is the sum of Supra-Laplacian centrality of v_i in S and $\sum_{i,j \in S} E_M(e_{ij})$ is the sum of Supra-Laplacian energy of edge e_{ij} in S. Now, we propose a greedy algorithm to mine the key node set S to maximize the collective influence based on minimal coupling effect.

Algorithm 1. Collective influence maximizing algorithm based on Supra-Laplacian energy (SLE)

Input: Graph G, K: the size of influential node set
Output: The influential nodes set S

1: $S = \varnothing$, $E = \varnothing$, $max = 0$, $t = e = 0$, $sum = 0$
2: **for** $i := 1$ to K **do**
3:    **for** $v \in V$ **do**
4:       **if** $v \in S$ **then**
5:          continue
6:       $S = S \cup v$
7:       calculate $E_G(v)$
8:       $t' = t + E_G(v)$
9:       $sum = 0$
10:      **for** $j \in S$ **do**
11:         **if** $e_{vj} \notin S$ **then**
12:            continue
13:         calculate $E_G(e_{vj})$
14:         remove e_{vj} from G
15:         $E = E \cup e_{vj}$
16:         $sum+ = E_G(e_{vj})$
17:      $e' = e + sum$
18:      calculate $\Delta E(S) = t' - e'$
19:      **if** $\Delta E(S) > max$ **then**
20:         $max = \Delta E(S)$
21:         $h_1 = v$
22:         $h_2 = E_G(v)$
23:         $h_3 = sum$
24:      remove v from S
25:      $G \cup E$
26:      $E = \varnothing$
27:      $max = 0$
28:   **if** $h_1 \notin S$ **then**
29:      $S = S \cup h_1$
30:   $t+ = h_2$
31:   $e+ = h_3$

---

4   Experimental Analysis

4.1   Baseline Methods

We compare the results of the collective influence maximizing algorithm based on Supra-Laplacian energy with the classical methods, including Degree centrality (DC), Closeness centrality (CC), and Betweenness centrality (BC).

4.2   Evaluation Metrics

In this subsection, we introduce several metrics as criteria for evaluating the merits of SLE. The details are as follows:

1) **Connected component number (c):** After the deletion of key nodes, the larger the number of connected omponents, the more severe the network function decline, the more vulnerable the network.

2) **Size of giant component (g):** After multiple cascading failures, the interdependent network finally reaches steady state and decomposes into several components. The connected component with the most nodes is called the giant component, which is another factor characterizes cascading failures is the size of the giant component.

3) **Shortest distance (d):** The sparser the node group is, the smaller the coupling effect is. The most intuitive metric for sparsity of key nodes is the average shortest distance

$$d = \frac{2}{\sum_{i,j \in S} e_{ij}} \sum_{i,j \in S,\ i \geq j} d_{ij}, \tag{2}$$

where e_{ij} is an edge between two nodes i and j, d_{ij} is the shortest diatance between two nodes i and j.

4) **Coupling Supra-Laplacian energy (p):** The coupling Supra-Laplacian energy is a straightforward method to measure the influence overlap between S

$$p = \frac{\sum_{i,j \in S} E_M(e_{ij})}{\sum_{i \in S} E_M(v_i)}. \tag{3}$$

According to the previous analysis, the smaller p is, the better the algorithm is.

4.3   Monolayer and Interdependent Network

In order to verify the effectiveness of SLE, four real monolayer networks (see Fig. 2) are introduced for mining important nodes.

1) **Jazz [13]:** A collaboartion network between Jazz musicians with 198 nodes and 2742 edges.

2) **The 2-layer interdependent network:** The network is composed of two ER random networks, each layer has 50 nodes and the probability of connections in Y_1 and Y_2 are 0.2 and 0.6, respectively. The nodes in the Y_i layer $(i = 1, 2)$ depends on at most one node in the other network layer.

3) **Zachary Karate Club [14]:** This network is a member of a university karate club related to data (see Fig. 5). ZACHE indicates whether there are connections between club members; ZACHC represents the relative strength of the association. Each layer of the network has 34 nodes.

4.4   Experimental Results

In this subsection, we evaluate the performance of SLE. In Fig. 1, the number of connected components changes with the number of key nodes. Normally, as the number of influential nodes increases, the number of connected components

increases. It is obvious that SLE has the best performance among the majority
of networks. In Jazz, although the SLE effect is not the best, it is better than
most algorithms. We also found that the larger the network size, the better
the algorithm performance. Compared with monolayer network, SLE performs
better on interdependent network.

Another variable related to network vulnerability is the size of giant component. It is easy to see from Fig. 2, as the size of S increases, the size of the giant
component decreases to 0. Obviously, SLE, comparing with other algorithms,
can dismantle the network more quickly.

The smaller the coupling effect between nodes is, the more sparse the nodes
are. The straightforward metric of network sparsity is the average distance.
Whether in monolayer network or interdependent network, SLE can find influence nodes with larger average distance than other algorithms (see Fig. 3).

Our ultimate aim not only makes the coupling effect small, but also requires
the nodes to have a large collective influence. The node influence is proportional to the Supra-Laplacian energy. Figure 4 shows that, compared with the
traditional centrality algorithms, the nodes selected by SLE have less coupling
Supra-Laplacian energy. It is proved that the traditional centrality algorithms
have strong coupling connections. Figure 5 shows the Supra-Laplacian energy
of the remaining network after the deletion of the influential nodes. The Supra-
Laplacian energy of the remaining network is inversely proportional to the Supra-
Laplacian energy of the deleted influential nodes. It is easy to see from Figs. 4
and 5 that the nodes identified by the SLE not only have the largest collective
influence, but also ensure the minimum coupling effect.

The increase of network size inevitably leads to the increase of edges, we
find that the final result of SLE in the interdependent network is better, compared with the monolayer network. If the influence nodes identified by SLE are
deleted, the network performance will drop sharply, which is more obvious in
interdependent networks. Obviously, the monolayer network can achieve a similar effect only by deleting more nodes. It shows that interdependent networks
are easier to decompose. Because of the interdependence of each layer network
in the interdependent network, the network becomes more vulnerable after the
nodes are attacked.

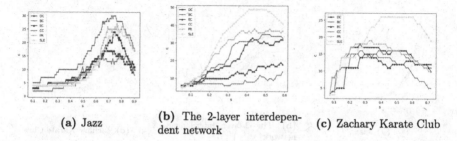

(a) Jazz   (b) The 2-layer interdependent network   (c) Zachary Karate Club

Fig. 1. The number of connected components (c) of the survival network after removing
S (where the x-axis is $s = \frac{|S|}{N}$).

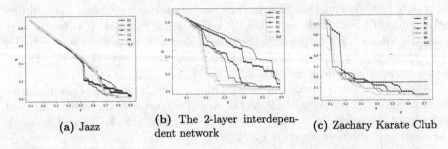

(a) Jazz

(b) The 2-layer interdependent network

(c) Zachary Karate Club

Fig. 2. The size of giant component (g) of the survival network after removing S.

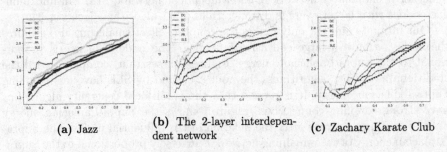

(a) Jazz

(b) The 2-layer interdependent network

(c) Zachary Karate Club

Fig. 3. The shortest distance (d) of S.

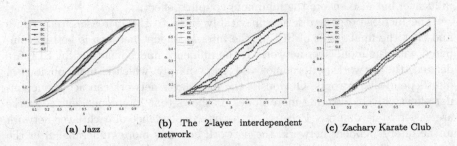

(a) Jazz

(b) The 2-layer interdependent network

(c) Zachary Karate Club

Fig. 4. The coupling Supra-Laplacian energy (p) of S.

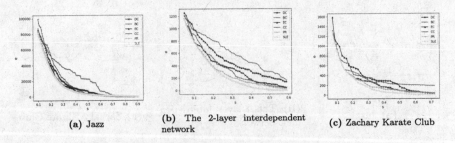

(a) Jazz

(b) The 2-layer interdependent network

(c) Zachary Karate Club

Fig. 5. The Supra-Laplacian energy (e) of the survival network after removing S.

5   Conclusion

The vulnerability of interdependent network is one of the core problems in the research of complex networks. Because the interlayer connections, interdependent networks are very fragile. Based on Laplacian energy of the Supra-Laplacian matrix, we propose a greedy algorithm to select a set of nodes to minimize the coupling effect and maximize the collective influence. In monolayer networks and interdependent networks, compared with the classical algorithms, it is obvious that SLE shows better performance. Meanwhile, SLE algorithm provides a new strategy for protecting the key nodes of the network.

Acknowledgment. This work was partly supported by National Natural Science Foundation of China (Nos. 61977016, 61572010), Natural Science Foundation of Fujian Province (Nos. 2020J01164, 2017J01738 and JAT170118), Middle-aged and Young of the Education Department of Fujian Province of China (Nos. JAT200958, JAT191119) and Research Foundation of Concord University College Fujian Normal University (Nos. KY20200204).

References

1. Wen, T., Deng, Y.: The vulnerability of communities in complex networks: an entropy approach. Reliab. Eng. Syst. Saf. **196**, 106782 (2020)
2. Gu, Y., Fu, X., Liu, Z., Xu, X., Chen, A.: Performance of transportation network under perturbations: reliability, vulnerability, and resilience. Transp. Res. Part E: Logist. Transp. Rev. **133**, 101809 (2020)
3. Yu, D., Ding, T.: Assessment on the flow and vulnerability of water footprint network of Beijing city, China. J. Clean. Prod. **293**, 126126 (2021)
4. Weintraub, S., Rader, B., Coventry, C., et al.: Familial language network vulnerability in primary progressive aphasia. Neurology **95**(7), 847–855 (2020)
5. Wu, Z.-N., Di, Z.-R., Fan, Y.: The structure and function of multilayer networks: progress and prospects. J. Univ. Electron. Sci. Technol. China **50**(1), 106–120 (2021)
6. Chen, K., Chen, L., Wu, T.: Survey on community detection in multi-layer networks. J. Front. Comput. Sci. Technol. **14**(11), 1801–1812 (2020)
7. Qi, X., Fuller, E., et al.: Laplacian centrality: a new centrality measure for weighted networks. Inf. Sci. **194**, 240–253 (2012)
8. Ma, Y., Cao, Z., Qi, X.: Quasi-Laplacian centrality: a new vertex centrality measurement based on Quasi-Laplacian energy of networks. Phys. A **527**, 121130 (2019)
9. Lazic, M.: On the Laplacian energy of a graph. Czechoslov. Math. J. **56**(131), 1207–1213 (2006)
10. Qi, X., Duval, R.D., et al.: Terrorist networks, network energy and node removal: a new measure of centrality based on Laplacian energy. Soc. Netw. **2**, 19–31 (2013)
11. Zheng, Y., Li, W., et al.: Laplacian energy maximization for multi-layer air transportation networks. J. Southeast Univ. (Engl. Ed.) **33**(3), 341–347 (2017)
12. Yang, Y., Tu, L., et al.: Spectral properties of Supra-Laplacian for partially interdependent networks. Appl. Math. Comput. **365**, 124740 (2020)
13. See [SPSurl1urlSPS] for "Jazz"
14. Zachary, W.: An information flow model for conflict and fission in small groups. J. Anthropol. Res. **33**, 452–473 (1977)

DWT-DQFT-Based Color Image Blind Watermark with QR Decomposition

Liangcheng Qin, Ling Ma[✉], and Xiongjun Fu

School of Information and Electronics, Beijing Institute of Technology, Beijing, China

Abstract. In order to improve the performance of color image digital watermarking, a watermarking algorithm based on integration of Discrete Wavelet Transform (DWT) and Discrete Quaternion Fourier Transform (DQFT) combined with QR matrix decomposition is proposed. The three channels of a color image are processed as a whole to embed watermark information. Experimental results show that the watermarking algorithm has good robustness against attacks such as JPEG compression, cropping, and median filtering.

Keywords: DWT transform · Quaternion · DQFT transform · QR decomposition · Blind watermark

1 Introduction

For multimedia content owners and service providers, the protection of digital multimedia content has become an increasingly important issue. Taking into account the human visual system and the redundancy property of the image, watermark such as copyright information is embedded into the digital image to track the use of the host image, so as to achieve the copyright protection and integrity verification of the digital image.

A lot of algorithms of digital watermark have been proposed yet, mainly including embedding the watermark directly in the pixel values of host images [1], or altering the coefficients in the transform domain, such as Fourier transform, discrete cosine transform [2–4], Fourier-Mellin transform, wavelet transform [5, 6], et al. And the studies of watermarking based on the feature point [7] of original images were proposed. Matrix decomposition was also considered during the watermark embedding, such as the self-embedding fully blind watermarking algorithm based on QR matrix decomposition [8,9], and the blind digital watermarking algorithm of QR decomposition of gray-scale image DWT-FRFT transformation [10], so that image watermarking has good robustness and invisibility. Literature [11] proposed the quaternion polar harmonic transform watermarking algorithm and realized the three-channel integral watermarking of the color image.

The watermark embedding algorithm based on DWT transform and DQFT [12] transform with QR matrix decomposition [13, 14] is proposed, which combines the better robustness of the transform domain, embedding the watermark by processing the three channels of color images as a whole. It shows good transparency as a blind watermarking algorithm, that the watermark is extracted without original image.

© Springer Nature Switzerland AG 2021
W. Lu et al. (Eds.): SciSec 2021, LNCS 13005, pp. 214–224, 2021.
https://doi.org/10.1007/978-3-030-89137-4_15

2 Related Theories

2.1 Discrete Wavelet Transform

Discrete Wavelet Transform (DWT) is a conversion in the time-frequency domain, with the characteristics of multi-scale. Two dimensional wavelet transform includes scaling function $\varphi(x, y)$ and wavelet functions $\psi^H(x, y), \psi^V(x, y)$ and $\psi^D(x, y)$, in which ψ^H denotes the transform in column direction, ψ^V denotes the transform in row direction, ψ^D denotes the transform in diagonal direction.

The scaling and translation basis function defines like

$$\varphi_{j,m,n}(x, y) = 2^{j/2}\varphi\left(2^j x - m, 2^j y - n\right) \tag{1}$$

$$\psi^i_{j,m,n}(x, y) = 2^{j/2}\psi^i\left(2^j x - m, 2^j y - n\right), \quad i = \{H, V, D\} \tag{2}$$

in which i denotes direction H,V,D.

The wavelet transform of the image $f(x,y)$ is stated as follows,

$$W_\varphi(j_0, m, n) = \frac{1}{\sqrt{MN}} \sum_{x=0}^{M-1} \sum_{y=0}^{N-1} f(x, y)\varphi_{j_0,m,n}(x, y) \tag{3}$$

$$W^i_\psi(j, m, n) = \frac{1}{\sqrt{MN}} \sum_{x=0}^{M-1} \sum_{y=0}^{N-1} f(x, y)\psi^i_{j,m,n}(x, y) \quad i = \{H, V, D\} \tag{4}$$

the inverse discrete wavelet transform is

$$f(x, y) = \frac{1}{\sqrt{MN}} \sum_m \sum_n W_\varphi(j_0, m, n)\varphi_{j_0,m,n}(x, y)$$
$$+ \frac{1}{\sqrt{MN}} \sum_{i=H,V,D} \sum_{j=j_0}^{\infty} \sum_m \sum_n W^i_\psi(j, m, n)\psi^i_{j,m,n}(x, y) \tag{5}$$

2.2 Quaternion and Quaternion Fourier Transform

Quaternion is an effective representation of a high-dimensional space. A quaternion q has one real part and three imaginary parts, which can be expressed as $q = a + bi + cj + dk$, in which i, j and k satisfies the relational expression [15].

$$i^2 = j^2 = k^2 = -1, \; ij = -ji = k, \; jk = -kj = i, \; ki = -ik = j$$

Quaternion can express the rotation and scaling of four-dimensional space through addition, subtraction, multiplication, and division. Due to the limitation of the relationship between i, j, k, quaternion does not satisfy the commutative law of multiplication.

Because of the constraints of the relationship between the three imaginary parts of the quaternion i, j, k, the two-dimensional quaternion Fourier transform can be divided into several types, including the right-sided quaternion Fourier transform, the left-sided quaternion Fourier transform and the two-sided quaternion Fourier transform. The left-sided quaternion Fourier transform and the corresponding inverse transform is illustrated as following [16].

$$F(w, v) = \frac{1}{\sqrt{MN}} \sum_{m=0}^{M-1} \sum_{n=0}^{N-1} exp\left[-\mu 2\pi \left(\frac{mw}{M} + \frac{nv}{N}\right)\right] f(m, n) \qquad (6)$$

Inverse left-sided Quaternion Fourier Transform of is stated as below

$$f(m, n) = \frac{1}{\sqrt{MN}} \sum_{m=0}^{M-1} \sum_{n=0}^{N-1} exp\left[\mu 2\pi \left(\frac{mw}{M} + \frac{nv}{N}\right)\right] F(w, v) \qquad (7)$$

In which μ is an orthogonal unit pure quaternion, w and v is the frequency component.

2.3 The Quaternion Matrix Representation of Color Image

A color image has three color channels Red, Green, and Blue. For a color image of $M \times N$ size, $f_R(x, y), f_G(x, y), f_B(x, y)$ can be used to represent the pixel values of the three channels, $1 \le x \le M, 1 \le y \le N$. Then the elements in the $M \times N$ quaternion matrix can be expressed as a quaternion matrix[5] with 0 as a real part, $f(x, y) = f_R(x, y)i + f_G(x, y)j + f_B(x, y)k$, because of which all channels of the color image are taken into account as a whole.

While, the quaternion of the watermarking scheme proposed in this paper is constituted with the low-frequency coefficients $LL_R(x, y), LL_G(x, y), LL_B(x, y)$ of discrete wavelet transform of R, G, B components as three imaginary parts, instead of $f_R(x, y), f_G(x, y), f_B(x, y)$, to represent a pure quaternion matrix, namely $Q(x, y) = LL_R(x, y)i + LL_G(x, y)j + LL_B(x, y)k$ (Fig. 1).

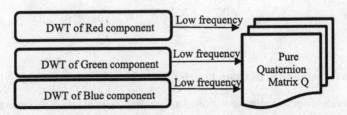

Fig. 1. The quaternion matrix constituted with wavelet transform low frequency coefficients

2.4 Watermark Embedding Combined with Matrix QR Decomposition

A non-singular matrix A of size N×N can be decomposed as follows

$$A = QR \qquad (8)$$

Where Q is the $N \times N$ matrix with orthonormal vectors, and R is the upper triangular matrix of $N \times N$. Let $A = [a_1, a_2, \cdots, a_N]$, $Q = [q_1, q_2, \cdots, q_N]$,

$R = [r_1, r_2, \cdots, r_N]$, where a_i, q_i and r_i ($i = 1, 2,..., N$) are the column vectors of A, Q, and R. The R matrix has an important property, that is the first row elements of the R matrix is larger than the other row elements, so the first row elements of the R matrix are selected to embed the watermark.

$$A = [a_1, a_2, a_3, a_4] = \begin{bmatrix} a_{1,1} & a_{1,2} & a_{1,3} & a_{1,4} \\ a_{2,1} & a_{2,2} & a_{2,3} & a_{2,4} \\ a_{3,1} & a_{3,2} & a_{3,3} & a_{3,4} \\ a_{4,1} & a_{4,2} & a_{4,3} & a_{4,4} \end{bmatrix}$$

$$A = [q_1, q_2, q_3, q_4][r_1, r_2, r_3, r_4]$$

$$= \begin{bmatrix} q_{1,1} & q_{1,2} & q_{1,3} & q_{1,4} \\ q_{2,1} & q_{2,2} & q_{2,3} & q_{2,4} \\ q_{3,1} & q_{3,2} & q_{3,3} & q_{3,4} \\ q_{4,1} & q_{4,2} & q_{4,3} & q_{4,4} \end{bmatrix} \begin{bmatrix} r_{1,1} & r_{1,2} & r_{1,3} & r_{1,4} \\ 0 & r_{2,2} & r_{2,3} & r_{2,4} \\ 0 & 0 & r_{3,3} & r_{3,4} \\ 0 & 0 & 0 & r_{4,4} \end{bmatrix}$$

$$= \begin{bmatrix} q_{1,1}r_{1,1} & q_{1,1}r_{1,2}+q_{1,2}r_{2,2} & q_{1,1}r_{1,3}+q_{1,2}r_{2,3}+q_{1,3}r_{3,3} & q_{1,1}r_{1,4}+q_{1,2}r_{2,4}+q_{1,3}r_{3,4}+q_{1,4}r_{4,4} \\ q_{2,1}r_{1,1} & q_{2,1}r_{1,2}+q_{2,2}r_{2,2} & q_{2,1}r_{1,3}+q_{2,2}r_{2,3}+q_{2,3}r_{3,3} & q_{2,1}r_{1,4}+q_{2,2}r_{2,4}+q_{2,3}r_{3,4}+q_{2,4}r_{4,4} \\ q_{3,1}r_{1,1} & q_{3,1}r_{1,2}+q_{3,2}r_{2,2} & q_{3,1}r_{1,3}+q_{3,2}r_{2,3}+q_{3,3}r_{3,3} & q_{3,1}r_{1,4}+q_{3,2}r_{2,4}+q_{3,3}r_{3,4}+q_{3,4}r_{4,4} \\ q_{4,1}r_{1,1} & q_{4,1}r_{1,2}+q_{4,2}r_{2,2} & q_{4,1}r_{1,3}+q_{4,2}r_{2,3}+q_{4,3}r_{3,3} & q_{4,1}r_{1,4}+q_{4,2}r_{2,4}+q_{4,3}r_{3,4}+q_{4,4}r_{4,4} \end{bmatrix} \quad (9)$$

As seen from the above formula that $a_{11} = r_{11}q_{11}$, if r_{11} is modified, meanwhile, the value of a is changed, and the pixel value is altered to affect the invisibility of the watermark. While if $r_{1,4}$ and $a_{1,4}$ is modified, the indirect impact will be less. So $r_{1,4}$ is the proper element to embed the watermark.

3 Watermarking Algorithm

3.1 Watermark Embedding Algorithm

The proposed algorithm of watermark embedding is shown in Fig. 2. The principle steps of watermark embedding are illustrated as follows:

(1) The first-level wavelet transform is performed on the R, G, B channels of the original color image. Then the three low-frequency components $LL_R(x, y)$, $LL_G(x, y)$, $LL_B(x, y)$ are obtained.
(2) Coefficients of $LL_R(x, y)$, $LL_G(x, y)$, $LL_B(x, y)$ constitute a pure quaternion matrix $Q = LL_R(x, y)i + LL_G(x, y)j + LL_B(x, y)k$, and the left quaternion Fourier transform is performed to get the matrix $F_q(w, v) = W(w, v) + X(w, v) i + Y(w, v)j + Z(w, v)k$.
(3) The real part $W(w, v)$ of $F_q(w, v)$ is divided into 4×4 blocks. QR decomposition is done for each sub-block. The watermark is embedded in the $r_{1,4}$ element in the first row and fourth column of the R matrix obtained by QR decomposition.
(4) Different modification ranges T_1 and T_2 according to the watermark information w is selected.

(5) The possible results C_1 and C_2 of the modification based on T_1 and T_2 are determined as below,

$$C_1 = 2kt + T_1 \tag{10}$$

$$C_2 = 2kt + T_2 \tag{11}$$

in which $k = \text{floor}(\text{ceil}(r_{1,4}/t)/2)$, $\text{floor}(x)$ is the largest integer not greater than x, $\text{ceil}(x)$ is the smallest integer not less than x, and t is the quantization step size, the value of which can be determined through experiments.

(6) $r_{1,4}*$ is calculated after embedding the watermark

$$r_{1,4}^* = \begin{cases} C_2 \; if \; abs(r_{1,4} - C_2) < abs(r_{1,4} - C_1) \\ C_1 \; otherwise \end{cases} \tag{12}$$

(7) Instead of $r_{1,4}$, $r_{1,4}*$ is used to perform inverse QR decomposition to obtain 4×4 matrix $\mathbf{A}*$ with watermarked information

$$\mathbf{A}^* = \mathbf{Q} \times \mathbf{R}^* \tag{13}$$

(8) Inverse-QDFT and Inverse-DWT is done to obtain a watermarked color image.

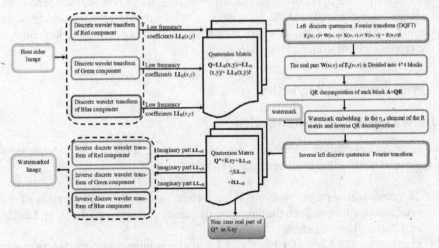

Fig. 2. Watermark embedding algorithm flowchart

3.2 Watermark Extraction Algorithm

Since the real part quantity obtained after DQFT transformation is modified, the quaternion matrix obtained by inverse-DQFT is no longer a pure quaternion matrix. A non-zero real part will be generated, which is stated as the key, which is used to extract the watermark information.

The proposed algorithm of watermark extraction is shown in Fig. 3, the principle steps of which are illustrated as follows:

(1) The first-level wavelet transform is performed on the **R, G, B** channels of the watermarked color image. And the three low-frequency components $LL_R^*(x, y), LL_G^*(x, y), LL_B^*(x, y)$ are obtained.

(2) Coefficients of $LL_R^*(x, y), LL_G^*(x, y), LL_B^*(x, y)$ constitute a quaternion matrix $Q^* = key + LL_R^*(x, y)i + LL_G^*(x, y)j + LL_B^*(x, y)k$, and the left quaternion Fourier transform is performed to get the matrix $F_q^*(w, v)$

$$F_q^*(w, v) = W^*(w, v) + X^*(w, v)i + Y^*(w, v)j + Z^*(w, v)k$$

(3) The real part $W^*(w, v)$ of $F_q^*(w, v)$ is divided into 4×4 blocks. QR decomposition is performed for each sub-block, the watermark is extracted from the $r_{1,4}^*$ element in the first row and fourth column of the **R** matrix obtained by QR decomposition.

$$w^* = mod\left(ceil\left(\frac{r_{1,4}^*}{t}, 2\right)\right) \tag{14}$$

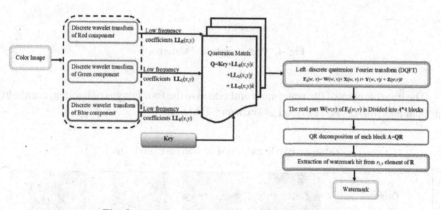

Fig. 3. Watermark extraction algorithm flowchart

4 Experiment and Analysis

The experimental simulation environment is windows10 and Matlab R2017a. The 8-bit true color images, such as baboon, cornfield, sailboat, and flowers, with the size of 512 × 512, are the test images as shown in Fig. 4. The wavelet basis function of the wavelet transform is Haar wavelet, and the watermark image is 64 × 64, shown in Fig. 5. PSNR and SSIM are used to evaluate the invisibility of the watermark. The larger the PSNR and SSIM, the more similar the watermarked image and the original image. The correct decoding rate (CDR) is used to evaluate the robustness of the image watermark under

220   L. Qin et al.

the attack of noise, JPEG compression, cropping, and median filtering. The closer to 1 the CDR is, the better the robustness of the watermark is.

$$\text{CDR} = \frac{1}{MN} \sum_{i=1}^{M} \sum_{j=1}^{N} xnor\big(\mathbf{W}(i,j), \mathbf{W}^*(i,j)\big) \tag{15}$$

Where $M \times N$ is the size of the watermark, $\mathbf{W}(i,j)$ and $\mathbf{W}^*(i,j)$ refer to the original watermark and the extracted watermark respectively, and the quantization step is $t = 40000$.

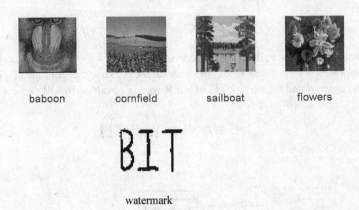

baboon   cornfield   sailboat   flowers

BIT

watermark

Fig. 4. Host images and watermark

The transparency of the watermark embedded in the four images of baboon, cornfield, sailboat and flowers is described as shown in Table 1.

Table 1. PSNR and SSIM of watermarked images.

Original image				
Watermarked image				
PSNR（dB）	28.2189	25.2308	22.9226	22.8766
SSIM	0.9744	0.9723	0.9628	0.9275

The experimental results show that the watermarked color image and the color original image can basically remain the same in human vision, and the PSNR value between the water-marked image and the color original image is between 20 dB and 30 dB. The value of the image SSIM can reach above 0.95, and the SSIM index has a good description of watermark invisibility.

JPEG compression is the most common attack in image processing. As the compression factor Q decreases, the compression effect on the images gradually appear, meanwhile, the quality of the image decreases significantly. The comparison results of some JPEG compression attacks are shown in Table 2. Under JPEG compression attacks with different compression factors, the correct decoding rate (CDR) of the watermark can basically be maintained above 90%. The watermark algorithm in this paper has good robustness against image compression attacks.

Table 2. CDR of watermark undergone JPEG attack.

CDR \ image \ Q				
90	0.9736	0.9668	0.9644	0.9551
85	0.9758	0.9607	0.9570	0.9504
75	0.9783	0.9631	0.9648	0.9563
65	0.9546	0.9424	0.9324	0.9326
45	0.9111	0.9241	0.8962	0.8948

In order to test the robustness of the watermarking algorithm against clipping attacks, the four images are clipped, and the correct decoding rate of the watermark is tested as shown in Table 3. The experimental results show that the proposed watermarking algorithm is effective. The shear attack has good robustness.

Noise is a common attack for image watermarking. Gaussian noise and salt-and-pepper noise with different variances to attack the image is used to test the correct decoding rate CDR of the watermark. The experimental results are shown in Tables 4 and 5.

Table 3. Experimental results of watermark undergone Clipping attack.

Clipped image				
Extracted watermark	BIT	BIT	BIT	BIT
CDR	0.9324	0.9363	0.9473	0.9109
Clipped image				
Extracted watermark	BIT	BIT	BIT	BIT
CDR	0.9382	0.9421	0.9141	0.9119
Clipped image				
Extracted watermark	BIT	BIT	BIT	BIT
CDR	0.9355	0.9084	0.9080	0.9207
Clipped image				
Extracted watermark	BIT	BIT	BIT	BIT
CDR	0.9316	0.9324	0.9138	0.9114

Table 4. Experimental results of watermark undergone Gaussian noise attack.

CDR \ image Gaussian variance				
0. 001	0.9272	0.9309	0.9150	0.9021
0. 002	0.9080	0.9114	0.8904	0.8906
0. 003	0.8960	0.8940	0.8728	0.8628
0. 004	0.8853	0.8882	0.8655	0.8513
0. 005	0.8679	0.8809	0.8352	0.8464
0. 01	0.8523	0.8433	0.8015	0.7937

Table 5. Experimental results of watermark undergone Salt & pepper noise attack.

CDR \ image				
Salt and pepper variance				
0.001	0.9661	0.9539	0.9456	0.9360
0.003	0.9548	0.9363	0.9268	0.9041
0.006	0.9275	0.9031	0.8955	0.8853
0.01	0.9199	0.8887	0.8726	0.8606
0.02	0.8901	0.8691	0.8389	0.8110

The experimental results show that the watermarking algorithm in this paper is less robust to Gaussian noise attacks, comparing with JPEG attack. After the variance is greater than 0.01, the CDR starts to be lower than 0.9, while it has good robustness to the attack on salt and pepper noise, and the CDR can be more than 85% under the attack of 0.02-variance salt and pepper noise.

Median filtering of different sizes of windows is used to perform filtering on watermarked images to test the robustness against filtering attacks. As the experimental results shown in Table 6 below, it has good robustness against filtering.

Table 6. CDR of watermark undergone Filtering attack.

CDR \ image				
Filter window				
[1x2]	0.8589	0.8560	0.8530	0.8408
[1x3]	0.9309	0.9365	0.9414	0.9170
[3x1]	0.8818	0.9497	0.9238	0.9434
[3x3]	0.8545	0.8923	0.8750	0.8889
[1x4]	0.8384	0.8438	0.8372	0.8147
[1x5]	0.8293	0.8428	0.8408	0.8308

5 Conclusion

The proposed watermarking algorithm of DWT-DQFT transformation combined with QR decomposition realizes the embedding of watermark information in the three color channels of color images, taking into account the correlation of the three channels of color images. The watermarking algorithm has good invisibility in SSIM indicators. And the corresponding experiments show good robustness in resisting compression attacks, clipping attacks and median filtering attacks. The watermark extraction process does not refer to the color original image and the original watermark image, that is the blind extraction of the watermark. It has greater practical value.

References

1. Guo, H., Du, Y., Xu, Q.: Quantum image watermarking algorithm based on blocked spatial domain. Chin. J. Quant. Electron. **35**(5), 527–532 (2018)
2. Zhang, X., Xiao, Y., Zhao, Z.: Self-embedding fragile watermarking based on DCT and fast fractal coding. Multimedia Tools Appl. **74**(15), 5767–5786 (2014)
3. Fu, J., Chen, D., Xu, D., Mao, J.: A watermarking algorithm for image content authentication in double-compression environment. Scientia Sinica Informationis **49**(4), 464–485 (2019)
4. Zhang, N.N., Yu, L., Yang, X.F.: Research of digital image watermarking robustness algorithm based on DCT[C]. Prog. Appl. Sci. Eng. Technol. Source Adv. Mater. Res. **926–930**, 3171–3174 (2014)
5. Ma, L., Zhang, X.: Characteristics of color images with watermark based on the relationship between non-void subspaces of inner space. Chinese J. Comput. **40**(5), 1204–1217 (2017)
6. Hai, F., Quan, Z., Kaijia, L.: Robust watermarking scheme for multispectral images using discrete wavelet transform and tucker decomposition. J. Comput. **8**(11), 2844–2850 (2013)
7. Liu, Q., Zhang, L., Zhang, Y., et al.: Geometrically synchronous watermarking algorithm based on the corner feature. J. Commun. **32**(4), 25–31 (2011)
8. Han, S., Zhang, H.: Self-embedding perfectly blind watermarking algorithm based on QR decomposition for color images. J. Graphics **36**(03), 345–351 (2015)
9. Chen, Y.: Structure-preserving QR algorithm of general quaternion eigenvalue problem with application to color watermarking. Jiangsu Normal Univeristy (2018)
10. Wu, Q., Peng, Y.: A blind digital watermarking algorithm based on DWT-FRFT transform and QR decomposition. Electron. Sci. Tech. **31**(10), 53–55 (2018)
11. Liu, Y., Zhang, S., Yang, J.: Color image watermark decoder by modeling quaternion polar harmonic transform with BKF distribution. Signal Process.: Image Commun. **88**, 115946 (2020)
12. Guo, J., Ma, Y.: Color image digital watermarking algorithm based on quaternion Fourier transform. Packag. Eng. **38**(3), 155–159 (2017)
13. Rasti, P., Anbarjafari, G., Demirel, H.: Colour image watermarking based on wavelet and QR decomposition. In: 2017, 25th Signal Processing and Communications Applications Conference (SIU), Antalya, pp. 1–4 (2017). doi: https://doi.org/10.1109/SIU.7960259
14. Liu, Y., Wang, J., Hu, H., et al.: Robust blind digital watermarking scheme based on contourlet transform and QR decomposition. J. Optoelectr. Laser **27**(3), 317–324 (2016)
15. Ding, J., Pei, S., Chang, J.: Efficient implementation of quaternion Fourier transform, convolution, and correlation by 2-D complex FFT. IEEE Trans. Signal Process. **49**(11), 2783–2797 (2001). Author, F.: Article title. Journal **2**(5), 99–110 (2016)
16. Zhou, K., Wu, C., Li, C.: Quality assessment of blind color images using quaternion fourier transform. Laser Optoelectr. Prog. **57**(18), 181021 (2020)

A Multi-level Elastic Encryption Protection Model

Caimei Wang, Zijian Zhou(✉), Hong Li, Zhengmao Li, and Bowen Huang

School of Artificial Intelligence and Big Data, HeFei University, Hefei 230601, China

Abstract. Most of the existing file encryption models are based on international cryptographic algorithms, and lack of flexibility when facing the changing security environment. To solve these problems, we propose a multi-secret-level flexible encryption protection model (Muselfen-PM), which is suitable for environments with the requirement of safe storage. There are three levels of encryption protection, including low, medium and high levels of security. Domestic cryptographic algorithms SM3 and SM4 with high security are used in the model. In order to improve the security of the key, a dynamic key generation and inverse key storage mechanism are designed in the high security protection mode. The model is used in a cloud storage system, which runs well and can effectively protect the confidentiality and security of documents.

Keywords: Encryption protection model · Elastic encryption · Dynamic key · Inverse key storage

1 Introduction

With the development of information science, electronic storage methods occupy the main position of current storage methods. How to protect the confidentiality and security of sensitive documents has always been one of the most concerning issues. The current main encryption protection methods are mainly divided into three categories, the first is hardware encryption machine, the second is software encryption system and the third is Cloud-of-clouds technology [1, 2]. Most of these encryption protection methods are based on cryptographic algorithms. The mainstream encryption algorithms currently used are AES, DES, 3DES, SHA256, MD5, etc. [3]. However, most of these algorithms are international cryptographic algorithms, which have been proven to have certain security risks. At present, the more secure algorithm is the SM series algorithm, which is a commercial cryptographic algorithm independently developed by China.

A more comprehensive comparative analysis of SM3 cryptographic algorithms is conducted by Wang et al. [4]. The analysis results show that SM3 cryptographic algorithms are more secure than the current internationally popular hash cryptographic algorithms. Lv et al. also stated that the SM4 cipher algorithm has higher security than other current block cipher algorithms [5]. In 2018, the SM3 algorithm became an ISO international standard, and in 2020, SM4 became a draft supplement to the ISO standard. The application of SM series of algorithms will be used more and more widely.

© Springer Nature Switzerland AG 2021
W. Lu et al. (Eds.): SciSec 2021, LNCS 13005, pp. 225–235, 2021.
https://doi.org/10.1007/978-3-030-89137-4_16

Based on SM3, SM4 cryptographic algorithms, a **M**ulti-**S**ecret-**L**evel **F**lexible **En**cryption **P**rotection **M**odel (Muselfen-PM) is proposed in this paper. In this model, a dynamic key generation algorithm based on input characteristic information and a key grouping inverse order storage algorithm are proposed to protect and store the key.

2 Rated Work

Sudha devi dorairaj et al. proposed an adaptive multi-level security framework for the data stored in a cloud environment [6]. The processing object of multi-level encryption in the framework is sensitive information data, which is based on different security classifications of data sensitivity. In this paper, the sensitivity is divided into three levels: low, medium and high. The data are segmented and the sensitive data are treated with sensitivity reduction. At the same time, the normal segment and sensitive segment data are protected by different algorithms. However, the multi-level information classification in this mode is more complicated. In addition, the author points out that the framework does not provide effectively protect key management, and there is a risk of key leakage.

The current key management mode is mainly database storage or trusted third-party storage. For example, Yu et al. proposed a TPM dynamic key management mechanism with the function of revoking a single key, which is a trusted third-party key storage operation at the hardware level [7]. In this paper, the trusted third party's key related operation is relatively complex, and the cost of storage, communication, calculation and other aspects is high.

Based on the predecessors, we propose a new multi-level encryption model and key management mechanism. Our model adopts multiple levels of encryption mode, and does not carry out sensitivity classification for data. According to the user's security needs, there are three protection modes of low EPL (**E**ncryption **P**rotection **L**evel), medium EPL and high EPL. Users only need to choose freely according to their own security needs, so as to realize an elastic encryption mode. For the key management, we adopt the mixed storage and processing of the key and ciphertext, combined the key protection and the key loss prevention, and designed a unique key management mode, which protects the encryption key to the greatest extent.

3 Model Design

According to the security requirements of different users, three encryption protection levels are designed in Muselfen-PM: low, medium and high encryption, which can be flexibly selected by users according to their actual security needs. In low EPL mode, no encryption algorithm is involved, only sensitive information of the file is hidden. The framework of Muselfen-PM is sketched in Fig. 1. In medium EPL mode, the SM4 cryptographic algorithm is used to encrypt and decrypt files, and the encryption key is the static secret key. In high EPL mode, the dynamic key generation algorithm is used to generate a unique dynamic key, which is used as the encryption and decryption key of the SM4 cipher algorithm. At the same time, the unique key management mechanism of hybrid storage of key and encrypted ciphertext is adopted, which not only protects the key, but also prevents the situation where the key is lost and the file cannot be recovered.

For better readability, the explanation of the parameters involved in model are shown in Table 1.

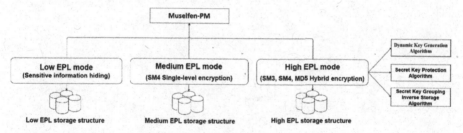

Fig. 1. The frame work of Muselfen-PM

Table 1. Explanation of the parameters involved

Parameter	Meaning
calcu SM3()	SM3 hash value calculation function
R	Random value
F	File
$File_{KEY}$	The key of file
sizeof()	File memory measurement function

Different storage structures for the three security levels are designed in Muselfen-PM, in which the low and medium classified storage structures are the same. Different storage structures of Muselfen-PM are sketched in Fig. 2.

The storage structure of low or medium security levels is divided into two layers. The first layer is the storage root directory, and the subdirectories of the SM3 hash value of each file are stored in the root directory. The second level is the actual storage directory for the files, which contains the ciphertext files and the "logs.dat" file that records the number of file uploads. The calculation method of the SM3 hash value of the file in low EPL and medium EPL storage structures is different. For file { F }, in low EPL mode, the calculation formula is:

$$Hash\ Value\ =\ calcu\ SM3(F) \tag{3.1}$$

In medium EPL mode, the calculation formula is:

$$Hash\ Value\ =\ calcu\ SM3(calcu\ SM3(F) + File_{KEY}) \tag{3.2}$$

Among (3.2), $File_{KEY} = sizeof(F)$.

There is only one layer in high EPL storage structure, that is, the file storage root directory. All are single encrypted files in this directory. The ciphertext file naming formula is:

$$Filename\ =\ calcu\ SM3(calcu\ SM3(F) + File_{KEY}) + R \tag{3.3}$$

In the cloud storage system with Muselfen-PM:

$$File_{KEY} = \text{sizeof}(F), R = \text{upload time} \tag{3.4}$$

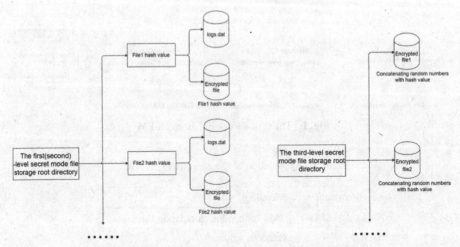

Fig. 2. The different storage structures of Muselfen-PM

4   Implementation of the Mode

4.1   The Generation Method of Dynamic Encryption Key

The dynamic key generation algorithm is the core algorithm in high EPL mode, which is mainly used to dynamically generate encryption and decryption key. According to the characteristic information of the file, the algorithm calculates the SM3 hash value in two steps, calculates the MD5 hash value and generates the random number. The input of the algorithm is the content of the file, and the output is a 256-bit dynamic key.

Table 2. Parameter description of dynamic key generation algorithm

Parameter	Meaning
$SM3_1$	SM3 hash value calculated for the first time
$SM3_2$	SM3 hash value calculated for the second time, also used as the output of the algorithm
$MD5_i$	MD5 hash value calculation result
R	Random number generated randomly

The dynamic key algorithm process is as follows:

Step 1: Calculate the hash value of the first 4096 Bytes of the file, recorded as $SM3_1$. If the file size is less than 4096 Bytes, the calculation unit is the entire file.

Step 2: Calculate the MD5 value of the entire file, the calculation result is recorded as $MD5_1$.

Step 3: Generate a random number R randomly.

Step 4: Calculate the combined hash value $SM3_2$ and output it.

$$SM3_2 = \text{calcu SM3}(SM3_1 + MD5_1 + R) \tag{4.1}$$

$SM3_2$ is the encryption and decryption key of the SM4 block cipher algorithm.

The parameters description of the dynamic key generation algorithm are shown in Table 2.

4.2 Inverse Ordered Key Blocking Storage Scheme

The Inverse Ordered Key Blocking Storage Scheme consists of two parts, the first part is the key protection algorithm, and the second part is the key group inverse storage algorithm. The overall structure of key storage technology is sketched in Fig. 3.

Secret Key Protection Algorithm

The purpose of the secret key protection algorithm is to protect the encryption and decryption key of the file, which is realized by the XOR algorithm. The input of the algorithm is the 256-bit key generated by the dynamic key generation algorithm, and the output of the algorithm is the 256-bit encryption key with the same length as the input. The main idea of the algorithm is to divide the key into 32 groups, transform and protect them according to the number of dynamically generated iteration rounds and the key parameter K of the algorithm, and then concatenate the changed results of each group into a protection key. The parameters of this algorithm are shown in Table 3.

Table 3. Parameter Description of Dynamic Key Protection Algorithm

Parameter	Meaning
Hex_1	Algorithm input
Hex_2	Algorithm output
R	Random number generated randomly
$Hash(x)$	Hash function
$Round$	Iteration rounds
K	Key parameter value of dynamic key protection algorithm
K_i	Intermediate iteration value, $i \in [0, Round + 3]$
G_i	Grouping of input data
O_i	Transformation result
(a, b)	Grouping of G_i, $i \in [0, 31]$
(c, d)	Grouping of O_i, $i \in [0, 31]$

The calculation formula of Hash(x) is as follows:

$$\text{Hash}(x) = \begin{cases} \begin{cases} K = (x+5) \ mod \ 17 \\ Round = [(x+1)*K] \ mod \ 32 \end{cases}, x \ mod \ 2 = 1 \\ \begin{cases} K = (x+7) \ mod \ 17 \\ Round = [(x-1)*K] \ mod \ 32 \end{cases}, x \ mod \ 2 = 0 \end{cases} \quad (4.2)$$

The algorithm process is as follows:

Step 1: Generate a random number R, where R is an integer.
Step 2: According to the SM3 hash algorithm standard, the output is 256 bits, and the hash value is converted into a hexadecimal number string, which should be 64 characters in length.
Step 3: Divide Hex_1 into 32 groups and record as G_i, $i = 0, 1, ..., 31$.
Step 4: Divide G_i into two groups and mark as (a_i, b_i), $i = 0, 1, ..., 31$. The original can be expressed as:

$$\text{Hex}_1 = \{G_i | G_i = (a_i, b_i) \ \text{and} \ i = 0, 1, ..., 31\}. \quad (4.3)$$

Step 5: Calculate the $Round$ value and K value according to Hash(x).
Step 6: Transform all G, and get the corresponding O for each group of G.
Step 7: Combine 32 groups into output Hex_2, Hex_2 can be expressed as:

$$\text{Hex}_2 = \{O_i | O_i = (c_i, d_i) \ \text{and} \ i = 0, 1, ..., 31\}. \quad (4.4)$$

Step 8: output Hex_2.

The transformation method of G to O is as follows:

Step 1: $K_0 = a \oplus K$.
Step 2: $K_1 = b \oplus K$.
Step 3: Iterate Round rounds, each round calculate K_i

$$K_i = K_{i-1} \oplus K_{i-2}, i = 2, 3, ..., Round + 1 \quad (4.5)$$

Step 4: $K_{Round+2} = K_{Round} \oplus K$.
Step 5: $K_{Round+3} = K_{Round+1} \oplus K$.
Step 6: Output c, d, $c = K_{Round+3}$, $d = K_{Round+2}$, $O_i = (c , d)$.

The input during key restoration is the output during encryption, and the decryption algorithm structure is consistent with the encryption structure. In the entire key generation and encryption protection process, only the value of R needs to be stored in the database.

Secret Key Grouping Inverse Storage Algorithm

The purpose of the key grouping inverse storage algorithm is to protect and store the file encryption and decryption keys. The input of this algorithm is 256-bit data output by the key protection algorithm without output. The algorithm writes files directly during the transformation process. The parameters of algorithm are shown in Table 4.

Table 4. Parameter Description of Secret Key Grouping Inverse Storage Algorithm

Parameter	Meaning
Hex_2	Algorithm input
Hex_{2i}	Grouping of Hex_2, $i = 0, 1, 2, 3$

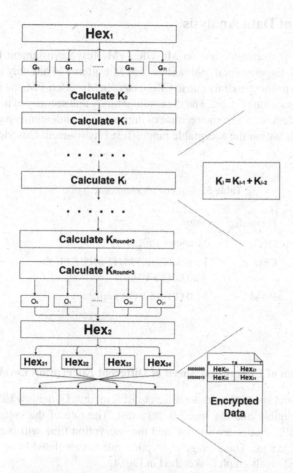

Fig. 3. The overall structure of key storage technology

The algorithm process is as follows:

Step 1: Divide Hex_2 into 4 groups, record as Hex_{2i}, $i = 0, 1, 2, 3$.
Step 2: Write the four groups to the beginning of the ciphertext file in reverse order. The writing order is Hex_{2i}, $i = 3, 2, 1, 0$.

The key grouping inverse storage technology breaks through the traditional storage schemes that writing keys in the database and other methods. The ciphertext and the key coexist. When Muselfen-PM needs to decrypt the ciphertext, it can directly read the ciphertext file, and the decryption key is directly parsing from the ciphertext. Writing the key in the ciphertext file not only protects the key to a certain extent, but also prevents the loss of the key from causing the file to be unrecoverable.

5 Experiment Data Analysis

We performed a performance test on Muselfen-PM. Test Environment Description is shown in Table 5. Experimental results show that Muselfen-PM has only a small performance impact on the host, mainly due to CPU usage. In Muselfen-PM, the file encryption rate is fast, the operation is stable, and the confidentiality and security of the file are guaranteed to a high degree. Under the premise of improving confidentiality and security, the influence value is within the acceptable range. Test Environment Description is shown in Table 5.

Table 5. Test environment description

Parameter	Value
OS	Windows 10 X64
CPU	Intel(R) Core(TM) i7-8700 CPU @ 3.20 GHz 3.19 GHz
RAM	16.0 GB (15.8 GB available)

5.1 Comparison of Encryption Speed of Different Encryption Levels

We have carried out speed tests under different EPL modes. Under low EPL, the encryption time is negligible and the speed is very fast. The rate of the system in medium EPL and high EPL modes are similar, and the encryption time will increase with the increase of the file size. The average encryption rate is calculated to be about 7 Mb/s. The experimental result graph is sketched in Fig. 4.

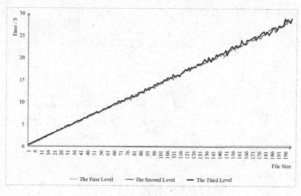

Fig. 4. Experimental result graph

5.2 The Impact of Security Level on Host Hardware Performance

We have tested the impact on the performance of the host while calculating three levels of encryption calculations for files with a size of 0–200 MB. In different protection modes, when the file size is increased from 0 to 200 MB, the calculation will stop. The increment unit is set to 0.5MB. We have used a script to monitor the performance consumption of the host computer, which was shown in Table 6.

Table 6. Host performance monitor

Encryption type	CPU usage rate/%	Memory usage rate/%
Free Time	8.32	28.23
Low EPL	13.02	29.95
Medium EPL	16.86	28.86
High EPL	16.90	29.27

It can be concluded from Table 6 that low EPL mode has almost no impact on host performance, while medium EPL and high EPL modes have a slightly higher impact on host performance than low EPL, and mainly have a certain consumption on CPU. However, as the cost of improving security, these impacts are acceptable. Muselfen-PM can largely guarantee the confidentiality and security of files.

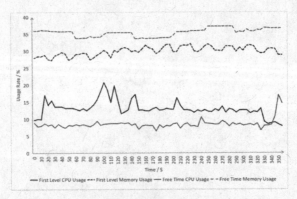

Fig. 5. First-level host performance monitoring

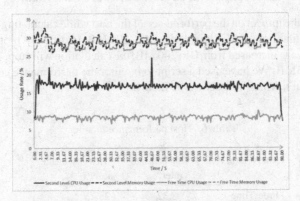

Fig. 6. Second-level host performance monitoring

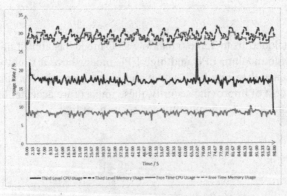

Fig. 7. Third-level host performance monitoring

In Figs. 5, 6, and 7, the solid line represents the monitoring of the CPU occupancy rate, and the dotted line is the monitoring of the memory occupancy rate. Figure 5 shows the experimental results of low EPL. There is little difference between CPU and memory usage in this mode. Figures 6 and 7 are two similar images, representing the experimental results in the medium EPL and high EPL modes, respectively. In general, the impact of the two EPL modes on the memory occupancy rate is not very htabobvious, and the CPU occupancy rate is slightly higher than that in Fig. 5, which is about 10% higher than in the idle situation. However, due to the increased security of the two modes, the impact of this part is acceptable.

6 Conclusion and Future Work

A high security Muselfen-PM is designed in this paper, which can be used in a variety of classified storage environments. The model has been applied to a cloud storage system, which runs stably and effectively guarantees the confidentiality and security of files in the system. In the next step of research, we will further reform the key grouping technology proposed by Muselfen-PM, such as combining the Galois field when storing keys in reverse order to strengthen the confidentiality and security of the keys.

Acknowledgments. This work is supported by the major science and technology projects of Anhui Province under Grant (No. 201903a05020011), the Anhui Provincial Quality Engineering Project (No. 2020szsfkc0752), Anhui Province Online Teaching Demonstration University Project (No. 2020xssfgx14) and Hefei University Quality Engineering Project (No. 2020hfukcsz02).

References

1. Masoumi, M.: A highly efficient and secure hardware implementation of the advanced encryption standard. J. Inf. Secur. Appl. **48**, 102371 (2019)
2. Niknia, A., Correia, M., Karimpour, J.: Secure cloud-of-clouds storage with space-efficient secret sharing. J. Inf. Secur. Appl. **59**, 102826 (2021)
3. Matta, P., Arora, M., Sharma, D.: A comparative survey on data encryption techniques: big data perspective. Mater. Today: Proc.
4. Wang, X., Yu, H.: SM3 cryptographic hash algorithm. J. Inf. Secur. Res. **2**(11), 983–994 (2016)
5. Lv Shuwang, S., Bozhan, W.P., Yingying, M., Lili, H.: Overview on SM4 algorithms. J. Inf. Secur. Res. **2**(11), 995–1007 (2016)
6. Devi Doraira, S., Kaliannan, T.: An adaptive multilevel security framework for the data stored in cloud environment. Sci. World J. **2015**, 1–11 (2015)
7. Yu, F., Chen, Y., Zhang, H.: Dynamic key management with individual key revocation for TPM. Tsinghua Univ. (Sci. Technol.) **60**(6), 464–473 (2021)

An Event-Based Parameter Switching Method for Controlling Cybersecurity Dynamics

Zhaofeng Liu[1]($\boxtimes$), Wenlian Lu[1,2], and Yingying Lang[1]

[1] Fudan University, No. 220 Handan Road, Shanghai, China
{wenlian,18110180026}@fudan.edu.cn
[2] Shanghai Key Laboratory for Contemporary Applied Mathematics,
Shanghai 200433, China

Abstract. This paper proposes a new event-based parameter switching method for the control tasks of cybersecurity in the context of preventive and reactive cyber defense dynamics. Our parameter switching method helps avoid excessive control costs as well as guarantees the dynamics to converge as our desired speed. Meanwhile, it can be proved that this approach is Zeno-free. A new estimation method with adaptive time windows is used to bridge the gap between the probability state and the sampling state. With the new estimation method, several practical experiments are given afterwards.

Keywords: Event-based method · Preventive and reactive cyber defense dynamics · Cybersecurity dynamics

1 Introduction

The emerging research field 'cybersecurity dynamics' [22,23] is an interdisciplinary field, conceived from the methodology of several studies in *biological epidemiology* (e.g., [1,3,6,11,16]) and its variants in *cyber epidemiology* (e.g., [10,17,19]), *interacting particle systems* [13], and *microfoundation in economics* [7]. Different from the classical researches oriented to specific tools, such as Cryptography and Database Security, cybersecurity dynamics studies the offensive and defensive models under various circumstances from a whole-network perspective, which has opened the door to a new research field.

1.1 Our Contributions

In this paper, we investigate how to control the evolution of cybersecurity dynamics more efficiently and effectively in the context of *preventive and reactive cyber defense dynamics*, and guarantee its globally convergence to a safe state.

With regard to the control problem of the highly nonlinear network dynamics system, the traditional method is to use a single control strategy, that is, to adjust the dynamic parameters and maintain them, so that the security dynamics of the

W. Lu et al. (Eds.): SciSec 2021, LNCS 13005, pp. 236–251, 2021.
https://doi.org/10.1007/978-3-030-89137-4_17

network space converges to a safe state globally. However, maintaining a high level of dynamic defense strategy may result in excessive prevention and control cost, lead to a waste of control resources, and even affect on the stable operation of the network systems.

In order to solve this problem, this paper proposes an event-based parameter switching approach to save control resources and control the evolution of cybersecurity dynamics in a decentralized manner. It is also proved that this approach is Zeno-free, that is, it will not fall victim to the Zeno behavior. Numerical examples show that the maintenance hours of high-cost control strategies can be reduced by more than 40% with our parameter switching approach.

In addition, this paper provides an estimation method to bridge the gap between the probability state and the sampling state when using the method in practice. Different from the equilibrium state estimation problem [14], the new control method requires considering the timeliness of probability estimation. A new adaptive estimation method is proposed to verify the effectiveness of the parameter switching method through numerical examples.

1.2 Related Work

Similar event-based methods have been employed in many other application settings before (see, for example, [2,5,21]). In practical application, one of the essential problems is that this method should not fall victim to the Zeno behavior, which can lead to infinitely many events within a finite period of time, thus invalidate the method [9].

The first cybersecurity dynamics model was proposed in [12]. Ten years later, [27] demonstrated that a certain class of cybersecurity dynamics is globally convergent in the entire parameter universe, which laid a foundation for our further research. The preventive and reactive cyber defense dynamics is a particular kind of cybersecurity dynamics. Several other kinds of cybersecurity dynamics have been demonstrated in early studies, such as the models aiming to accommodate adaptive defenses [25], active defenses [26], and proactive defenses [4]. It is worth mentioning that the event-based parameter switching method may be extended and applied to the various kinds of dynamics.

1.3 Paper Outline

In Sect. 2, we briefly review the preventive and reactive cyber defense dynamics model and its global convergence in the entire parameter universe [27]. And then we state the problems we addressed in this paper. In Sects. 3, we present an event-based parameter switching method for controlling the cybersecurity dynamics, and prove the effectiveness of the control method (without Zeno behavior). Then in Sect. 4, we show how to apply this event-based parameter switching method in practice by bridging the gap between the probability-state in the theoretical model and the sample-state in practice, using an stochastic process method with adaptive time windows. In Sect. 5, we conclude the paper with open problems.

2 Problem Statement

2.1 Review of Preventive and Reactive Defense Dynamics

As a particular kind of cybersecurity dynamics, the preventive and reactive defense dynamics model was first introduced in [12], and the convergence properties of the dynamics is studied in [24]. Later [27] fully analyzed the convergence issues, not only considered the common situation with node homogeneity (i.e., the parameters are node-independent), but also a more general situation with node heterogeneity (i.e., the parameters are nodes-dependent). The paper proved that this dynamics model is globally convergent in the entire parameter universe, that is, there is always a unique equilibrium, whose exact value (or position) depends on the specific parameter values instead of the initial state of the dynamics.

In the preventive and reactive defense dynamics model, we consider two classes of defenses: *preventive defenses* and *reactive defenses*, and two classes of attacks: *push-based attacks* and *pull-based attacks*.

Suppose that the attack-defense interaction occurs over an *attack-defense graph structure* $G = (V, E)$, where V is the vertex set representing computers and $(u, v) \in E$ means computer u can directly attack computer v using push-based attack strategy (i.e., the communication from u to v is allowed by the security policy). G can be derived from the security policy of a networked system and the physical network in question. Without loss of generality, we do *not* make any restrictions on the structure of G (e.g., G may be directed or undirected). Denote the adjacency matrix of G by $A = [a_{vu}]_{n \times n}$, where $a_{vu} = 1$ if and only if $(u, v) \in E$. Since the model aims to describe the attacks between computers, we set $a_{vv} = 0$. Let $N_v = \{u \in V : (u, v) \in E\}$.

In this paper, we consider the continuous-time model described in [27]. At any time point, a node $v \in V$ is in one of two states: "0" means *secure* but vulnerable, or "1" means *compromised*. Let $s_v(t)$ and $i_v(t)$ be the probability that v is *secure* and *compromised* at time t respectively. It is obvious that $s_v(t) + i_v(t) = 1$, $s_v(t)$ and $i_v(t)$ explain the term *probability-state*.

For a node $v \in V$ at time t, let $\theta_{v,1\rightarrow0}(t)$ abstract the effectiveness of the reactive defenses and $\theta_{v,0\rightarrow1}(t)$ abstract the capability of attacks against preventive defenses. $\beta_v \in (0, 1]$ represents the probability that the *compromised* computer v changes to the *secure* state because the attacks are detected and cleaned up by the reactive defenses. Then, $\theta_{v,1\rightarrow0}(t) = \beta_v$. Let $\alpha_v \in [0, 1]$ denote the probability that the *secure* computer v becomes *compromised* despite the presence of the preventive defenses (i.e., the preventive defenses are penetrated by the pull-based attacks). And let $\gamma_{uv} \in (0, 1]$ denote the probability that a *compromised* computer u wages a successful attack against a *secure* computer v despite the preventive defenses (i.e., the preventive defenses are penetrated by push-based attacks), where $(u, v) \in E$. Under the assumption that the attacks are waged independent of each other, it holds that

$$\theta_{v,0\rightarrow1}(t) = 1 - (1 - \alpha_v) \prod_{u \in N_v} (1 - \gamma_{uv} i_u(t)). \tag{1}$$

The dynamics can be rewritten as a system of n nonlinear equations for $v \in V$ [27]:

$$\frac{\mathrm{d}i_v(t)}{\mathrm{d}t} = f_v(i) = -\beta_v i_v(t) + \left[1 - (1 - \alpha_v) \prod_{u \in N_v} \left(1 - \gamma_{uv} i_u(t)\right)\right] \left(1 - i_v(t)\right).$$
$$(2)$$

Notice that system (2) is globally stable (i.e., there exists a unique equilibrium $i^* \in [0,1]^n$ such that every trajectory of system (2) converges to i^*) no matter whether the parameters are nodes-dependent or nodes-independent [27]. If the parameters of the network system are nodes-independent (i.e., $\alpha_v = \alpha$, $\beta_v = \beta$ for any $v \in V$ and $\gamma_{uv} = \gamma$ for any $u, v \in V$, $(u, v) \in E$), the global convergence of system (2) can be summarized as follows:

- If the attacker wages both push-based and pull-based attacks on some nodes $v \in V$ (i.e., $\alpha_v > 0$ for some nodes $v \in V$), system (2) is globally convergent in the entire parameter universe and the dynamics converges to a unique *nonzero* equilibrium exponentially.
- If the attacker only wages push-based attacks (i.e., $\alpha_v = 0$ for any nodes $v \in V$), system (2) is still globally convergent in the parameter universe but the convergence speed depends on all the model parameters (β_v, γ_{uv}) and the largest eigenvalue $\lambda_{A,1}$ of adjacency matrix A.

In this paper, we need to control the dynamics with nodes-dependent parameters converging to equilibrium zero. Despite the complexity of nodes heterogeneity, we can still take advantage of the convergence properties of the dynamics with nodes-independent parameters.

2.2   Problem Statement: Controlling Cybersecurity Dynamics

In this paper, we focus on controlling the convergence process of the cybersecurity dynamics model in a decentralized control manner, thus we only need to observe the state of the target node v during the control process of v, with no need to observe the states of its neighbors within the network. For each node v of the network, we need to control $i_v(t)$ converging to zero at our target convergence speed with relatively low control cost by switching its parameter β_v according to our trigger rule.

Before presenting the control method, we need to finish two pre-control steps to assure the effectiveness of our method. As introduced before, we need to control the dynamics converging to equilibrium zero globally. So firstly, as discussed in Sect. 2.1, we need to force the parameter $\alpha_v = 0$ for each node v, which means that the threats of pull-based attacks are eliminated after the first step of the control process (e.g., connections between some compromised websites and the network system in which the pull-based epidemic spreading takes place are all cut off). This is the first step of the pre-control process. Then the corresponding push-based dynamics model we focus on can be rewritten as:

$$\frac{\mathrm{d}i_v(t)}{\mathrm{d}t} = f_v(i) = -\beta_v i_v(t) + \left[1 - \prod_{u \in N_v} \left(1 - \gamma_{uv} i_u(t)\right)\right] \left(1 - i_v(t)\right). \quad (3)$$

As for β_v, we select two reactive defense strategies with different control cost for our parameter switching method, including one relatively strict defense strategy with higher control cost, denoted by β_+, and one relatively relaxed defense strategy with lower control cost, denoted by β_-, $\beta_+ > \beta_-$. These two strategies should satisfy the condition that they should both ensure the dynamics to converge to equilibrium zero. The key difference between them is, comparing to our target convergence speed, the dynamics with $\beta_v = \beta_+$ should converge faster than the target speed for all nodes in V, while the dynamics with $\beta_v = \beta_-$ may converge more slowly than the target speed.

The classical approach to control the dynamics through adjusting the reactive defense strategy is the trivial method that forcing $\beta_v = \beta_+$ during the entire control process, which is inefficient and costs excessive defense resources to maintain the strict strategy. Besides, under high-cost control, the convergence speed may be faster than what we actually need, causing redundancies and wastes of defense resources to some extent.

As discussed above, both the relatively strict defense strategy and the relatively relaxed one need to guarantee the dynamics to converge to equilibrium zero. So a safe method to get equilibrium zero is to make sure $\beta_v/\gamma_{max} \geq \lambda_{A,1}$ for both $\beta_v = \beta_+$ and $\beta_v = \beta_-$, where γ_{max} denotes the maximum value of probability γ_{uv} for all neighbor nodes pair $(u, v) \in E$. However, γ_{max} may be relatively large in practice, leaving little choice for parameter β_v. Therefore, the second step of the pre-control process is to force γ_{max} to a relatively small value, which means we need to permanently reinforce the preventive defense strategy for the nodes which are more vulnerable to push-based attacks launched by the attacker (e.g., a stronger network firewall or filter is deployed).

After the two pre-control steps, in which all the pull-based attacks have been eliminated and γ_{max} is relatively small, we now employ a parameter switching method to control the convergence speed with relatively low cost of defense resources. We use an event-based mechanism to define the parameter switching rule.

2.3 Notations

Table 1 summarizes the major notations used in the paper.

3 An Event-Based Parameter Switching Method

In this section, we propose an event-based trigger rule for the parameter switching method We first show that the global dynamics under control will converge to equilibrium zero at our target convergence speed. Then we prove that there is no Zeno behavior during the entire control process.

3.1 Designing Event-Based Parameter Switching Rule

We apply the control method on all nodes of the network system. But for the purpose of clarification, we focus on one target node v to explain the control process corresponding to the decentralized control manner as discussed above.

Table 1. Notations used throughout the paper.

I_n	The $n * n$ identity matrix
$\mathbb{R}$	The set of real numbers
$\mathbb{N}$	The set of positive integers and zero
$\|i\|_1$	$\|i\|_1 = \sum_{v=1}^{n} \|i_v\|$ is the l_1-norm for an n-dimensional vector $i = [i_1, \ldots, i_n] \in \mathbb{R}^n$. Note that the result equally holds with respect to other norms
$G = (V, E), A$	The attack-defense graph structure G with adjacency matrix $A = [a_{vu}]_{n \times n}$ where $a_{vu} = 1$ if and only if $(u, v) \in E$
N_v	$N_v = \{u \in V : (u, v) \in E\}$
$\alpha_v \in [0, 1]$	The probability that *secure* node v becomes *compromised* because pull-based attack penetrates preventive defense
$\beta_v \in (0, 1]$	The probability that *compromised* node v becomes *secure* because reactive defense detects and cleans compromise
$\gamma_{uv} \in (0, 1]$	The probability that a *compromised* neighbor node u wages a successful push-based attack against *secure* node v
$\gamma_{max} \in (0, 1]$	The maximum value of probability γ_{uv} for all neighbor nodes pair $(u, v) \in E$
β_-, β_+	The value of parameter β_v for all nodes $v \in V$ in low-cost (high-cost) reactive defense setting
$i_v(t), i(t)$	The probability v is in *compromised* state at time t; $i(t) = [i_1(t), \cdots, i_n(t)]$
$\varphi_{up}(s), \varphi_{up}(s)$	The decision functions that trigger high-cost (low-cost) control events
t_k^v, τ_k^v	The time for the k-th high-cost (low-cost) control event at $v \in V$ in the event-based control method; $t_1^v = \tau_0^v = 0$
T_-^v, T_+^v	The total time of maintaining the parameter β_v of the target node in low-cost (high-cost) reactive defense setting during control process
$\mathcal{S}(t), \mathcal{S}_v(t)$	The exponential speed index of the convergence speed of $i(t)$ $(i_v(t))$ when the dynamics converge exponentially
$\chi_v(t)$	The sample-state of node v at time t; 0 means *secure* and 1 means *compromised*
$\widehat{i_v(t)}, \widehat{s_v(t)}$	The probability v is in the *compromised* (*secure*) state at time t as estimated from the sample-states
$\mathcal{W}, \mathcal{W}'(t)$	The time window with fixed (adaptive) time length for estimating the probability-states from sample-states

We switch the parameter β_v of the target node v between the low-cost parameter β_- and the high-cost parameter β_+. Denote by T_-^v and T_+^v the total time of maintaining the two parameters β_- and β_+ respectively during the entire control process for node $v \in V$. We expect the dynamics to converge with a relatively low cost, which means to make the mean of time ratio $\frac{1}{n}\sum_{v\in V}\frac{T_+^v}{T_+^v+T_-^v}$ relatively small.

Before defining the event-trigger rule, we first review the following lemma.

Definition 1 ([8]). *A non-singular $n*n$ real matrix U is said to be a monotone matrix (M-matrix), if every component of U^{-1} is non-negative.*

Lemma 1 ([15]). *Let $U = (u_{ij})$ be a non-singular $n * n$ real matrix with $u_{ij} \leq 0, i \neq j$. Then all the following statements are equivalent:*

(a) *U is a M-matrix, that is, all the successive principal minors of U are positive.*
(b) *The real parts of all eigenvalues of U are positive.*
(c) *There is a positive diagonal matrix P such that $UP+P^TU$ is positive definite.*

For all nodes $v \in V$, let $n * n$ real matrix $K = \{\gamma_{uv}\}_{u,v=1}^n$, where $\gamma_{vv} = 0$ for all nodes $v \in V$, and let non-singular $n*n$ real diagonal matrix $B = diag(\{\beta_v\}_{v=1}^n)$. Notice that β_v takes values in $\{\beta_-, \beta_+\}$. Let $B_+ = \beta_+I_n$ and $B_- = \beta_-I_n$.

Lemma 2. *If there exists some positive constant number ι, so that $J = B_+ - K - \iota I_n$ is a monotone matrix (M-matrix), then there exists a positive diagonal matrix $P = diag(\{p_v\}_{v=1}^n)$ such that $[(-J)P + P^T(-J)]$ is negative definite.*

Apparently, our target convergence speed should be faster than the dynamics with $\beta_v = \beta_-$ for all nodes in V, and slower than the dynamics with $\beta_v = \beta_+$ for all nodes in V. Set our target convergence speed as $Ce^{-\iota t}$ with $\iota > 0$ satisfying Lemma 2, where C is a positive constant number.

In our event-based parameter switching method, we switch the parameter β_v when an event is triggered (e.g. certain conditions are satisfied). Between two consecutive events, the parameter β_v holds. We define two criterion functions according to our target speed of the convergence process:

$$\begin{cases} \varphi_{up}(t) &= e^{-\iota t}, \forall t \geq 0, \\ \varphi_{low}(t) &= L * e^{-\iota t}, \forall t \geq 0, \end{cases}$$

where L is a constant number satisfying $0 < L < 1$. Note that $\varphi_{up}(t)$ represents the ideal convergence process at our target convergence speed. Theoretically, $\varphi_{up}(t)$ can be a polynomial function if the original dynamics converges polynomially. But from the Sard's Lemma [20], the parameter regime that causing polynomial convergence speed is in a zero measure set and cannot be chosen in practice. So without loss of generality, let $\varphi_{up}(t)$ be an exponential function for the simplification of narrative. It is also worth mentioning that $\varphi_{low}(t)$ can be defined in other functional form as long as it satisfies the conditions of convergence speed.

With the matrix P defined in Lemma 2, we now define rigger rule as follows:

Definition 2 (event-based trigger rule). *$P = diag(\{p_v\}_{v=1}^n)$ is as defined in Lemma 2. Let $m_v(t) = p_v^{-1}i_v(t)$, then for $k = 1, 2, \ldots$, the trigger rule is defined as:*

– *if $m_v(0) \geq 1$, then let $t_1^v = 0$, and*

$$\begin{cases} \tau_k^v = & \inf\left\{ s \geq t_k^v : m_v(s) \leq \varphi_{low}(s) \right\} \\ t_{k+1}^v = & \inf\left\{ s \geq \tau_k^v : m_v(s) \geq \varphi_{up}(s) \right\} \end{cases}$$

– *if $m_v(0) < 1$, then let $\tau_0^v = 0$, and*

$$\begin{cases} t_k^v = & \inf\left\{ s \geq \tau_{k-1}^v : m_v(s) \geq \varphi_{up}(s) \right\} \\ \tau_k^v = & \inf\left\{ s \geq t_k^v : m_v(s) \leq \varphi_{low}(s) \right\} \end{cases}$$

which specifies two sequences of parameter switching events:

– *High-cost control event: At time t_k^v, parameter β_v switches to β_+.*
– *Low-cost control event: At time τ_k^v, parameter β_v switches to β_-.*

As discussed above, both β_- and β_+ should be able to ensure the dynamics converges to equilibrium zero in the parameter regime after pre-control. So system (3) can be written as: for target node $v \in V$,

– If $t \in [t_k^v, \tau_k^v)$,

$$\frac{di_v(t)}{dt} = -\beta_+ i_v(t) + \left[1 - \prod_{u \in N_v} \left(1 - \gamma_{uv} i_u(t) \right) \right] (1 - i_v(t)), \qquad (4)$$

– If $t \in [\tau_k^v, t_{k+1}^v)$,

$$\frac{di_v(t)}{dt} = -\beta_- i_v(t) + \left[1 - \prod_{u \in N_v} \left(1 - \gamma_{uv} i_u(t) \right) \right] (1 - i_v(t)). \qquad (5)$$

For $k = 1, 2, \ldots$, we regard the two control steps (4) and (5) during $t \in [t_k^v, t_{k+1}^v)$ as the k-th *control cycle*.

3.2   Analyzing the Event-Based Parameter Switching Method

Under the control procedure proposed above, we will prove the effectiveness of the event-based parameter switching method, that is, the new dynamics of the target node under control will converge to zero at our target convergence speed, and what's more important, with no Zeno behavior.

Theorem 1. *For any node $v \in V$, system (4) (5) generated by the event-based parameter switching control strategy (trigger rule Definition 2) will converge to zero at the convergence speed same as $\varphi_{up}(t)$, with no Zeno behavior.*

Proof. We first prove that $m_v(t) = p_v^{-1} i_v(t)$ under parameter switching control strategy (trigger rule Definition 2) could never exceed $\varphi_{up}(t)$ after time τ_1^v for all nodes $v \in V$ (i.e., it always holds that $p_v^{-1} i_v(t) \le \varphi_{up}(t)$ after time τ_1^v). For any node $v \in V$, we have the following inequality (see [14,27])

$$\frac{\mathrm{d}}{\mathrm{d}t} i_v(t) \le -\beta_v i_v(t) + \sum_{w \in N_v} \gamma_{wv} i_w(t). \tag{6}$$

At time τ_1^v, we have $m_v(\tau_1^v) = \varphi_{low}(\tau_1^v) < \varphi_{up}(\tau_1^v)$ for all nodes $v \in V$. Let $M(t) = \max_{v \in V} m_v(t)$. Assume there is some time point t^* so that $M(t^*) = \varphi_{up}(t^*)$, then for each $v^* \in V$ so that $m_{v^*}(t^*) = M(t^*)$, by inequality (6) we have

$$\frac{\mathrm{d}}{\mathrm{d}t} \Big[i_{v^*}(t) e^{\iota t} \Big] \Big|_{t=t^*} \le \Big(-\beta_v^* p_{v^*} + \sum_{w \in N_{v^*}} \gamma_{wv^*} p_{w^*} + \iota p_{v^*} \Big) m_{v^*}(t^*) e^{\iota t^*}$$

According to the event-based trigger rule Definition 2, the reactive defense strategy switches to high-cost setting β_+ right after time point t^*. Recall Lemma 2, we have $-\beta_v^* p_{v^*} + \sum_{w \in N_{v^*}} \gamma_{wv^*} p_{w^*} + \iota p_{v^*} < 0$, thus

$$\frac{\mathrm{d}}{\mathrm{d}t} \Big[i_{v^*}(t) e^{\iota t} \Big] \Big|_{t=t^*} < 0.$$

This implies that $m_{v^*}(t) e^{\iota t} = p_v^{-1} i_{v^*}(t) e^{\iota t}$ is strictly decreasing after time point t^*. Finally we have $m_v(t) \le \varphi_{up}(t)$ for all nodes $v \in V$ at any time point t.

Next we prove that the parameter switching events will continue to exist till infinite time. That is to say, $t \to +\infty$ implies $k \to +\infty$ for both $\{t_k^v\}$ and $\{\tau_k^v\}$ (i.e., there are infinitely many parameter switching events). Besides, we prove that there is no Zeno behavior during the entire control process.

For any $k = 1, 2, 3 \cdots$, with respect to the k-th *control cycle* during $t \in [t_k^v, t_{k+1}^v)$, We analyze the two control steps respectively.

i) *Step one:*

With regard to the high-cost control step (4) during $t \in [t_k^v, \tau_k^v)$, notice that $m_v(t_k^v) = \varphi_{up}(t_k^v)$, $m_v(\tau_k^v) = \varphi_{low}(\tau_k^v)$, and $i_v(t)$ converges to zero faster than $\varphi_{up}(t)$ and $\varphi_{low}(t)$. We prove that there is no Zeno behavior in the high-cost control step (4) during $t \in [t_k^v, \tau_k^v)$.

According to the dynamic, we have

$$\left| \int_{t_k^v}^{\tau_k^v} \frac{\mathrm{d}}{\mathrm{d}t} \Big[m_v(t) \Big] \mathrm{d}t \right| = \Big| \varphi_{up}(t_k^v) - \varphi_{low}(\tau_k^v) \Big|$$

For the left side, we have

$$\left| \int_{t_k^v}^{\tau_k^v} \frac{\mathrm{d}}{\mathrm{d}t} \Big[m_v(t) \Big] \mathrm{d}t \right| \le M \int_{t_k^v}^{\tau_k^v} \Big| e^{-t \mathcal{S}_+^v(t)} \Big| \mathrm{d}t \le M e^{-\iota t_k^v} (\tau_k^v - t_k^v),$$

where $e^{-t\mathcal{S}_+^v(t)}$ represents the convergence speed when $\beta_v = \beta_+$, $\mathcal{S}_+^v(t) > \iota$, M is a positive constant.

For the right side, we have

$$\left| \varphi_{up}(t_k^v) - \varphi_{low}(\tau_k^v) \right| = i_v(0)e^{-\iota t_k^v} - L * i_v(0)e^{-\iota \tau_k^v} \geq (1 - L)i_v(0)e^{-\iota \tau_k^v}$$

Thus, with the two inequalities above, it can be easily proved that $(1 - L)i_v(0)e^{-\iota(\tau_k^v - t_k^v)} \leq M(\tau_k^v - t_k^v)$, which shows the existence of a positive number η_v, which is the root of the transcendental equation $(1-L)i_v(0)e^{-\iota \eta_v} \leq M\eta_v$ and satisfies $\tau_k^v - t_k^v \geq \eta_v$, which essentially means that for every $v \in V$, $\inf\{\tau_k^v - t_k^v\} > 0$. That is to say, there is no Zeno behavior in the high-cost control step (4) during $t \in [t_k^v, \tau_k^v)$.

ii) *Step two*:

With regard to the low-cost control step (5) during $t \in [\tau_k^v, t_{k+1}^v)$, notice that the parameter β_v switches to low-cost setting β_- since $m_v(\tau_k^v) = \varphi_{low}(\tau_k^v)$, and $\varphi_{up}(t)$ and $\varphi_{low}(t)$ converge to zero faster than $i_v(t)$. Similarly, we have $m_v(t_{k+1}^v) = \varphi_{up}(t_{k+1}^v)$ as well.

Now we prove that there is no Zeno behavior in the low-cost control step (5) during $t \in [\tau_k^v, t_{k+1}^v)$. Notice that $i_v(t)$ converges to zero, so we have $\varphi_{up}(t_{k+1}^v) \leq \varphi_{low}(\tau_k^v)$, thus $e^{-\iota(t_{k+1}^v - \tau_k^v)} \leq L$, which essentially means that for every $v \in V$, $\inf\{t_{k+1}^v - \tau_k^v\} \geq -\ln L / \iota > 0$. That is to say, there is no Zeno behavior in the low-cost control step (5) during $t \in [\tau_k^v, t_{k+1}^v)$.

From the proof above, we have shown that $m_v(t) = p_v^{-1}i_v(t)$ continues to touch $\varphi_{up}(t)$ but could never exceed $\varphi_{up}(t)$ till infinite time, so i_v converges to zero at the convergence speed same as $\varphi_{up}(t)$.

Note that the proof under periodic reference setting (see also [14]) is similar.
□

3.3 Numerical Examples

We use numerical examples to illustrate the convergence process of the dynamics under control. The settings of the examples are defined as follows.

For graph G in the dynamics model, we conduct experiments on both undirected graph and directed graph to put the method into practice. The following network structures are obtained from http://snap.stanford.edu/data/. Note that the extraction of G in practice demands access to the enterprise's physical network topologies and security policies, which are usually confidential data unavailable to academic researchers.

- Enron email network: This is an undirected graph with $|V| = 5242$ nodes, $|E| = 28980$ edges, maximal node degree 81 and $\lambda_{A,1} = 45.6167$.
- Gnutella peer-to-peer network: This is a directed graph with $|V| = 8,717$ nodes, $|E| = 31,525$ links, maximal node in-degree 64 and $\lambda_{A,1} = 4.7395$.

We set $\beta_+ = 0.8$, $\beta_- = 0.1$ with respect to β_v for all nodes $v \in V$. As for γ_v, we randomly select the values for all nodes $v \in V$ with an upper bound $\gamma_{max} = 0.002$

for undirected Enron email network and $\gamma_{max} = 0.013$ for directed Gnutella peer-to-peer network. With respect to the criterion functions $\{\varphi_{up}, \varphi_{low}\}$ of the event-based trigger rule Definition 2, we set $\iota = 0.5$ and $L = 0.5$ for both networks. *Thus, the pre-control process is finished.* We calculate the matrix $P = diag(\{p_v\}_{v=1}^{n})$ in Lemma 2 for each graph respectively. As for the initial values, each node $v \in V$ is assigned with an initial compromise probability $i_v(0) \in_R [0, 1]$ where $\in_R$ means sampling uniformly at random. Besides, we consider $t \in [0, 500]$ with a fixed step-length $h = 0.025$. The convergence processes of dynamics are shown in Fig. 1, which shows consistence with the proof of Theorem 1. Notice that the grey curve (i.e., the dynamics under control) refers to $i_v(t)$, while the blue curve (i.e., the adjusted control target) refers to $m_v(t) = p_v^{-1} i_v(t)$.

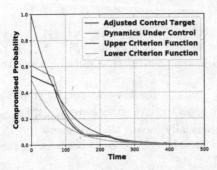 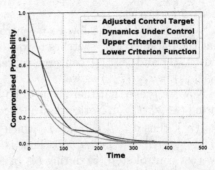

(a) Node 1855 of undirected Enron email network

(b) Node 6992 of directed Gnutella peer-to-peer network

Fig. 1. The convergence processes of dynamics under parameter switching control for both undirected and directed graph. (Color figure online)

In order to compare the convergence speeds, we define the following indicator of convergence speed and name it *exponential speed index*: $\mathcal{S}(t) = -\frac{1}{\Delta t} \ln \frac{i(t+\Delta t)}{i(t)}$. Notice that the target speed ,i.e., the exponential speed index of the criterion function, is equal to $\iota = 0.5$ in our settings. The exponential convergence speed indexes of the dynamics $i(t)$ under parameter switching control for both undirected and directed graph are calculated, denoted by $\mathcal{S}_i$. The threshold of effectiveness is defined as $\frac{|\mathcal{S}_i - \iota|}{\iota}$, which equals to 3.72% and 2.60% respectively, which shows the effectiveness.

Next, it comes to the control cost, which is indicated by the mean of time ratio $\frac{1}{n} \sum_{v \in V} \frac{T_+^v}{T_+^v + T_-^v}$. Suppose the control cost of the classical control approach without parameter switching is equal to 1. In the present experiments, by using the event-based parameter switching method, the control cost is reduced to 0.50 in the case of undirected Enron email network and 0.53 in the case of directed Gnutella peer-to-peer network respectively. That is to say, the new control method should save at least 40% of the cost incurred by the classical approach, which shows the efficiency.

4 Putting the Event-Based Method into Practice

Similar to [14], we need to bridge the gap between the following two kinds of states for utilizing the event-based parameter switching control method in practice. In the aforementioned model, the state of node $v \in V$ at time t is represented by $i_v(t)$, namely the probability that v is in *compromised* state at time t. In practice, this state is often measured as a Boolean value, with "0" indicating v is *secure* but vulnerable and "1" indicating v is *compromised*. In other words, the *sample-state* of node $v \in V$ at time t can be denoted by

$$\chi_v(t) = \begin{cases} 0 & v \text{ is in the } secure \text{ state at time } t \\ 1 & v \text{ is in the } compromised \text{ state at time } t. \end{cases} \quad (7)$$

This difference underlines the gap between the probability-states in the model and the sample-states in practice.

4.1 Estimation via 0-1 State Sequences Within a Time Window

Motivated by the theorem of two-valued processes introduced in [18, Chapter 1], we propose a new method to bridge the aforementioned gap by obtaining an estimation $\widehat{i_v(t)}$ of probabilities $i_v(t)$ and an estimation $\widehat{s_v(t)}$ of probabilities $s_v(t)$ from a 0-1 state sequence within a time window, as indicated by (7).

In our present scenario, unlike the equilibrium estimation task [14] in which the accuracy of estimation is of vital importance, the timeliness is the main focus in our event-based parameter switching dynamics control. The time-averaged estimations in [14] suffer from an increasing time lag as $t \to \infty$, so we need a new estimation method with less time lag and faster reaction. For simplicity, let $\mathcal{W}$ represent the time window which covers the $\mathcal{W}$ most recent time points before t. We use the Lebesgue measure $\mathcal{M}$ to define

$$\begin{cases} \mathcal{T}_{v0}^{\mathcal{W}}(t) = \mathcal{M}(\{t - \mathcal{W} < \tau \leq t : \chi_v(\tau) = 0\}) \\ \mathcal{T}_{v1}^{\mathcal{W}}(t) = \mathcal{M}(\{t - \mathcal{W} < \tau \leq t : \chi_v(\tau) = 1\}). \end{cases} \quad (8)$$

Then we let

$$\begin{cases} \widehat{s_v(t)} = \dfrac{\mathcal{T}_{v0}^{\mathcal{W}}(t)}{\mathcal{W}} \\ \widehat{i_v(t)} = \dfrac{\mathcal{T}_{v1}^{\mathcal{W}}(t)}{\mathcal{W}}. \end{cases}$$

Notice that the smaller $\mathcal{W}$ implies the less time lag and the lower accuracy the probability estimation exhibits. So we face the immediacy-accuracy trade-off dilemma when selecting the proper time window $\mathcal{W}$. To cope with this dilemma, we propose a new design of adaptive time windows

$$\mathcal{W}'(t) = \max(\mathcal{W}, \frac{t}{C_0}).$$

4.2   Using the Event-Based Control Method in Practice

With the aid of the newly proposed estimation method with adaptive time windows, which exhibits less time lag and faster response, the gap between probability-states and sample-states has been properly bridged. We now use the aforementioned event-based parameter switching method in practice to control the preventive and reactive cyber defense dynamics. Since undirected networks are a special case of directed networks, only experiments on the directed Gnutella peer-to-peer Network are performed here. Let the time window $W = 30$. As proposed above, we use an adaptive time window $W'(t)$ to replace the original time window W with a fixed time length, where C_0 is a positive constant number.

In the settings of our numerical examples, let $C_0 = 3$ for $W'(t)$. Figure 2 shows the convergence process of the dynamics under control, using a time window with adaptive time length to estimate the probability $m_v(t)$. We can find that there are still some events triggered in the advanced stage $t \in [300, 500]$ when probability $i_v(t)$ has fully converged to equilibrium zero, which means the event-based parameter switching method becomes effective by using the adaptive time window. With respect to the convergence speed indexes, notice that the threshold for it defined in Sect. 3.3 is 10%. Figure 3(b) shows the effectiveness of the time window with adaptive time length, with $\frac{|S-\iota|}{\iota} = 6.79\% < 10\%$, while $\frac{|S-\iota|}{\iota} = 27.27\% > 10\%$ for the time window with fixed time length exhibited in Fig. 3(a). Besides, with respect to the control cost, which is indicated by the mean of time ratio $\frac{1}{n}\sum_{v \in V} \frac{T_+^v}{T_+^v + T_-^v}$, recall the statement in Sect. 3.3, the threshold of efficiency is defined as 40% of the cost. The control cost in the current numerical example is 0.60, which means the reactive defense setting is under low-cost setting for 40% of the time. (the low-cost reactive defense setting takes up 40% of the time)

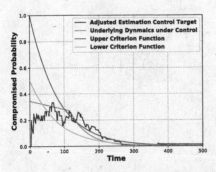
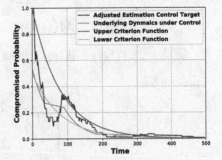

(a) Node 2688 using a time window with adaptive time length

(b) Node 4011 using a time window with adaptive time length

Fig. 2. The convergence processes of dynamics under parameter switching control aiming at adjusted sample-states estimation, using a time window with adaptive time length.

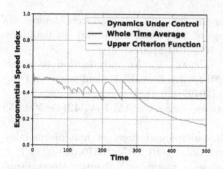
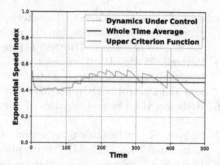

(a) The convergence speed index, using a time window with fixed time length

(b) The convergence speed index, using a time window with adaptive time length

Fig. 3. The exponential convergence speed indexes of the dynamics under parameter switching control, using a time window with fixed or adaptive time length.

5 Conclusion

In this paper, an event-based parameter switching method is proposed for the control tasks of cybersecurity, which helps avoid excessive control costs as well as guarantees the dynamics to converge as our desired speed. The Zeno-free property is proved, implying the feasibility of the method. Meanwhile, we designed a new estimation method with adaptive time windows in order to bridge the gap between the probability state and the sampling state with less time lags. Both theoretical and practical experiments are given to illustrate the parameter switching method, which show the effectiveness and efficiency of our new method.

There are many open problems for future research: Do there exist some better event-based parameter switching trigger rules so as to save more defense resources and guarantee the convergence speed? Can this parameter switching approach be applied to other dynamics control? Furthermore, similar parameter switching approaches regarding the parameter γ for push-based attacks are worth further studying.

References

1. Anderson, R., May, R.: Infectious Diseases of Humans. Oxford University Press, Oxford (1991)
2. Astrom, K.J., Bernhardsson, B.M.: Comparison of Riemann and Lebesgue sampling for first order stochastic systems. In: Proceedings of the 41st IEEE Conference on Decision and Control 2002, vol. 2, pp. 2011–2016 (2002)
3. Bailey, N.: The Mathematical Theory of Infectious Diseases and Its Applications, 2nd edn. Griffin, London (1975)

4. Han, Y., Lu, W., Xu, S.: Characterizing the power of moving target defense via cyber epidemic dynamics. In: Proceedings of 2014 Symposium and Bootcamp on the Science of Security (HotSoS'14), pp. 10:1–10:12 (2014)

5. Heemels, W.P.M.H., Johansson, K.H., Tabuada, P.: An introduction to event-triggered and self-triggered control. In: 2012 IEEE 51st IEEE Conference on Decision and Control (CDC), pp. 3270–3285 (2012)

6. Hethcote, H.: The mathematics of infectious diseases. SIAM Rev. **42**(4), 599–653 (2000)

7. Hoover, K.D.: Idealizing reduction: the microfoundations of macroeconomics. Erkenntnis **73**(3), 329–347 (2010). https://doi.org/10.1007/s10670-010-9235-1

8. Horn, R.A., Johnson, C.R.: Matrix Analysis. Cambridge University Press, Cambridge (2012)

9. Johansson, K.H., Egerstedt, M., Lygeros, J., Sastry, S.: On the regularization of zeno hybrid automata. Syst. Control Lett. **38**(3), 141–150 (1999)

10. Kephart, J., White, S.: Directed-graph epidemiological models of computer viruses. In: IEEE Symposium on Security and Privacy, pp. 343–361 (1991)

11. Kermack, W., McKendrick, A.: A contribution to the mathematical theory of epidemics. Proc. R. Soc. Lond. A **115**, 700–721 (1927)

12. Li, X., Parker, T., Xu, S.: Towards quantifying the (in)security of networked systems. In: Proceedings of IEEE International Conference on Advanced Information Networking and Applications (AINA'07), pp. 420–427 (2007)

13. Liggett, T.: Interacting Particle Systems. Springer, Heidelberg (1985). https://doi.org/10.1007/978-1-4613-8542-4

14. Liu, Z., Zheng, R., Lu, W., Xu, S.: Using event-based method to estimate cybersecurity equilibrium. IEEE/CAA J. Automatica Sinica **8**(2), 455–467 (2020)

15. Lu, W., Chen, T.: New conditions on global stability of Cohen-Grossberg neural networks. Neural Comput. **15**(5), 1173–1189 (2003)

16. McKendrick, A.: Applications of mathematics to medical problems. Proc. Edin. Math. Soc. **14**, 98–130 (1926)

17. Moreno, Y., Pastor-Satorras, R., Vespignani, A.: Epidemic outbreaks in complex heterogeneous networks. Eur. Phys. J. B **26**, 521–529 (2002)

18. Parzen, E.: Stochastic Processes. SIAM (1999)

19. Pastor-Satorras, R., Vespignani, A.: Epidemic dynamics and endemic states in complex networks. Phys. Rev. E **63**, 066117 (2001)

20. Sard, A.: The measure of the critical values of differentiable maps. Bull. Am. Math. Soc. **48**(12), 883–890 (1942)

21. Tabuada, P.: Event-triggered real-time scheduling of stabilizing control tasks. IEEE Trans. Autom. Control **52**(9), 1680–1685 (2007)

22. Xu, S.: Cybersecurity dynamics. In: Proceedings of Symposium and Bootcamp on the Science of Security (HotSoS'14), pp. 14:1–14:2 (2014)

23. Xu, S.: Cybersecurity dynamics: a foundation for the science of cybersecurity. In: Wang, C., Lu, Z. (eds.) Proactive and Dynamic Network Defense. Advances in Information Security, vol. 74. Springer, Heidelberg (2019). https://doi.org/10.1007/978-3-030-10597-6_1

24. Xu, S., Lu, W., Xu, L.: Push- and pull-based epidemic spreading in arbitrary networks: thresholds and deeper insights. ACM Trans. Auton. Adapt. Syst. (ACM TAAS) **7**(3), 32:1–32:26 (2012)

25. Xu, S., Lu, W., Xu, L., Zhan, Z.: Adaptive epidemic dynamics in networks: thresholds and control. ACM Trans. Auton. Adapt. Syst. (ACM TAAS) **8**(4), 19 (2014)

26. Zheng, R., Lu, W., Xu, S.: Active cyber defense dynamics exhibiting rich phenomena. In: Proceedings of 2015 Symposium and Bootcamp on the Science of Security (HotSoS'15), pp. 2:1–2:12 (2015)
27. Zheng, R., Lu, W., Xu, S.: Preventive and reactive cyber defense dynamics is globally stable. IEEE Trans. Netw. Sci. Eng. 5(2), 156–170 (2017)

RansomLens: Understanding Ransomware via Causality Analysis on System Provenance Graph

Rui Mei[1,2], Han-Bing Yan[3(✉)], and Zhi-Hui Han[3]

[1] Institute of Information Engineering, Chinese Academy of Sciences,
Beijing 100093, China
[2] School of Cyber Security, University of Chinese Academy of Sciences,
Beijing 100049, China
[3] National Computer Network Emergency Response Technical Team/Coordination
Center of China (CNCERT/CC), Beijing 100029, China
yhb@cert.org.cn

Abstract. Malware analysis technology has been one of the most important research topics of cyber security. The recent surge in adoption of ransomware is rapidly changing the malware landscape. A large body of researches in security community have given us an understanding of ransomware individuals and families. However, to the best of our knowledge, there are currently few works that explore common and distinct malicious behaviors on large scale ransomware dataset. Our insight is that although the implementation of each ransomware vary widely, its malicious behaviors inevitably interact with the underlying operating system, which will be exposed and captured by system event tracing mechanism. In this paper, we propose a novel ransomware analysis pipeline, a system provenance graph based approach for better understanding the ransomware's behaviors. Then we leverage the analysis framework to analyze on large scale ransomware dataset and present some interesting findings on diverse ransomware and their families. Furthermore, our analysis on ransomware also reveals that system provenance graph is an ideal tool, with strong abstract expression ability and relatively high efficiency.

Keywords: Ransomware analysis · Data provenance · Causality dependency graph

1 Introduction

In the past year, many fields around the world have faced severe challenges, and the field of cyber security is not optimistic. Among them, the spreading of ransomware has risen, and new blackmail models have emerged. Although ransomware infections account for about 3% of the total malware incidents [1], they are more destructive than other malware. Once they encounter ransomware, enterprises or other organizations will face the risk of business interruption and high ransom.

© Springer Nature Switzerland AG 2021
W. Lu et al. (Eds.): SciSec 2021, LNCS 13005, pp. 252–267, 2021.
https://doi.org/10.1007/978-3-030-89137-4_18

The security community has been paying attention to ransomware for a long time. Several previous researches have conducted in-depth studies on the spread posture, impact, and attack vectors of ransomware. However, it's worth noting that there are few studies aiming at the common and distinct behaviors of ransomware clusters. The main reason is probably lack of automated and effective software behavior analysis tools that can be used on large scale ransomware dataset. DARPA has launched a project called Transparent Computing [2], trying to find a high-fidelity and visible method to abstract the interaction between components in the opaque system. According to previous research on Transparent Computing project, scholars believe that system provenance graph has the potential to become the next generation of more robust attack investigation and detection mechanism.

In this paper, we propose a novel analysis approach based on system provenance graph, and use to analyze our ransomware dataset. To summarize, we make the following contributions:

- We design an effective and efficient ransomware analysis pipeline, a system provenance graph based approach for analyzing the common and distinct behaviors of ransomware dataset.
- To accurately identify malicious behaviors of ransomware dataset, we implement an end-to-end analysis framework including ransomware sample collection, system event tracing, graph generation and graph-based analysis.
- Leveraging the approach in this paper, we conduct an in-depth analysis of the inter-family and intra-family characteristics on ransomware dataset, and present some previously undiscovered findings.

2   Background and Motivation

There are mainly two types of ransomware, crypto and locker ransomware. The former encrypts all personal data existed on the target machine, leaving it hostage until the victim pays the ransom and obtains the decryption key from the attacker. Some variants of crypto ransomware will progressively delete hostage files or release them to the public if the victim failed to pay the ransom on time. The latter works by preventing the victim from reaching to his/her personal files through denying access to computing resources (e.g., locking desktop) and then demanding a ransom to regain access [3].

Traditional ransomware analysis usually includes static analysis and dynamic analysis. The former extracts the byte or opcode characteristics of the ransomware file, while the latter runs ransomware sample in the sandbox and enumerates the captured dynamic behavior. It is worth mentioning that all state-of-the-art dynamic behavior analyzers (e.g., VirusTotal) only output structured dynamic behaviors list, such as creating process list, opening file list, etc. Due to lack of those behaviors' correlationship (e.g., causal dependency), it is difficult to understand the interdependency between those dynamic behaviors and conduct in-depth analysis by relying solely on dynamic behaviors list.

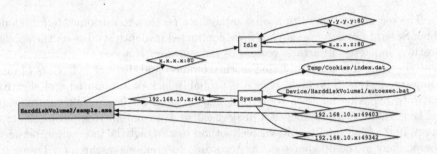

Fig. 1. Motivation example of system provenance graph. The nodes use shapes of rectangle, oval, and diamond to represent process, file, and network connection respectively. The node marked in red is ransomware sample process. IP address is masked for privacy reason. (Color figure online)

To gain insight into the activities of ransomware in underlying system, a naive thought is finding a mechanism that provides a highly interactive and visualized way to represent system event tracking. Based on this intuition, we consider system provenance graph to be a potential tool. Figure 1 shows a simplified example of system provenance graph of a *Wannacry* sample. It can be seen that the graph not only reveals the behaviors of the sample during running, but more importantly, the graph contains the spatial and temporal sequence between the behaviors, i.e., control dependency and data dependency. Furthermore, we can conduct graphs or network algorithms on the graph to dig deeper into the behavioral characteristics of ransomware.

3   Related Work

In the past decade, a large body of researches had laid the foundation for the analysis of this paper.

Large Scale Malware Analysis. As mentioned in Sect. 2, traditional malware detection and analysis have two main methods: static analysis and dynamic analysis. Recent studies show that traditional methods of malware analysis cannot be carried out on large scale samples effectively. Some studies began to combine data science to large scale malware analysis. Microsoft and Intel researchers proposed an approach called STAMINA [4] which convert malware binary to grayscale image in order to leverage image algorithms for analysis. MALALERT [5] proposed an efficient analysis framework for detection of malware in large scale network traffic, which is via generalizing the statistical features of network communication behavior of malware. MGET [6] got inspiration from biological gene sequence and generate malware genes for malware classification by identifying the specific behavior sequence of malware. In addition, several works leverage machine learning to automatically or semi-automatically extract the feature vectors of malware for classification and further analysis [7–10].

Host Level Event Analysis. Host level event log is one of key data sources of host-based intrusion detection system (HIDS), which is used for threat detection or attack investigation. It includes two types, namely, system level and application level. Due to the diversity and complexity of application level logs, previous studies for threat analysis and investigation are almost based on system level logs. Caselli et al. [11] proposed an approach which builds a normal model using N-gram from benign system call tracing for anomaly detection on new system call tracing. Research by Dong et al. [12] found that intrusion activities usually consist of a series of low-level heterogeneous events, especially it was necessary to consider that there were a large number of "noisy events" filled in event sequence. This work proposed a graph-based intrusion detection technique that could accurately identify the abnormal event sequence from a large number of heterogeneous process tracing. Siddiqui et al. [13] proposed a multi-view anomaly detection framework in order to solve the challenge that different cyberattacks will have different indicators of suspicion, in which multiple "views" of data designed by experts were created to capture features that may be potential indicators. In addition, several studies focus on attack investigation and forensics. OmegaLog [14] proposed a multi-layer log analysis framework, which blended system level logs and application level logs (e.g., Apache Tomcat web access logs) to trace and investigate security incidents from both levels. UISCOPE [15] focused on the attack investigation of GUI applications, and proposed an attack investigation solution which established a unified correlation analyzer by capturing both GUI events (e.g., mouse click) and system events.

Graph-Based Solutions. A great deal of previous works leverage graph structure to solve problems in multiple domains, e.g., threat intelligence knowledge representation, attack reconstruction and anomaly detection. BackTracker [16] proposed an approach to automatically identify the sequence of steps that may occur in an intrusion, find out related files or processes that may affect check point, and visualize the chain of events in the dependency graph. UNICORN [17] proposed a novel framework by leveraging historical sketches to construct an incrementally updated graph data structure for anomaly detection of log stream. MORSE [18] proposed a tag propagation technique based on system provenance graph, which mitigated the dependency explosion problem in attack investigation. HOLMES [19] focused on mapping system provenance graph to high-level attack activity graph for attack investigation. This approach was based on MITRE's ATT&CK framework, which described tactics, techniques, and procedures (TTPs) observed in attack scenarios. Hazem et al. [20] proposed a graph-based partitioning technique, which was based on intrusion model such as the Cyber Kill Chain model to decompose the alarm graph into a set of smaller subgraphs and reduce the impact of false alarms. HINTI [21] focused on threat intelligence representation, proposed an approach of Indicator of Compromise (IoC) identification based on multi-granular attention by leveraging Heterogeneous Information Network (HIN) to model the interdependency between IoCs.

Table 1. The system entities and their relations we consider.

Subject	Object	Attributes	Operations
Process	Process	Executable Path, PID, First Seen Timestamp	Start, Stop
		Last Seen Timestamp, Count	
	File	File Path, First Seen Timestamp	Read, Write, ImageLoad
		Last Seen Timestamp, Count	
	Socket	Src IP, Src Port, Dst IP, Dst Port, First Seen Timestamp	Send, Receive
		Last Seen Timestamp, Count	

4   Threat Model and Definitions

In this section, we discuss the ransomware threat model considered in this paper, based on which we make several basic assumptions. In addition, we define several concepts for later use in the rest of this paper.

4.1   Threat Model

As discussed earlier, while the ransomware ecosystem includes multiple aspects, we focus on the malicious behaviors of ransomware for ransom (e.g., file encryption, screen locking and bitcoin mining). Since our dataset is gathered from antivirus (AV) aggregators (e.g., VirusTotal), our analysis does not account for differences in how ransomware deliver to victim (e.g., exploiting vulnerability or phishing email). Actually, previous work shows that different propagation paths could rarely effect the malicious behaviors of ransomware [1].

  We make the following assumptions about our analysis. First, we assume that the system log collector is in the trusted computing base (TCB), i.e., the logic of log record collection is trusted. Second, we also assume that the log data cannot be tampered without authorization, i.e., the integrity of log records is maintained at all time. Third, we do not consider implicit flow (side channel) attacks, so ransomware's malicious behavior can always be caught by the system log tracker. Finally, since we collect the provenance of ransomware log records by running samples in the virtual machine (VM), we ignore the subtle differences between the ransomware samples running in VM and real environment. Actually, according to our observation, unlike other malware (e.g., backdoor or remote access trojan), ransomware rarely use the anti-virtualization technique for self-protection or detection avoidance.

4.2   Definitions

System Subject and Object. A subject refers to a system entity that performs an operation. Correspondingly, any target that the subject operates is called system object. In the rest of this paper, subjects and objects are denoted by u and v, respectively. Similar to previous works, our analysis considers three types of system entities: processes, files, and network connections. Only processes can be system subjects, while the process, files, and network connections can all be system objects.

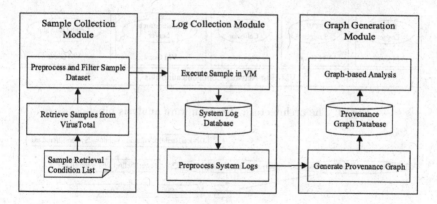

Fig. 2. The workflow of ransomware analysis pipeline

System Event refers to the operation from subjects to objects. An event can be denoted by a quad $<u, v, o, t>$, which is subject, object, operation, and timestamp respectively. It is worth noting that the type of operations depends on the type of the subject and object. For example, if the subject is a process and the object is a file, the operation can be read, write, or imageload. In Table 1, we show the system entity attributes and relations we consider.

System Provenance Graph. Given a ransomware sample r, the system provenance graph of r is constructed by all system events collected when r is running in VM. The provenance graph shows the control dependency (e.g., process create child process) and data dependency (e.g., process sending data via network socket) between subjects and objects. Formally, the system provenance graph of r is defined as $G(r) = <S, O, E>$, which are the sets of subjects, objects and events respectively. In the graph, subjects and objects are represented as vertices, and events are represented as edges.

Causality Dependency. Two events $e_1 = <u_1, v_1, o_1, t_1>$ and $e_2 = <u_2, v_2, o_2, t_2>$ have causal dependency if and only if $v_1 = u_2$ and $t_1 < t_2$. Causal dependency indicates the possible control flow or data flow between the two events, but it does not mean that there must be control dependency or data dependency between them. In system provenance graph, two adjacent edges can naturally represent causal dependency.

Backward Tracing. Starting from a selected checkpoint (e.g., a suspicious file or process), backward tracing tries to find all nodes that affect the checkpoint in the provenance graph.

Forward Tracing. Starting from a selected checkpoint, forward tracing tries to find all affected nodes that depend on that checkpoint in the provenance graph.

5   Analysis Infrastructure

In this section, we detail the design and implementation of an effective and efficient ransomware analysis pipeline. Figure 2 shows the workflow of this pipeline,

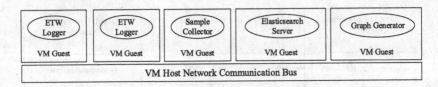

Fig. 3. The architecture of ransomware analysis pipeline

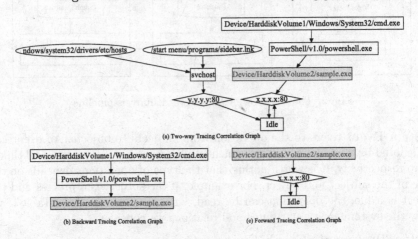

Fig. 4. Example tracing correlation subgraph from the provenance graph.

which involves three main steps: 1) The ransomware sample collection module gathers a set of ransomware samples from AV aggregator VirusTotal for further analysis;. 2) We run each sample of our dataset in VM for tracing and storing required system event logs; 3) Graph generation module filters and normalizes system event logs and generates corresponding system provenance graph for graph-based analysis. As mentioned above, we implemented the analysis pipeline using about 3K lines of Python code.

Sample Collection Module. To gather sufficient ransomware samples for further analysis, we used VirusTotal API [22] to retrieve all sample files that were submitted between Jul 2020 and Dec 2020 for 6 months. Noting that the labels of each sample (e.g., family name, packer type, compiler type) in VirusTotal not only come from its built-in 70+ AV engines, but may also come from crowdsourced YARA rule matching, so incorrect labels may be introduced. To eliminate the deviation that YARA rules may cause by detecting whether a sample is ransomware or not based only on the static characteristics of the binary code, we retrieved the malware analysis report of each sample by VirusTotal API, and took advantage of AVClass [23] to label the most likely malware type (e.g., ransomware, backdoor), malware family name, and malicious behavior (e.g., file encryption, kill process, info stealing). These labels of samples helped to better identify ransomware as well as in-depth analysis in Sect. 6.

Log Collection Module. Once we collected ransomware sample dataset, we needed to trace system event logs when the ransomware sample was running. We deployed several VMs as sandboxes for ransomware execution to prevent the system and data from being damage by ransomware. Modern operating system (e.g., Windows, Linux) generally has system event tracing mechanism, such as Event Tracing for Windows [24] and Linux Auditing Framework [25]. We implemented a system event collector as an agent in VMs based on the system event tracing mechanism built into the operating system. Our collector was optimized based on FireEye's project SilkETW [26] which is an event tracing framework for Windows. By registering our ETW logger agent to a Windows Service in VMs, system event logs would be collected continuously while the ransomware sample is running. It is noteworthy that although our implementation only focuses on ransomware analysis on Windows, the approach presented in this paper is still effective for Linux platform ransomware.

Particularly, considering that ransomware often encrypts files on the entire disk after running which included event log files themselves if we use VM guest file system for log storage or cache, we deployed a standalone Elasticsearch server (ES) for receiving logs from VM guests. On the one hand, Using ES ensures the integrity and availability of event logs, on the other hand, with the help of ES's capability, it can accelerate the performance of further analysis. Thus the architecture of our analysis pipeline is shown in Fig. 3. All modules are located in VM guests and interact via the VM host network communication bus.

System Provenance Graph Generation. To characterize the control dependency and data dependency between system events, we used the approach in previous study BackTracker [16] to generate the whole system provenance graph of ransomware execution in VM guests. Furthermore, focusing on the system events related to the ransomware sample, we leveraged naive tracing method which set sample file or process node in the provenance graph as the checkpoint and adopts forward tracking, backward tracking and bidirectional tracking to generate corresponding system provenance subgraphs, i.e., correlation graph, so as to more accurately analyze the behavior of ransomware. Figure 4 shows an example of the subgraphs generated by three types of tracing mentioned above.

6   Under the Hood

In this section, we use the aforementioned analysis pipeline to explore our ransomware dataset.

6.1   Dataset

As previously mentioned, we use our analysis infrastructure especially sample collection module to retrieve sample from VirusTotal. Then we filter the dataset in multiple steps. Our final dataset, after all filtering stage, consists of 3993 samples within 17 families. Table 2 shows the summary of our dataset with each step and corresponding filtering strategy. First, we retrieve 27110 ransomware

Table 2. Summary of our dataset

Steps	Filtered categories	#
Retrieval from VirusTotal	Time frame: Jul–Dec 2020	27110
	Format: peexe	
	Tag: ransomware	
	Positive: 40+	
AVClass	Type: ransomware	−15679
	Positive: 5+	−5342
File Corruption	Launch error	−1929
	Exit error	
Family Scale	Number of samples: 10+	−167
Total		**3993**

Table 3. Ransomware dataset detail grouped by families

Family	#	Raw event logs (Avg. per sample)		Whole system graph (Avg. per sample)			Correlation graph (Avg. per sample)		
		#Event (K)	Size (MB)	#Ver.	#Edg.	Size (KB)	#Ver.	#Edg.	Size (KB)
gandcrab	2152	59.31	13.95	2970	2982	621.58	491	499	95.49
wannacry	554	54.53	13.01	2786	2797	582.8	1800	1814	351.95
tofsee	420	60.28	14.07	2712	2721	567.94	1146	1153	224.24
locky	406	57.04	13.5	2547	2556	533.58	996	1004	195.4
poison	121	60.65	14.07	2861	2871	599.37	1771	1784	347.55
cerber	54	49.6	12.67	2342	2347	488.67	349	352	67.77
zusy	53	58.02	13.86	2670	2675	558.91	63	62	12.08
gimemo	50	58.24	13.65	2461	2468	515.57	6	5	0.94
lukitos	32	59.41	13.96	2398	2410	503.24	1848	1865	362.97
genkryptik	29	62.92	14.73	2659	2667	557.9	9	8	1.56
gandcrypt	28	47.66	13.15	2621	2652	543.19	1350	1384	259.69
purgen	20	54.93	13.21	2624	2630	549.09	157	158	30.83
virut	19	49.19	12	2072	2081	433.3	1621	1636	316.91
sodinokibi	17	62.86	14.64	2674	2688	562.26	279	281	54.86
ryuk	15	54.08	13	2456	2461	513.63	159	160	31.08
vbklog	12	62.89	14.73	2335	2348	490.88	1321	1333	259.08
fullscreen	11	63.8	15.02	2965	2974	621.88	3	2	0.44

samples from VirusTotal with search patterns described in Table 2. Second, we leverage AVClass to further identify ransomware to eliminate potential deviations introduced from VirusTotal's crowdsourced YARA rules. After this step, we get 6089 samples accounted for 22.5% of the result in previous step. Third, considering some samples submitted to VirusTotal is malware author's attempt at detection avoidance, there are several samples cannot execute but only test whether AV engines can identify they are malware samples. We execute these samples in the VM tentatively to observe if they run and handle exceptions well.

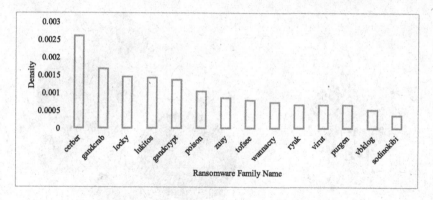

Fig. 5. Average graph density of ransomware families

Then we filter out 1929 samples which have launch errors or exit errors, and get 4160 samples. Lastly, to better understand the characteristics of each family, we filter out some families which the number of samples is less than 10, so we get 3993 samples as our dataset finally.

As mentioned in Sect. 5, our analysis pipeline captures raw system event data when the ransomware sample is running in the VM, then generates the whole the system provenance graph of each sample. To better understand behaviors of the ransomware, we further generate causality dependency subgraph, aka correlation graph, by using forward tracing and backward tracing. Through the above steps, we have greatly reduced the size of the logs data while maintaining the semantics of event logs. At the same time, the system provenance graph also provides a better way for further analysis. Table 3 shows a comparison of raw event log data, whole system graph, and correlation graph grouped by ransomware families. We find out that the correlation graphs generated by our analysis pipeline are two orders of magnitude smaller than raw event logs on average.

6.2 Inter-family Analysis

Not surprisingly, the basic function of ransomware is to encrypt files and demand a ransom, and recently several variants also perform information stealing, denial of service (DoS) and other malicious behaviors. In-depth analysis on ransomware has been carried out by security vendors and community. In this paper, we use the analysis framework discussed in Sect. 5 to support conclusions of those reports. Furthermore, we also have some interesting findings, which will be discussed in the rest of this section.

Concurrency of File Encryption. Encryption of disk files by ransomware is a time-consuming task. We found that some ransomware families encrypt files using concurrent operations for saving time. To measure the concurrency of file encryption in the system provenance graph, we use the indicator of graph density.

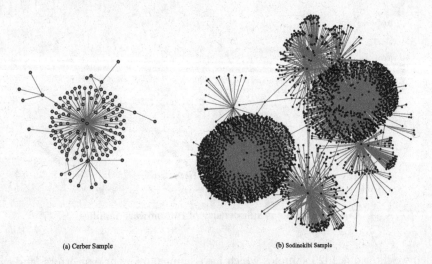

(a) Cerber Sample   (b) Sodinokibi Sample

Fig. 6. Graph Density of Cerber v.s. Sodinokibi. The pink, green, and yellow nodes in the graph represent processes, files, and network sockets respectively. (Color figure online)

For a directed graph, the graph density D is defined as:

$$D = \frac{|E|}{|V|(|V|-1)} \tag{1}$$

where $|E|$ is the number of edges and $|V|$ is the number of vertices in the graph.

Our insight is that the system provenance graph of concurrent encrypted samples has a low edge density, since each encryption process encrypt a large number of files, and there is no correlation between the files encrypted by different processes. Based on this intuition, we calculate the density of all samples in the dataset. Average density of each ransomware family is shown in Fig. 5. Taking into account the bias caused by the excessive small scale of the graph, we filtered out the samples with vertices less than 100. Thus only 14 ransomware families were in comparison for analysis.

As we can see from Fig. 5, the family of *Cerber* have the largest average edge density, i.e., those samples have the least concurrency. On the contrary the *Sodinokibi* family has the most encryption concurrency. To verify our inference, we randomly selected each sample of those two families respectively whose system provenance graph is as shown in Fig. 6. It can be seen clearly that the sample of *Cerber* family has only one cluster which is single thread file encryption, while *Sodinokibi* sample have multiple clusters which can encrypt files concurrently.

Detection Evasion. Due to ransomware does not need to maintain persistence, it is supposed that detection evasion requirement is not as strong as backdoor and other malware used in APT attacks. To our surprise, we manually observed some system provenance graphs of samples and found that process of encrypting

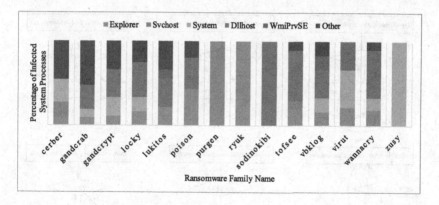

Fig. 7. Percentage of Infected or Impersonated Processes that execute encryption

files used by ransomware were almost infected system processes or built-in system management tools which had been usually added in the whitelist of HIDS. Based on the observation, we use closeness centrality indicator to measure importance of nodes in the graph, which is defined as:

$$CC(i) = \frac{N-1}{\sum_j d(i,j)} \tag{2}$$

where $i \neq j$, $d(i, j)$ is the length of the shortest path between nodes i and j in the graph. N is the number of nodes.

We calculate the closeness centrality value for each node in the system provenance graph and mark the type and name of the node which has maximum value (i.e., the most important node in the graph). We found that the node having maximum value of the closeness centrality is always a process node. As shown in Fig. 7, we count the number of different names of nodes having maximum value of closeness centrality in each family, i.e., process name that executes file encryption. According to the statistics result, we found that the vast majority of ransomware families execute file encryption by infecting or impersonating system processes.

Non-instant File Encryption. As discussed earlier, we found that some sample's provenance graphs have only fewer nodes. To explore the behavior of these samples, we retrieve samples with no more than 3 nodes for further analysis (considering the VM agent and launcher process, samples with no more than 3 nodes in the graph doing nothing actually). Although all samples in our dataset are labeled "filecrypt" in VirusTotal, about 30.6% of the samples do not execute file encryption instantly when they are running. Furthermore, we selected 5 samples per family (85 samples in total) for manual malware analysis. According to the results, the main findings are as follows: 1) Some samples only lock the screen and display the ransom message, but actually do not encrypt files; 2) Samples need to contact with command and control (C2) server to get the encryption key. If the network connection is not available, no operation is executed; 3) The sample releases a dropper and

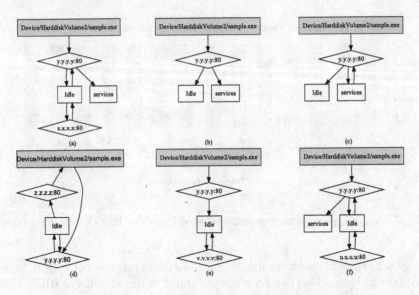

Fig. 8. Visualized variation in the same ransomware family.

adds it to the OS startup list, then the ransomware will automatically be launched while the system starts again.

6.3 Intra-family Analysis

In the analysis of Sect. 6.2, we note that samples belonging to the same family sometimes have different characteristics, probably due to version evolution or configuration variation.

As an example of this variety, we want to discuss the case of a popular ransomware family in our dataset, *Gandcrab*. To capture the subtle differences between samples of the same family, that is, the research question is how to find the least common subgraphs or paths in the system provenance graph. We use an anomaly detection approach based on the previous work ProvDetector [27]. This method calculates the regularity score of each edge on the graph, and finally finds the top K uncommon paths which are top K system event sequences of the sample most differing from other samples in the same family. the regularity score of an edge $e = <u, v>$ is defined as:

$$R(e) = OUT(u)\frac{|S(e)|}{|S|}IN(v) \tag{3}$$

In Eq. 3, $S(e)$ is the set of samples that event (i.e., edge in the graph) e happens while S is the set of all samples in the same family. The definitions of OUT, IN and other formulas are the same as ProvDetector [27].

As a case study, we retrieve 6 *Gandcrab* samples submitted to VirusTotal on the same day and use the algorithm mentioned above. The result is visualized as shown in Fig. 8. We found that these 6 samples are tiny different in the infected target system process and network communication, which probably be caused by configuration variation of each sample.

7   Conclusion

In this paper, we present a novel analysis framework based on system provenance graph. Leveraging this analysis pipeline, we conduct an end-to-end analysis procedure on ransomware dataset. Through the steps of data collection, pre-processing, log tracking, and in-depth analysis, our approach has an excellent effect on our ransomware dataset. However, frankly speaking, we only use three types of system events: process, file, and network communication, this limits the further extension of our approach. This will be our further research goal.

Acknowledgments. The authors would like to thank the anonymous reviewers for their valuable comments and suggestions. This work is supported by National Natural Science Foundation of China (No. U1736218) and National Key R&D Program of China (No. 2018YFB0804704). The analysis infrastructure and dataset of this work are partially supported by CNCERT/CC.

References

1. The State of Ransomware (2020). https://www.sophos.com/en-us/medialibrary/Gated-Assets/white-papers/sophos-the-state-of-ransomware-2020-wp.pdf. Accessed 16 Apr 2021
2. DARPA Transparent Computing. https://www.darpa.mil/program/transparent-computing. Accessed 30 Dec 2020
3. Ransomware: Attack Techniques and Countermeasures. https://www.secjuice.com/attack-techniques-countermeasures-ransomware/. Accessed 28 Apr 2021
4. Chen, L., Sahita, R., Parikh, J., Marino, M.: STAMINA: scalable deep learning approach for malware classification. https://www.intel.com/content/dam/www/public/us/en/ai/documents/stamina-scalable-deep-learning-whitepaper.pdf. Accessed 20 Mar 2021
5. Piskozub, M., Spolaor, R., Martinovic, I.: Malalert: detecting malware in large-scale network traffic using statistical features. In: ACM SIGMETRICS Performance Evaluation Review, pp. 151–154. ACM (2019)
6. Ding, J., Chen, Z., Zhao, Y., Su, H., Guo, Y., Sun, E.: MGeT: malware gene-based malware dynamic analyses. In: Proceedings of the 2017 International Conference on Cryptography, Security and Privacy, pp. 96–101. ACM (2017)
7. Yuan, Z., Lu, Y., Wang, Z., Xue, Y.: Droid-Sec: deep learning in android malware detection. In: Proceedings of the 2014 ACM Conference on SIGCOMM, pp. 371–372. ACM (2014)
8. Kolosnjaji, B., Zarras, A., Webster, G., Eckert, C.: Deep learning for classification of malware system call sequences. In: Kang, B.H., Bai, Q. (eds.) AI 2016. LNCS (LNAI), vol. 9992, pp. 137–149. Springer, Cham (2016). https://doi.org/10.1007/978-3-319-50127-7_11

9. HaddadPajouh, H., Dehghantanha, A., Khayami, R., Choo, K.K.R.: A deep recurrent neural network based approach for internet of things malware threat hunting. In: Taufer, M., Cambria, E., Abramson, D. (eds.) Future Generation Computer Systems, vol. 85, pp. 88–96. ScienceDirect (2018)

10. Hardy, W., Chen, L., Hou, S., Ye, Y., Li, X.: DL4MD: a deep learning framework for intelligent malware detection. In: Proceedings of the International Conference on Data Science (ICDATA), pp. 61–67. CSREA Press (2016)

11. Caselli, M., Zambon, E., Kargl, F.: Sequence-aware intrusion detection in industrial control systems. In: Proceedings of the 1st ACM Workshop on Cyber-Physical System Security, pp. 13–24. ACM (2015)

12. Dong, B., Chen, Z., Wang, H., Tang, L. A., Zhang, K., Lin, Y., et al.: Efficient discovery of abnormal event sequences in enterprise security systems. In: Proceedings of the 2017 ACM on Conference on Information and Knowledge Management, pp. 707–715. ACM (2017)

13. Siddiqui, M. A., Fern, A., Wright, R., Theriault, A., Archer, D. W., Maxwell, W.: Detecting cyberattack entities from audit data via multi-view anomaly detection with feedback. In: Workshops at the 32th AAAI Conference on Artificial Intelligence, pp. 277–284. OpenReview (2018)

14. Hassan, W. U., Noureddine, M. A., Datta, P., Bates, A.: OmegaLog: high-fidelity attack investigation via transparent multi-layer log analysis. In: Network and Distributed System Security Symposium (NDSS). The Internet Society (2020)

15. Yang, R., Ma, S., Xu, H., Zhang, X., Chen, Y.: UISCOPE: accurate, instrumentation-free, and visible attack investigation for GUI applications. In: Network and Distributed Systems Symposium (NDSS). The Internet Society (2020)

16. King, S.T., Chen, P.M.: Backtracking intrusions. In: Proceedings of the 9th ACM Symposium on Operating Systems Principles, pp. 223–236. ACM (2003)

17. Han, X., Pasquier, T., Bates, A., Mickens, J., Seltzer, M.: Unicorn: runtime provenance-based detector for advanced persistent threats. In: Network and Distributed Systems Symposium (NDSS). The Internet Society (2020)

18. Hossain, M.N., Sheikhi, S., Sekar, R.: Combating dependence explosion in forensic analysis using alternative tag propagation semantics. In: 2020 IEEE Symposium on Security and Privacy (SP), pp. 1139–1155. IEEE (2020)

19. Milajerdi, S.M., Gjomemo, R., Eshete, B., Sekar, R., Venkatakrishnan, V.N.: HOLMES: real-time apt detection through correlation of suspicious information flows. In: 2019 IEEE Symposium on Security and Privacy (SP), pp. 1137–1152. IEEE (2019)

20. Soliman, H.M.: An optimization approach to graph partitioning for detecting persistent attacks in enterprise networks. In: 2020 International Symposium on Networks, Computers and Communications (ISNCC), pp. 1–6. IEEE (2020)

21. Zhao, J., Yan, Q., Liu, X., Li, B., Zuo, G.: Cyber threat intelligence modeling based on heterogeneous graph convolutional network. In: 23rd International Symposium on Research in Attacks, Intrusions and Defenses (RAID), pp. 241–256. USENIX Association (2020)

22. VirusTotal API v3 Overview. https://developers.virustotal.com/v3.0/reference. Accessed 10 Jan 2021

23. Sebastián, S., Caballero, J.: AVCLASS2: massive malware tag extraction from AV labels. In: Annual Computer Security Applications Conference (ACSAC), pp. 42–53. ACM (2020)

24. Event tracing for windows. https://docs.microsoft.com/en-us/windows/win32/etw/about-event-tracing. Accessed 10 Mar 2021

25. Linux auditd. https://linux.die.net/man/8/. Accessed 25 Dec 2020
26. SilkETW. https://github.com/fireeye/SilkETW. Accessed 1 Apr 2021
27. Wang, Q., Hassan, W.U., Li, D., Jee, K., Yu, X., Zou, K., et al.: You are what you do: hunting stealthy malware via data provenance analysis. In: Network and Distributed Systems Symposium (NDSS). The Internet Society (2020)

Correction to: Science of Cyber Security

Wenlian Lu, Kun Sun, Moti Yung, and Feng Liu

Correction to:
W. Lu et al. (Eds.): *Science of Cyber Security*, **LNCS 13005,**
https://doi.org/10.1007/978-3-030-89137-4

In the original version of this book, the affiliation of Feng Liu was presented incorrectly. This has been corrected to Institute of Information Engineering, Chinese Academy of Sciences, Beijing, China.

The updated version of the book can be found at
https://doi.org/10.1007/978-3-030-89137-4

© Springer Nature Switzerland AG 2021
W. Lu et al. (Eds.): SciSec 2021, LNCS 13005, p. C1, 2021.
https://doi.org/10.1007/978-3-030-89137-4_19

Author Index

Printed in the United States
by Baker & Taylor Publisher Services